Designed to meet the needs of scholars in various disciplines, this bibliography is the first comprehensive reference work to the extensive critical literature and many editions and facsimiles related to medieval music in its broadest sense.

As the subtitle suggests, the book considers music as *musica*, that is, as discipline, philosophy, and mathematical science, as well as craft and performing art. Drawing on publications in all European languages, the author has organized material concerned with the history of music from *circa* 400 to 1400 in the following categories: reference works; general histories; collections of texts, miscellaneous facsimiles, and anthologies; philosophy and speculative music literature; notation and rhythm; technical matters (tuning, compositional procedures, etc); iconography; instruments; the Near East, Islam, Byzantium; plainsong; tropes and liturgical drama; eastern Europe; treatises; the lyric (*conductus*, troubadour and trouvère, the minnesang, lauda, and cantiga); polyphony (organized by century and geographical area); the British Isles; Germany; Spain; Scandinavia; instrumental music and dances; and performance practices.

Although the scope is comprehensive, the collection is selective, listing the best recent works, but referring to earlier works when appropriate. Professor Hughes provides annotation and gives detailed indexes of authors, names, titles, subjects, and terms.

This bibliography will help the scholar more fully to understand the purpose of music in the medieval world and to glimpse what the phrase *musica mundana* expresses — the medieval vision of a unified ordering of the universe.

MEDIEVAL MUSIC: THE SIXTH LIBERAL ART

TORONTO MEDIEVAL BIBLIOGRAPHIES 4

General editor: John Leyerle

Published in association with
the Centre for Medieval Studies, University of Toronto

ANDREW HUGHES

Medieval Music

THE SIXTH LIBERAL ART

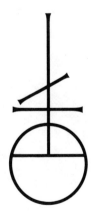

UNIVERSITY OF TORONTO PRESS

© University of Toronto Press 1974
Toronto and Buffalo
Printed in USA
ISBN 0-8020-2094-1
LC 73-85087

Contents

Editor's preface

The study of the middle ages has been developed chiefly within university departments such as English or history. This pattern is increasingly being supplemented by an interdisciplinary approach in which the plan of work is shaped to fit the subject studied. The difference of approach is between Chaucer the English poet and Chaucer the civil servant of London attached to the court of Richard ii, a man interested in the Ptolemaic universe and widely read in Latin, French, and Italian. Interdisciplinary programs tend to lead readers into areas relatively unfamiliar to them where critical bibliographies prepared with careful selectivity by an expert are essential. The Centre for Medieval Studies at the University of Toronto takes such an interdisciplinary approach to the middle ages, and the need for select bibliographies has become apparent in our work. The centre has undertaken to meet this need by sponsoring the Toronto Medieval Bibliographies.

In his valuable guide, *Serial Bibliographies for Medieval Studies*,* Richard H. Rouse describes 283 bibliographies; the number is surprisingly large and indicates the considerable effort now being made to list, in many categories, items relevant to medieval studies. The total amount in print is already vast; for one unfamiliar with a subject significant work is difficult to locate and the problem grows worse with each year's output. The reader may well say, like the throng in *Piers Plowman* seeking the way to *Treuth*, 'This were a wikked way but who-so hadde a gyde' (B.vi.). The Toronto Medieval Bibliographies are meant to be such guides; each title is prepared by an expert and gives directions to important work in the subject.

Each title presents a list of work selected with three specific aims. One is to aid students relatively new to the area covered by the title, for example, Old Norse and Icelandic. Another is to guide more advanced readers in a subject where they have had little formal training, for example, medieval rhetoric or Old English literature; and the third is to assist new libraries in forming a basic collection in the subject presented. Individual compilers are

*Publications of the Center for Medieval and Renaissance Studies 3 (Berkeley and Los Angeles 1969)

given scope to organize a presentation that they judge will best suit their subject and also to make brief critical comments as they think fit. Clarity and usefulness of a volume are preferred over any demand for exact uniformity from one volume to another.

In *Medieval Music* Andrew Hughes surveys a field far wider in time and space than those covered in earlier volumes in this series. Consequently this volume is substantially larger and more complex to use than the previous titles. The reader must give careful attention to the 'Key to the bibliography,' as well as to the list of abbreviations and the indices, if the volume is to have its full value.

JL
Ithaca, New York 1973

Author's preface

Music in the presently accepted sense of the word is but a very restricted part of the medieval conception of *musica*. Many items of this bibliography, especially **81**, **93**, **94**, and **123a**, make the medieval attitude clear: *musica ad omnia extendit se videtur*. The chronological, geographical, and intellectual limits of 'all things' to be found in this compilation will be quickly evident from the 'Key to the bibliography' (pp 3–8) and from the headings in the body of the work. At present there is a dichotomy between music and her sister disciplines, wherein she can know only the art of sound and they only the closest of their relatives; the medieval vision of a unified ordering of the universe expressed by the phrase *musica mundana*, today fully understood by few, has disappeared. This bibliography is dedicated to those who have helped me glimpse the purpose of music in the medieval world, in particular to those who have helped me complete this work, and to all who understand that *sine musica nulla disciplina potest esse perfecta*.

THE SELECTION

Some 40 per cent of the material originally collected was discarded. The selection was made by weighing, among others, these factors: quality of scholarship and presentation; the amount of information available on a topic; the originality and soundness of the views put forward; the date. Certain kinds of item, notably facsimiles, catalogues, and editions, more closely concerned with the primary sources, were treated somewhat favourably regardless of date, on the grounds that in medieval music 'the real need is to find out what is there, without trying to prove this or that about it' (**759**.367). Furthermore some entries regarded as poor by scholars in other disciplines were included because, from the musical viewpoint, they treat material only scantily researched.

The problems of discrimination in this multi-disciplinary field proved, as expected, very taxing: the character and worth of an entry may be assessed from the bibliographical details and from the annotation. The arrangement of the items does *not* imply discrimination.

THE ARRANGEMENT

I have tried to impose a structure on the discipline, placing adjacent those entries and sections which are related. The music of Islam, for example, considered mainly as an influence on European music, appears within the section on music treatises, within the section on the twelfth-century lyric, as well as independently. The organisation of items in detail was perhaps in large part intuitive and in any case does not lend itself to verbalisation. Frequently chronological and evolutionary, this disposition of topics in relation to each other should not be regarded as a universal principle by which the development of medieval music may be understood.

In larger sections the bibliography proceeds from the general, such as histories, anthologies, collections of facsimiles, to more specific items dealing, for example, with individual sources, composers, or compositions. This arrangement is superseded in some categories by a chronological order or by alphabetical order of subject: where no other arrangement is apparent, items are listed alphabetically by author. Where necessary the order may be stated at the beginning of a section. The division into sections is often necessarily somewhat arbitrary, and in particular the later geographical distinctions, while useful in general, apply very tenuously to certain items. The thirteenth-century motet, for instance, falls most naturally into the section on France, although numerous English and Spanish relatives are included. Moreover the topic of one section may also be discussed in items of immediately adjacent sections devoted to other topics, as well as quite elsewhere in the bibliography. Many items could easily be placed in several different categories, and this most common of problems could never be solved quite satisfactorily. *Entries of major importance to a topic may not be listed specifically under that heading.* **1418c** is a case in point: its text is the most comprehensive investigation of modal rhythm; however, since its transcriptions form the only complete edition of the *Magnus Liber*, it is listed under that heading. Within the body of the book, then, there are cross-references. More important, the General Index serves as a comprehensive guide to the work and should always be consulted.

THE BIBLIOGRAPHICAL STYLE

For a single entry the bibliographical information is listed first, with the annotation following. Items are sometimes placed in groups before their annotations, also grouped together. The main bibliographical information follows the item number in bold type: the annotations, which begin on a new line, are identified by the item number, again in bold type. Bold type always refers to entries in the bibliography: when a stop and figures in lightface follow an entry number, these latter refer to volume and page numbers in the item cited. An asterisk (*) indicates that the item was not seen. References consisting of a letter and number (e.g., **F-7**) relate to collections, listed on pp 261–9.

The bibliographical information is invariably taken from the item itself. Discrepancies in spelling, as with the name Higinio Angles, are thus repeated here. For articles I have given only the initials of authors' first names; otherwise, where it is necessary to go to catalogues as in the case of independent books and editions, I have given the first name in full. This too causes apparent inconsistency. Titles of series, or their abbreviations, are printed in small capitals, and often, where the whole series was published in the same city or edited by a single person, the place of publication or editor's name is omitted from the entry and appears only in the list of abbreviations. The information conveyed in the bibliographical description and in the annotation forms the basis for assessment and discrimination. Annotations of items in languages I do not read are derived where possible from other summaries or reviews.

TERMINOLOGY

The annotations necessarily demanded some use of technical terms not familiar to all users. Many terms could be defined briefly only at great risk, and to be useful a glossary would have amounted to a small dictionary. The user is referred to items **1, 2, 3, 3a**.

A BRIEF SURVEY

Some users may wish to obtain a broad general knowledge of the topic and at the same time to take advantage of more specialised information. The following list presents a selection from the bibliography of some items outstanding because of their excellence or their simplicity. These are arranged in what I believe is a convenient order for studying medieval music. Most are articles and quite brief; many appear in publications not likely to be listed in general histories of music.

Not all areas are represented, and, while some items, such as those from *The Listener*, are elementary surveys, most should be regarded as supplementary to more comprehensive textbooks, probing deeper or putting central issues very clearly. Textbooks, editions of the music itself, and reference books, obviously essential, are not included here.

Medieval music: its essential differences from later music, and its underlying characteristics **78 123a 50**; its philosophical and intellectual aspects **94 95 112**; its Judaeo-Arabic roots **39 41 42 382**; its Arabic parallels **1019 1021**; its melodic system: the modes **197 32.49–164 213**; its rhythm and notation **168 134 160**; its mathematics **185**; its performance **1958 1959**; its instruments **321 375 1952 345**; its dances **1914**; its role in society **272 273 274**

ACKNOWLEDGMENTS

Amongst those who understand the role of music in the medieval world I must single out John Leyerle, whose wise and patient criticism has always been combined with persuasive encouragement. JoAnna Dutka has suffered with great goodwill much of the tedium of collecting, arranging, and checking. Sister Frances Nims and Robert Taylor of the University of Toronto read several sections of the typescript and offered useful suggestions. Diane has waited, as wives do. All have my deep appreciation and thanks. So do the staff of the Music Library and Interlibrary Loan Department of the University of Toronto, whose services I have severely overworked; Professor James Pruett and the staff of the Music Library of the University of North Carolina at Chapel Hill; a number of student helpers, in particular Pierre Lacasse, at the University of Toronto; and most warmly the staff of University of Toronto Press.

   This book has been published with the help of grants from the Research Board of the University of Toronto and from the Humanities Research Council of Canada, using funds provided by the Canada Council.

ANDREW HUGHES
Toronto 1973

MEDIEVAL MUSIC: THE SIXTH LIBERAL ART

MUSICAM NOSSE NIHIL ALIUD NISI
CUNCTARUM RERUM ORDINEM SCIRE

Key to the bibliography

4 Key to the bibliography

5 Key to the bibliography

PLAINSONG 476–714

Bibliography 476–81
Introductions 481a–2
Histories and surveys 483–95
Anthologies, indices, catalogues 496–501
Liturgical books 502–34
Notation 535–45
Rhythm 546–60
Eastern and Greek elements in plainsong 561–73
Folk elements in plainsong 574–5
Repertories and Uses 576–604

Gregorian chant 605–714

The central problem 605–31
Style, form, dialect 632–47
Mass 648–75
Offices 676–89
Processions 689a
Special Offices 689b–703
The Tonary 703a–11
Miscellaneous 712–14

TROPES 715–83

Catalogues and sources 715–29
Origins, history, and significance of tropes 730–43
St Martial and Aquitaine 744–51
Alleluias and the Sequence 752–83

LITURGICAL DRAMA 784–837

General histories 785–801
Facsimiles and editions 802–22
Performing editions 823–9
The music 830–7

EASTERN EUROPE 838–99

Bibliographies, catalogues, surveys 838–59
Individual countries 860–99

TREATISES 900–1016

Catalogues, sources 900–17
Histories 918–24
Editions and anthologies 925–7

6 Key to the bibliography

Theory and theorists up to 800 **928–40**
The ninth and tenth centuries **941–50**
The eleventh and twelfth centuries **951–79a**
Arabic influence **980–2**
The thirteenth century **983–1005**
The fourteenth and fifteenth centuries **1006–16**

MUSIC IN ISLAM **1017–37**

Bibliography, sources, histories **1017–20**
Philosophical, scientific, and aesthetic concepts **1021–4a**
Instruments 1025–7
Theory **1028–37**

THE LYRIC IN LATIN AND THE VERNACULAR **1038–1334**

Surveys **1038–52**
The earliest lyrics, epics, etc **1053–75**
Continuations of the Sequence **1076–1104**

Conductus **1105–24**

Reference, sources **1105–17**
Rhythm **1118–24**

Arabic influence **1125–39**

Vernacular song in Provence and northern France **1140–1236**

Reference, bibliography, sources **1140–53**
Transmission and variants **1154–9**
Rhythm **1160–72**
The forms **1173–80**
Troubadours **1180a–1201**
Trouvères **1202–30**
Latin lyrics and sacred songs **1231–6**

The lyric in Germany and Switzerland: Minnesinger **1237–1322**

Reference **1237**
Anthologies **1239–45a**
Origins, contrafacta **1246–68**
Sources, editions, facsimiles **1268a–88**
The poets **1290–1313**
Sacred song, Geisslerlied **1313a–22**

7 Key to the bibliography

The lauda **1323–34**

Origins and evolution **1323–5**
Sources **1326–30**
Laudesi **1331–4**

THE THEORY AND PRACTICE OF
POLYPHONY **1335–1748**

Catalogues of manuscripts **1335**
Before the twelfth century **1336–55**
The twelfth century **1356–89**

France: Notre Dame and the thirteenth-century motet **1390–1494**

The *Magnus Liber* **1390–1434**
Discant, clausula, motet **1435–46**
Conductus
The thirteenth-century motet **1447–65**
Major sources, facsimiles, editions **1466–82**
Anthologies **1483**
Specific stylistic characteristics **1484–94**

France and Flanders: The fourteenth century **1495–1611**

Ars nova **1495–1579**
Ars subtilior (ca 1377–1417) **1580–1601**
Places **1602–11**

France: Fourteenth-century theory **1612–30a**

Italy and Sicily **1631–1748**

Reference and bibliography **1631–45**
Texts and poets **1646–64**
Sources, facsimiles, editions **1665–93**
The forms **1694–1703**
Composers **1704–21**
Specific pieces and techniques **1722–6**
Italian theory, fourteenth and fifteenth centuries **1727–48**

THE BRITISH ISLES **1749–1815**

References and surveys **1749–51**
Before the twelfth century **1752–9**
The twelfth and thirteenth centuries **1760–78**
The fourteenth and fifteenth centuries **1779–95**
Sources **1796–1806**
The Celtic lands **1807–9**

Thirteenth- and fourteenth-century theory **1810–15**

8 Key to the bibliography

THE IBERIAN PENINSULA **1816–48**

Surveys and the Cantigas **1816–28**
Sources **1829–34**
Areas **1835–46**
Treatises **1847–48**

THE GERMANIC COUNTRIES **1849–75**

Lyric song and Minnesinger
Catalogues and sources of polyphony
1849–75

SCANDINAVIA **1876–86**

Denmark **1876–80**
Iceland **1881–3**
Sweden **1884–6**

MISCELLANEOUS MANUSCRIPTS WITH
POLYPHONY **1887–1907**

INSTRUMENTAL MUSIC, DANCES **1907a–28**

Dances **1908–23**
Keyboard music **1924–8**

PERFORMANCE PRACTICE **1929–62**

General discussions **1929–32**
More specific discussions **1933–7**
Plainsong **1938–46**
Instruments in church **1947–53a**
Conducting, tempo **1954–7**
Practical suggestions **1958–62**

THE RENAISSANCE **1963–2003**

Sources **1970–90a**
Polyphony in archaic style **1991–8**
Well-known melodies **1999–2003**

CONGRESSES, FESTSCHRIFTEN,
AND OTHER COLLECTIONS

Congresses **A-1–6 B-1–4 C-1–2**
Miscellaneous congresses **D-1–14**
Miscellaneous collections **E-1–8**
Collections dedicated to, or written by,
noted scholars **F-1–36**

General reference works

DICTIONARIES

1 *Die M in Geschichte und Gegenwart* [MGG] 14 vols ed Friedrich Blume (Kassel 1949–) suppl vols in progress
This is the most comprehensive and excellent dictionary available, lavishly illustrated and with lists of works and bibliographies. It is particularly valuable for references to European dissertations.

2 *Grove's Dictionary of M and Musicians* 9 vols ed Eric Blom (1 suppl vol ed Denis Stevens 1961) (5th ed London 1954)
A new edition is in preparation.

3 Riemann, Hugo *Musik Lexikon* 3 vols ed Wilibald Gurlitt (12th ed Mainz):
3a vol 1 *Personenteil A-K* (1959) xv + 986 (suppled Carl Dahlhaus 1972, xv + 698); vol 2 *Personenteil L-Z* (1961) xv + 976; vol 3 *Sachteil* (1967) xv + 1087 **3a** *Harvard Dictionary of M* ed Willi Apel (2nd ed Cambridge, Mass. 1969) xviii + 935, illus, M exx, diagrams
3 The third volume is greatly superior to **3a**; both deal only with subjects and terms.

MORE SPECIALISED REFERENCE WORKS

4 *Encyclopédie des M sacrées* 2 vols ed Jacques Porte (Paris 1968, 1969) 524, 573
This comprehensive work, lavishly illustrated with plates and facsimiles, comprises substantial articles by noted scholars. Vol 1 deals with the Far East, Middle East, Musulman, and Jewish traditions; vol 2 deals with Christian traditions.

5 *Directory of M Research Libraries* 3 vols comp Rita Benton INTERN. ASSOCIATION OF M LIBRARIES, Commission of Research Libraries (Iowa City 1967, 1970, 1972) ix + 70; xix + 235; xviii + 342 + separate list of errata
The directory is intended primarily for use with series A and B of RISM. Vol 1: Canada and the US; vol 2: thirteen European countries, excluding those of volume 3; vol 3: Spain, France, Italy, Portugal.

6 *Historical Musicology, a Reference Manual for Research in* M ed Lincoln B. Spiess MS 4 (Brooklyn 1963) xiii + 294, index
S surveys editions, monographs, periodicals, publishers, dictionaries, histories, and reference works, with a brief review of the development of musicology (153–72), showing its main fields, journals, and publications, and its principal scholars up to ca 1960. There is no discrimination.

7 *Historical Atlas of* M ed Paul Collaer and Albert Van der Linden (transl Allan Miller from original ed Paris 1960) (Cleveland and New York 1968) xii + 176, illus, maps, facss, glossary, b, index / rev R.E. Wolf *MQ* 47 (1961) 413–16 (French ed); E. Taylor *ML* 49 (1968) 251–3
The text is sketchy. Pp 1–24 deal with the oral tradition and non-western M, 25–39 with the M of ancient Greece, plainsong, and the MA.

MANUSCRIPT CATALOGUES

The following are singled out because they are exclusively musical or medieval, and have useful indices of incipits, or numerous facsimiles. Many subsequent sections refer to more specific catalogues: the RISM series should be especially noted (**8b 8c 900 901 1335 1503**); it is described more fully in the list of abbreviations. In **8** Stäblein shows the difficulties in using catalogues prepared by persons not trained in M, and lists the basic information needed about a M source.

8 Stäblein, B. 'Erfassung und Erschliessung ma. M-hss' **B-4**.339–40

8a Plante, J.G. 'The Monastic Manuscript Microfilm Library' *Notes* 25 (1968/9) 12–14
P describes the library (Collegeville, Minn.) and lists some of the med. M treatises included.

8b *Hss mit mehrstimmiger* M *des 14., 15. und 16. Jh.* 2 vols ed Kurt von Fischer
8c and Max Lütolf RISM ser B IV³ (*Austria bis France*) (1972) and RISM ser B IV⁴ (*Gt Britain bis Yugoslavia*) (1972) 592; iv + 593–1221, index of incipits and composers
See under series abbreviations.

9 London. *Catalogue of Ms* M *in the British Museum* 3 vols ed Augustus Hughes-Hughes (London 1906, 1908, 1909) xxvi + 616; xxvi + 962; xxiv + 544
Each volume has indices of titles, incipits, names, and subjects, and a table of mss. Vol 1 lists polyphonic sacred vocal M according to form and type; vol 2 lists secular vocal M; vol 3 lists instrumental M, treatises, histories, dictionaries, drawings, and descriptions of M instruments, etc, and has addenda.

10 Madrid. *Catálogo* M *de la Biblioteca Nacional de Madrid.* I: *Manuscritos* ed

Higinio Anglés and José Subirá IEM (Barcelona 1946) xix + 492 + 28 facss, indices of names, incipits, etc.

11 Paris. The CENTRE NATIONAL DE LA RECHERCHE SCIENTIFIQUE has begun to
12 publish a series of catalogues under the general title 'Répertoire de mss méd. contenant des notations M' ed Solange Corbin. Published so far are: 11 Vol 1 *Bibliothèque Sainte-Geneviève-Paris* ed Madeleine Bernard (Paris 1965) 160 + 26 facss / rev Bruno Stäblein *CCM* 12 (1969) 191–3 12 Vol 2 *Bibl Mazarine-Paris* ed Madeleine Bernard (Paris 1966) 194 + 16 facss / rev P. Peacock *ML* 49 (1968) 187–8

BIBLIOGRAPHIES

13 *Répertoire intern. de littérature* M (RILM) 1– (New York 1967–)
This is a computer-indexed bibliography of significant literature on M. Established in 1966, it appears four times a year and is cumulated annually. It publishes abstracts of books, articles, essays, reviews, dissertations, catalogues, etc.

14 *The Music Index* 1– (Detroit 1949–)
This is a comprehensive subject/author guide to current M literature from almost 200 periodicals of 20 countries. It is published monthly, cumulated annually. It includes reviews of books, M, recordings, and performances.

15 Lesure, F. 'La Musicologie méd. d'après des travaux récents' *Rom* 74 (1953) 271–8
L surveys important publications.

16 'Das gegenwärtige Geschichtsbild der ma. M' comp J. Smits van Waesberghe *KmJb* 46 (1962) continuing
Annually since 1962 *KmJb* has included an annotated 'bibliography' of outstanding articles on med. M drawn from yearbooks, periodicals, congress reports, and festschriften of the previous year(s). The publications searched include organs of musicology, liturgy, and general med. studies. Articles are listed under headings such as: ethnomusicology, liturgical M of the East, Greg. M, paleography, organology, monophony, polyphony, M theory, tropes and Sequences, vernacular M, notation, rhythm, etc. The listings from publications not solely devoted to M makes this an important supplement to 13 and 14. Vol 53 (1969) has a cumulative index of subjects, areas, manuscripts, names, and authors.

17 *Historical Sets, Collected Editions and Monuments of* M ed Anna H. Heyer (2nd ed Chicago 1969) xiv + 573
H describes series, mainly editions but including some texts, without annotation. There is a good index.

18 *An Index to* M *Festschriften and similar Publications* comp Walter Gerboth (New York 1969) ix + 188

12 General reference works

This bibliography, revised and enlarged from the section in **F-23**, is divided principally into eras with an index of authors and subjects. Cf *Notes* 21 (1963/4) 94–108.

DISSERTATIONS

19 *Doctoral Dissertations in Musicology* comp Helen Hewitt (4th ed Philadelphia 1965) 152
This is a detailed and cross-referenced index, divided mainly by era. Additions appear in periodical supplements, cumulated as necessary in the next edition.

20 *Verzeichnis deutschsprachiger mw Dissertationen 1861–1960* comp Richard Schaal, MwArb 19 (Kassel 1963) 167

RECORDINGS

21 *Med. and Renaissance* M *on Long-playing Records* comp James Coover and Richard Colvig DETROIT STUDIES IN M B 6 (Detroit 1964) 122
A new edition is promised for 1973. Many of the older discs listed in the first edition do not present performances acceptable by more recent standards and opinions about how the M should sound.

22 'French and Provençal Poet-musicians of the MA: a Biblio-discography' comp E. Jahiel *Romance Philology* 14 (1960/1) 200–7
J lists songs alphabetically under composer.

23 Reaney, G. 'Med. M on the Gramophone' *ML* 38 (1957) 180–90
R discusses perennial problems, including those of performance practice and authenticity.

General histories

These items are listed alphabetically by author; the *New Oxford History* and *Pelican History* are under N and P.

24 Besseler, Heinrich *Die M des Ma und der Renaissance* HbMw (Potsdam 1931) Med. M is discussed on pp 1–183, num pll, facss, M exx, ext index and b
This is a standard work.

25 Chailley, Jacques *Histoire M du ma* (2nd ed revd Paris 1969) iii + 336, index / rev C. Van den Borren *RBM* 4 (1950) 150–2

26 Coussemaker, Edmond de *Histoire de l'harmonie au ma* (Paris 1852; repr Hildesheim 1966) xvi + 374, 38 pll, index
Used with great caution, there is valuable information to be found. C quotes theorists, and texts, and gives diplomatic facsimiles of lesser known sources.

27 Crocker, Richard L. *A History of M Style* (New York 1966) xi + 573, m exx, b, index / rev J. Pruett *JMTh* 11 (1967) 144–9
Med. M is discussed on pp 1–153, beginning ca 700 with plainsong and troping. C deals stylistically with written-down M, and ignores the origins of the philosophical, ethical, and aesthetic attitudes of the MA. The period receives better treatment than is usual, and the opinions are stimulating, original, and sometimes unconventional, but founded on firm understanding and solid research rather than on second-hand information. Unfortunately documentation is sacrificed in favour of readability.

28 Harman, Alec *Med. and Early Renaissance M* MAN AND HIS M vol 1 (London 1958) xii + 268, 17 pll, illus, exx, indices / rev R. Tidmarsh *ML* 39 (1958) 398–9
This is an excellent elementary textbook. Defects are its omission of the English school of the 13–14c and of M treatises, and its scant documentation and bibliography. Virtues are its M examples, usually of complete pieces

with translated texts, and its necessarily simple suggestions for their performance, and its enthusiasm for aesthetic appreciation of the M.

29 Lang, Paul H. *M in Western Civilisation* (New York 1941)
Greek, Byz., and med. M are discussed on pp 1–180. There are plates, maps, comprehensive index and bibliography. The facts are sometimes incorrect, but L's grasp of cultural generalisation is masterly.

30 THE NEW OXFORD HISTORY OF M (NOHM), accompanied by a set of discs, *The History of M in Sound,* with its own set of explanatory booklets. There are better recordings available. Vol 1 *Ancient and Oriental M* ed Egon Wellesz (London 1957) xxiii + 530 / rev C. Sachs *Notes* 15 (1957/8) 97–9. Vol 2 *Early Med. M up to 1300* ed Anselm Hughes (revd ed London 1955) xviii + 434 / rev J. Noble *ML* 36 (1955) 65–70. Vol 3 *Ars Nova and the Renaissance, 1300–1540* ed Anselm Hughes and Gerald Abraham (London 1960) xv + 565 / rev T. Dart *ML* 42 (1961) 57–60
All volumes have numerous plates, M examples, bibliography, and index. Vol 1: chapters 7–11 discuss Judaic, Greek, Roman, and Islamic M; vol 2: this volume deals with med. M before its contamination with humanistic ideals; vol 3: chapters 1–7 carry the survey to 1450.

31 THE PELICAN HISTORY OF M Vol 1 *Ancient Forms to Polyphony* ed Denis Stevens and Alec Robertson (London 1960) 343, 16 pll, M exx, index, brief b, discography / rev T. Dart *ML* 44 (1963) 55–6
This is a detailed but undocumented introduction, beginning with non-western M, and the Greek, Arabic, and Jewish background. The section devoted to plainsong includes chapters on Byz., Russian, and other rites. The chief defects are its failure to refer to original sources or modern transcriptions, its avoidance of speculative, aesthetic, and ethical matters, and its neglect of the social function of M. It concentrates on style and form.

32 Reese, Gustave *M in the MA* (New York 1940) xviii + 502, 8 pll, M exx, b, record list, index / rev G. Sarton *Isis* 34 (1942/3) 182–6
This detailed and comprehensive survey begins with ancient times and ends ca 1450, including some discussion of Byz. and Arabic M. Its heavily factual and documented text makes it slow reading but indispensable as a reference work. It is concerned with stylistic and bibliographical information rather than with opinions about social function, aesthetic significance, and performance practices. A new edition is promised and needed.

33 Testi, Flavio *La M italiana nel Medioevo e nel Rinascimento* 2 vols (Milan 1969)
Med. M is discussed in vol 1, pp 1–236, with numerous plates and facsimiles, many in colour. The plates are excellent. Vol 2 has a bibliography and index.

34 Valois, J. de 'La M religieuse française des origines à 1180 environ' *RM* 222 (1953/4) 9–20; J. Chailley '... au XIIIe siècle' 21–9; A. Machabey '... au XIVe siècle' 30–43
The first section has some unusual information.

15 General histories

The earliest centuries

35 Arro, E. 'Das Ost-West-Schisma in der Kirchenmusik' *MOst* 2 (1963) 7–83
A discusses essential differences between church M of East and West.

36 Behn, Friedrich *Musikleben im Altertum und frühen-MA* (Stuttgart 1954) xxiv
+ 180, 100 pll, b, index / rev C. Astruc *L'Antiquité classique* 24 (1955) 284–6
Reviewer says this is essentially a catalogue based on a selection of
reproductions of M instruments best illustrating the MA to the 9c.

37 Gamberini, Leopoldo *La Parola e la M nell'antichità: Confronto fra documenti
M antichi e dei primi secoli del medio evo* HISTORIAE MUSICAE CULTORES: Bibl
15 (Florence 1962) xii + 448, b, indices of examples and subjects / rev J.M.
Barbour *JAMS* 18 (1965) 81–3
G discusses the relationship between Greg. chant and preceding Greek,
Hebrew, Gnostic, Syrian, Byz., and Ambrosian M.

38 Quasten, Johannes *M und Gesang in den Kulten der heidnischen Antike und
Christlichen Frühzeit* LITURGIEGESCH QUELLEN UND FORSCHUNGEN 25 (Münster in Westfalen 1930) xii + 274, 38 pll, index / rev J. Handschin *Acta* 12
(1940) 61–2
Q examines M in cult, ceremony, ritual, and private life, up to ca 4–5c.

39 Werner, Eric *The Sacred Bridge* (London 1959) xxi + 618, glossary, indices
40 / rev E. Leahy *JAMS* 14 (1961) 394–8 **40** Werner 'The Conflict between Hel-
41 lenism and Judaism in the M of the Early Christian Church' *HUCA* 20 (1947)
407–70 **41** Werner 'The Common Ground in the Chant of Church and
Synagogue' **D-9**.134–48, 6 pp transcc
39 The book deals with the interdependence of liturgy and M in synagogue
and church during the first millenium. **40** Summarizing the sources of information, W shows that opposing forces, such as conservatism and syllabic
exactitude (Hellenistic) and flexibility and melismatic freedom (Eastern),
were combined to create Christian M. **41** Identifiable Jewish M converts
transmitted the synagogal tradition to the church. The *tonus peregrinus* is
of synagogal origin. These and other features demonstrate the source of
Christian M tradition.

Church Fathers
42 Werner, Eric 'Notes on the Attitude of the Early Church Fathers towards
Hebrew Psalmody' *Rev of Religion* 7 (1942/3) 339–52 + 1 table, M exx
This is an excellent survey.

43 Stefani, G. 'L'Etica M di S. Agostino' *Jucunda Laudatio* (Venice 1968) 1–65
St Augustine's *De Musica* is examined from philosophical, ethical, and
aesthetic, and from numerological and mystical aspects. Plainsong and its
relation to words and to pagan song is interpreted in the same way.

16 General histories

THE CAROLINGIAN PERIOD

44 Corbin, Solange *L'Eglise à la conquête de sa* M (Paris 1960) 309, 16 pll,
b, chronological table / rev E.J. Leahy *Spec* 38 (1963) 112–16
Discursive and highly documented, this outlines the social conditions and
M development up to the 10c.

45 Jammers, E. 'Byz. in der karolingischen M' *Berichte zum XI. Intern. Byz.-
Kongress, München 1958* (Munich 1958) section v², 1–29 and 46–7
With certain exceptions, Greek influence is much more evident than Byz.
Cf **F-23**.27–39.

46 Schuberth, Dietrich *Kaiserliche Liturgie: die Einbeziehung von Musikin-
strumenten, insbesondere der Orgel, in den früh ma. Gottesdienst* VER. DER
EVANGELISCHEN GES FÜR LITURGIEFORSCHUNG 17 (Göttingen 1968) 155 + 4
pll, b, index / rev H. Reifenberg *LJb* 19 (1969) 252–4
S examines the use of instruments in, and the relation between, court and
church, Byz. and the West.

47 Sesini, Ugo, ed Giuseppe Vecchi *Poesia e* M *nella latinità cristiana dal* III *al
X secolo* NUOVA BIBL ITALIANA 6 (Turin 1949) xvi + 275, 5 facss, b, index / rev
E. Gianturco *Spec* 27 (1952) 250 –4
S deals with sacred and serious poetry, as well as hymns, Sequences, and
tropes. Various transcriptions are included.

48 Schuler, M. 'Die M an der Höfen der Karolinger' *AMw* 27 (1970) 23–40
S accumulates the evidence, mostly scattered in chronicles and other
literature.

THE LATER MIDDLE AGES

These are listed alphabetically by author.

49 Besseler, H. 'Studien zur M des MA' *AMw* 7 (1925) 167–252 and 8 (1926)
137–258
With descriptions and inventories B relates the major sources of med. M and
theory. The documentation is good and the inventories are often the only
ones available. The first part deals with polyphony in the 14c and early 15c;
the second deals with the motet from Franco to Vitry. B prints some texts
and transcribes some important pieces.

50 Bukofzer, M.F. 'Changing Aspects of Med. and Renaissance M' *MQ* 44
(1958) 1–18
B considers some problems and underlying traits of the M in the light of
sources not well known at the time.

51 Coussemaker, Edmond de *L'Art harmonique aux* XII*ᵉ et* XIII*ᵉ siècles* (Paris

1865; repr Hildesheim 1964) xii + 292 + i–cv dipl facss + 1–138 M transcc, index

There is still useful factual information here, if the item is used with caution. C prints many texts and indices, and gives an inventory of the Montpellier Ms.

52 Gennrich, F. 'Internationale ma. Melodien' *ZMw* 11 (1928/9) 259–96, 321–48, 6 facss, index of transcc

With extensive comparative transcriptions showing variants, G shows that many plainsongs, secular tunes, and polyphonic pieces were common currency for sacred and secular works in many parts of Europe, from 12–16c. Where a tune is missing, but known, G sometimes combines different sources to make a conflated, fictitious example: the origins should always be checked.

53 Handschin, J. 'Die Rolle der Nationen in der ma. Mg' *SJbMw* 5 (1931) 1–42
54 54 Günther, U. secretary, Round Table 'Die Rolle Englands, Spaniens, Deutschlands, und Polens in der M des 14. Jh.' A-5.II.188–200

53 This is a general survey, designed to emphasise the role of nations other than France. Pp 31–42 have an excursus on instruments and performance practices. **54** Several scholars contribute information about sources and styles.

55 Ludwig, F. 'Die geistliche nichtliturgische, weltliche einstimmige und die mehrstimmige M des MA bis zum Anfang des 15. Jh.' *Handbuch der Mg* vol 1 ed Guido Adler (2nd ed Vienna 1929) 157–295, 2 facss, num M exx / rev *Musikerziehung* 6 (1929) 13–20

This is a standard survey.

56 Ludwig, Friedrich *Studien über die Geschichte der mehrstimmigen M im MA* SMMA 16 (1966) vii + 146 (original pagination at the top of the page)

This reprints or retypes articles in journals and festschriften, but the references are inaccurate or confusing. The sections and their sources are as follows: 1 'Die mehrstimmige M des 14. Jh.' *SIMG* 4 (1902/3) 16–69; 2 'Die 50 Beispiele Coussemakers aus der Hs von Montpellier' *SIMG* 5 (1903/4) 177–224; 3 'Die mehrstimmige M der ältesten Epoche im Dienste der Liturgie' *KmJb* 19 (1924) 1–16; 4 'Über die Entstehung und die erste Entwicklung der lateinischen und französischen Motette in M Beziehung' *SIMG* 7 (1905/6) 514–28; 5 'Die liturgischen Organa Leonins und Perotins' F-24. 200–13.

Texts

editions **56a 59 63** indices **56a–59** metrical studies **60–61a** surveys **58 59 62 64**

56a *Analecta Hymnica* 55 vols (all pub Leipzig); Guido Maria Dreves ed vols 1–24 (1886–96) and 26 28 30 32 35 36 38 41 43 45a 45b (with Clemens Blume) 46 (with Blume) 48 50 (1897– 1907); Blume ed vols 25 27 29 31 33 34 37 39 42 44 47 (with Henry M. Bannister) 49 51 52 53–54 (with Bannister) 55 (1897–1922); Bannister ed vol 40 (1902)
A large proportion of the texts edited in this invaluable collection have M settings, a few of which the editors include, in very old-fashioned transcriptions. All volumes have indices of incipits; some have indices of saints or feasts. Several 'series' are incorporated, as follows:
HYMNS *Hymni Inediti: Liturgische Hymnen I–VII* vols 4 11 12 19 22 23 43 (270 274 272 280 300 306 324 pp). *Hymnographi Latini: Lateinische Hymnendichter I–II* vols 48 50 (543 664 pp). *Die Hymnen des Thesaurus Hymnologicus H.A. Daniels I–II* vols 51 52 (372 358 pp). *Das Hymnar der Abtei Moissac im 10. Jh* vol 2 (174 pp). *Das Hymnar der Abtei S. Severin* vol 14a (143 pp). *Hymnodia Hiberica: Spanische Hymnen* vol 16 (290 pp); see also vol 17 below, under Rhymed Office and under Misc. *Hymnodia Gotica: Die mozarabischen Hymnen* vol 27 (296 pp).
RHYMED OFFICES AND PRAYERS *Historiae Rhythmicae: Liturgische Reimoffizien I–VII* vols 5 13 18 24–6 45a (278 266 266 288 291 292 212 pp); also vol 17 (Spanish offices) (pp 1–188) and vol 52 (pp 329–51). *Pia Dictamina: Reimgebete und Leselieder I–VII* vols 15 29–33 46 (273 240 312 218 238 350 395 pp). *Psalteria Rhythmica: Gereimte Psalterien I–VII* vols 35–6 (275 274 pp). *Ulrich Stöcklins von Rottach: Reimgebete und Leselieder* and *… Reimpsalterien* vols 6 38 (204 248 pp).
TROPES AND SEQUENCES *Tropi Graduales: Tropen des Missale I–II* vols 47 (Ordinary of the Mass) 49 (Propers) (424 404 pp). *Sequentiae Ineditae: Liturgische Prosen I–IX* vols 8–10 34 37 39 40 42 44 (231 296 336 305 304 323 350 332 352 pp). *Liturgische Prosen erster Epoche: Notkerus Balbulus* and *… des Übergangsstiles und der zweiten Epoche: Adam von Sanct Victor* and *… zweiter Epoche* vols 53–5

(414 443 418 pp). *Prosarium Lemovicense: Die Prosen der Abtei St Martial* vol 7 (282 pp).
MISCELLANEOUS *Hymnodia Hiberica: Carmina Compostellana* (Codex Calixtinus) vol 17 (pp 189–236); see **1374**. *Cantiones et Muteti: Lieder und Motetten I-III* vols 20–1 45b (264 226 179 pp); these volumes print texts from very important M manuscripts, which are described. In this bibliography see items **1317 1330 1411 1413 1414 1416 1470 1858**: also BM Egerton 274, BN lat. 3549, 3719, 11412, 15131, St Gall 383, Graz 258, Stuttgart I Asc. 95. Vol 45b deals with Bohemian and Swedish texts: *Cantiones Bohemicae: Leiche, Lieder und Rufe* vol 1 (204 pp). *Konrads von Haimburg* vol 3 (200 pp). *Origo Scaccabarozzi's Liber Officioroum* vol 14b (pp 146–262).

57 Walther, Hans *Initia carminum ac versuum medii aevi posterioris Latinorum* CARMINA MA POSTERIORIS LATINA 1 (2nd ed Göttingen 1969) xiv + 2nd ed 1186, b, index of names and subjects / rev R.W. Hunt *MAe* 40 (1971) 64–6
This is a catalogue of 21,254 med. Latin poems, many of which are set to M (not indicated).

58 Szövérffy, Josef *Weltliche Dichtungen des lateinischen MA.* I: *Von den Anfängen bis zum Ende der Karolingerzeit* (Berlin 1970) 771
This comprehensive survey includes lists of incipits and indices of names and subjects. Subsequent volumes have not yet appeared.

59 Szövérffy, Josef *Die Annalen der lateinischen Hymnendichtung: Ein Handbuch.* I: *Die lateinischen Hymnen bis zum Ende des 11. Jh.* II: *... bis zum Ausgang des MA* (Berlin 1964, 1965) 464; 554 / rev F.J.E. Raby *MAe* 35 (1966) 49–50
Both volumes have bibliographies including editions and anthologies, and indices of textual incipits and names and subjects. S comprehensively surveys the composition of Latin sacred poetry, much of which exists in M settings. Many texts are printed complete. There are references to M (conductus, Sequence, motet, cantio, rondeau, etc).

60 Meyer, Wilhelm *Gesammelte Abhandlungen zur mittellateinischen rythmik* 2
61 vols (Berlin 1905) vii + 375; iii + 403 **61** Chailley, J. 'Essai sur la formation de la versification latine d'accent au ma' *MAe* 29 (1960) 49–80
60 This is a comprehensive account of metre, accent, rhythm, etc. **61** Basing his work on Meyer, C attempts to relate the Carolingian poems of the ms Paris, BN lat. 1154 to the change from quantitative to accentual verse.

61a Norberg, Dag *Introduction à l'étude de la versification latine méd* AUS, Studia Latina Stockholmiensia 5 (Stockholm 1958) 218 + b, indices of texts, etc
In pp 86–183 N discusses Sequences, tropes, motets, rondeaux, and other texts set to M.

62 Spanke, Hans *Deutsche und französische Dichtung des MA* (Stuttgart 1943) viii + 117, index
This is a general survey, not ignoring the M. Pp 18–19 have a list of titles of Sequence tunes.

63 Vecchi, Giuseppe ed *Poesia Latina Medievale* (2nd ed Parma 1958) xl + 522, 34 M transcc, 14 pll and facss, index, index of incipits / rev G. Falco *SM* 18 (1952) 174–85
This is an edition of texts of hymns, Sequences, planctus, conductus, tropi, etc, with the M printed where necessary.

64 Menéndez Pidal, Ramón *Poesía juglaresca y juglares* PUBL DE LA 'REVISTA DE FILOLOGÍA ESPAÑOLA' 7 (Madrid 1924) viii + 488, index, num small facss
This is a general survey, with references to M.

Collections, editions

The collected works of single composers or groups of composers and publications of single sources or genres should be sought under the more specific headings. Of editions in general, scholarly editions, seeking to present with a minimum of editorial alteration the version of the original manuscript, are the most numerous: these are rarely suitable for immediate performance. Publications designed for performance require substantial editorial 'arrangement' in the form of addition of parts for instruments, addition of ornamentation, transposition and adaptation of various kinds (see the section on 'Performance Practice'). In view of the paucity of information editors are reluctant to publish in apparently fixed and unchangeable form music which undoubtedly could be realised in numerous different ways: editions for performance are thus rather rare. The choice of editions which are performable as they stand or with a minimum of arrangement is a matter of very personal judgement. My own cautious selection is as follows:

PERFORMANCE EDITIONS 70 1111 1294 1312 1419 1510 1511 1536 1571–2 1670 1699 1708 1784 1962 liturgical dramas 823–9

ANTHOLOGIES

Apart from **69–71**, which are somewhat more specific, these general collections are arranged alphabetically by title. Others are under genre headings.

65 Gleason, Harold ed *Examples of M before 1400* ESM 10 (revd ed Rochester, NY 1945) xi + 117
This contains 100 pieces from all repertories. It needs substantial revision and the addition of notes and translations of texts. The piano reductions are useful for beginners.

66 *Historical Anthology of M I: Oriental, Med. and Renaissance M* ed Archibald

T. Davison and Willi Apel (revd ed Cambridge, Mass. 1949) xi + 258 / rev
Anselm Hughes ML 29 (1948) 173–4
60 items antedate 1400. There are notes and translations of texts. Especially
useful are the items illustrating the development

plainsong–organum–clausula
plus secular refrain (no. 19d) } to motet (nos 28a–i)
(no. 32d)

and the different organa, clausulae, and motets on the same plainsong (nos
29–32).

67 Entry deleted

68 Parrish, Carl ed *Masterpieces of M before 1750* (New York 1951) x + 235 and
A Treasury of Early M (New York 1958) x + 331
Masterpieces ... has 14, *Treasury* ... has 17 items antedating 1400. Both have
indices, notes, and translations of texts.

69 Husmann, Heinrich ed *Med. Polyphony* transl Robert Kolben, AnthM 9
(Cologne 1962) 62, 1 facs / rev J.A. Westrup ML 45 (1964) 290
H is forced to be highly selective in his choice from the 11–14c, but the
anthology is useful.

70 Lütolf, Max *Die mehrstimmigen Ordinarium Missae-Sätze* 2 vols (Bern 1970)
338 + 32 facss, index of mss, ext b; 236
Vol 1 is a detailed study of the sources, 11–14c. L traces plainsongs and tropes.
Vol 2 consists of transcriptions, with critical apparatus and an introduction
on the notation.

71 Göllner, Theodor *Die mehrstimmigen liturgischen Lesungen* 2 vols, MVM 15
(Tutzing 1969) xxx, 12 facss + 359; 200, 2 facss, b, index
Vol 1 contains diplomatic facsimiles, with commentary and ms references;
vol 2 contains a stylistic analysis.

FACSIMILES

These are general collections. Other facsimiles should be sought under more
specific headings.

72 Bannister, Henry M. ed *Monumenti Vaticani di paleografia M latina* 1 vol, 1
portfolio (Leipzig 1913; repr London 1968) lxi + 284; x facss + 130 facss
The text is in Italian. The sources are mostly of plainsong. Vol 1 is essentially
a catalogue of sources and notations, with an index of incipits. Vol 2 (portfolio) has 206 reproductions (9–14c) preceded by 10 plates illustrating and
classifying more than 200 neumes.

73 EARLY BODLEIAN M Sir John Stainer ed *Sacred and secular M from Mss in the*
74 *Bodleian Library* EBM vol I (London 1901; repr Farnborough 1967) xxviii + 223

facss (black and red), with introduction and indices of texts and mss
74 Edward B. Nicholson ed *Introduction to the study of some of the oldest Latin M Mss in the Bodleian Library, Oxford* EBM vol III (London 1913; repr Farnborough 1967) xciv + 71 facss
73 These are mostly sources from the later MA. Vol II contains old-fashioned transcc. **74** N describes the pre-12c sources.

75 Jammers, Ewald *Tafeln zur Neumenschrift* (Tutzing 1965) 151, 43 facss / rev M. Huglo *RdM* 51 (1965) 98–9
J studies early notation, describing each plate in detail.

76 Thibaut, Jean-Baptiste ed *Monuments de la Notation Ekphonétique et Neumatique de l'église latine* (St Petersburg 1912) xix + 104, 50 facss + 94 pll with 376 facss
These are facsimiles of French and Polish mss in the Imperial Library of Leningrad before 1912, with a copious introduction describing the notation and sources.

77 Vecchi, Giuseppe ed *Atlante paleografico M* (Bologna 1951) 16 + 12 facss
V describes the notation exemplified in his plates (9–15c).

Philosophy and speculative music literature

This section deals with M's intellectual, physical, moral, and mystical functions, i.e., with *musica speculativa*, and with the medieval conception of M. These topics are unfamiliar to the modern western world and a re-Orientation is essential (see especially **78**). Philosophical attitudes stem from classical antiquity. Aesthetics, as **79–81** show, cannot be understood in the modern, subjective sense, and aesthetic quality is determined by philosophy, mathematics, and metaphysics.

78 Sachs, C. 'Primitive and Med. M: a Parallel' *JAMS* 13 (1960) 43–9
S discusses oral transmission, voice production, tuning (or intonation), melodic construction, rhythm, form, and polyphony. This study should be the starting point for studies of med. M.

79 Hollander, John *The Untuning of the Sky* (Princeton 1961) xiii + 467, 16 pll / rev J. Stevens *ML* 43 (1962) 137–8
Ostensibly concerned with 'Ideas of M in English Poetry 1500–1700,' H presents much information about med. M. The book traces the philosophical, aesthetic, and ethical attitude to M from classical antiquity to the 17c and avoids technical aspects. The nature of M, its relation to poetry and mathematics, and its speculative and social functions are illustrated with quotations from contemporary poetry.

80 Abert, Hermann *Die Musikanschauung des MA* (Halle 1905; repr with foreword by H. Hüschen, Tutzing 1964) ix + 274, index
Cassiodorus was more influential than Boethius: medieval aesthetics were based on Pythagorean and Neo-Platonic ideas.

81 Bruyne, Edgar de *Etudes d'esthétique méd.* 3 vols I: *De Boèce à Jean Scot Erigène.* II: *L'Epoque romane.* III: *Le XIII* siècle RIJKSUNIVERSITEIT TE GENT: WERKEN UITGEGEVEN DOOR DE FACULTEIT VAN DE WIJSBEGEERTE EN LETTEREN 97e, 98e, 99e AFLEVERING (Bruges 1946) xiv + 371; x + 420; x + 400 (B's one-vol abridgement, publ Louvain 1946, transl Eileen B. Hennessy as *The Esthetics of the MA* (New York 1969) viii + 232) / rev of the original

and the author's abridgement by S. Clercx *RBM* 2 (1947) 59–64
The abridgement omits the copious citations from original sources. The section on M is excellent and B shows that the speculative view of M is identical with the fundamental principles on which med. aesthetics is based. The whole book may be recommended.

82 Portnoy, Julius *M in the Life of Man* (New York 1963) xx + 300, glossaries, b, index / rev S. Benedict *Notes* 20 (1963) 656–7
P gives cultural information in a highly unusual manner which cuts across historical sequence. He exposes the relation between med. M and philosophy, mathematics, therapy, science, metaphysics, etc.

83 Portnoy, Julius *The Philosopher and M* (New York 1954) xv + 268 / rev C.
84 Palisca *JAMS* 8 (1955) 223–4 **84** Portnoy 'Similarities of M Concepts in
85 Ancient and Med. Philosophy' *JAAC* 7 (1948/9) 235–43 **85** Hüschen, H.
'Antike Einflüsse in der ma. Musikanschauung' *Miscellanea mediaevalia* I.
Antike und Orient im MA THOMAS-INST (Cologne 1962) 80–95
83 In pp 1–106 P examines what M was to med. man, tracing the origins to Greek concepts. **84** Platonic aesthetic theory becomes artistic actuality in the MA. Chinese, Hebrew, Greek, and med. theories are all similar. **85** This is an excellent summary of the speculative legacy derived mainly from the Greeks.

86 Schrade, L. 'M in the Philosophy of Boethius' *MQ* 33 (1947) 188–200 **87**
87 Eggebrecht, H. 'Ars musica. Musikanschauung des MA und ihre Nachwirkungen' *Die Sammlung. Zs für Kultur und Erziehung* 12 (1957) 306–22
86 Boethius' *Musica* is primarily an 'exhortation' to philosophy, with elements of an 'introduction' to M itself. **87** The med. view of M as a mathematical introduction to philosophy lingers until the 18c.

88 Bukofzer, M.F. 'Speculative thinking in med. M' *Spec* 17 (1942) 165–80, 1 facs
Things unrelated in sound and effect may be related by the intellect through proportion and number: B thus shows how speculative ideals may be demonstrated in practical M. See **754** for some factual corrections. B also shows that troping is analogous to glossing.

89 Handschin, J. 'Die Musikanschauung des Johannes Scotus Erigena' *DVLG* 5 (1927) 316–41
Scotus (9c) transmits (neo-)Platonic number symbolism and speculative theory of the cosmos.

MUSIC OF THE SPHERES

Musica mundana, as it appears in poetry, art, etc, is a symbol of world order.

89a Spitzer, Leo *Classical and Christian Ideas of World Harmony* (Baltimore 1963)
xv + 232, index

S comprehensively examines the philosophical, literary and philological context of *stimmung*, showing its connection with *musica mundana*. This expands articles in *Traditio* 2 (1944) 409–64 and 3 (1945) 307–64.

90 Handschin, J. 'Ein ma. Beitrag zur Lehre von der Sphaerenharmonie' *ZMw*
91 9 (1926/7) 193–208, 3 facss **91** Schneider, M. 'Die M Grundlagen der
92 Sphärenharmonie' *Acta* 32 (1960) 136–51 **92** Meyer-Baer, Kathi *M of the Spheres and the Dance of Death* (Princeton 1970) xxvii + 376, 174 pll / rev M.W. Bloomfield *Spec* 46 (1971) 172–4
90 H quotes literary passages and a complete M piece which relate M and cosmology. **91** S examines the symbolism. **92** M deals with abstract concepts of symbolism in M iconology.

93 Zitmann, R. 'Wort und Weise im ordo des MA' *DVLG* 21 (1943)
94 437–61 **94** Chamberlain, D.S. 'Philosophy of M in the *Consolatio* of Boethius' *Spec* 45 (1970) 80–97
93 Z refers to features which could demonstrate the universal order of *musica mundana* in theoretical and practical M. **94** C recognizes the essential role of M in the med. conception of all physical and spiritual states.

95 Tolnay, C. de 'M of the Universe' *JWAG* 6 (1943) 83–104, 23 pll **96** Cham-
96 berlain, D.S. '*Anticlaudianus*, III 412–445, and Boethius' *De Musica*,' *Msct*
97 13 (1969) 167–9 **97** Chamberlain 'The M of the Spheres and *The Parlement of Foules*,' *ChR* 5 (1971) 32–56
95 T traces the importance of representations in art, mosaics, murals, etc. **96** This passage of the poem mirrors Boethius' threefold division of M. **97** Rhyme scheme, metre, structure, length, and many other features of the poem are strictly determined by M concepts of number and harmony (cf the article immediately preceding this one, pp 22–31, not listed here).

SOME LATER WRITERS AND WRITINGS

Albertus Magnus and Aquinas

98 Hüschen, H. 'Albertus Magnus und seine Musikanschauung' **F-15.**
99 205–18 **99** Burbach, Hermann-Josef *Studien zur Musikanschauung des Thomas von Aquin* KBMf 34 (Regensburg 1966) 142 / rev C.D. EG 9 (1968) 112 These are general introductions.

Echecs amoureux

100 Abert, H. 'Die Musikästhetik der *Echecs amoureux*,' *Romanische Forschungen* 15 (1904) 884–925 and *SIMG* 6 (1904/5) 346–55
A prints the section on M from this 14c poem, and in *SIMG* comments on the attitude towards traditional concepts, that the spheres are not actual, only intellectual.

101 Entry deleted

Gundisalvi, Hildegard, Jacobus of Liège

102 Oberti, E. 'La M nel *De divisione philosophiae* di Domenico Gundisalvi'
103 *Rivista di Estetica* 7 (1962) 58–82 **103** Schmidt-Görg, J. 'Die Musikan-
104 •schauung in den Schriften der hl. Hildegard' *Der Mensch und die Künste: Fs
für Heinrich Lützeler zum 6o. Geburtstage* (Düsseldorf 1962) 230–7 **104** Smith,
F.J. 'A Med. Philosophy of Number: Jacques de Liège and the *Speculum
Musicae*' D-7.1023–39
102 This is a very general examination of the place of M in philosophical and
aesthetic thought. **103** Hildegard's letters, quoted extensively, rehearse
largely conventional views. **104** The *Speculum* is a *summa* of the mathematical and philosophical basis for med. M.

MUSICUS AND *CANTOR*

This section concerns the difference between reason and sense in understanding M.

105 Meyer-Baer, K. 'Psychologic and Ontological Ideas in Augustine's *De
106 Musica*' *JAAC* 11 (1952) 224–30 **106** Corbin, Solange '*Musica* spéculative et
cantus pratique. Le rôle de Saint Augustin dans la transmission des sciences M' *CCM* 5 (1962) 1–12
105 Augustine explains that both reason and feeling are necessary to understand M fully, and emphasises the movement of M through time, two aesthetic factors not to reappear for many centuries. **106** His attitude brings *cantor*
and *musicus* into communication. Despite Augustine's influence, the two
split profoundly.

107 Hammerstein, Reinhold *Die M der Engel: Untersuchungen zur Musikanschauung des MA* (Bern, Munich 1962) 303 + 144 pll, b, index / rev
TLS June 1963, 416
The angels stand in the same relationship to the *cantor* as the spheres do
to the *musicus*. H interprets 'angelic' appearances in literature and art.

108 Gurlitt, Willibald *Zur Bedeutungsgeschichte von 'musicus' und 'cantor' bei
109 Isidor von Sevilla* AKW UND DER LITERATUR IN MAINZ, Geistes- und sozialwissenschaftliche Klasse, Abh, Jahrgang 1950, no. 7 (Wiesbaden 1950) 20
(originally pp 541–58) **109** Pietzsch, G. 'Bildung und Aufgaben des Kantors
im MA und Frühprotestantismus' *Die Musikpflege* 4 (1933) 221–35
108 Historically *musicus* relates to the Greek and speculative, *cantor* to the
Roman and practical. **109** P discusses the *cantor/musicus* distinction, and the
training and responsibilities of the former.

110 Hüschen, H. 'Berufsbewusstsein und Selbstverständnis von Musicus und

Cantor im MA' *Miscellanea mediaevalia* III. *Beiträge zum Berufsbewusstsein des ma. Menschen* ed Paul Wilpert (Berlin 1964) 225–38
Cantor comprehends the distinctly separate concepts of artifice and spontaneity (*musica artificialis/naturalis*), to which composer/performer and church singer/entertainer correspond.

111 Ellinwood, L. 'Ars Musica' *Spec* 20 (1945) 290–9
E discusses the different views taken by academicians and theorists, mainly in the 13c.

112 Kresteff, A.D. 'Musica Disciplina and Musica Sonora' *JRMEd* 10 (1962) 13–29
Practical M, tolerated in the ecclesiastical tradition of St Augustine, eventually acquired intellectual justification by incorporating elements from the quadrivium of Boethian tradition.

RELATED TOPICS

imagery **123a** magic **113 113a 115–19** mysticism **113 122** numbers **115 117 118** science and medicine **114 120 123** symbolism **115 121**

113 Stege, Fritz M, *Magie, Mystik* (Remagen 1961) 323, 8 pll **113a** Stege *Das*
113a *Okkulte in der M* (Münster i.W. 1925)
These are comprehensive studies.

114 Liessem, Franz M *und Alchemie* (Tutzing 1969) 179, with 182–item b / rev C.W. Warren *Notes* 27 (1970) 55–6

115 Vogel, Martin *Die Zahl Sieben in der spekulativen Musiktheorie* (Bonn 1954) 339
The number 7 is significant acoustically, magically, and symbologically. Cf **117.**

116 Combarieu, Jules *La M et la magie* EPM 3 (Paris 1909) viii + 375, M exx, index
Religious song is fundamentally magical. C's references provide a useful start.

117 Ruelle, C.E. 'Le Chant gnostico-magique des sept voyelles grecques' *Con-*
118 *grès intern. d'histoire de la M, Paris 1900* (Solesmes 1901) 15–27 **118** Poirée, E. 'Chant des sept voyelles: formules M des papyrus magiques' ibid 28–38

119 Wagner, P. 'Das *Media vita' SJbMw* 1 (1924) 18–40
W gives the basic information. Meyer (**311.83**) refers to its connections with magic.

120 Vecchi, G. 'Medecina e musica, voci e strumenti nel *Conciliator* (1303) di Pietro da Abano' *Quad* 8 (1967) 5–22
The physician relies on M to transcend the purely corporal with spiritual therapy.

121 Schneider, Marius *El Origen Musical de los Animales-Simbolos en la Mitología*

y la Escultura Antiguas IEM (Barcelona 1946) vii + 472, 45 pages of pll / rev
N. Fraser *ML* 29 (1948) 213–14
Comparing an Indian theory of the 13c, S shows definite evidence relating
animal symbols and M pitches. Cf **312**.

122 Machabey, A. 'Remarques sur le lexique M du *De Canticis* de Gerson' *Rom*
79 (1958) 175–236, 3 facss
From the edition of 1606, M abstracts the important terms and explains them
in the form of a glossary. Gerson's treatise (early 15c) is much concerned
with mystical aspects of M.

123 Machabey, A. 'Notions scientifiques disseminées dans les textes
musicologiques du ma.' *MD* 17 (1963) 7–20
M shows the way in which M was allegorically and symbolically or actually
related to the sciences.

123a Chamberlain, D.S. 'Wolbero of Cologne (d1167): a Zenith of M imagery'
Med. Studies 33 (1971) 114–26
'In exegetical and contemplative tradition, all aspects of M activity are
figures or metaphors for moral or religious activity' and 'all imaginable
moral and religious qualities can be signified by M imagery.'

Notation

See separate sections under 'Byzantium' and 'Plainsong.' Items **124–8** deal with concepts of notation and some scribal preliminaries.

124 Chailley, Jacques *La M et le Signe* (Lausanne 1967) 128, num illus, facss / rev D. Launay *RdM* 54 (1968) 114–15
This is a comprehensive history of the representation and ornamentation of M in notation, gesture, art, etc. There are few references.

125 Karkoschka, Erhard 'Darmstadt hilft der Notation neuer M' *Melos* 33 (1966) 76–85, 6 facss
Comparing med. and 20c scores, K shows that note symbols are only one means of notation and are not indispensable.

126 Huglo, M. 'Règlement du XIIIᵉ siècle pour la transcription des livres notés' **F-29.**121–33
H prints and discusses rules for copying and noting plainsong. He remarks on the use of the *custos*.

127 Van, G. de 'La Pédagogie M à la fin du ma.' *MD* 2 (1948) 75–97
V shows how late med. notation reflects the attitude that M was an esoteric science.

128 Van Dijk, S.J.P. 'An advertisement sheet of an early 14c writing master at Oxford' *Scrip* 10 (1956) 47–64
The master probably specialised in liturgical texts and chants. V describes how the scribe set about writing text and M.

INSTRUCTION MANUALS

These items explain to the present-day reader how to transcribe into some form of modern notation. See next section.

129 Wolf, Johannes *Geschichte der Mensural-Notation von 1250–1460* 3 vols

(Leipzig 1904; one-vol repr Hildesheim 1965) x + 424, index; viii + 150; vii + 202 / rev F. Ludwig *SIMG* 6 (1904/5) 597–641: a detailed, complementary and descriptive review, to which W replies in *SIMG* 7 (1905/6) 131–8
Vol 1 has a comprehensive discussion, with index, of all notations and of sources, many of which are inventoried. Some matters of detail are to be corrected. Vol 2 includes 78 pieces in two-colour dipl facs. Vol 3 includes transcriptions (in long note values) of the pieces in vol 2.

130 Wolf, Johannes *Handbuch der Notationskunde* 2 vols (Leipzig 1913, 1919; repr Hildesheim 1963) xii + 488, num facss (some col, some dipl) and M transcc (alphabetically listed, xi–xii), index; xvii + 519
Vol 1 *Tonschriften des Altertums und des ma. Choral- und Mensuralnotation.* W deals with paleography and notation (Byzantine, accent, letter, plainsong, mensural, and modal). There is copious reference to mss, facsimiles, and theoretical evidence. Vol 2 deals with 16–17c.

131 Apel, Willi *The Notation of Polyphonic M, 900–1600* MAA 38 (5th ed revd and enl Cambridge, Mass. 1961) xxv + 462 + appendix (transcc), num facss, M exx / rev (4th ed) O. Gombosi *Notes* 7 (1949/50) 283–5
This is a standard work, but complex and detailed, and omits many areas such as plainsong notation and other relevant disciplines: in this respect **130** is more useful.

132 Parrish, Carl *The Notation of Med. M* (London 1958) xvii + 228, 62 facss / rev T. Dart *ML* 40 (1959) 79–80
This is simple and brief. P does not transcribe complete pieces, but gives translations of the texts and other useful information.

132a *Abriss der frankonischen Mensuralnotation des XIV. Jh. und der ersten Hälfte des XV. Jh.* 2 vols, MwSb 1–2 (2nd enl ed 1956) and MwSb 3–4 (1948 [2nd ed not seen]) 36 + separate booklet 6 + 30 facss; 28 including 27 col facss + separate booklet 31 + 6 col M exx
This introduction is less comprehensive than **131**, more difficult to use than **132**.

EDITING FROM MEDIEVAL NOTATION

These items, and **1929,** discuss what forms of modern notation are preferable. A related editorial problem is that of 'Chromaticism' (**250–61**).

133 Carapetyan, A. 'A Preface to the Transcription of Polyphonic M' *MD* 5 (1951) editorial 3–14
C discusses the general principles of editing old M and the major problems facing the transcriber. Cf **135**.

134 Sachs, C. 'Some remarks about old Notation' *MQ* 34 (1948) 365–70

Discussing notation, tempo, and transcription, S rightly attacks many editors of the first half of the 20c.

135 Stevens, D. 'Problems of Editing and Publishing Old M' A-4.1.150–8
This is very general. Joel Newman reports discussion of the paper in II.101–4, and there is an editorial response by Armen Carapetyan in *MD* 15 (1961) 5–14.

NOTATION PRIOR TO THE TWELFTH CENTURY

This section mainly, but not exclusively, concerns plainsong, and is basically chronological in arrangement.

Accents and neumes: origins, dissemination, and meaning

136 Suñol, Dom Grégoire M. *Introduction à la paléographie M grég.* (Paris, Rome 1935) 660, 154 facss, M exx, several bb, analytical index, indices of neumes, notations, scripts, places, persons, mss; map and tables showing comparative notations / rev W.H. Frere *ML* 17 (1936) 265–7
This is an exhaustive compendium of early plainsong notation, dealing with the origin and development of plainsong itself, of neumes, alphabetic notations, etc, emphasising local variations. The question of plainsong rhythm is broached. The book is difficult and specialised, but the plates are useful for illustrating the wide range and distribution of early notation.

137 Cardine, E. 'Sémiologie grég.' *EG* 11 (1970) 1–158 (first appeared independently, in Italian, as *Semiologia greg.* (Rome 1968) 185)
Different signs are transcribed identically in modern Vatican editions. Semiology investigates graphic distinctions. C concludes that variations indicate not mensural (i.e., fixed and proportional) but rhythmic (i.e., flexible and variable) values. Modern notation used at Solesmes tries to show these irrational rhythms.

138 Agustoni, L. 'Notation neumatique et interprétation' *RG* 30 (1951) 173–90, 223–30 and 31 (1952) 15–26, complemented by E. Cardine on pp 55–65
Graphic distinctions justify modern notation and performance.

139 Thibaut, Jean-Baptiste *Origine byz. de la notation neumatique de l'église latine* BIBL MUSICOLOGIQUE 3 (Paris 1907) viii + 108 + 28 facss, transcc, diagrams, b
T traces the development of Byz. notation and tries to show that from it originated the western neumes.

140 Jammers, E. 'Die materiellen und geistigen Voraussetzungen für die Ent-
141 stehung der Neumenschrift' *DVLG* 32 (1958) 554–75 **141** Jammers 'Studien zu Neumenschriften, Neumenhss und neumierter M' *Bibliothek und Wissenschaft* 2 (1965) 85–161, 4 facss (partial repr in F-16.70–87)

J discusses in **140** the earliest hints of notation, prior to the 9c, and the relationship with prosody, and in **141** the connection between accent and M inflection in several mss of 9–10–11c.

142 Corbin, S. 'Les Notations neumatiques en France à l'époque carolingienne'
143 *R d'hist de l'église de France* 38, no. 131 (Paris 1952) 225–32 **143** Jammers, E.
144 'Die paläofränkische Neumenschrift' *Sçrip* 7 (1953) 235–59 (repr in **F-**
145 **16**.35–58, 4 facss) **144** Jammers 'Zur Entwicklung der Neumenschrift im
146 Karolingerreich' *Otto Glauning zum 60. Geburtstag* (Festgabe aus *Wis-*
147 *senschaft und Bibliothek*) (Leipzig 1936) 89–98 (repr in **F-16**.25–34)
145 Tintori, G. 'La Più antica tradizione melodica del R.G. *Dilexisti iusti-tiam' CHM* 2(Florence 1957) 433–46, 3 facss, 4 tables **146** Sesini, Ugo *La Notazione comasca nel cod. Ambrosiano E. 68 sup.* STUDI E TESTI LITURGICO-MUSICALI (Milan 1932) 34, 5 facss, index of incipits **147** Handschin, J. 'Eine alte Neumenschrift' *Acta* 22 (1950) 69–97, 1 facs, and 25 (1953) 87–8 These items describe the origin and dissemination of different notational styles about the 9c. In **145** T compares a 'bilingual' ms.

Neumes: *punctum* and *pes*
148 Arbogast, P.M. 'The small Punctum as isolated Note in Codex Laon 239' *EG*
149 3 (1959) 83–133 **149** Lipphardt, W. 'Punctum und Pes im Cod. Laon 239 [249 in title and list of contents]' *KmJb* 39 (1955) 10–40
148 The symbol indicates brief duration and rapid execution. **149** Statistical comparisons illuminate the melodic meaning.

Neumes: *quilisma*
150 Wiesli, Walter *Das Quilisma im Codex 359 der Stiftsbibliothek St Gallen* (Immensee 1966) xiii + 341 + 90
This is a minutely detailed paleographic study.

Neumes: *flexa* and *torculus*
151 Lipphardt, W. 'Flexa und Torculus im Codex Laon 239' *KmJb* 41 (1957)
152 9–15 **152** Kelly, Columba *The Cursive Torculus Design in the Codex St Gall 359 and its Rhythmical Significance* (St Meinrad, Indiana 1964) xiii + 546, col frontispiece / rev J.A. Emerson *JAMS* 20 (1967) 124–6
152 With extensive documentation and tables, K describes the ms and its notation, concluding that there is a close relation between paleographical forms and verbal and melodic context.

Neumes: transcription
153 Sanden, Heinrich *Die Entzifferung der lateinischen Neumen* (Kassel 1939)
154 91 **154** Sanden *Entzifferungsvorgang neumatischer Tonzeichen* (Regensburg 1959) 54
See also *KmJb* 46 (1962) 35–42. In **153** S deduces from med. theorists nine rules for the clarification of adiastematic neumes: there is a devastating review by W. Lipphardt in *AMf* 6 (1941) 185–8.

* Announced: Sanden, Heinrich *Entzifferung der lateinischen und west-gotisch-mozarabischen Neumen* (in preparation for the series MS)

Neumes: rhythm

155 Jammers, E. 'Grundsätzliches zur Erforschung der rhythmischen Neumenschriften' *Buch und Schrift* ns 5/6 (1942/3) 83–105 (repr in **F-16**.9–24, 2 facss)
J thinks that neumes indicate rhythm, but that the principles differ with each source.

Neumes: terminology

156 Huglo, M. 'Les Noms des neumes et leur origine' *EG* 1 (1954) 53–67
Listing mss, H concludes that terminology began in the early 11c, borrowing Greek words. In the 12c component elements of neumes were analysed, with a corresponding simplification in terminology.

Neumes: non-musical uses

157 Jammers, E. 'Neumen im lateinunterricht' *Fs Martin Bollert zum 80. Geburtstag* (Dresden 1956) 64–8
Neumes are used pedagogically to indicate grammatical structure.

158 Dreimüller, K. 'Neumen als Korrekturzeichen im ma. hss' *Mf* 7 (1954) 210–11

Alphabetic notations

159 Vogel, M. 'Boetius und die Herkunft der modernen Tonbuchstaben' *KmJb* 46 (1962) 1–19
V thinks Boethius' letters are of both theoretical and practical significance.

160 Smits van Waesberghe, J. 'Les Origines de la notation alphabétique au ma.' *AnuarioM* 12 (1957) 3–16
S distinguishes letters denoting pitches from those denoting geometrical points on the monochord, and explains why the instrumental series differs from the vocal.

161 Corbin, S. 'Valeur et sens de la notation alphabétique, à Jumièges et en Normandie' **D-10**.II.913–24, 2 facss facing 913: addenda in *RdM* 50.226
C localises the notation in northern France, and lists sources.

Alphabetic notations: complements to other notations. See 'bilingual' notation.

162 Jammers, E. 'Rhythmen und Hymnen in einer St Galler Hs. des 9. Jh.' **F-29**.134–42, 2 facss
J describes the pitch and rhythmic indications of the *litterae significatae*.

35 Notation

Early notation on lines

163 Wagner, P.J. 'Aus der Frühzeit des Liniensystems' *AMw* 8 (1926) 259–76, 3
164 col facss (dipl ?) **164** Emerson, J.A. 'The Recovery of the Wolffheim
Antiphonal' *JAMS* 12 (1959) 263–4
Red neumes on a stave are entered over earlier heighted black neumes to
define the pitches exactly.

165 Smits van Waesberghe, J. 'The M Notation of Guido of Arezzo' *MD* 5 (1951)
15–53, 4 pll, 1 col table
This is a valuable exposition of Guido's notation and clefs. Numerous mss
are listed to show the wide distribution of the system in 11–12c, and to support the claim for Guido's originality. See **954.**

Ligatures and plicas

These are more important in the notation of the later MA.

166 Anglès, H. 'Die Bedeutung der Plika in der ma. M' **F-11.**28–39
Stressing that it is not a grace-note, A examines various plica symbols and
quotes relevant theoretical passages.

167 Tischler, H. 'Ligatures, Plicae and Vertical Bars in Premensural Notation'
RBM 11 (1957) 83–92
T suggests meanings and interpretations.

Rhythm

The two main systems of the later Middle Ages, the modal succeeded by the mensural system, are fundamentally for use in part-music and through their ligatures are related to the text. In monophonic music – in plainsong and secular song – and in textless passages of the sort which occur in conductus the application of these systems, or any others, is extremely difficult and often doubtful. Items dealing with special problems of this nature will be found under the specific genre: **168** discusses them more generally. **169** points to the special meaning of medieval rhythmic terms.

168 Sachs, Curt *Rhythm and Tempo* (New York 1953) 391 / rev T. Dart *ML* 35 (1954) 45–6
Pp 147–97 have a useful exposition of the character and problems of rhythm in the MA. With an admirably commonsense and practical attitude S takes a position on each of the major controversies.

169 Crocker, R.L. '*Musica Rhythmica* and *Musica Metrica* in Antique and Med. Theory' *JMTh* 2 (1958) 2–23
C examines the abstruse and technical meaning of the two terms. See also *KmJb* 39 (1955) 3–9.

THE MODAL SYSTEM

The standard manual on 'Modal Notation' is **1418c**, W. Waite *The Rhythm of 12c Polyphony*, which deals exclusively with works of the Notre Dame school.

170 Husmann, H. 'Les Epoques de la M provençale au ma.' *Actes et mém du premier congrès intern. de langue et littérature du midi de la France* (Avignon 1957) 197–201
This is a simple explanation of pre-modal, modal, and mensural theories, which H sees in chronological sequence.

171 Machabey, A. 'Problèmes de notation M (notations méd. des mss d'Evreux)'
172 F-12.361–87 + 1 facs 172 Machabey 'Hégémonie de la rhythmique M au
173 XIIIe siècle' R d'Esthétique 7 (1954) 10–30 173 Machabey Notations non-
modales des XIIe et XIIIe siècles (3rd ed corrected and enl Paris 1959) iv + I–III
+ 122
171 Briefly reviewing earlier opinions, M concludes that rhythmic modes
in purely ternary form are modern abstractions from philosophical prefer-
ences of the 13c. Ignoring possible inconsistency in the original, M points
to inconsistent modern interpretation, and shows how 12c notation can be
transcribed in binary rhythm. 172 Orthography in some periods does not
correspond to pronunciation, and may therefore be useless for establishing
M rhythm. 13c literary teaching was 'mécanisé' (Gilson): mechanical modal
rhythms may then be justified. 173 M accompanies his M exx with parallel
diplomatic facsimiles. He gives his conclusions regarding the rhythmic
implications, on pp 119–21.

174 Knapp, J. 'Two 13c Treatises on Modal Rhythm and the Discant (Discantus
175 positio vulgaris and De musica libellus [Anon VII])' JMTh 6 (1962)
176 201–15 175 Chailley, J. 'Sur la rythmique des proses victoriennes' F-
11.77–81 176 Flindell, E.F. 'Aspekte der Modalnotation' Mf 17 (1964) 353–77
174 K translates the two tracts without giving the original. 175 C concludes
that modal rhythm owed nothing to the 12c Sequence. 176 F demonstrates
the inadequacy of Waite's uncritical application of theoretical rules (1418c).
Stressing the ambiguity rather than the consistency of modal notation, he
seeks rhythmic clarification through an examination of melodic motives
(colores). Relating the Vatican Organum treatise (1389), F suggests a
development of the typical Notre Dame characteristics.

177 Gennrich, F. 'Die Deutungen der Rhythmik der Kalenda-maya-Melodie'
Romanica: Fs für Gerhard Rohlfs (Halle 1958) 181–92
G discusses various rhythmic interpretations, claiming only one to be cor-
rect. Cf 246.

Binary rhythm

178 Sanders, E.H. 'Duple Rhythm and Alternate Third Mode in the 13c' JAMS
179 15 (1962) 249–91 179 Dittmer, L.A. 'Binary Rhythm, M Theory and the Worcester Fragments' MD 7 (1953) 39–57
178 Somewhat dogmatically reviewing contemporary and modern
accounts, S interprets the slippery and ambiguous evidence to suggest a
binary form of the third mode. 179 This article calls for expertise in 13c notation and may confuse even the expert. [There is as yet no unambiguous
information about chronology, geography, notation, and terminology.
Most scholars agree that there is a theoretical basis for assuming binary
rhythm: the disagreement lies in the method by which it is rendered in
notation, and how it may be identified.]

38 Rhythm

THE MENSURAL SYSTEM, TO 1400

The following items, arranged in approximately chronological order, deal with specific problems. General discussions are in **129–32a**.

180 Reckow, F. '*Proprietas* und *Perfectio*' Acta 39 (1967) 115–43
Quoting relevant passages, R examines the use of these terms in 13c rhythmic theory. See also *ZMw* 8 (1925/6) 103–9 on the *longa*.

181 Dittmer, L.A. 'The Ligatures of the Montpellier Ms' *MD* 9 (1955) 35–55. See also **A-2**.146–54
Demanding an expertise in 13c notation, D tries to show how ligatures reflect the change from modal to mensural principles.

182 Bockholdt, R. '*Semibrevis minima* und *Prolatio temporis*. Zur Entstehung der Mensuraltheorie der Ars Nova' *Mf* 16 (1963) 3–21
Relating mensural to modal system, B traces theoretical terminology and the actual use of the note symbol. He concludes that Vitry's discussion illustrates practice.

183 Günther, U. 'Die Mensuralnotation der Ars nova in Theorie und Praxis' *AMw* 19/20 (1962/3) 9–28
G notes ambiguities and difficulties in 14c notation, especially concerning syncopation, and draws useful conclusions about the development of rhythm in the 14c.

184 Josephson, N.S. 'Vier Beispiele der *Ars subtilior*' *AMw* 27 (1970) 41–58
J describes the rhythmic complexities in, and transcribes, the examples.

Technical matters

Mathematics, through the monochord, is the basis for determining M intervals and their aesthetic value, occasionally for determining precise pitches, and for building M instruments (185–92). Through rhythm, symmetry, and symbolism, the mathematics of M may control features of iconography, poetry, and, as in isorhythm, the M structure itself.

185 Crocker, R.L. 'Pythagorean Mathematics and M' *JAAC* 22 (1963/4) 189–98, 325–35
C shows that the tone 9:8 was the basic unit from which the system was constructed. Essentially C goes through the operations of many M theorists, but in English.

186 Zoubov, V. 'Nicole Oresme et la M' *Med. and Renaissance Studies* 5 (1961) 96–107
Oresme (14c) suggests that aesthetically beautiful M may be produced by irrational as well as by simple mathematical proportions, and rejects the monopoly of the M of the spheres.

187 Adkins, C. 'The Technique of the Monochord' *Acta* 39 (1967) 34–43 **188**
188 Chailley, J. 'La Monocorde et la théorie M' F-28.11–20 **189** Wantz-
189 loeben, Sigfrid *Das Monochord als Instrument und als System* (Halle 1911) iii + 131
All three authors discuss the mathematical theory of acoustics demonstrable on the instrument.

190 Irtenkauf, W. 'Der *Computus ecclesiasticus* in der Einstimmigkeit des MA' *AMw* 14 (1957) 1–15, 2 facss
Mnemonic songs deal with the mathematics and astronomy of the calendar; their note pitches relate to the Dominical letters and Golden numbers of Easter tables.

191 Sachs, C. 'A Strange Med. Scale' *JAMS* 2 (1949) 169–70 **192** Adler, I. 'Les
192 Mensurations des tuyaux d'orgue dans le ms Héb. 1037 de la BN de Paris' *Acta* 40 (1968) 43–53

A shows that S's 'strange scale' (consisting of tones which are 8:7 rather than the usual 9:8) is a misinterpretation of theory which takes into consideration the diameter as well as the length of organ pipes.

THE MELODIC MODES

The word *modus* can mean simply 'method.' It also has three technical meanings (melodic mode, rhythmic scheme, musical interval), as Hüschen (193) demonstrates.

193 Hüschen, H. 'Der Modus-Begriff in der Musiktheorie des MA und der Renaissance' *MlatJb* 2 (1965) 224–32

Surveys

194 Auda, Antoine *Les Gammes* M (Woluwé-St-Pierre nd [rev says 1947]) xxxi
195 + 393, 10 tables / rev J.M. Barbour *JAMS* 4 (1951) 40–2 195 Machabey,
196 Armand *Essai sur les formules usuelles de la* M *occidentale des origines ...*
(Paris 1928) 229 / rev J. Marnold *Mercure de France* 208 (1928) 207–16 196
Machabey *Genèse de la tonalité* M *classique des origines ...* BIBL D'ETUDES M
(Paris 1955) 303, indices of names and terms

Origins and medieval adoption of the modes

197 Werner, E. 'The Origin of the Eight Modes of M (Octoechos). A Study in M
Symbolism' *HUCA* 21 (1948) 211–55. Cf A-2.428–37
W summarizes terms and previous conclusions. His own conclusions are
that (a) the concept dates back to 1000 BC, (b) cosmological, numerical, calendar, and magical religious reasons provide the motivation. From Syrian,
Byz., Jewish and western M evidence, W shows that *post facto* theoretical
systems do not account for every circumstance. Cf 379.

198 Vogel, M. 'Die Entstehung der Kirchentonarten' B-4.101–6 (cf 159) 199
199 Chailley, Jacques *L'Imbroglio des modes* (Paris 1960) 92 / rev H. Potiron *RdM*
200 47 (1961) 126–8 200 Chailley 'La Naissance de la notion modale au ma.' F-
201 2.I.203–10 201 Gombosi, O. 'Studien zur Tonartenlehre des frühen MA' *Acta*
202 10 (1938) 149–74; 11 (1939) 28–39, 128–35; 12 (1940) 21–52 202 Machabey, A.
203 'De Ptolémée aux Carolingiens' *Quad* 6 (1964) 37–56 203 Auda, Antoine *Les
Modes et les tons de la* M *et spécialement de la* M *méd.* ACAD ROYALE DES
SCIENCES, DES LETTRES ET DES BEAUX-ARTS DE BELGIQUE: CLASSE DES BEAUX-
ARTS, Mém Collection in-8°, Tome 3, fasc. 1 (Brussels 1931) 204, 1 facs /
rev Ch. Van den Borren *RUB* 37 (1931/2) 16*–17*
198 V seeks the med. modes in the inversion of the Greek system. 199 200
C questions the Greek origin and suggests several co-existent sources. 201
G concludes that, the modes of antiquity unknown, the med. modes

originated elsewhere. He examines and quotes Byz. theory in this respect. **202** M attempts to clarify the transmission of the modal system via Byzantium and via Boethius. **203** A distinguishes mode (=essence) from tone (=sensible form). The former was inherited directly from the Greeks; the latter is totally different.

Plainsong and the modes

The only major studies of this in English appear in larger histories: the best are **484**.133–78 and **32**.149–64 passim.

203a Jammers, E. 'Einige Anmerkungen zur Tonalität des greg. Gesänges' **F-**
204 **11**.235–44 **204** Chailley, J. 'Une nouvelle méthode d'approche pour l'analyse modale du chant grégorien' **F-15**.85–92. Cf **F-34**.84–93
203a J speculates about the inadequacy of the usual 8 church modes. **204** C, isolating nuclear intervals of a pentatonic scale transposed to make the ornamental notes diatonic, tries to establish a better analytical system than that adopted by med. theorists.

205 Krasuski, Florian *Über den Ambitus der greg. Messgesänge* GAkF 1 (Freiburg 1903) 132, 3 tables
K examines range, final and mode.

206 Claire, Dom Jean 'L'Evolution modale dans les répertoires liturgiques occidentaux' *RG* 40 (1962) 196–211; 41 (1963) 8–29 + 10 tables, 49–62 + 4 tables, 77–102 + 7 tables, 127 –151 + 4 tables
These are special studies of certain styles and modes.

*207 Haberl, F. 'Die Modelltöne der Choraltonarten und ihre Entwicklung in den Gesängen des Messpropriums' *Musica Sacra* 80 (1960) 195–202

Miscellaneous modal matters

208 Gmelch, Joseph *Die Viertelstonstufen im Messtonale von Montpellier* GAkF 6 (Eichstätt 1911) 75
G claims that prior to the 11c plainsong used quartertones, more frequently in the solo sections.

209 Mocquereau, Dom A. and Dom Gabriel M. Beyssac 'De la transcription sur
210 lignes des notations neumatique et alphabétique à propos du Répons *Tua sunt*' **F-24**.137–53, facss **210** Bomm, Urbanus *Der Wechsel der Modalitätsbestimmung in der Tradition der Messgesänge im IX. bis XIII. Jh.* (Einsiedeln 1929) 196 / rev J. Handschin *Acta* 9 (1937) 138–43
Both items refer to (apparent) modal transposition to avoid chromaticism. M and Beyssac illustrate the danger of assuming that written pitch indicates a particular frequency. Bomm analyses the modal characteristics of numerous plainsongs.

211 Kunz, L. 'Ursprung und textliche Bedeutung der Tonartensilben Noeane, Noeagis' *KmJb* 30 (1935) 5–22. See also 23–35
In an ingenious theory K links the syllables with pitches specifying modal characteristics. See **565**.

212 Wagner, P.J. 'Zur ma. Tonartenlehre' **F-1**.29–32
W finds evidence for the *paracter*, co-equal, or *circumaequales* with authentic and plagal modes. Cf Byz. *mesoi* modes, *RdM* 55 (1969) 84.

Extension of the modal system

213 Sachs, C. 'The Road to Major' *MQ* 29 (1943) 381–404 **213a** Aarburg, U.
213a 'Melodiesprache im G-Modus' *Helmuth Osthoff zu seinem 70. Geburtstag* ed Ursula Aarburg and Peter Cahn (Tutzing 1969) 33–49
213 Using ethnomusicological parallels, S analyses melodies according to superimposed thirds, etc, rather than by modal or pentatonic structure. 213a Characteristic formulae such as GAC are modified by the use of B and D, giving pentatonic the flavour of major.

214 Niemöller, K.W. 'Zur tonus-Lehre der italienischen Musiktheorie des ausgehenden MA' *KmJb* 40 (1956) 23–32
N reviews the expansion of the modal system, 14–15c, supposedly centred in Italy.

Polyphony and the modes

The conventional modern assumption is that the modes, designed for plainsong, also apply to part-music.

215 Reaney, G. 'Modes in the 14c, in particular in the M of G. de Machaut' **F-28**.137–43
Assuming that modes are applicable to polyphony, R relates the modal system and solmisation.

215a Hoppin, R.H. 'Tonal Organization in M before the Renaissance' *Paul A. Pisk: Essays in his Honor* ed John Glowacki (Austin, Texas 1966) 25–37
Preservation of cadence formula forces tonal development elsewhere than at ends of phrases. Late 14c secular M often demonstrates clear tonal organization in its opening bars.

TECHNIQUES OF COMPOSITION, HARMONY, AND COUNTERPOINT

Melodic structure, phrasing, symmetry

216 Karp, T. 'Rhythmic Architecture in the M of the High MA' *MH* ns 1 (1970)

217 67–80 **217** Treitler, L. 'm Syntax in the MA: Background to an Aesthetic Problem' *Perspectives of New M* 4 (1965/6) 75–85
216 K examines symmetry achieved by rhythmic patterns in Notre Dame pieces. **217** T shows examples of balanced phrasing, and analyses their melodic and tonal direction.

218 Handschin, J. 'Zur Frage der melodischen Paraphrasierung im MA' *ZMw* 10 (1927/8) 513–59 and 12 (1929/30) 192
This is an important article presenting the case for melodic ornamentation of parallel voices, of repeated sections, and of voices allegedly based on plainsong. Original chants are not given; the last feature is probably overstated.

219 Monterosso, R. 'L'Ornamentazione nella monodia med.' *RCCM* 7 (1965) 724–44, 1 facs
M tries to distinguish essential and ornamental melody notes, using variant transmissions.

220 Schmidt, G. 'Zur Frage des Cantus firmus im 14. und beginnenden 15. Jh.' *AMw* 15 (1958) 230–50
S reviews theories and practice of *cantus firmus* usage.

Part writing

This section is alphabetical by author: the subjects are harmony, consonance, and dissonance **221–3 226 227 229–31 234** cadence **225 230** counterpoint, imitation, and canon **224 226 229 235** tonality **225 232 233**

221 Hüschen, H. 'Der Harmoniebegriff im Musikschrifttum des Altertums und des MA' **A-3**.143–50
H examines the meanings of the word *harmonia*.

222 Dahlhaus, C. 'Über den Dissonanzbegriff des MA' **A-3**.87–8
D traces the definitions of dissonance.

223 Yasser, Joseph *Med. Quartal Harmony* (New York 1938) 103 (repr of *MQ* 23 (1937) 170–97, 333–66; 24 (1938) 351–85) / rev L. Ellinwood *Spec* 15 (1940) 127–8
Y exaggerates his claim for harmonic preference for 4ths rather than 5ths, although his assertion is tenable for melodic structure.

224 Apel, W. 'Imitation in the 13c and 14c' **F-31**.25–38
Imitation is to be found in med. M and it antedates canon.

225 Apfel, E. 'Die klangliche Struktur der spätma. M als Grundlage der Dur-Moll-Tonalität' *Mf* 15 (1962) 212–27 and 16 (1963) 153–6
A examines the development of cadential formulae.

226 Crocker, R.L. 'Discant, Counterpoint, and Harmony' *JAMS* 15 (1962) 1–21

Pursuing the conclusions of **1810**, C shows that imprecision of med. terminology can allow two interpretations of theoretical discant: as a combination of separate horizontal lines, or as a sequence of vertical sonorities. C
stresses the latter, opposing the conventional view.

227 Davis, S. 'The Solus Tenor in the 14c and 15c' *Acta* 39 (1967) 44–64 and 40
228 (1968) 176–8 **228** Hughes, Andrew 'Some Notes on the Early 15c Contratenor' *ML* 50 (1969) 376–87
227 Listing the known examples, D discusses the general principles. Often
the *solus tenor* makes clear a latent or incipient harmonic foundation. **228**
Translating a 14c passage on the function of the contratenor, H examines
the stylistic characteristics of the voice and its position as an essential or
inessential part of the piece.

229 Harbinson, D. 'Consonance and Dissonance in the Old Corpus of the Montpellier Motet Ms' *MD* 22 (1968) 5–13
H sees two-part writing as the key to consonance practices and suggests
abandoning contemporary theoretical statements. He tries to establish
empirical rules for two-part writing in a presentation much too short to support his arguments.

230 Marggraf, W. 'Tonalität und Harmonik in der französischen Chanson
zwischen Machaut und Dufay' *AMw* 23 (1966) 11–31
Without carefully defining criteria M examines the significance of cadences
and the notes of the scale they emphasise, and concludes that tonal coherence increases between 1360 and 1450.

231 Reaney, G. 'Notes on the Harmonic Technique of G. de Machaut' **F-3**.63–8
Analysing three pieces, R concludes that Machaut's technique was not
arbitrary.

232 Salzer, F. 'Tonality in Early Med. Polyphony: towards a History of Tonality'
The M Forum 1, ed W.J. Mitchell and Felix Salzer (New York 1967) 35–98
Assuming that 'motion directed towards a goal' is an elemental factor of
med. M, S reduces Notre Dame compositions to skeletons in order to show
tonal coherence. Ambiguities in his premises and data make them so
adaptable that some analyses are bound to appear convincing. Nevertheless
the attempt is illuminating.

233 Sanders, E.H. 'Die Rolle der englischen Mehrstimmigkeit des MA in der
Entwicklung von Cantus-firmus-Satz und Tonalitätsstruktur' *AMw* 24
(1967) 24–53
S investigates the relation between the treatment of plainsong in polyphony
and the concept of 'tonality.' Accepting some of Lowinsky's criteria for tonality, S maintains that they are present in 13c and 14c English M.

234 Schrade, L. 'Diabolus in musica' *Melos* 26 (1959) 361–73: repr **F-27**.537–55
Without documentation S discusses the categorical prohibition and the use

of the tritone in general. [I do not know of any use of the phrase *diabolus in musica* in the med. period: see **258** passim.]

235 Spratt, J.F. transl 'Contrapuntal Theory of the 14 and 15c from the *Geschichte der Musiktheorie* by Hugo Riemann' *Studies in M Hist and Theory* ed Lee Rigsby, FLORIDA STATE U STUDIES 18 [17 on inner title page] (Tallahassee 1955) 41–128 / rev W. Kimmel *Notes* 13 (1955/6) 435–6. See **919**

CONTRAFACTA

The principle of adapting pre-existent M to new words was widespread and applied to monophony and polyphony. For the former, some indices are available (**238 243** and **1160**). For the latter, indices are being compiled: the *clausula* and motet refrain are central. Later, contrafactum technique is allied to the 14c principle of parody.

236 *Die Kontrafaktur im Liedschaffen des MA* SMMA 12 (1965) xviii + 278, b, indices of songs and names, M exx, dipl facss
This is a discussion of borrowing and adapting.

237 *Lateinische Liedkontrafaktur: Eine Auswahl lateinischer Conductus mit ihren volkssprachigen Vorbildern* MwSb 11 (1956) x + 18 dipl facss + separate booklet viii + 23 dipl facss
Latin and vernacular versions may easily be compared.

238 Gennrich, F. 'Die beiden neuesten Bibliographien altfranz. und altprovenz. Lieder' *ZrPh* 41 (1921) 289–346
G prints catalogues and concordances of large and small mss of French and Provençal songs, with a table showing the various sigla. He complements earlier publications with lists of contrafacta. Cf **243** and *ZrPh* 39 (1919) 330–61.

239 Gennrich, F. 'Liedkontrafaktur in mhd. und ahd. Zeit' *ZdA* 82 (1948/50)
240 105–41; revd in **E-4.**330–77 **240** Gennrich 'Lateinische Kontrafakta altfranzösischer Lieder' *ZrPh* 50 (1930) 187–207, 2 facss
These are general discussions.

241 Husmann, H. 'Die M Behandlung der Versarten im Troubadourgesang der Notre Dame-Zeit' *Acta* 25 (1953) 1–20
H discusses the rhythm and texts of some famous contrafacta and their models.

242 Jammers, E. 'Der Vers der Trobadors und Trouvères und die deutschen Kontrafakten' **F-8.**147–60
J examines the relation between German and French accentuation and the rhythmic differences entailed.

243 Spanke, H. 'Das öftere Auftreten von Strophenformen und Melodien in der altfranzösischen Lyrik' *ZfSL* 51 (1928) 73–117, 1 facs
S lists and analyses secular models for sacred contrafacta, comparing the metrical schemes. He complements **238**.

244 Aarburg, U. 'Ein Beispiel zur ma. Kompositionstechnik. Die Chanson R. 1545 von Blondel de Nesle und ihre mehrstimmigen Vertonungen' *AMw* 15 (1958) 20–40
From complex M and poetical analyses A finds for the priority of the monophonic version.

245 Gennrich, F. 'Zwei altfranzösische Lais' *SM* ns 15 (1942) 1–68, 2 facss
Discussing part of a fragmentary ms and with complete transcriptions (Rh), G shows the M and textual relations between Latin and French contrafacta of the Provençal *Lai Markiol* and derives a stemma from the 12c to the 14c *Roman de Fauvel*. He also transcribes and discusses two versions of the *Lai de Chievrefeuil* and the conductus *Pater sancte dictus Lotharius*.

246 Husmann, H. 'Kalenda maya' *AMw* 10 (1953) 275–9
H shows that *Souvent souspire* is contrafactum rather than model. Cf **177**.

Philippe the Chancellor's contrafacta

247 Falck, R. 'Zwei Lieder Philipps des Kanzlers und ihre Vorbilder' *AMw* 24
248 (1967) 81–98 **248** Husmann, H. 'Ein Faszikel Notre-Dame-Kompositionen
249 auf Texte des Pariser Kanzlers Philipp in einer Dominikaner Hs (Rom, Santa Sabina XIV L 3)' *AMw* 24 (1967) 1–23 **249** Paganuzzi, E. 'L'Autore della melodia della *Altercatio cordis et oculi* di Philippe le Chancelier' *CHM* 2 (1957) 339–43
247 F identifies 12c melodies in a complex of 13c mss and shows that Philipp's songs are different contrafacta of related models. **248** Comparing it with other sources, H describes the ms, transcribes some pieces and texts, and shows how they contribute to knowledge about Philipp. **249** P transcribes six versions of the melody, with contrafactum texts, taking Ventadorn's as the original.

CHROMATICISM, *MUSICA FICTA*

Chromatic notes were sometimes extemporised according to principles based on hexachords and solmisation but stated only generally: these are nowadays the responsibility of the modern editor. Other chromatic notes were written into the manuscripts as accidentals.

Unwritten chromaticism

250 Clercx, S. 'Les Accidents sous-entendus et la transcription en notation moderne' **D-14**.167–95

In a very general manner C examines the editor's problems regarding bar-lines and *musica ficta*.

251 Hibberd, L. '*Musica ficta* and Instrumental M c.1250–c.1350' MQ 28 (1942) 216–26
H denies that instruments played any part in the introduction of chromaticism.

252 Vogel, M. 'Musica falsa und falso bordone' F-36.170–6
With exhaustive etymology V examines *bourdon* and *faux*.

253 Apel, W. 'The partial signatures in the sources up to 1450' Acta 10 (1938) 1–13
254 and 11 (1939) 40–2 254 Lowinsky, E.E. 'The Function of Conflicting Signa-
255 tures in Early Polyphonic M' MQ 31 (1945) 227–60 255 Hoppin, R.H. 'Partial
256 Signatures and Musica Ficta in some early 15c Sources' JAMS 6 (1953)
257 197–215 256 Lowinsky, E.E. 'Conflicting Views on Conflicting Signatures'
JAMS 7 (1954) 181–204 257 Hoppin, R.H. 'Conflicting Signatures Reviewed'
JAMS 9 (1956) 97–117
253 A stresses the use of practical rather than theoretical sources. He pro-poses rules despite his own warnings. 254 L sees conflicting signatures arising because of new cadence structures. Much of his evidence is 15c and 16c. 255 H disputes L's theories and proposes that conflicting signatures indicate different pitch levels, agreeing partly with A. 256 Dealing with M and theory from 13–16c as though a common practice existed, L criticizes H and confirms his own deductions based on the change in cadential patterns. 257 Replying to L, H restates his claim that the phenomenon reflects the simultaneous use of different modes. [None of these theories is truly convincing. New explanations are offered in 257a and 258.]

Manuscript accidentals, hexachords, and the modes

Item 261 concerns a composition lavishly supplied with incomprehensible accidentals.

257a Allaire, Gaston G. *The Theory of Hexachords, Solmization and the Modal System* MSD 24 (1972) 165, 7 facss, num M exx, index / rev Andrew Hughes JAMS (forthcoming)
This is a highly technical study. A juxtaposes med. and renaissance theory, attempting to relate solmisation and modes in order to determine principles for extemporized chromaticism. There is much new material and imaginative re-thinking which makes this an important contribution, but serious errors cast doubt on the reliability of the evidence presented.

258 Hughes, Andrew *Ms accidentals: ficta in focus 1350–1450* MSD 27 (1972) 143,
259 1 pl, index 259 Reaney, G. 'Accidentals in early 15c M' F-18.223–31
258 This is a complex technical study, based on the cosmopolitan Old Hall Ms (1784), of accidentals and key-signatures written into sources, and what

they imply regarding extemporised (i.e., nowadays, editorial) chromaticism. The book repeats the practical editorial suggestions of **1784**. Margaret Bent is writing a parallel theoretical investigation. Research into the visible ms evidence has otherwise been virtually ignored: the only other study is **259**, which in nine pages cannot do justice to the topic.

260 Reaney, G. 'Musica ficta in the works of G. de Machaut' **D-14**.196–213
R assumes the relevance of modes while considering chromaticism.

261 Seay, A. 'The beginnings of the coniuncta and Lorenzo Masini's "L'Antefana"' **D-5**.51–65
S's attempt at a solution does not answer all the questions. He collates his own version with the original and with Lowinsky's attempts.

TEXTUAL CRITICISM

This section presents attempts to derive manuscript filiations from analysis of variant and error in M scores. Text and M are inseparable in this respect.

262 Aarburg, U. 'Muster für die Edition ma. Liedmelodien' *Mf* 10 (1957) 209–17
Adapting textual analysis to M, A attempts filiation techniques and invents analytical symbols.

263 *Die autochthone Melodie* MwSb 21 (1953) xvi + 59
Friedrich Gennrich explains principles and methods of M 'Textkritik.' He includes an index of texts and 37 diplomatic transcriptions.

264 Bittinger, Werner *Studien zur M Textkritik des ma. Liedes* LMw 11 (Würzburg 1953) xx + 171 + 36 pp separate M appendix, 5 facss, b, index / rev H. Husmann *Neue Zs für M* 117 (1956) 359–60
B seeks to establish the M stemma of four songs from different nations.

265 Hughes, D.G. 'The Sources of *Christus manens*' **F-23**.423–34
H deduces a stemma, and discusses its implications.

266 Mužík, František *Úvod do kritiky hudebního zápisu* [*Introduction to the*
267 *Criticism of M Texts*] AUC-PH 3 (Prague 1961) 101, 16 facss / rev C. Schoenbaum *JbLH* 8 (1963) 274–5 **267** Mužík 'Nejstarší nápěv písně "Jesu Kriste, štědrý kněže" a jeho vztah k husově variantě' AUC-PH 1 (Prague 1958) 31–53, 1 table, 8 facss (at end of vol)
266 There is an English summary, pp 97–100: M considers the art of transcription of med. melodies from oral transmission, and examines how far it is possible to use traditional methods of textual criticism in M. Incidentally, he concludes that Záviš and Záviš of Zap are not the same. **267** M uses textual criticism to establish the oldest version of the tune. There is a German summary, pp 52–3.

268 Gennrich, Friedrich *Musikwissenschaft und romanische Philologie* (Halle

269 1918) 54 **269** Bittinger, W. 'Fünfzig Jahre Mw als Hilfswissenschaft der romanischen Philologie' *ZrPh* 69 (1953) 161–94

268 Using rhythmic problems for support, G stresses the inseparability of philological and M investigation. **269** To demonstrate the necessity for examining all evidence, B uses textual and M evidence to establish correct readings and attributions in secular songs and to relate the sources to each other.

∗269a Sesini, Ugo *Musicologia e filologia. Raccolta di studi sul ritmo e sulla melica del Medio Evo* BIBL M BONONIENSIS, section 5, no. 8 (Bologna 1968) 200

Music in everyday life

The items in this section are mainly based on contemporary accounts, records, and poems.

SOCIAL AND CIVIC FUNCTIONS AND CUSTOMS, MINSTRELS

270 Salmen, Walter *Der fahrende Musiker im europäischen MA* DIE M IM ALTEN
271 UND NEUEN EUROPA 4 (Kassel 1960) 244 / rev E.A. Bowles *JAMS* 16 (1963) 74–5 **271** Salmen 'Zur Geschichte der Ministriles im Dienste geistlicher Herren des MA' **F-2.II.**811–19
270 S deals mainly with German evidence, including literary quotations. His extensive bibliography lists older publications. **271** This is a general survey, with good references to secondary literature. S stresses clerical patronage. [See also *Mens en Melodie* 15 (1960) 332–6 (Netherlands), *BMw* 3 heft 2 (1961) 67–9 (Weismar).]

272 Bowles, E.A. 'M Instruments at the Med. Banquet' *RBM* 12 (1958) 41–51
273 **273** Bowles 'Tower Musicians in the MA' *BQ* 5 (1961/2) 91–103 **274**
274 Bowles 'M Instruments in Civic Processions during the MA' *Acta* 33
275 (1961) 147–61 **275** Bowles 'M Instruments in the Med. Corpus Christi Procession' *JAMS* 17 (1964) 251–60, 2 pll
272 Contemporary accounts offer information about performance practices. **273** Musicians were installed as watchmen at the gates of the med. town. B quotes contemporary accounts and refers to the development of the trumpet. **274** B comments on contemporary accounts from various countries and for various occasions. His references are very useful. **275** B quotes contemporary accounts to show the type of instruments used.

Women

276 Rokseth, Y. 'Les Femmes musiciennes du XIIe au XIVe siècle' *Rom* 61 (1935) 464–80
Numerous literary passages, quoted, show that women participated in

vocal M and dance, less commonly playing instruments, prior to the 14c. Church documents denounce women singing.

Ecclesiastical functions and musicians: Precentor and Succentor

277 Aubry, P. 'La M et les musiciens d'église en Normandie aux XIIIᵉ siècle d'après le "Journal des visites pastorales" d'Odon Rigaud' *Le Mercure* M 2¹ (1906) 337–47, 455–62, 505–12, 556–68 and 2² (1906) 17–26, 58–63
A quotes and discusses references to M. He summarizes the repertory and M practice of the area.

278 Meyer, K. 'Das *Amtbuch* des Johannes Meyer' *AMw* 1 (1918/19) 166–78, 1 facs
279 279 Fischer, K. von 'Das Kantorenamt am Dome von Siena zu Beginn des
280 13. Jh.' F-11.155–60 280 Müller, Karl F. *Der Kantor. Sein Amt und seine Dienste* (Gütersloh 1964) 224
278 Comparing a 15c nun's version in German with an earlier Latin text, M prints references to the offices of Precentor and Succentor. 279 F prints and discusses the chapter of an *Ordo* which outlines the Precentor's M functions. 280 Pp 1–55 refer to the MA.

281 Goldine, N. 'Les Heuriers-matiniers de la cathédrale de Chartes jusqu'au XVIᵉ siècle. Organisation liturgique et M' *RdM* 54 (1968) 161–75
G gives a general survey of the institution, daily life, and function of the *heuriers*. She shows how the services were sung, where polyphony was used, and emphasises the memorising of the M. Some rules for conduct are printed from an original source.

*282 Lipphardt, W. 'Das älteste Ordinarium missae und seine Bedeutung für die Volkschoralpraxis' *Musik und Altar* 5 (1952/3) 168–76

Poems and archives

283 Maillard, J. 'Coutumes M au ma. d'après le *Tristan* en prose' *CCM* 2 (1959) 341–53
M quotes and comments on lengthy passages referring most usefully to M.

284 Van der Linden, A. 'Les Comptes de la ville d'Ypres de 1267 à 1329' *RBM* 2 (1948) 150–6
V prints M references from archives.

FOLK MUSIC AND ORAL TRANSMISSION

There can be no doubt about the interaction of folk and high culture, nor about the oral transmission of much M either written down later or, for us, lost. A number of scholars claim to detect folk melodies or folk influence in plainsong and secular song, but such claims are based on general overall resemblances: the evidence is not factual but circumstantial. The folk tunes used for comparison were mostly collected in this century.

285 Lord, Albert B. *The Singer of Tales* HARVARD STUDIES IN COMPARATIVE LITERATURE 24 (Cambridge, Mass. 1960) xv + 309 / rev *TLS* 27 Jan. (1961) 58
Not primarily concerned with either M or the med. period, this study has insights into processes and results of oral composition directly relevant in many ways to the known features of much med. M. A M version of this book needs to be written.

286 Avenary, H., Secretary, Round Table 'Mündliche und schriftliche Tradition
287 im Mittelmeerraum' **A-5**.121–42 **287** Apfel, E. 'Volkskunst und Hochkunst in der M des MA' *AMw* 25 (1968) 81–95
These items have some useful references.

288 Wiora, W. 'Die vergleichende Frühgeschichte der europäischen M als
289 methodische Forschung' **A-1**.212–21 **289** Wiora 'Jubilare, sine verbis' **F-14**.39–65
288 W quotes interestingly similar melodies from plainsong, folksong, secular art song, far and near East, stressing the importance of comparative research. In 289 he seeks similar practices in folk M and in classical literature.

290 Menard, R. 'Le Problème de la mémorisation en M copte garant de fidélité à la tradition' **A-3**.191–3
M discusses an example of oral preservation and its relation to ornamentation and centonizing. Cf **E-3**.III.135–43.

EDUCATION

In specific institutions and countries **291 299 302–5** the Liberal Arts **294–301**

291 Carpenter, Nan C. *M in the Med. and Renaissance Universities* (Norman, Oklahoma 1958) xiv + 394, 8 pll, b footnotes, index / rev E.C. Krohn *Msct* 4 (1960) 106–7
Beginning with the Greeks, C traces the history of M education through Europe up to 1600. She quotes from theorists, med. scholars, archives, and statutes. Parts appeared earlier in *JRMEd* 1 (1953) 11–20 (Oxford); 2 (1954) 119–33 (Paris); 3 (1955) 136–44 (general summary).

292 Smits van Waesberghe, Joseph *School en Muziek in de Middeleeuwen: De muziekdidactiek van de vroege middeleeuwen* MUZIEKBIBL (Amsterdam 1949) 174, 24 pll and facss / rev C. Van den Borren *RBM* 5 (1951) 38–40
This deals with M education, 9–12c.

293 Beichner, Paul E. 'The Med. Representative of M, Jubal or Tubalcain?' *Texts and Studies in the History of Med. Education* 2, THE MED. INST, U OF NOTRE DAME (Indiana 1954) 27, 6 pll
Jubal, the source of M according to Scripture, is often incorrectly referred

to as Tubal⌊cain⌋: the latter, a blacksmith, comes in Christian accounts to replace Pythagoras as the originator of M.

294 *Artes Liberales* ed Josef Koch, STUDIEN UND TEXTE ZUR GEISTESGESCH DES MA 5 (Cologne 1959) xii + 155, index
This is a collection of articles, two of which are annotated below (296 300), most of which refer in more or less detail to M (see index).

295 Lippman, E.A. 'The Place of M in the System of Liberal Arts' F-23.545–
296 59 296 Fellerer, K.G. 'Die musica in den Artes Liberales' 294.33–
297 49 297 Bachmann, W. 'Bilddarstellungen der M im Rahmen der *artes*
298 *liberales*' B-3.46–55, 8 facss 298 Hüschen, H. 'Die M im Kriese der *artes liberales*' B-3.117–23
295 L concentrates on the Greek background. 296 With quotations, F shows the primacy of M in the liberal arts, and the function of speculative and practical M as propaedeutic to theology and philosophy and its relation to rhetoric and literature. This attitude perseveres until the 18c. 297 B examines ten depictions of M as one of the liberal arts. 298 H discusses M as *scientia* and *ars* and its place in the quadrivium-trivium.

299 Pietzsch, G. 'Der Unterricht in den Dom- und Klosterschulen von der Jahrtausendwende' *AnuarioM* 10 (1955) 3–22
The former emphasise the practical, the latter the liberal arts.

300 Klinkenberg, H.M. 'Der Verfall des Quadriviums im frühen MA' 294.1–32
Christian theology disrupts the quadrivium, destroying the pre-eminent place of M within it.

301 Müller, U. 'Zur M Terminologie der antiken Rhetorik: Ausdrücke für Stimmanlage und Stimmgebrauch bei Quintilian, *Institutio oratoria* 11, 3' *AMw* 26 (1969) 29–48, 105–24
The orator's training was comparable to the musician's.

302 Pietzsch, G. 'Zur Pflege der M an den deutschen Universitäten bis zur Mitte
303 des 16. Jh.' *AMf* 3 (1938) 302–30; 5 (1940) 65–83; 6 (1941) 23–56; 7 (1942) 90–110,
304 154–69 303 Pietzsch 'Zur Pflege ... deutschen Universitäten im Osten ...' *AMf* 1 (1936) 257–92, 424–51 304 Pirro, A. 'L'Enseignement de la M aux universités françaises' *Acta* 2 (1930) 26–32, 45–56
302 303 Discussing theoretical and practical study and quoting statutes, etc, P gives biographical information about a multitude of musicians at Leipzig; Heidelberg and Cologne; Erfurt, Rostock, Greifswald, Basel, Freiburg im Breisgau, Ingolstadt, Trier, Mainz, Tübingen, and Dillingen; Wittenberg, Frankfurt, Marburg, Königsberg, Jena, Helmstedt, Herborn, and Göttingen; and 303 Prague, Vienna, and Krakow. 304 Pirro refers to numerous off the beaten track instances of M in education in France.

305 Kristeller, P.O. 'M and Learning in the Early Italian Renaissance' *MD* 1 (1946/7) 255–74
This is a general but well documented study.

Iconography

306 Winternitz, E. 'The Visual Arts as a Source for the Historian of M' **A-**4.I.109–20. Cf **F-35** passim.
W reviews pitfalls and degrees of realism in the interpretation of pictures. See **316 376**.

307 Bandmann, Günther *Melancholie und M: Ikonographische Studien* (Cologne 1960) 196, 61 pll / rev F.W. Sternfeld *ML* 42 (1961) 170 (S says that B emphasises the visual arts and their symbolism, from 12–16c, rather than M *per se*) / also rev E. Winternitz *Burlington Magazine* 104 (1962) 166–7 (W says there is scanty new evidence for the historian of art or M, but the uninitiated reader will be fascinated)

COLLECTIONS

308 *Musikgeschichte in Bildern* ed Heinrich Besseler and Max Schneider, published in several vols and fascc
Two fascicles of vol III M *des MA und der Renaissance* have appeared (**922 1019**). Excellent plates are accompanied by text and tables.

309 Goldron, Romain (pseudonym of A. Lewis Burkhalter) *History of M* I: *Ancient and Oriental M* transl Stella A. Sterman (np 1968) II: *Byzantine and Med. M* transl Doris C. Dunning (np 1968) III: *Minstrels and Masters* transl J.V. Williams (np 1968) / rev E. Helm *Notes* 25 (1968/9) 485–7
The text of all three vols in highly unreliable and out of date; there is no index or bibliography; documentation is minimal, from secondary sources. However, the multitudinous plates and diagrams, many in colour, make this a delightful and extremely useful source of visual information. There are facsimiles of notation, theoretical works, illuminations, liturgical mss, paintings, sculptures, instruments, frescoes, etc.

SCULPTURE (ROMANESQUE)

310 Reuter, Evelyn *Les Représentations de la M dans la sculpture romane en France*

COLLECTION FORME ET STYLE (Paris 1938) 104 + 32 pll + 3 pp / rev V. Denis
RHE 35 (1939) 821–2
This is an iconographical and symbological study.

311 Meyer, K. 'The Eight Greg. Modes on the Cluny Capitals' *AB* 34 (1952) 75–94
(+ the following unnumbered page), 3 pll and facss (not all the capitals are
included in these photographs)
This is the most convincing of a number of studies of this enigmatic topic
(cf *DVLG* 7 (1929) 229–66, 6 pll and *Spec* 5 (1930) 278–87, 3 pp of pll). The best
complete set of photographs is in Joan Evans *Cluniac Art of the Romanesque
Period* (Cambridge 1950) pll 202–7 and pp 116–19. M's conclusions are that
the mottoes are paraphrases of the texts of the 'key' antiphons in contemporary Tonaries: the sculptures are of jongleurs similar to those in ms Prosaria
(cf **831**). Mottoes and sculptures have no direct relationship. Cf **313** and **F-27**.
113–51.

312 Schneider, Marius *Singende Steine. Rhythmus-Studien an drei katalanischen
Kreuzgängen romanischen Stils* GES FÜR MF: MwArb (Kassel 1955) 92 + 16 pp
of pll, 3 tables / rev F. Feldmann *Mf* 9 (1956) 345–6 and P.C. [P. Collaer ?]
RBM 9 (1955) 162–4
S makes a good case for his assertion that animals carved on the capitals
around 12c cloisters serve mnemonically to denote the pitches of the hymns
of patron saints. There is more detail in **121**.

313 Schapiro, M. 'From Mozarabic to Romanesque in Silos' *AB* 21 (1939) 313–74,
13 pll and facss
Pp 339–48: representations in art and sculpture are of secular musicians,
jongleurs, watchmen, etc, unrelated to the text or surroundings. Cf **311**.

MISCELLANEOUS

314 Stauder, W. 'Asinus ad lyram' *Helmuth Osthoff zu seinem 70. Geburtstag* ed
Ursula Aarburg and Peter Cahn (Tutzing 1969) 25–32, 8 pll
This is a common iconographical motive. Cf **310** passim.

315 Smits van Waesberghe, J. 'Ein merkwürdige Figur und ihr musikgeome-
trisches Geheimnis' **F-29**.234–8, 4 pll
S argues that the mathematical proportions of certain miniatures are those
of musical intervals.

316 Droysen, D. 'Die Darstellungen von Saiteninstrumenten in der ma.
Buchmalerei und ihre Bedeutung für die Instrumentenkunde' **B-4**.302–5
This is a general résumé of the kinds of sources and their reliability.

317 Hardy, C.F. 'On the M in the Painted Glass of the Windows in the
Beauchamp Chapel at Warwick' *Arch* 61, part 2 (1909) 583–614, 9 facss, 1 table
15c stained glass depicts in detail M instruments, plainsong, and a little
polyphony. H's comments are faulty.

318 Hammerstein, R. 'Die M am Freiburg Münster; ein Beitrag zur M Ikono-
graphie' *AMw* 9 (1952) 204–18, 4 pll
H gives the literary, historical, and allegorical background.

Instruments

This section does not deal with the role of instruments in performance. The separation of M into vocal and instrumental styles and genres is of modern origin (**319 320**). The med. classification of instruments was by volume of sound and by social status (**321–2a**).

318a Crane, Frederick *Extant Med.* M *Instruments* (Iowa City 1972) xiv + 105, 30 illustrations, b
This provisional catalogue lists an astonishing number of archeological remains, fragmentary and complete, and its categorisation of instrument types, with a brief description, will prove very useful. Also astonishing is its extensive bibliography.

319 Apel, W. 'Stimme als Instrument' *Stimmen. Monatsblätter für M* 1 (1947/8)
320 404–10 **320** Hibberd, L. 'On "Instrumental Style" in Early Melody' *MQ* 32 (1946) 107–30
319 A quotes several examples, four from the MA, which show the voice to be, in effect, instrumental in melismas. **320** H re-examines earlier criteria and rejects distinctions between vocal and instrumental style for the MA.

321 Bowles, E. 'Haut and Bas: the Grouping of M Instruments in the MA' *MD*
322 8 (1954) 115–40 **322** Bowles 'La Hiérarchie des instruments de M dans l'Europe féodale' *RdM* 42 (1958) 155–69
With many quotations from original sources, B shows in **321** the aesthetic reasons for classifying instruments as loud or soft, and in **322** that instruments assume characteristics of the stratum with which they are most associated.

322a Spruit, J.E. *Van vedelaars, trommers en pijpers* (On fiddlers, drummers and pipers) (Utrecht 1969) 141, illus, 28 pp facss, index, b
S examines the legal and social status of *ioculatores* in northern Europe 13–16c.

58 Instruments

HISTORIES AND COLLECTIONS OF ILLUSTRATIONS

322b *M Instruments in Art and History* ed Roger Bragard and Ferdinand J. de Hen, transl Bill Hopkins (London 1968) 281 / rev Mary Remnant *ML* 50 (1969) 301–3: R says there are many inaccuracies in the med. section (31–64).

323 Galpin, Francis W. *Old English Instruments of M: their History and Character* (4th ed revd Thurston Dart, London 1965) xxviii + 254 + 57 pll, appendices, index / rev G. Oldham *MT* 107 (1966) 38–40
Most of the solid information dates from the 15c at the earliest.

324 Harrison, Frank Ll. and Joan Rimmer *European M Instruments* (London 1964) 1–23 and pll 1–88, indices / rev T. Dart *ML* 46 (1965) 348–50

325 Sachs, Curt *The History of M Instruments* (New York 1940) 505, num illuss
Pp 207–93 deal with the med. period, including the Orient.

KEYBOARD INSTRUMENTS

This section is mostly concerned with the organ, but **333** and the following section on stringed instruments refer to the early 'harpsichord.'

The organ: general

326 Perrot, Jean *L'Orgue de ses origines hellénistiques à la fin du XIIIe siècle* (Paris 1965) xii + 434, illus, 28 pll, appendix with original texts, index of names, b, footnotes (transl Norma Deane as *The Organ: from its Invention ...*, Oxford 1970) / rev W.L. Sumner *ML* 47 (1966) 165–6
P translates a multitude of contemporary accounts and theoretical references, including eastern and Arabic sources. He comments on construction, mechanism, and tuning. Pp 255–67 summarize the previous information about the organ of antiquity; 269–371 relate to 8–13c.

327 Hardouin, P. 'De L'orgue de Pépin à l'orgue méd.' *RdM* 52 (1966) 21–54, 1 pl, 8 diagrams
H claims that Pépin's instrument is identical with that described by Muristos and that portrayed in the Utrecht Psalter. He contrasts this with the later med. organ. Perrot (**326**) disagrees on pp 54–5.

328 Flade, E. 'Literarische Zeugnisse zur Empfindung der *Farbe* und *Farbigkeit* bei der Orgel und beim Orgelspiel' *Acta* 22 (1950) 97–127
F reviews early descriptions of the instrument.

329 Handschin, J. 'Antiochen, jene herrliche Griechenstadt' *AMf* 7 (1942) 193–204
A 5c poem, part of which H gives in German translation, has evidence relating to the organ of the Near East.

59 Instruments

Water organs

330 Schneider, Thekla 'Organum Hydraulicum' *Mf* 7 (1954) 24–39, pll and dia-
331 grams **331** Hyde, W.W. 'The Recent Discovery of an Inscribed Water-organ at Budapest' *Transactions of the American Philological Association* 69 (1938) 392–410
330 With many diagrams S explains the construction. **331** The instrument, of ca 2C AD, is quite well preserved.

Portative organs

332 Hickmann, Hans *Das Portativ* (Kassel 1936) iv + 260, 16 pll, b, index / rev F.W. Galpin *ML* 18 (1937) 415–16
This is a comprehensive history of the portative organ, 12–18c, including details of construction, range, and playing technique. H examines its use in solo and ensemble performance.

The organ: construction (keyboard mechanism and organ-pipes)

333 Bowles, E. 'On the Origin of the Keyboard Mechanism in the late MA' *Technology and Culture* 7 (1966) 152–62, 7 pll
13c development of mechanisms for clocks and animated models precedes the construction of linkages for keyboards of stringed instruments.

334 Hawthorne, John G. and Cyril S. Smith transl *On Divers Arts. The Treatise of Theophilus* (Chicago 1963) xxxv + 216
Chapters 81–7, pp 158–79, describe metal-casting and other work involved in making organs and bells.

335 Bormann, Karl*Die gotische Orgel zu Halberstadt: Eine Studie über ma. Orgelbau* VER. DER GES DER ORGELFREUNDE 27 (Berlin 1966) 192, illus, 24 pll, index / rev W.L. Sumner *Organ* 45 (1965/6) 190
B deals with the construction and other relevant evidence.

336 Casimiri, R. 'Un Trattatello per organisti di *Anonimo* del sec. XIV' *NASM* 19 (1942) 99–101
C edits a 14c treatise implying a completely chromatic keyboard and forbidding consecutive semitones.

337 Chailley, J. 'Un Clavier d'orgue à la fin du XIᵉ siècle' *RdM* 18 (1937) 5–11
The keyboard has note pitches inscribed.

338 Avenary-Loewenstein, H. 'The Mixture Principle in the Med. Organ' *MD* 4 (1950) 51–7, 2 pll
A suggests that an 11c treatise implies the presence of mixtures.

339 Fellerer, K.G. 'Die *Mensura fistularum*: Ein Beitrag zur Geschichte des ma. Orgelbaus' *KmJb* 30 (1935) 36–50

In spite of 'korrektionsfaktors' med. treatises on the mathematics of organ pipes are theoretical rather than practical.

340 Handschin, J. 'Aus der alten Musiktheorie: 1. Zur Mensuration der Orgel-pfeifen' *Acta* 14 (1942) 1–19
H prints and discusses relevant passages of theory.

341 Nef, W. 'Der sogenannte Berner Orgeltraktat' *Acta* 20 (1948) 10–20, 21 (1949) 8–18
N prints and translates (German) this important 11c treatise, with comments.

342 Weiler, K. '*De Mensura Fistularum*, ein gladbacher Orgeltraktat aus dem Jahre 1037' *KmJb* 40 (1956) 16–22
W discusses the acoustical mathematics and the history of this treatise.

*342a Sachs, Klaus J. *Mensura fistularum: Die Mensurierung der Orgelpfeifen im MA* SCHRIFTENREIHE DER WALCKERSTIFTUNG Bd 1 (Stuttgart 1970)

STRINGED INSTRUMENTS

Keyboard instruments

342b Steger, Hugo *Philologia Musica: Sprachzeichen, Bild und Sache im literarisch-m. Leben des MA: Lire, Harfe, Rotte und Fidel* MÜNSTERSCHE MA-SCHRIFTEN 2 (Munich 1971)176 + 37 facss, index, b
S accumulates factual information about stringed instruments.

343 Machabey, A. 'A propos du clavicorde du pseudo-Jacques de Liège' *Rom* 77 (1956) 26–38, 2 facss
The mid-14c evidence, consisting of a diagram and a passage involving the word *chorda* (see **344**), presents only string-lengths: there is no evidence of a mechanism.

344 Nef, W. 'The Polychord' *GSJ* 4 (1951) 20–4
A confusion between 'string' and 'sound' as a translation of *chorda* accounts for the early 'many-stringed' monochord. The later 'polychord,' after ca 1400, is the clavichord.

Bowed instruments

345 Bachmann, Werner *The Origins of Bowing and the Development of Bowed Instruments up to the 13c* (London 1969) xvi + 178, 98 pll and diagrams, 1 map, index, excellent b, and list of pictorial sources (transl Norma Deane from *Die Anfänge des Streichinstrumentenspiels*, 2nd ed Leipzig 1966) / rev M. Remnant *ML* 51 (1970) 309–10
Using ethnological and all available evidence, B concludes that bowing originated in Asia, ca 10c. Including the hurdy-gurdy, he describes playing techniques and social functions for all members of the fiddle family.

346 Andersson, O. 'The Bowed Harp of Trondheim Cathedral and Related Instruments in East and West' *GSJ* 23 (1970) 4–34, 4 pll
The instrument is related to the crwth: both seem to have been stopped with the left-hand fingers.

347 Puccianti, Anna 'La Descrizione della *viella* e della *rubeba* in Girolamo di Moravia' *CHM* 4 (1966) 227–37
P prints the text (13c) with notes on the readings, and translates it. There is no attempt to solve the problems of meaning.

348 Remnant, M. 'Rebec, Fiddle and Crowd in England' *PRMA* 95 (1968/9) 15–28
349 and 96 (1969/70) 149–50, 2 pll **349** Remnant 'The Use of Frets on Rebecs and Med. Fiddles' *GSJ* 21 (1968) 146–51, pll xvii and xviii (following p 152)
348 Cautious of the inconsistency of med. terminology, R relies heavily on the accuracy of med. art and of later writers. She discusses methods of playing the instruments. **349** Frets were certainly known from the late 13c.

350 Steger, H. 'Die Rotte. Studien über ein germanisches Musikinstrument im MA' *DVLG* 35 (1961) 96–147, 8 pll and facss
In this comprehensive article S identifies the instrument by terminology and geographical distribution, and claims to have established its social position and its use in practical m.

351 Remnant, M. 'The Gittern in English Med. Art' *GSf* 18 (1965) 104–9, pll xi and xii (following p 112)
R comments on several depictions, mostly 14c.

Plucked instruments

352 Geiringer, K. 'Vorgeschichte und Geschichte der europäischen Laute bis zum Beginn der Neuzeit' *ZMw* 10 (1927/8) 560–603, 8 pll
G outlines the lute's development in the Orient and its later transference to the West. Cf *ZMw* 1 (1918/19) 89–107, 27 pll.

353 Kasha, M. 'A New Look at the History of the Classic Guitar' *The Guitar*
354 *Review* 30 (1968) 2–12, num illus **354** Bowles, E. 'The Guitar in Med. Literature' *The Guitar Review* 29 (1966) 2–7, 3 pll

355 Rensch, Roslyn *The Harp* (London 1969) 1–65 and pll 1–20, 26, 27, b,
356 index **356** Rimmer, Joan *The Irish Harp* IRISH LIFE AND CULTURE 16 (Cork 1969) 1–38, num pll

357 Bessinger, J.B. 'The Sutton Hoo Harp Replica and Old English m Verse' *Old English Poetry: Fifteen Essays* ed Robert P. Creed (Providence, Rhode Island 1967) 3–26 and frontispiece
The quadrangular shape confirms carvings, etc. B adduces literary references in support of his conclusions about the probable capabilities of the original. Cf *Proceedings of the Royal Institution of Great Britain* 34 (1947–50) 446–8 and pl ii. See also **1752–5**

WIND INSTRUMENTS

358 Baines, Anthony *Woodwind Instruments and Their History* (2nd ed London 1962) 209–36 / rev E. Winternitz *JAMS* 12 (1959) 254–9

359 Becker, Heinz *Zur Entwicklungsgeschichte der antiken und ma. Rohrblattinstrumente* MW INST DER U HAMBURG, Schriftenreihe 4 (Hamburg 1966) 187, 64 pll
B deals chiefly with instruments of antiquity and their early med. descendants.

360 Buhle, Edward *Die m. Instrumente in den Miniaturen des frühen MA: Ein Beitrag zur Geschichte der Musikinstrumente. 1: Die Blasinstrumente* (Leipzig 1903; repr 1971) 120, frontispiece, 9 drawings, diagrams, list of mss
Translating theoretical and other evidence, and reproducing original drawings, B gives much basic evidence. The second vol was never published.

361 Bowles, E. 'Unterscheidung der Instrumente Buisine, Cor Trompe und Trompette' *AMw* 18 (1961) 52–72
With many quotations, B distinguishes instruments by size, material, and tone quality.

362 Karstädt, G. 'Zur Geschichte des Zinken ... Die Frühgeschichte' *AMf* 2 (1937) 386–97, pll

363 Megaw, J.V.S. 'A Med. Bone Pipe ...' *GSJ* 16 (1963) 85–94, pl VIII (facing p 65) and 17 (1964) 116–17
M describes the 13c pipe and its potential scale. It could possibly have been used by jongleurs.

364 Block, E.A. 'Chaucer's millers and their bagpipes' *Spec* 29 (1954)
365 239–43 **365** Jones, G. Fenwick 'Wittenwiler's *becki* and the med. Bagpipe' *J of English and Germanic Philology* 48 (1949) 209–28
364 The bagpipe generally symbolizes gluttony and lechery. **365** J gives much information about its social status.

BELLS, PERCUSSION

366 *Cymbala* ed Joseph Smits van Waesberghe MSD 1 (1951 or 1952) 64, 8 pll, index / rev L. Ellinwood *Notes* 9 (1951/2) 618
This is an edition of texts relevant to bells. The introduction deals with the use of bells in church and for teaching M, and the physical structure and casting process. Cf **334**.

367 Montagu, J. 'On the Reconstruction of Med. Instruments of Percussion' *GSJ* 23 (1970) 104–14, 4 pll (the first two are between pp 96 and 97), line diagrams
Assuming the reader's knowledge of pictorial evidence, M offers practical advice. Believing that drum names are onomatopoeic, he concludes that the

use of *tam-* rather than *trom-* roots before the 16c implies the preference for strokes rather than rolls.

INSTRUMENTS IN LITERATURE, ART, AND ARCHAEOLOGY

368 Hammerstein, R. 'Instrumenta Hieronymi' *AMw* 16 (1959) 117–34, 4
369 pll 369 Avenary, H. 'Hieronymus' Epistel über die Musikinstrumente und ihre altöstlichen Quellen' *AnuarioM* 16 (1961) 55–80
Both authors quote the 9c text. H comments on the terminology, drawings, and allegories. A shows that the value of the letter lies mainly in the field of biblical exegesis rather than in the history of instruments.

370 Cesari, G. 'Tre tavole de strumenti in un "Boezio" del x secolo' F-
371 1.26–8 371 Hollander, H. 'Das Engelskonzert zu Gloucester' *Musica* 12
372 (1958) 715–18, 2 pll 372 Pope, I. 'King David and his Musicians in Spanish
373 Romanesque Sculpture' **F-23**.693–703, pll 24a–d, 25a–c, 26a–h 373 Schünemann, G. 'Die Musikinstrumente der 24 Alten' *AMf* 1 (1936) 42–58, illus
370–3 The authors describe instruments from various 11–15c sources.

374 Devoto, D. 'La enumeración de instrumentos M en la poesía med. Castellana' **F-2**.I.211–22
D quotes obviously non-realistic passages and cautions against literal interpretation of others.

375 Winternitz, E. 'Bagpipes for the Lord' *The Metropolitan Museum of Art, Bull* 16 (1958) 276–86, num facss
In the Hours of Jeanne D'Evreux, ca 1320, marginalia depict a wide range of instruments, some with amazing precision.

376 Droysen, D. secretary, Round Table 'Die Musikinstrumente in Europa vom 9. bis 11. Jh.' **A-5**.II.176–87
Several scholars present information on archaeological remains, oriental influence, iconographical sources, etc. See also **316**.

The Near East and Byzantium

This section concerns principally the northeastern Mediterranean, whose
M culture influenced plainsong, especially in the earlier Middle Ages.
Islamic and North African M culture, which affected secular developments
of the 12th and later centuries, are dealt with in items **1017–37** and **1125–39**.

SYRIA

377 Husmann, Heinrich ed *Die Melodien des chaldäischen Breviers Commune nach*
378 *den Traditionen vorderasiens und der Malabarküste* ORIENTALIA CHRISTIANA
ANALECTA 178 (Rome 1967) xi + 204 **378** Husmann transl and ed *Die Melo-*
dien des Wochenbreviers (Šḥīmtā) gesungen von Qurillāos Ja'qub Kas Görgös,
Metropolit von Damaskus in *Die Melodien der jakobitischen Kirche* VER. DER
KOMMISSION FÜR MF, general ed E. Schenk, vol 9: ÖSTERREICHISCHE AKW,
p.h.Kl., Sitzungsberichte, Bd 262, Abh 1 (Vienna 1969) 216
377 378 These are editions of the melodies of the East Syrian rites, with short
commentaries.

379 Husmann, H. 'Die Tonarten der chaldäischen Breviergesänge' *Orientalia*
Christiana Periodica 35 (1969) 215–48
H places modal forms within a scheme of an expanded octoechos.

PALESTINE AND JEWISH MUSIC

380 Sendrey, Alfred *Bibliography of Jewish* M (New York 1951) xli + 404 / rev E.
Werner *Notes* 8 (1950/1) 353–4
This is a comprehensive encyclopaedia of some 10,000 titles, using translit-
eration. Relevant entries include those under 'The early Church Fathers on
M,' 'Med. Judeo-Arabic Writings on M,' 'Jewish Minstrels, Troubadours
and Jongleurs,' etc.

381 Idelsohn, Abraham Z. ed *Hebräisch-Orientalischer Melodienschatz* 10 vols
(Leipzig 1914–32)

This is an anthology of tunes, and a comprehensive analysis of the M and culture.

382 Werner, E. and Isaiah Sonne 'The Philosophy and Theory of M in Judaeo-Arabic Literature' *HUCA* 16 (1941) 251–319; 17 (1942/3) 511–73
Translating Hebrew quotations (pp 312–19) and giving a table of M terms (Hebrew, Greek, Arabic, English, 305–11), W comprehensively surveys the topic. S edits and translates sections of 7 texts (511–57) to which W writes descriptive appendices (558–73), the second rewritten and revised in **1629**.

383 Adler, I. 'Le Traité anonyme du ms. Hébreux 1037 de la BN de Paris' *Yuval* 1 (1968) 1–47
A describes and edits with parallel French translation a 14c Hebrew version of earlier western theory.

384 Werner, E. 'M Aspects of the Dead Sea Scrolls' *MQ* 43 (1957) 21–37
Marginal signs resemble Slavonic neumes; instruments and performances are mentioned; some 'hymns' may illuminate the evolution of the antiphon.

385 Farmer, H.G. 'Jewish Genizah Fragments on M' *GUOS* 19 (1961/2) 52–62
F summarizes the contents, which derive from Arabic theory.

386 Werner, E. 'The Oldest Sources of Synagogal Chant' *Proceedings of the American Acad for Jewish Research* 16 (1946/7) 225–34, 1 facs

387 Adler, I. 'Les Chants synagogaux notés au XIIᵉ siècle (ca 1103–1150) par
388 Abdias, le prosélyte normand' *RdM* 51 (1965) 19–51, 2 pp facss **388** Scheiber,
389 A. 'Der normannische Proselyt Obadja, der Aufzeichner der ersten hebräischen Melodie' *StuMus* 8 (1966) 173–87, 4 facss **389** Golb, N. 'Obadiah the proselyte: scribe of a unique 12c Hebrew Ms containing Lombardic neums' *The J of Religion* 45 (1965) 153–6, 2 facss
387 A describes the sources and the problems of transcription. **388** The Jewish melody from Egypt uses Italian neumes. **389** The ms is of Near Eastern rather than European origin and shows that the Jews of eastern countries absorbed something of Gregorian chant through the medium of European converts. See also *Ongaku gaku* 14 (1969) 213–22.

Byzantium

SURVEYS AND SOURCES

Other important items are Wellesz, *Eastern Elements* ... **561** and Fellerer **481a**.

390 Wellesz, E. 'Byz. M and its Place in the Liturgy' *PRMA* 59 (1932/3) 1–22 and 81 (1954/5) 13–28
This is an excellent brief introduction.

391 Wellesz, Egon *A History of Byz. M and Hymnography* (2nd ed Oxford 1961)
392 xiv + 461, 8 facss, b, index, transcc (371–427) / rev D. Stefanović *ML* 44 (1963)
169–70 **392** Wellesz *M of the Byz. Church* AnthM 13 (Cologne 1959) 63, 2 facss
/ rev of original German ed E. Jammers *Mf* 14 (1961) 119–20
391 This is a standard work. **392** W gives a concise introduction and bibliography dealing with history, sources, and notation and gives a good selection of the M. He includes translations of the texts.

393 Wilson, Nigel and Dimitrije I. Stefanović *Mss of Byz. Chant in Oxford* (Ox-
394 ford 1963) 56, 6 facss **394** Dévai, G. 'Mss en notation byz. dans les bibliothèques publiques de Budapest' *AA* 1 (1951/2) 247–60; 2 (1954) 361–3

395 Strunk, O. 'H.J.W. Tillyard and the Recovery of a Lost Fragment' *SEC* 1
(1966) 95–103
Tillyard had photographed 6 pages and copied by hand the remainder of the Chartres fragment. Cf **396**.

NOTATION

396 Gastoué, Amédée *Introduction à la paléographie M byz.* (np, nd [Paris 1907])
ix + 107, 7 facss / rev H. Villetard *Bull critique* 3. ser, 2 (1908) 328–30
This is an introduction to the notation and the books of the Byz. liturgy, and a catalogue of the ms sources in Paris, Besançon, Carpentras, and Chartres. G includes facsimiles of the destroyed Chartres fragments 1754 (cf **395**).

397 Strunk, William *Specimina Notationum Antiquiorum* MMB-P 7 (Copenhagen
1966) xiii + 40 + portfolio of 187 plates
These are photographs of selected folios of 10–12c mss.

398 Tillyard, H.J.W. 'The Stenographic Theory of Byz. M' *BZ* 25 (1925) 333–8
T exposes the incorrectness of the then traditional view of the notation.

399 Tillyard, H.J.W. 'The Stages of Early Byz. M Notation' *BZ* 45 (1952)
400 29–42 **400** Tillyard 'Early Byz. Neums: a New Principle of Decipherment'
401 *Laudate* 14 (1936) 183–7 **401** Wellesz, E. 'Early Byz. Neumes' *MQ* 38 (1952)
68–79
399 T gives some basic information. **400** A single symbol over a syllable need not be an interval sign but indicates the rhythmic framework of a stereotyped melodic formula. This deduction proved to be the major clue to the decipherment. **401** The neumes are performance marks rather than a notation.

402 Tillyard, H.J.W. 'Byz. Neumes: the Coislin Notation' *BZ* 37 (1937)
403 345–58 **403** Strunk, O. 'The Notation of the Chartres Fragment' *AnnM* 3
(1955) 7–37, 11 facss
402 T describes the last stage of early Byz. notation, which gives clues to the decipherment of more archaic systems, as well as to Russian sematic

notation. 403 Comparing Round, Coislin, and Chartres notation for the same piece, S attempts to limit date and place for changes in notation, ca 11c.

404 Biezen, J. van *The Middle Byz. Kanon-Notation of Ms H* UTRECHTSE BIJDRAGEN
405 TOT DE MUZIEKWETENSCHAP 5 (Bilthoven 1968) x + 141, 1 facs / rev M.
406 Velimirović *ML* 50 (1969) 482–5 (transcc 65–125) 405 Di Salvo, B. 'La
407 Trascrizione della notazione paleobyzantina. I°: I sýndesmoi e i sýndesmoi
408 con il klásma nel modo primo. II°: Il xerònklásma e il kýlisma nel modo primo' *BBG* ns 5 (1951) 92–110, 220–35 406 Floros, C. 'Die Entzifferung der Kondakarien-Notation' *MOst* 3 (1965) 7–71, 2 facss, 52 unnumbered pp M exx and 4 (1967) 12–44, 40 unnumbered pp M exx 407 Raasted, J. 'A primitive palaeobyz. M notation' *ClMed* 23 (1962) 302–10 408 Tillyard, H.J.W. 'Byz. M about A.D. 1100' *MQ* 39 (1953) 223–31
404–8 These items describe the notations, often listing sources.

STYLE, STRUCTURE, PERFORMANCE

Specific genres are listed under 424–63.

409 Calí, L. 'Innografia med. bizantina' *RIM* 2 (1967) 36–53
The same melody may take on a different character according to the destination of the book which preserves it for soloist ('professional'), choir, or congregation.

410 Di Salvo, B. 'L'Essenza della M nelle liturgie orientali' *BBG* ns 15 (1961) 173–91
This generally relates styles, forms, modal character, and traditional or popular use. See F-14.97–106.

411 Di Salvo, B. 'La Tradizione M bizantina delle colonie Italo-albanesi di Sicilia e quella manoscritta dei codici antichi' *BBG* ns 6 (1932) 3–26
D believes that the traditional Sicilian chant can be a precise aid to the study of Byz. M. Cf D-8.229–35.

412 Levy, K. 'Three Byz. Acclamations' F-30.43–57
L publishes and discusses chants not normally written down.

413 Marzi, Giovanni *Melodia e nomos nella M bizantina* STUDI ... DI FILOLOGICA CLASSICA 8 (Bologna 1960) vi + 225, 20 facss, index
M studies cadential endings and ornaments.

414 Raasted, J. 'Some Reflections on Byz. M Style' *SEC* 1 (1966) 57–66
The kylisma is an optional ornament suggesting an old layer of oral transmission.

415 Wellesz, E. 'Melody Construction in Byz. Chant' C-1.1.135–51
W discusses the Byz. form of centonization, with examples. Strunk complements the paper, on pp 365–73, relating formulaic construction to the simul-

taneous oral and written traditions. On pp 375–84, with 5 facss, Stefanović extends W's conclusions to Slavonic chant.

416 Wellesz, E. 'Über Rhythmus und Vortrag der byz. Melodien' *BZ* 33 (1933) 33–66
W gives some basic information.

MODES, SIGNATURES, INTONATIONS

417 Petresco, I.D. *Etudes de paléographie* M *byz.* (Bucharest 1967) 679 + 31 facss, index of incipits / rev M. Huglo *RdM* 55 (1969) 83–4
The first part is a general discussion of the modal characteristics of Byz. M based on the comparative transcriptions in the second half.

417a Husmann, H. 'Modalitätsprobleme des psaltischen Stils' *AMw* 28 (1971) 44–72
H links Byz. with Greek scale systems.

418 Tillyard, H.J.W. 'The Byz. Modes in the 12c' *ABSA* 48 (1953) 182–90
T traces the development of signatures specifying precise modal identification.

419 Raasted, Jørgen *Intonation Formulas and Modal Signatures in Byz.* M *Mss* MMB-S 7 (1966) xii + 238, index of incipits / rev F. de Meeûs *Scrip* 24 (1970) 92–5
R deals with notation and transcription.

420 Husmann, H. 'Modulation und Transposition in den bi- und tri-modalen
421 Stichera' *AMw* 27 (1970) 1–22 **421** Husmann 'Die oktomodalen Stichera und
422 die Entwicklung des byz. Oktoëchos' *AMw* 27 (1970) 304–25 **422** Thodberg, C. 'Chromatic alterations in the Sticherarium' **C-1**.II.607–12
420 Deducing modulation and transposition from internal signatures, H takes this to mean that the octoechos modes are applicable to the Hirmologium as well as the Sticherarium. **421** H describes the modal principles of, and transcribes, three examples. **422** 'Wrong' signatures imply exact interval transposition.

423 Strunk, O. 'The Antiphons of the Oktoechos' *JAMS* 13 (1960) 50–67, 2 facss
S examines modal formulae used in the troparia.

STYLES AND GENRES

Listed alphabetically by genre, these items are mainly editions and facsimiles.

Akathistos

424 Wellesz, Egon ed *The Akathistos Hymn* MMB-T 9 (1957) xcii + 108 **425**

425 Wellesz *The 'Akathistos': A Study in Byz. Hymnography* DOP 9, 10
426 (Cambridge, Mass. 1956) 141–74 **426** Wellesz 'Das Prooemium des
Akathistos' *Mf* 6 (1953) 193–206
  424 W edits the hymn. **425 426** Confirming Romanos as the author, W gives
the basic informaïon, with a partial transcription.

Asmatikon

427 Di Salvo, B. 'Gli *Asmata* nella M bizantina' *BBG* ns 13 (1959) 45–50, 127–45;
14 (1960) 145–78
  D discusses the repertory in some detail, having given a comparative index
of sources. The continuation cannot be traced, but D has an article entitled
'Asmatikon' in *BBG* ns 16 (1962) 135–58, where he describes the books containing the repertory.

Hirmos

428 Høeg, Carsten ed *Hirmologium Athoum* MMB-P 2 (1938) 28 + 151
429 facss **429** Jakobson, Roman ed *Fragmenta Chiliandarica Palaeoslavica*, part
430 B *Hirmologium* MMB-P 5 (1957) 14 + 72 fos facss **430** Raasted, Jørgen ed
431 *Hirmologium Sabbaticum* 2 vols MMB-P 8^1, 8^2 (Copenhagen 1968, 1970) xii +
126; 8 + 116 fos facss and 4 + 117–223 fos facss **431** Tardo, Laurentius ed
Hirmologium Cryptense MMB-P $3^{1,2}$ (Rome 1950, 1951) 4 + 337 fos facss; 96
These are facsimile editions.

432 Koschmieder, Erwin ed *Die ältesten Novgoroder Hirmologien-Fragmente* 3
vols BAYERISCHEN AKW, p.h.Kl., Abh ns 35, 37, 45 (Munich 1952, 1955, 1958)
iii + 317; vii + 106, 8 facss; 169 / rev A.J. Swan *JAMS* 7 (1954) 86–7
Vol 1: transcriptions; vol 2: description of mss and commentary; vol 3:
indices of incipits and words.

433 Wellesz, Egon ed *Trésor de M byz.* vol 1 EOL (Paris 1934) 23 and 39
Part 1 has an introduction in German and French, with the texts in Greek
and French; part 2 contains transcriptions of hirmologion melodies of the
first mode, mainly from 13c mss. Subsequent volumes were not published.

434 Stöhr, M. 'Reflections on Transcribing the Hirmoi in Byz. M' *SEC* 1 (1966)
89–94
Which of two melodic traditions is the earlier cannot yet be established.

Hymn

435 Ayoutanti, Aglaïa ed *The Hymns of the Hirmologium*, part 1 (with Maria
436 Stöhr) revd and annotated Carsten Høeg, MMB-T 6 (1952) 1 +
334 **436** Ayoutanti part 3, revd and annotated H.J.W. Tillyard MMB-T 8
(1956) x + 96
These are editions.

437 Tillyard, H.J.W. ed *The Hymns of the Octoechus* part 1, MMB-T 3 (1940) xxiv
438 + 192 **438** Tillyard part 2 MMB-T 5 (1949) xx + 216 **439** Tillyard *The Hymns*
439 *of the Pentecostarium* MMB-T 7 (1960) xxxvi + 174 **440** Wellesz, Egon ed *Die*
440 *Hymnen des Sticherarium für September* MMB-T 1 (1936) xlviii + 158 **441**
441 Tillyard, H.J.W. *The Hymns of the Sticherarium for November* MMB-T 2 (1938)
xx + 180
These are editions.

442 Wellesz, Egon *Die Hymnen der Ostkirche* BASILIENSES DE MUSICA ORATIONES
1 (Basel 1962) 27, 1 pl

443 Tillyard, H.J.W. 'A M Study of the Hymns of Casia' *BZ* 20 (1911) 420–85, 5
facss, 10 transcc
With a brief section on the notation, T prints, from 13–17c mss, the text and
tunes of hymns written by Casia (9c). He concludes that the tradition in the
East was continuous from 14–17c; how it related to earlier forms is still
obscure.

Kanon

444 Tillyard, H.J.W. *Twenty Canons from the Trinity Hirmologium* MMB-T 4
(American ser, 2) (Oxford 1952) xii, 1 pl + 130
This is an edition.

445 Jammers, E. 'Die jambischen Kanones des Johannes von Damaskus' F-
446 16.195–256 **446** Jammers 'Der Kanon des Johannes Damascenus für den
Ostersonntag' *Polychronion: Fs für Franz Dölger zum 75. Geburtstag* ed Peter
Wirth (Heidelberg 1966) 266–86
J describes and transcribes the pieces from mss of the 11–13c.

447 Tillyard, H.J.W. 'A Canon by Saint Cosmas' *BZ* 28 (1928) 25–37
Translating the text, T transcribes the 8c canon from a 13c ms.

Kontakion

448 Bugge, Arne ed *Contacarium Palaeoslavicum Mosquense* MMB-P 6 (1960) xxviii
449 + 10 + 204 fos facss **449** Høeg, Carsten ed *Contacarium Ashburnhamense*
MMB-P 4 (1956) 48 + 265 fos facss

450 Petresco, J.-D. ed *Les Idiomèles et le canon de l'office de Noël* ETUDES DE
PALEOGRAPHIE M BYZ. 1 (Paris 1932) viii + 70, 34 facss + 123 transcc / rev
H.J.W. Tillyard *BZ* 37 (1937) 135–7
P transcribes and comments on the notation and structure of six versions
from Greek mss, 11–14c.

451 Wellesz, E. 'Kontakion and Kanon' *D-9*.131–33 **452** Wellesz 'Zum Stil der
452 Melodien der Kontakia' *F-2*.II.965–75
In **451** W explains the late 7c adoption of Kanon and neglect of Kontakia,

and in **452**, using the Akathistos Hymn for comparison, traces the stylistic development, 10–13c.

453 Floros, C. 'Das Kontakion' *DVLG* 34 (1960) 84–106, 2 facss + p. 104$^{1-8}$ M exx
Identifying models for *prooemion* and *oikoi* of *prosomoia* and *idiomela*, F analyses the form and compares it to the Sequence.

454 Thodberg, Christian *The Tonal System of the Kontakarium* DANSKE VIDENSKABERNES SELSKAB, Historisk-filosofiske Meddelelser 37, Nr 7 (Copenhagen 1960) 50
'Wrong' signatures suggest a separate origin (perhaps *pré-octoéchique*) for the modal system of the Kontakarium.

455 Levy, K. 'An Early Chant for Romanus' *Contacium trium puerorum*?' *ClMed* 22 (1961) 172–5
Quotations of kontakia texts in stichera may carry with them fragmentary M of the lost syllabic kontakion tradition. Part of Romanus' kontakion is cited in a sticheron.

Psaltikon

456 Thodberg, Christian *Der byz. Alleluiarionzyklus: Studien im kurzen Psaltikonstil* transl Holger Harmann MMB-S 8 (1966) 239 / rev M. Huglo *RdM* 54 (1968) 249–50

Sticheron

457 Høeg, Carsten, H.J.W. Tillyard, and E. Wellesz edd *Sticherarium* MMB-P 1
458 (1935) 66 + 326 facss **458** Jakobson, Roman ed *Fragmenta Chilianderica Palaeoslavica*, part A: *Sticherarium* MMB-P 5 (1957) 26 + 110 fos facss

459 Raasted, J. 'Some Observations on the Structure of the Stichera in Byz. Rite' *Byzantion* 28 (1958) 529–41
R discusses the relationships between thought, syntax, and M.

460 Tillyard, H.J.W. 'The Stichera Anastasima in Byz. Hymnody' *BZ* 31 (1931)
461 13–20 **461** Strunk, O. 'Intonations and Signatures of the Byz. Modes' *MQ* 31 (1945) 339–55
460 T finds empirically that signatures indicate specific starting pitches and formulae. **461** S finds theoretical support.

Troparion

462 Levy, K. 'A Hymn for Thursday in Holy Week' *JAMS* 16 (1963) 127–75
The original troparion melody cannot yet be reconstructed either from Ambrosian or late Byz. versions.

463 Strunk, O. 'Tropus and Troparion' **F-15**.305–11

Setting aside forms which differ, S concentrates on prefatory additions to liturgical texts, which take similar form in western and Byz. rites.

THEORY

464 Dévai, G. 'The M Study of Koukouzeles in a 14c Ms' *AA* 6 (1958) 213–35, 4 facss
D corrects and complements his earlier study in *AA* 3 (1955) 151–79, 7 pp col facss. He transcribes and describes a didactic poem preserved in an 18c copy.

465 Richter, L. 'Antike Überlieferungen in der byz. Musiktheorie' *DJbMw* 6 (1961) 75–115, 1 pl
Theory originates in non-Pythagorean as well as Pythagorean thought: L reviews the chief researchers and surveys the topic, describing the writings of Psellos (ca 1000), Pachymeres and Bryennios (ca 1300), and Gregoras (14c).

466 Tillyard, H.J.W. 'Fragment of a Byz. M Handbook in the Monastery of Laura
467 on Mt. Athos' *ABSA* 19 (1912/13) 95–117, pll XIII and XIV (end of vol)
467 Tillyard 'A Byz. M Handbook at Milan' *JHS* 46 (1926) 219–22
466 The first treatise throws some light on earlier notation. 467 This is a very brief introduction to a singer's manual.

INSTRUMENTS

468 Anoyanakis, F. 'Ein byz. Musikinstrument' *Acta* 37 (1965) 158–65, 2
469 pll 469 Bachmann, W. 'Das byz. Musikinstrumentarium' *E-1*.125–38, pll
468 469 A and B describe instruments, their use, and some sources. See *JRAS* (1925) 299–304.

CHIRONOMY

470 Di Salvo, B. 'Qualche appunto sulla chironomia nella M bizantina' *Orientali christiana periodica* 23 (1957) 192–201
Chironomy is associated with more florid chants.

MISCELLANEOUS

471 Høeg, Carsten and Günther Zuntz edd *Prophetologium* MMB-L 1 Copenhagen 1939) 499

*472 Levy, K. 'The Byz. Sanctus and its Modal Tradition in East and West' *AnnM* 6 (1958/63) 7–67

473 Strunk, O. 'The Byz. Office at Hagia Sophia' DOP 9, 10 (Cambridge, Mass. 1956) 175–202, 8 facss
About 1400 an archbishop gives detailed descriptions of the services, including M performance.

474 Strunk, O. 'The Latin Antiphons for the Octave of Epiphany' *Mélanges Georges Ostrogorsky* vol 2 RECEUIL DE TRAVAUX DE L'INST D'ETUDES BYZ. 8² (Belgrade 1964) 417–26
Using the knowledge that the Latin texts are translations, S tries to reconstruct the Greek melodies. Cf **568**.

475 Wellesz, E. 'Words and M in Byz. Liturgy' *MQ* 33 (1947) 297–310
Byz. hymnographers were extremely careful in setting words to M.

Plainsong

BIBLIOGRAPHY

Three major periodicals deal with the liturgy and its music, but are only selectively recorded here. The *Rev grégorienne* contains many analyses of plainsong of the modern liturgy, often more or less identical with chants from the Middle Ages: the *Rev du chant grégorien* has many useful articles on medieval tropes, sequences, liturgical books, etc, and also has analyses of chants, old and new: *Etudes grégoriennes* deals with medieval and historical matters more in its earlier volumes than in volumes later than 6 or 7; thereafter the emphasis is on the 19–20c revival, restoration, and reformation of plainsong. This periodical is itemised in more detail under **E-3**. The following items refer to recent literature and current problems; most include comments or annotations: **476–81** [also **16 902a**].

476 Bomm, U. 'Gregorianischer Gesang' *ALw* 1 (1950) 397–443; 4 (1955) 184–222;
477 6 (1959) 256–336; 7 (1962) 470–511; 9 (1965) 232–77 **477** Guentner, F.J. rev of
478 *Etudes grégoriennes* 1, 2 (1954, 1957) *MQ* 45 (1959) 550–9 **478** Lipphardt, W.
479 'Neue Forschungen zur Gregorianik' *JbLH* 2 (1956) 134–41 **479** Lipphardt
480 secretary, Round Table 'Der Gegenwärtige Stand der Gregorianik-
481 Forschung' **A-5**.II.156–66 **480** Smits van Waesberghe, J. 'Etat des recherches scientifiques dans le domaine du chant grég.' *La M sacrée au 3ᵉ congrès intern. de M sacrée, Paris 1957* RM (Paris 1957) 87–99, 62–item b **481** Stäblein, B. 'Veröffentlichungen MA M' *DMk* 9 (1944) 52–61 (refers to facss and includes some secular material)

INTRODUCTIONS

Item **481a** will probably be encyclopaedic. **482** is a useful 'nutshell' introduction.

★481a Fellerer, Karl G. ed *Geschichte der katholischen Kirchenmusik* vol 1 (Early

Christianity, The Eastern Church, The Western Church up to the Council of Trent) to be published

482 Wellesz, E. 'Recent Studies in Western Chant' *MQ* 41 (1955) 177–90
W surveys the history and problems of plainsong.

HISTORIES AND SURVEYS

These are listed alphabetically by author.

483 Agustoni, Luigi *Greg. Choral: Elemente und Vortragslehre mit besonderer Berücksichtigung der Neumenkunde* (Freiburg, Basel, Vienna 1963) 279, indices of incipits and subjects
A deals with basic elements, with notation, with modern interpretations, and with theories, especially about rhythm.

484 Apel, Willi *Gregorian Chant* (Bloomington, Indiana 1958) xiv + 529, 8 pll, index, b, M exx / rev Alec Robertson *ML* 40 (1959) 76–9
This is the most useful book in English on the M styles and structures of plainsong, surveying in some detail the history, notation, and function of chant. Its biggest fault is its extensive reliance on secondary sources for information and on editions designed for modern use. Pp 3–86, introducing the Kalendar and liturgy, are also drawn from modern use and are much too abbreviated and general. There is no attempt to show the use of med. documents as sources for tunes, texts, or performance practices. As a guide for investigation of med. chant, then, the book is of very limited use. In a purely M sense the analyses are useful, and the section on church modes, pp 133–78, is excellent.

485 Jammers, Ewald *M in Byzanz, im päpstlichen Rom und im Frankenreich; Der Choral als M der Textaussprache* HEIDELBERGER AKW / p.h.Kl., Jahrgang 1962, Abh 1 (Heidelberg 1962) 344, b, index / rev W. Lipphardt *JbLH* 10 (1965) 177–9
J deals with problems of text, polyphony, and instrumental M.

486 Jammers, Ewald *Der ma. Choral* NEUE STUDIEN ZUR MW 2 (Mainz 1954) 102 / rev J. Hourlier *EG* 2 (1957) 219–22
J traces the general evolution and decadence after the Cluniac reforms, concentrating on rhythm and tonality.

487 Ursprung, Otto *Die katholische Kirchenm* HbMw (Potsdam 1931) 312, num pll, facss, and exx / rev K.G. Fellerer *Theologische R* 34 (1935) 250–1
Pp 1–155 deal with plainsong (from earliest Christian times) in East and West, sacred polyphony, and M theory, up to ca 1500.

488 Wagner, Peter J. *Introduction to the Greg. Melodies* 2nd ed revd and enl transl, Agnes Orme and E.G.P. Wyatt PMMS (London 1901?; repr Hildesheim 1962)

viii + 311 / This is the only volume to be translated from *Einführung in die greg. Melodien* 3 vols (Leipzig 1911, 1912, 1921; repr Hildesheim 1962) xi + 360, index; xvi + 505, num facss, index; xi + 540, index

Vol 1 deals mainly with history and formal development of the M items of the liturgy and with their ritual significance rather than with M matters. There is much documentation from med. sources, but no bibliography or lists of mss. Vol 2 deals with paleography, notation, and rhythm. Vol 3 deals with the style of chant.

More specialised surveys

489 Hucke, H. 'Die Entwicklung des christlichen Kultgesangs zum Greg. Gesang' *RQ* 48 (1953) 147–94

Examining closely the relationship of soloist with psalm and reading, and of choir with antiphon and responsory, H quotes documents dealing with antiphonal and other performance practices. He concludes that liturgical song develops into the art M of Greg. chant.

490 Jammers, E. 'Rhythmische und tonale Studien zur M der Antike und des MA. I: Die erhaltenen Denkmäler antiker M, analytisch untersucht. II: Auf dem Wege zum MA' *AMf* 6 (1941) 94–115, 151–81 and 8 (1942) 27–45, 87–101 (further continuation not publ)

Hymns belong tonally and metrically to the world of antiquity: the way to the MA lies through the Carolingian court and liturgical poetry.

491 Smits van Waesberghe, J. 'Einleitung zu einer Kausalitätserklärung der Evolution der Kirchenmusik im MA (von etwa 800 bis 1400)' *AMw* 26 (1969) 249–75

From 800–1050 S sees 'holding in holy respect' (*sanktifikationsprinzip*) as the cause for development, superseded later by 'sanctioning by holy authority' (*sanktionierung*).

Gregory the Great

492 Anglès, H. 'Sakraler Gesang und M in den Schriften Gregors des Grossen' *F-34.* 33–42

Gregory knew well the allegorical clichés of med. M.

493 Burda, A. 'Gregor der Grosse als Musiker' *Mf* 17 (1964) 388–93 and 20 (1967)
494 154–66 **494** Hucke, H. 'Die Entstehung der Überlieferung von einer M
495 Tätigkeit Gregors des Grossen' *Mf* 8 (1955) 259–64 **495** Hucke 'War Gregor der Grosse doch Musiker?' *Mf* 18 (1965) 390–3

493 Quoting some of the evidence, B concludes that Gregory was at least capable in M, and replies to Hucke. **494 495** H discredits evidence used to support Gregory's musical role, and exposes some weaknesses in Burda's arguments.

496 Tack, Franz *Gregorian Chant* transl Everett Helm AnthM 18 (Cologne 1960) 152 + 46 facss / rev W. Irtenkauf *Mf* 14 (1961) 444
T gives a brief history, dealing with modern and old notation (the facss are especially useful), dialects, modes, forms, and sources. There are no translations of texts, and rubrics are left in Latin. A wide selection of chants is included.

497 Marbach, Carl *Carmina Scripturarum* (Strasbourg 1907; repr Hildesheim 1963) 144* + 596, indices
Starting from the scriptural source, this identifies the use, in plainsong, of texts drawn from the Bible.

498 *An Index of Gregorian Chant* comp John R. Bryden and David G. Hughes 2 vols (Cambridge, Mass. 1969) xx + 456; viii + 354 / rev Andrew Hughes *ML* 51 (1970) 317–19
This cumulative textual and melodic index of nineteen widely available sources and inventories of plainsong, including facsimiles and modern editions, is an invaluable time-saver.

499 Plummer, John *Liturgical Manuscripts for the Mass and the Divine Office* (New York 1964) 55, 24 facss
This catalogue describes the principal types of liturgical mss.

500 *Bibliotheca Musico-Liturgica* ed Walter Howard Frere 2 vols PMMS (London 1901, 1932; repr 1967) xiv + 215, 13 pll and facss; xvii, 4 facss + 189; indices in vol 2
F catalogues med. plainsong and liturgical mss in libraries of Great Britain and Ireland, including some polyphonic and theoretical sources.

501 Mearns, James *Early Latin Hymnaries* (Cambridge 1913; repr Hildesheim 1970) xx + 107, facss
This is an index of hymns and sources before 1100.

These items are editions, facsimiles, or major studies.

Antiphonals (noted Breviaries)

502 *L'Antiphonaire du b. Hartker (No. 390–391 de St-Gall, Xe siècle)* PalMus ser 2:
503 1 (1909; revd ed Berne 1970 ed Jacques Froger) 45 + 458 facss (see **549**)
504 **503** *L'Antiphonaire du Mont-Renaud (X–XIe siècle)* PalMus ser 1: 16 (1955) 47 + 133 facss + xxix **504** Beyssac, G.M. 'Le Graduel-antiphonaire de Mont-Renaud' *RdM* 40 (1957) 131–50
504 B describes the contents of the 10c ms, which originated at St Denis.

505 *Antiphonale Sarisburiense* (AS) ed Walter H. Frere PMMS (London 1901–24, separate reissue of Introduction 1927: originally issued in portfolios; repr bound 1966) Collation: 102 (Introduction and index) + 1–96 facss (97–100 are omitted, see Introduction p 76), 101–608 facss (609–32 are omitted, see Introduction p 76), 633–68 facss, a–z, A–Z, α, β, γ, δ facss
This is a facsimile of a deficient 13c Salisbury Antiphonal complemented, in somewhat confusing fashion (see Introduction pp 76–7), from other sources. The introduction, issued last, is comprehensive and extremely valuable, with analytical and stylistic information. The texts are completely indexed.

506 *Codex Albensis* (an Antiphonal of the 12c) ed Zoltán Falvy and László Mezey MON HUNGARIAE MUSICA 1 (Graz 1963) 179 + 321 facss
This is a superb colour facsimile, preceded by a comprehensive description of the ms, its paleography and neumatic notation, and of Hungarian rites in the MA. The German introduction is summarised in English, 167–70. There are indices of names, subjects, and texts.

507 *Pars Antiphonarii* ed Walter H. Frere PMMS (London 1923) iv + fos 136–59 facss
This is a facsimile of an 11c ms.

Graduals (Antiphonalia Missarum)

508 Bussi, Francesco *L'Antifonario Graduale della Basilica di S. Antonino in Piacenza (sec. XII)* BIBL STORICA PIACENTINA, promossa dal 'Boll Storica Piacentino' 27 (Piacenza 1956) xvii + 133, 2 facss / rev S. Corbin *RdM* 42 (1958) 225–7
B describes and indexes the source and compares it with other mss.

509 *Antiphonale Missarum sancti Gregorii, IX–Xe siècle, Codex 239 de la Bibl. de Laon* PalMus ser 1: 10 (Tournai 1909) 216 + 10* + 179 facss + i–l
This includes studies of an Introit and the Credo and notes on the rhythmic signs.

510 *Antiphonale Missarum sancti Gregorii, Xe siècle, Codex 47 de la Bibl. de Chartres* PalMus ser 1: 11 (Tournai 1912) 142 + 10* + 134 facss
This compares the notations of Chartres, St Gall, and Metz. Cf **539–40**.

511 *Antiphonarium Tonale Missarum. XIe siècle, Codex H. 159 de la Bibl. de l'Ecole de Médecine de Montpellier* 2 vols PalMus ser 1: 7, 8 (Tournai 1901) 377, M exx, indices; 25 + 324 pp facss, indices
The first volume introduces the bilingual notation used in the ms, and deals with rhythmic problems.

512 *Le Codex 121 de la Bibl. d'Einsiedeln* (x–xie siècle, Antiphonale Missarum sancti Gregorii) PalMus ser 1: 4 (1894) 215 + 108 pp facss + 4 facss
This contains an introduction to psalmody.

513 *Le Codex 123 de la Bibl. Angelica de Rome* (XIᵉ siècle, Graduel et Tropaire de Bologne) PalMus ser 1: 18 (Berne 1969) 71 + 265 fos facss

514 *Le Codex 339 de la Bibl. de St-Gall* (xᵉ siècle, Antiphonale Missarum sancti Gregorii) PalMus ser 1: 1 (1889) vi + 8* + 167 + 142 facss +xxxi fos facss
There is a general introduction and classification of neumatic scripts.

515 *Le Codex 903 de la BN de Paris* (XIᵉ siècle, Graduel de Saint-Yrieix) PalMus ser 1: 13 (1925) 228, 33 facss + 8* + 265 pll facss
The introduction deals with liturgy and history and with Aquitainian notation.

516 *Le Codex 10.673 de la Bibl. Vaticane, fonds latin* (XIᵉ siècle, Graduel Bénéventain) PalMus ser 1: 14 (Tournai 1931) 479 + 23 facss + 71 facss

517 *Le Codex VI 34 de la Bibl. Capitulaire de Bénévent* (XIᵉ–XIIᵉ siècle, Graduel de Bénévent avec Prosaire et Tropaire) PalMus ser 1: 15 (Tournai 1937) 194, 291 pp facss

*518 Haberl, F. 'Graduale pauperum' *Musica sacra* 81 (1961) 130–8

519 *Le Graduel de l'église cathédrale de Rouen au XIIIᵉ siècle* ed Henri Loriquet, Joseph Pothier, and Armand Collette 2 vols (Rouen 1907) iii + 338, index of incipits, 9 facss; xv + fos 2–264 facss
Vol 1 has a historical and liturgical study of the ms and comparable sources. Some liturgical dramas and polyphony are discussed. Vol 2 is a complete facsimile edition, especially useful because printed shoulder heads specify the liturgical date.

520 *Das Graduale der St Thomaskirche zu Leipzig* ed Peter Wagner 2 vols PÄM Jahrgänge 5 and 7 (Leipzig 1930, 1932; repr Hildesheim 1967) xxviii, 2 facss + 144 facss; lxiv + i–xiv + facss 145–249
Vol 1 introduces and describes the ms. Vol 2 has a valuable essay, with comparative tables, on the German plainsong dialect, followed by an index.

521 *Graduale Sarisburiense* (GS) ed Walter H. Frere PMMS (London 1894; repr 1966) cii + 294 facss
This is a facsimile of a 13c Salisbury Gradual. Where this ms has leaves missing, other sources are used to complete the book: these complementary leaves are not placed in the main sequence but are collected at the end. The comprehensive and so far unsurpassed introduction describes the development of the Gradual, and Mass chants in general, with lists of early sources. There is a stylistic discussion and a complete index of the texts. The introduction, with 4 facsimiles, was reprinted separately by Frere as *The Sarum Gradual ...* PMMS (London 1895) cii + facss.

Gregorian sources

These items include Antiphonals and Graduals forming the nucleus of Roman use.

522 *Corpus antiphonalium officii.* I: *Manuscripti 'Cursus romanus'* II: *Manuscripti 'Cursus monasticus'* III: *Invitatoria et Antiphonae* IV: *Responsoria, Versus, Hymni et Varia* ed René-Jean Hesbert RERUM ECCLESIASTICARUM DOCU-MENTA, Ser Major, Fontes 7, 8, 9, 10 (Rome 1963, 1965, 1968, 1970) xxiv + 6 facss + 445, indices of texts, etc; xxiv + 6 facss + 829, indices; xii + 551; xii + 527
Vol I is a comparative and descriptive inventory of 6 early sources, 9–12c. Vol II deals with monastic sources in the same way. Vols III and IV discuss the distribution of Invitatories, Responsories, etc, in the 12 sources of vols I and II, listing the items alphabetically.

523 *Antiphonale Missarum Sextuplex,* ed René-Jean Hesbert (Brussels 1935) cxxvi + 8 facss + 256 / rev C. Callewaert *RHE* 32 (1936) 943–7
Including numerous indices of plainsongs, etc, this is a detailed comparative inventory of 6 major mss of the 8–10c, whose relationship is comprehensively described.

524 Brou, Dom L. 'L'Antiphonaire Wisigothique et l'Antiphonaire Grég. au début du VIII⁰ siècle' **D-9.**183–6
The repertories correspond remarkably.

524a Stäblein, B. ' "Gregorius Praesul," der Prolog zum römischen Antiphonale' *Musik und Verlag; Karl Vötterle zum 65. Geburtstag* ed Richard Baum and Wolfgang Rehm (Kassel 1968) 537–61, 1 facs
S discusses its origins, and preservation as an Introit trope.

525 *Le Graduel Romain* ed Solesmes. Vol I not yet publ. II: *Les Sources* (Solesmes 1957) 235, maps / rev F. de Meeûs *Scrip* 14 (1960) 80–97
This is a catalogue of primary and secondary sources. Vol III not yet publ. IV: *Le Texte neumatique,* part 1, *Le Groupement des mss* (Solesmes 1960) 402 + num maps; part 2, *Les Relations généalogiques des mss* (Solesmes 1962) 93 / rev R. Weakland *Notes* 19 (1961/2) 62–4
This is a detailed reference work isolating geographical locations of chants and their sources, and the relations between them.

Other liturgical books and brief descriptions of sources

Antiphonal **533** Cantatorium **526** Hymnal **528** Ordinal **529** Processional **525a** Tonary **529** others **529–31 534**

525a Allworth, C. 'The Med Processional: Donaueschinger Ms 882' *EL* 84 (1970) 169–86
A describes the ms, with a comparative inventory.

526 *Cantatorium, No 359 de la Bibl. de St-Gall* (IX⁰ siècle) PalMus ser 2: 2 (Tournai 1924) 23 + 142 facss + 5* indices

527 Delaporte, Yves *L'Ordinaire chartraine du XIIIe siècle* SOC ARCH D'EURE-ET-LOIRE, Mém 19 (Chartres 1953) vii + 305, 4 facss, indices of names, places, texts, etc, list of mss (203–13) / rev S. Corbin *RdM* 36 (1954) 168–70
D describes and edits the text. There are eight references to *organum*.

528 Ebel, Basilius *Das älteste alemannische Hymnar mit Noten (Kodex 366 (472) Einsiedeln) (XII Jh.)* GAkF 17 (Einsiedeln nd) 116 + 9 facss
E describes the ms and its contents and transcribes a few chants.

529 Frere, Walter H. *The Use of Sarum* 2 vols (Cambridge 1898, 1901; repr 1969) lxxii + table + 314; xxxvi + 236 + i–lxxxvi
Vol 1: F edits the texts of a Consuetudinary and Customary. Vol 2: he edits the Ordinal and Tonary. Both volumes have useful introductions.

530 Härting, M. 'Die Fragment von Choral-Hss im Archiv der Stadt Peine' *KmJb* 49 (1965) 35–55
H describes and inventories fragments of plainsong books, mainly 14c.

531 Husmann, H. 'Eine Palimpsest-Jahrestabelle in der Hs Stiftsbibliothek St Gallen 381' **F-10**. 188–91
H dates the ms ca 980.

532 Lipphardt, W. 'Das Hymnar der Metzer Kathedrale um 1200' **F-29**. 160–77, 1 facs
L itemises 'concordances,' seeking to discover whether this small collection was a selection from, or a kernel creating a larger repertory.

533 Lipphardt, W. 'Ein Quedlinburger Antiphonar des 11. Jh.' *KmJb* 38 (1954) 13–24, 1 facs
L describes the ms.

534 *Les Mss M de Jumièges* MMS 2 (Mâcon 1954) 88 + 100 facss + 89–104. See **1606**.

NOTATION

A major study of early plainsong notation is Suñol, *Introduction* ... (**136**).

535 *La Notation M des chants liturgiques latins* PalMus, ser 2: 3 (1960) 3 unnumbered pp, 1 map + 39 + 43 pll facss

536 *The Musical Notation of the Middle Ages exemplified by Facsimiles of Mss. written between the 10th and 16th Centuries Inclusive* PMMS (London 1890)
This includes 16 facsimiles of plainsong notation, with brief description and introduction.

537 Bernoulli, Eduard *Die Choralnotenschrift bei Hymnen und Sequenzen* (Leipzig 1898; repr Hildesheim 1966) xiv, index of texts + 241, index of terms, 130 M transcc (Rh) + 14 facss
This is a study of comparative notations and variant melodic transmissions.

538 Werner, E. 'Preliminary Notes for a Comparative Study of Catholic and Jewish M Punctuation' *HUCA* 15 (1940) 335–66, 2 facss
W compares the accents, signs, and neumes and the musical tones of Jewish and Christian psalmody.

Regional notations

539 Hourlier, J. 'Le Domaine de la notation messine' *RG* 30 (1951) 96–113,
540 150–8 540 Vecchi, G. 'La Notazione neumatica di Nonantola' *Deputazione di Storia Patria per le antiche provincie Modenesi*, Atti e Mem, ser VIII, vol 5 (1953) 326–31, 2 facss
539 Listing sources, H describes the distribution of the notation. 540 Similarities with the notation of Metz do not indicate a descendant relationship (in either direction).

541 Huglo, M. 'Le Domaine de la notation Bretonne' *Acta* 35 (1963) 54–84
H isolates the characteristics and distribution of one of the oldest known notations, and discusses sources.

542 Hourlier, J. 'Remarques sur la notation clunisienne' *RG* 30 (1951)
543 231–40 543 Irtenkauf, W. 'Beiträge zur Einführung der Liniennotation im
544 südwestdeutschen Sprachraum um 1200' *Acta* 32 (1960) 33–9 544 Jammers,
545 Ewald *Die Essener Neumenhandschriften der Landes- und Stadtbibliothek Düsseldorf* VER. DER LANDES- UND STADTBIBL DÜSSELDORF 1 (Ratingen 1952) 36 + 16 pll facss 545 Smits van Waesberghe, J. 'Die rheno-mosamosellanische Neumenschrift' D-12. 599–602 and 1 facs
The authors study regional notations and their mss.

RHYTHM

General investigations

546 Rayburn, John *Greg. Chant: A History of the Controversy Concerning its Rhythm* (New York, 1964) xiv + 90
R comprehensively describes the various opinions of well known and little known scholars.

547 Hucke, H. 'Zum Probleme des Rhythmus im greg. Gesang' A-3. 141–2
H denies the possibility of a single rhythmic interpretation for all styles of chant. Cf *EG* 8 (1967) 21–8.

548 Jammers, Ewald *Der greg. Rhythmus* SMwAbh 25 (Strasbourg 1937) iii + 188
549 + 59 M transcc, index of incipits / rev O. Ursprung *Acta* 11 (1939) 44–6 549 Lipphardt, W. 'Studien zur Rhythmik der Antiphonen' *Mf* 3 (1950) 47–60, 224–36
548 J investigates the supposed rhythmic implications of neumatic notation. 549 L examines the rhythmic implications of the neumes in the Hartker Antiphonal (502) and compares the Solesmes editions.

550 Schmidt, James G. ed *Haupttexte der greg. Autoren betreffs Rhythmus* ... (Düsseldorf 1921) 20
S quotes ten passages, with German translation.

Major theories

551 Murray, Dom Gregory *Greg. Chant according to the Mss* (London 1963) vi +
552 97 + 31 M supplement / rev A. Milner *MT* 104 (1963) 486–7 **552** Vollaerts,
553 Jan W.A. *Rhythmic Proportions in Early Med. Ecclesiastical Chant* (2nd ed
Leiden 1960) xix + 245 / Rev ext in **553** Cardine, E. 'Le Chant grég. est-il
mesuré?' *EG* 6 (1963) 7–38
551 Interpreting the original M and theoretical sources and describing the
notation, M concludes that early chant was measured. He applies his findings in a number of examples. **552** With an impressive array of mss, comparison of notations, and translations of theoretical passages, V makes an
authoritative case for mensural interpretation prior to the 11c. **553** C attacks
the mensuralist theories in general, and M's and V's books in particular. His
view that both scholars base their theories on the assumption that plainsong
notation is consistent seems well grounded.

Numerical rhythm

554 Jammers, E. 'Greg. Studien. 1: Was Können wir den frühma. Theoretiken
555 über den Choralrhythmus entnehmen?' *Mf* 5 (1952) 24–37 **555** Kunz, L.
556 'Dürfen die Melodietöne des greg. Chorals gezählt werden?' *Mf* 5 (1952)
332–6 **556** Jammers, E. 'Dürfen die Melodietöne ...?' *Mf* 7 (1954) 68–70
554 J studies the treatises of Bede, *Musica Enchiriadis*, etc, to see whether
the theories of Kunz (**636**.11) and Lipphardt (**549**) about numerical rhythm
are valid. **555** K gives further examples. **556** J cites paleographical evidence.

Polyphony and plainsong rhythm

557 Kunz, L. 'Organum und Choralvortrag' *KmJb* 40 (1956) 12–15 **558** Meeûs,
558 Dom Francis de 'L'Introduction de la diaphonie et la rupture de la tradition
grég. au xie siècle' ed J. Vos *SE* 7 (1955) 177–218
557 Associating organum with tropes rather than chant, K questions Jammers' view (**1341**) that it causes a radical break in the rhythmic tradition of
chant. **558** The author, giving no convincing reasons, asserts that the onset
of parallel organum destroyed the rhythmic shape of plainsong. The article
is too confused to be an adequate explanation of the effect of polyphony on
chant.

Theory [also **550**]

559 Daras, Dom Michel *Etude de rhythmique grég.* 1: *Mora vocis Quilisma et*

épisèmes horizontaux. II: *Quilisma.* III: *Le vrai rythme grég.* (Louvain 1959, 1963?, 1965) 105, ?, 46
The subtitle is *Retour à la rythmique traditionelle (gréco-romaine) du Chant grég., sous la direction de Gui d'Arezzo.* Vol 2 was not seen and the information is taken from the Library of Congress catalogues. According to vol 3, p 10, there is a second edition of vol 1 (1964). The books are well documented in theory and practical evidence of the sources.

*560 Lipphardt, W. 'Zwei ma. Theoretikerzitate zum Choralrhythmus und ihre Deutung' *Zs für Km (Cäcilien-Vereins-Organ)* 69 (1949) 227–34

EASTERN AND GREEK ELEMENTS IN PLAINSONG

561 Wellesz, Egon *Eastern Elements in Western Chant* MMB-S 2 (American Ser 1) (Oxford 1947) xvi + 212, 11 pll, M exx, list of mss, index / rev E. Werner *MQ* 34 (1948) 430–5
W studies the relation between Byz. and Greg. chant, especially referring to bilingual items. He deals with the origin of sequences and tropes, and with problems of the Winchester Tropers. He includes an introduction to Byz. notation, '... a first attempt at ... a history of Byz. M.' The subject matter is complex, but presented clearly and easily. See *Mf* 5 (1952) 131–7 for W's Epilegomena.

Jewish elements

562 Gerson-Kiwi, E. 'Halleluia and Jubilus in Hebrew-Oriental Chant' F-
563 5.43–9 563 Gerson-Kiwi 'Justus ut palma' F-29.64–73 564 Idelsohn, A.Z.
564 'Parallelen zwischen greg. und hebräisch-orientalischen Gesangsweisen'
565 *ZMw* 4 (1921/2) 515–24 565 Werner, E. 'The Psalmodic Formula NEANNOE and its origin' *MQ* 28 (1942) 93–9
562 In the living tradition of Jewish communities G seeks similarities with med. western performance practices. 563 G compares Middle East tones for Pss 92 (especially v. 13) and 113. 564 Including 7 transcriptions, I sees melodic similarities. 565 W sees the origin in a Hebrew term. See 211.

Greek elements

566 Ursprung, O. 'Alte griechische Einflüsse und neuer gräzistischer Einschlag in der ma M' *ZMw* 12 (1929/30) 193–219
U thinks Greek forms in the liturgy and in M theory, etc, are not remnants of Greek roots, but are neologisms of the Carolingian renaissance.

Byzantine elements

567 Huglo, M. 'Relations M entre Byz. et l'Occident' C-2.267–80
H points to translations, adaptions, and parallels.

568 Handschin, J. 'Sur quelques tropaires grecs traduits en latin' *AnnM* 2 (1954) 27–60
H examines the origin of certain plainsongs. (In an appendix he reviews the problem of OR chant claiming that it is prior to Greg.) See also *SE* 1 (1948) 165–80 and 4 (1952) 226–38 and *EL* 72 (1958) 3–38.

569 Meersseman, Gilles G. *Der Hymnos Akathistos im Abendland* 2 vols
570 SPICILEGIUM FRIBURGENSE 2 (and 3?) (Freiburg 1958, 1960) xii + 228; xv + 390,
571 index of incipits, glossary **570** Huglo, M. 'La Prose de Notre-Dame de Grâce de Cambrai' *RG* 31 (1952) 112–18 **571** Huglo 'L'Ancienne version latine de l'hymne acathiste' *Le Muséon* 64 (1951) 27–61
569 This is a literary study. M prints numerous Latin Marian texts. **570** H transcribes the 'prose,' whose text is a 9c translation of the Akathistos hymn. **571** This is a textual and liturgical study.

572 Huglo, M. 'Origine de la mélodie du Credo *authentique* de la Vaticane' *RG*
573 30 (1951) 68–78 **573** Huglo 'La Mélodie grecque du *Gloria in excelsis* et son utilisation dans le Gloria XIV' *RG* 29 (1950) 30–40
572 A 14c ms preserves the Greek chant from which the Roman version is said to originate. **573** H lists Greek and bilingual sources, and compares text and melody. He transcribes the *Doxa en ypsistis,* and shows that the Latin Gloria XIV emerged from it in 10th or 11c. See also **E-7.**40–6.

FOLK ELEMENTS IN PLAINSONG

574 Chambers, George B. *Folksong-Plainsong. A Study in Origins and M Relationships* (London 1956) viii + 120, appendix of original texts, index / rev V. Žganec *JIFMC* 9 (1957) 90
C gives the evidence for folk origin of chant. He considers Jewish tradition and patristic references (giving translations of important passages, including Boethius and Augustine) and deals with tropes and notation. Although partisan, C gives an important point of view.

575 Járdányi, P. 'Über Anordnung von Melodien und Formanalyse in der Gregorianik' *Acta Ethnographica* 8 (1959) 327–37
J compares folk tunes collected by Bartok and Kodaly, etc, with plainsongs published by Rajeczky (**879**) and concludes that the relation between Greg. and folk music in Hungary is 'much deeper than we had supposed.'

REPERTORIES AND USES

These are listed alphabetically. Material on Benedictine and Sarum Uses will be found in the index.

Ambrosian

576 Husmann, H. 'Zur Geschichte der Messliturgie von Sitten und über ihren

Zusammenhang mit den Liturgien von Einsiedeln, Lausanne und Genf'
AMw 22 (1965) 217–47
This is a useful article for showing how a particular Use develops, and how
relationships between Uses may be demonstrated.

577 Huglo, Michel, Luigi Agustoni, Eugène Cardine, and E.T. Moneta-Caglio
578 *Fonti e paleografia del canto ambrosiano* ARCHIVIO AMBROSIANO 7 (Milan 1956)
579 xvi + 280 + 16 facss + 1 table, indices of plainsongs, mss, names and subjects
580 / rev S. Corbin *RdM* 39 (1957) 101–3 578 *Antiphonarium Ambrosianum du
British Museum, XIIe siècle* PalMus ser 1: 5, 6 (1896, 1900) viii + 200, 136 facss;
336 + 24 facss 579 Hucke, H. 'Die greg. Gradualeweise des 2. Tons und ihre
ambrosianischen Parallelen' *AMw* 13 (1956) 285–314 580 Husmann, H.
'Zum Grossaufbau der ambrosianischen Alleluia' *AnuarioM* 12 (1957) 17–33
577 This is a catalogue of 295 mss, 10–17c. Their notations are compared with
each other and with Greg. sources. 578 This has notes on the Ambrosian
liturgy; vol 2 contains transcriptions (Sq). 579 Using evidence which suggests some derivation from Frankish sources, Hucke argues against the
antiquity of Ambrosian chant. 580 Husmann uses form and performance to
conclude that Ambrosian chant originated from a layer earlier than Greg.

Augustinian

581 Husmann, H. 'Das Graduale von Ediger. Eine neue Quelle der rheinischen
Augustinerliturgie' **F-11.**224–34
H describes the ms and itemises some characteristic sections.

Cistercian

582 Marosszéki, Solutor *Les Origines du chant cistercien* ANALECTA SACRI ORDINIS
582a CISTERCIENSIS 8, fasc. 1–2 (Vatican 1952) xvi + 179, 10 tables, 8 facss, M exx,
583 indices of plainsongs, mss, names, b 582a Waddell, C. 'The Origin and
Early Evolution of the Cistercian Antiphonary: Reflections of Two Cistercian Chant Reforms' *The Cistercian Spirit: A Symposium* ed M. Basil Penning-
ton CISTERCIAN STUDIES 3 (Spencer, Mass. 1970) 190–223 583 Hammer,
Hubert-Gabriel *Die Allelujagesänge in der Choralüberlieferung der Abtei
Altenberg* BRMg 76 (Cologne 1968) 251
582 This is a comprehensive investigation. The reformers attempted to
reconcile a return to authentic tradition with the M theory of the time (12c).
582a W examines the 12c search for 'authentic' chant. 583 H discusses
characteristics of Cistercian usage.

Cluniac

584 Hourlier, J. 'Le Bréviaire de Saint-Taurin: Un Livre liturgique clunisien à
l'usage de l'Echelle-Saint-Aurin (BN lat. 12601)' *EG* 3 (1959) 163–73, 1 facs
H describes a Cluniac noted Breviary of ca 1100.

Dominican

585 Delalande, Dominique *Vers la version authentique du Graduel Greg.: Le Graduel des Prêcheurs* BIBL D'HIST DOMINICAINE 2 (Paris 1949) vii + 287, num tables with M, indices of plainsongs, mss
The reform responsible for the Dominican Gradual is dependent on the previous Cistercian reform (see **582**). D analyses the changes in several chosen plainsongs.

Gallican

586 Gastoué, Amédée *Le Chant gallican* (Grenoble 1939) repr from *RCG* 41 (1937) 101–6, 131–6 (origins and sources), 167–76 and 42 (1938) 5–12, 57–62, 76–80 (the Mass), 107–12 (psalms and ferial antiphons), 146–51 (antiphons), 171–6 and 43 (1939) 7–12 (hymns), 44–6
This is a general survey.

Manichean

587 Machabey, Armand *La Cantillation manichéenne: notation hypothétique, métrique, analogies* RM (Paris 1955) 22, 3 facss, b
M thinks certain signs in Manichean documents have M significance.

588 Puech, H.-C. 'M et hymnologie manichéennes' 4.1.354–86, num illuss
This gives the basic information.

Monastic

589 Daux, Camille, and (?) Morelot *Deux livres choraux monastiques des Xe et XIe siècles* (Paris 1899) xv + 151 + 8 leaves incl facss (some col) and transcc
D describes the Hymnary of Moissac and the Troper of Montauriol. M discusses the transcription of the neumes (pp 123–45).

590 Entry deleted

591 Entry deleted

592 *Antiphonaire Monastique, XIIe siècle, Codex 601 de la Bibl Capitulaire de Lucques*
593 PalMus ser 1: 9 (Tournai 1906) 56* + 218 + 560 facss + lviii, indices, tables, charts, M exx **593** *Antiphonaire Monastique, XIIIe siècle, Codex F. 160 de la Bibl de la Cathédrale de Worcester* PalMus ser 1: 12 (Tournai 1922) 181 + 422 facss + 12 facss
592 The introduction to this facsimile includes a comparison of two Tonaries. **593** This facsimile also includes a Tonary.

Mozarabic–Visigothic

594 Wagner, Peter *Der mozarabische Kirchengesang und seine Überlieferung*

SPANISCHE FORSCHUNGEN DER GÖRRESGES, ser 1 (GESAMMELTE AUFSÄTZE ZUR KULTURGESCHICHTE SPANIENS vol 1) (1928) 102–41, 1 facs
W gives much basic information, including sources, and compares the rite with contemporary Uses, especially Gallican.

595 *Antifonario Visigótico Mozárabe de la Catedral de León* ed Dom Louis Brou and José Vives 2 vols MON HISPANIAE SACRA, Ser litúrgica vol v[1,2] IEM (Barcelona, Madrid 1959, 1953) xix, 2 facss + 636, indices; iv + fos 29–307 facss, index of Offices / rev W. Apel *Spec* 30 (1955) 612–15
Vol 1 is an edition of the text, including that on fos 1v–28v, not given in the facsimile. There are extensive indices of texts, biblical sources, names, rubrics, etc. Vol 2 is a facsimile of the folios with M (in neumes) of the 10c ms.

596 Brou, Dom L. 'Notes de paléographie M mozarabe' *AnuarioM* 7 (1952) 51–76, 7 facss and 10 (1955) 23–44, 7 facss, 1 pl
B isolates signs and features peculiar to the Use.

597 Werner, E. 'Eine neuentdeckte mozarabische Hs. mit Neumen' F-2.II.977–91, 7 pll
With remarks on the rite and notation, W describes the oldest noted Mozarabic source (9–10c).

598 Brockett, Clyde W. *Antiphons, Responsories and other Chants of the Mozarabic Rite* MS 15 (Brooklyn 1968) xii + 294, 24 facss, num dipl facss, indices and lists, ext b / rev D.M. Randel *MQ* 56 (1970) 125–30
B deals with sources, history, notation, and analyses various forms.

599 Brou, Dom L. 'L'Alleluia dans la liturgie mozarabe' *AnuarioM* 6 (1951) 3–90, 22 facss and dipl facss
The Alleluia, or Laudes, is used also in the Mozarabic Offices and differs in some respects from the Greg. type.

600 Brou, Dom L. 'Séquences et tropes dans la liturgie mozarabe' *Hispania Sacra* 4 (1951) 27–41, 4 facss
These forms are very rare in the Mozarabic rite.

601 Messenger, R.E. 'The Mozarabic Hymnal' *The Hymn* 16 (1965) 49–63
M gives a general survey of the texts.

602 Randel, Don M. *The Responsorial Psalm Tones for the Mozarabic Office* PSM
603 3 (Princeton 1969) viii + 300, b / rev R. Steiner *MQ* 55 (1969) 575–80 603 Randel 'Responsorial Psalmody in the Mozarabic Rite' *EG* 10 (1969) 87–113
602 R includes an alphabetical list of Response and Verse (102–295) and information about history and sources. 603 R quotes and translates evidence relating to the performance of antiphons, responsories, and special items of the Mozarabic liturgy.

604 Rojo, R.P.C. 'The Greg. Antiphonary of Silos and the Spanish Melody of the Lamentations' *Spec* 5 (1930) 306–23
R describes the 12c ms, and transcribes chants peculiar to it.

Gregorian chant

THE CENTRAL PROBLEM

The problem concerns the origin of what we now know as Gregorian chant: does it stem from the Roman tradition of Gregory the Great, as was conventionally believed, or does it stem from a composition or radical revision which took place in Gaul? There is a special repertory of chant, existing in only four manuscripts of the thirteenth century, quite different from traditional Gregorian, but related in some aspects. There are no Gregorian sources in Rome from before the 13c. At first, the special repertory, usually called Old Roman (OR), was considered to date from the thirteenth century and no earlier.

605 Apel, W. 'The Central Problem of Greg. Chant' *JAMS* 9 (1956) 118–27
Clearly reviewing the issues, A confirms the 8–9c Frankish origin of Greg. chant. He does not examine whether OR is earlier or later.

606 Cutter, P.F. 'The Question of the 'Old-Roman' Chant: a Reappraisal' *Acta* 39 (1967) 2–20
C comprehensively reviews the literature, sources, problems, and modern opinions. He declines a firm stand but evidently leans towards Hucke's view (see 614–16).

607 Schuler, R.J. 'The Roman Chant' *Caecilia* 86 (1959) 129–37
This is an elementary survey of the dissemination of plainsong to the 13c, including the problem of OR chant. S has a useful list of M and non-musical sources bearing on the problem.

608 Smits van Waesberghe, J. 'Die Tradition des 'Altrömischen' und des Greg. Chorals' A-3.358–63
S poses several basic problems, to which the main scholars in the field reply: what are the *termini* of the repertories? why are Greg. mss not found in Rome until the 12–13c? whence stems the purest transmission? how can *cantus romanus* apply in the case of Frankish origin? will analysis not reveal Italian and non-Italian (i.e., Frankish) melodic traits?

Various solutions to the problem

Various solutions to the problem appear in the following items (609–23), beginning with the least valid, now virtually discarded, and ending with what I think to be the most convincing. In the immediately following section these items are listed: their annotations are then categorized according to the author of the theory presented. Moberg's article (624) interrupts these annotations. In the charts F stands for Frankish, G for Gregorian, OR for Old Roman.

609 Stäblein, B. 'Zur Frühgeschichte des römischen Chorals' **D-9.**271–5 **610**
610 Stäblein 'Alt- und neurömischer Choral' **B-1.**53–6 (see chart I)

611 Smits van Waesberghe, J. 'Neues über die Schola Cantorum zu Rom' **D-**
612 11.111–19 **612** Schmidt, H. 'Die Tractus des zweiten Tones in greg. und stat-
613 römischer Überlieferung' **F-25.**283–302 **613** Smits van Waesberghe, J.'De
Glorioso Officio ... Dignitate Apostolica ... (Amalarius): Zum Aufbau der
Gross-Alleluia in den Päpstlichen Ostervespern' **F-34.**48–73 (see chart II)

614 Hucke, H. 'Die Einführung des greg. Gesanges im Frankenreich' RQ 49
615 (1954) 172–87 **615** Hucke 'Greg. Gesang in altrömischer und fränkischer
616 Uberlieferung' AMw 12 (1955) 74–87 **616** Hucke 'Zu einigen Problemen der
Choralforschung' Mf 11 (1958) 385–414 (see chart III). Cf **D-11.**120–3.

617 Stäblein, B. 'Kann der greg. Choral im Frankenreich entstanden sein?' AMw
618 24 (1967) 153–69 **618** Stäblein 'Nochmals zur angeblichen Entstehung des
greg. Chorals im Frankenreich' AMw 27 (1970) 110–21 (see chart IV)

619 Gajard, J.' "Vieux-romain" et "Grégorien" ' EG 3 (1959) 7–26, 1 facs (see
chart V)

620 Jammers, E. 'Der greg. Choral und das byz. Kaisertum' Stimmen der Zeit 167
621 (1960/1) 445–52 **621** Van Dijk, S.J.P. 'The Urban and Papal Rites in 7 and 8c
622 Rome' SE 12 (1961) 411–87 **622** Van Dijk 'The OR Rite' Studia Patristica 5, Texte
623 und Untersuchungen 80 (1962) 185–205 **623** Van Dijk 'Recent Developments
623a in the Study of the OR Rite' Studia Patristica 8, Texte und Untersuchungen 93
(1966) 299–319 **623a** Van Dijk 'Gregory the Great, founder of the Urban
schola cantorum' EL 77 (1963) 335–56 (see chart VI)

Stäblein's first theory

Chart I

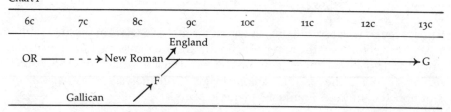

609 S sees OR as the 6–7c prototype, reformed ca 670, which with some Frankish additions became Greg. **610** The OR forms were transformed before
adoption in England. This solution is made difficult by the fact that the only
M sources for OR date from the 13c (but see **631**): S later changed his theory.

Smits van Waesberghe's theory
611 SvW proposes that the chant of the Greg. Schola in Rome was reformed
to produce the standard (Greg.) repertory and again to produce the special

Chart II

6c
7c
8c
9c
10c
11c
12c
13c
SCHOLA
(Gregorian)
G
F
OR (dies out)

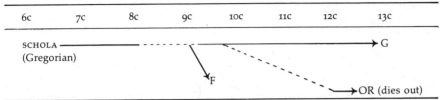

(OR) repertory. The former was used by regular, the latter by secular clergy. **612** Schmidt, comparing only the melismas of 2nd mode Tracts, concludes that the Greg. version is the older. **613** SvW identifies OR as the special repertory of the Schola (presumably later in its history).

Hucke's theory

Documentary and liturgical evidence (**625, 626**) suggests that OR must have originated earlier.

Chart III

6c
7c
8c
9c
10c
11c
12c
13c
OR
(dies out)
Gallican
F
G

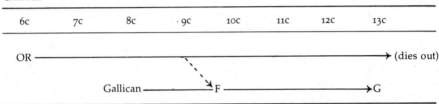

614–16 H, giving extensive quotations and M analyses, concludes that OR chant existed in Rome until the 13c: Frankish chant originated outside the OR tradition but adapted it, ca 9c, and eventually superseded it as Greg. chant.

Stäblein's second theory

Chart IV

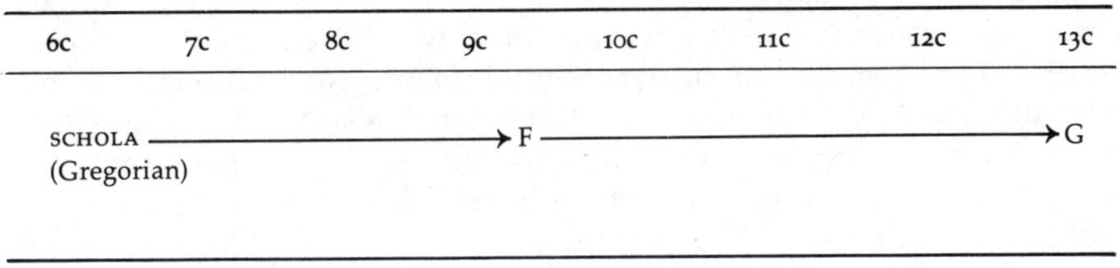

6c
7c
8c
9c
10c
11c
12c
13c
SCHOLA
(Gregorian)
F
G

617 Demolishing Hucke's arguments for Frankish origin, S maintains that Chrodegang (d 766) introduced it from Rome. **618** S investigates the source of text in Gallican or Roman Psalter, to confirm this thesis.

Moberg's argument

624 Moberg, C.-A. 'Greg. Reflexionen' F-2.II.559–83
M finds fault with the theories of both Hucke and Stäblein.

Gajard's theory

Chart v

6c	7c	8c	9c	10c	11c	12c	13c

⌐SCHOLA ――――――――――→ F ――――――――――→ G
¦ (Gregorian)
└OR ―――――――――――――――――――→ (dies out)

The two traditions are related

619 G finds evidence for the standard (Greg.) chant in Rome and 'almost all churches of the West' in the 9c. His evidence that it originated in Rome is weak. Opting for the traditional view (the priority and Roman origin of the standard repertory), G hypothesises that the OR chant could have existed simultaneously in Rome.

Jammers' and Van Dijk's theory

Chart vi

6c	7c	8c	9c	10c	11c	12c	13c

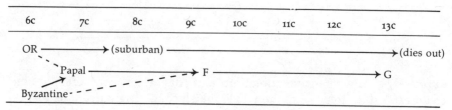

OR ―――――→ (suburban) ―――――――――――――→ (dies out)
Papal ―――――――――→ F ―――――――――→ G
Byzantine - - -

620 J tries to make a case for the standard repertory (Greg.) being developed only in the papal basilica, 7–8c, as a result of Byz. influence. Charlemagne, for similar political reasons, adopted this version rather than the more widespread OR version. **621** VanD examines the liturgical circumstances in Rome itself. He maintains that the 13c OR books are accidental preservations of rites, originally more widespread in Rome, which were relegated to local use only. The papal rite, taking over the style of Byz. court M for artistic and political reasons, developed Greg. 'professional' chant, and earlier chant was reduced to parochial use. This papal rite (not to be confused with Roman rite) was taken to Gaul, where it flourished. **622** This is a lighter, less documented version of the preceding article. **623** Taking Jammers' book (**485**) into account, VanD sees that it fits his theory. See also **620**. **623a** VanD distinguishes between the urban *schola* (St John's and St Peter's, OR chant) founded by Gregory I and the papal *schola* (Lateran, Greg. chant) founded by Vitalian.

Some evidence

625 Huglo, M. 'Le Chant "vieux-romain." Liste des mss et témoins indirects' *SE*
626 6 (1954) 96–124 **626** Frénaud, G. 'Les Témoins indirects du chant liturgique
en usage à Rome aux ix⁰ et x⁰ siècles' *EG* 3 (1959) 41–74
625 H lists and describes M and non-M sources, and tabulates some differences between OR and Greg. **626** F denies that the three most important
sources isolated by Huglo can be considered as evidence for the use of OR
chant in Rome before ca 1050.

627 Hourlier, J., and M. Huglo 'Un Important témoin du chant "vieux-romain."
Le Graduel de Sainte-Cécile du Trastévère … 1071' *RG* 31 (1952) 26–37
H and H describe the source.

628 Lipphardt, W. 'Ein unbekannter karolingischer Tonar und seine Bedeutung
für die fränkische Choralüberlieferung' **A-3**.179–81
The Tonary of Metz offers new evidence for the relation of Greg. to OR.

629 Smits van Waesberghe, J. 'Die Geschichte von Glastonbury (1082) und ihre
Folgen' **F-25**.372–8
Norman mss with bilingual notation suggest that after the Norman Conquest *cantus gregorianus* was replaced. OR chants had recently been
introduced into Normandy.

630 Stäblein, B. 'Der "altrömische" Choral in Oberitalien und im deutschen
Süden' *MF* 19 (1966) 3–9
S concludes that St Gall used OR chant at least till ca 9c.

631 Cutter, P.F. 'The OR Chant Tradition: Oral or Written?' *JAMS* 20 (1967) 167–81
Briefly comparing the consistency of many Greg. with the variability of few
OR mss, C concludes the latter use to have been primarily oral.

STYLE, FORM, DIALECT

Form, formula, analysis, centonization, adaptation

632 Ferretti, Paolo *Esthétique grég.* (Paris, etc 1938) xiv + 349, num M exx, tables,
transl A. Agaësse from *Estetica greg.: Trattato delle forme musicali del canto
greg.* vol 1 (Rome 1934); vol 2 *Estetica greg. dei recitativi liturgici* QUADERNI
DEI PADRI BENEDETTINI DI SAN GIORGIO MAGGIORE 3 (Venice, Rome 1964) 138
/ rev (vol 1 only) O. Ursprung *ZMw* 17 (1935) 474–6
Vol 1: F comprehensively examines word setting and accent, concepts of
musical composition, and chant in general. He then analyses psalmody. Vol
2: This volume, edited by Pellegrino M. Ernetti from F's unpublished notes,
forms the intended continuation. It deals with reciting tones, the Ordinary
of the Mass, and strophic chants.

633 Gevaert, François A. *La Mélopée antique dans le chant de l'église latine* (Gand

1895; repr Osnabrück 1967) xxxvi + 487, index of incipits / rev H.-I. Marrou
E-2.73
G's catalogue of melodic types underlying antiphons has not been super-
seded.

634 Holman, H.-J. 'Compositional Techniques and Concepts of Originality in
Monophonic Church M from the 9–13c' D-7.993–1005
Traditional centonization techniques for Tracts and Responsories give way
more commonly to free composition in the late MA.

*635 Dreimüller, K. 'Das Kunstprinzip der Wiederholung im greg. Gesang' Zs
für Km 74 (1954) 32–4

636 Kunz, Lucas Aus der Formenwelt des greg. Chorals 4 vols (Münster). I:
Antiphonen und Responsorien der heiligen Messe (1948) 48; II: Rhythmus und
Form (1947) 48; III: Metrische Gestaltung Textformen (1949) 54; IV: Antike Lied-
texte, moderne Choraltheorie, Satzarten und Choralvortrag (1950) 66, cumulative index / rev B. Stäblein Mf 3 (1950) 298–305 and 5 (1952) 385–7

Dialects

637 Brenn, F. 'Zur Frage greg. Lesarten' Mf 9 (1956) 442–3 638 Lipphardt, W.
638 'Une Source importante pour l'histoire de la tradition grég. en Allemagne
639 [Le Tonaire de Leipzig]' RG 31 (1952) 140–3 639 Wagner, P. 'Germanisches
640 und Romanisches im frühma. Kirchengesang' D-6.21–34 640 Falvy,
Z. 'Über Antiphonvarianten aus dem österreichisch-ungarischtschecho-
slowakischen Raum' StuMw 26 (1964) 9–24
637 B comments on the thesis of plainchant dialects. 638 The Leipzig
Tonary, 11c (711) does not demonstrate German dialect variants, which
therefore must be of 12c at the earliest. 639 The replacement of B and E by
C and F is a common northern variant. 640 F compares and prints 6 antiphons
from 19 sources, isolating Hungarian characteristics.

Recitation, cantillation, psalm-tones

641 Corbin, S. 'La Cantillation des rituels chrétiens' RdM 47 (1961) 3–36 642 Jam-
642 mers, E. 'Der Choral als Rezitativ' AMw 22 (1965) 143–68 643 Köllner, G.P.
643 'Zur Tradition des Accentus Moguntinus' KmJb 42 (1958) 39–46
641 Defining cantillation, C describes five liturgical recitatives transcribed
from modern rituals preserving ancient forms. 642 J stresses the essential
origin of plainsong in heightened speech. 643 K discusses liturgical recitation (accentus) of Mainz Use, 14–19c, and lists sources.

644 Berger, Hugo Untersuchungen zu den Psalmdifferenzen KBMf 37 (Regensburg
645 1966) vii + 170, index of incipits 645 Falvy, Z. 'Zur Frage von Differenzen
der Psalmodie' StuMw 25 (1962) 160–73

644 B analyses *differentia*. **645** F prints and compares the Psalm terminations from seven different countries.

646 Kunz, L. 'Psalmengliederungen und formale Probleme des greg. Chorals' *KmJb* 41 (1957) 4–8
This is a numerical analysis of formal structure. Cf *KmJb* 45 (1961) 1–37.

647 Herzog, A., and A. Hajdu 'A la recherche du *Tonus peregrinus* dans la tradition M juive' *Yuval* 194–203 + appendix of M exx, 1–15
The authors provide further documentation for Werner's conclusions (**39**) that the *tonus* originates in Hebrew melodies.

MASS

Some material on Introits is listed in the General Index.

648 Froger, J.'Les Chants de la Messe aux VIIIe et IXe siècles' *RG* 26 (1947) 165–72 (Introit), 218–28 (Kyrie, Gloria, Collect, Epistle, Gradual, Alleluia, Tract); 27 (1948) 56–62 (Gospel, Credo, Offertory, Secret), 98–107 (Preface, Sanctus, Canon, Pater noster, Agnus, Communion, Post-communion, Ite, Benediction); 28 (1949) 58–65 (general overview and conclusions and the role of priest, people, choir, organ, etc), 94–102 (the role of M)
Translating passages from *Ordines*, etc, F describes methods of performance. This is a step by step reconstruction of the service, in detail.

Kyrie

649 (Landwehr-)Melnicki, Margaretha *Das einstimmige Kyrie des lateinischen MA* FORSCHUNGSBEITR ZUR MW 1 (Regensburg, 1955) 151, 4 facss
M analyses Kyries from continental mss and gives a thematic inventory.

Gloria

650 Bosse, Detlev *Untersuchung einstimmiger ma. Melodien zum 'Gloria in excelsis Deo'* FORSCHUNGSBEITR ZUR MW 2 (Regensburg 1955) 102
This includes copious geographical and chronological lists of sources, and thematic index.

Alleluia

651 Schlager, Karl-Heinz *Thematischer Katalog der ältesten Alleluia-Melodien aus*
652 *Mss des 10. und 11. Jh., ausgenommen das ambrosianische, alt-römische und alt-spanische Repertoire* EArbMw 2 (Munich 1965) vii + 270 **652** Schlager *Alleluia-Melodien. I: bis 1100* MMMA 7 (Kassel 1968) xxxii + 682 / rev Andrew Hughes *Notes* 26 (1969/70) 598–9

651 is an index of themes, texts, and sources, etc. 652 This volume includes transcriptions of 410 melodies, indexed.

653 Cochrane, M.B. 'The Alleluia in Greg. Chant' *JAMS* 7 (1954) 213–20
C gives some basic information.

654 Huglo, M. 'Les Listes alléluiatiques dans les témoins du Graduel grég.' **F-15.**219–27
Seeking clarification of the early stages by comparing the sequence of Alleluia verses, H isolates five broad groups of Uses.

655 Treitler, L. 'On the Structure of the Alleluia Melisma: A Western Tendency in Western Chant' **F-30.**59–72, 1 facs
Parallel but differentiated phrase repetition probably entered the repertory late: the new melodic style forced a new system of notation.

656 Schlager, K.-H. 'Anmerkungen zu den zweiten Alleluia-Versen' *AMw* 24 (1967) 199–219
S documents, describes, and exemplifies different treatment of multiple verses.

657 Huglo, M. 'Une Composition monodique de Latino Frangipane' *RdM* 54 (1968) 96–8, 1 facs
H gives the biography of Frangipane (late 13c), with a description of the Alleluia ascribed to him.

Gradual and Tract

658 *Le Répons-Graduel 'Justus ut palma'* 2 parts, PalMus ser 1: 2, 3 (1891, 1892) ix + 88 + 107 facss, tables, M cxx; 89–191, 104 facss, tables, M exx, indices
These facsimile volumes trace the history of a single Gradual, 9–17c, through its notation and rhythm. Cf **563 766.**

659 Haberl, F. 'Die Gradualien des dritten Modus und ihre M Struktur' *AnuarioM* 16 (1961) 3–25
H analyses the formulaic patterns and their variants.

660 Kojima, S. 'Die Ostergradualien *Haec dies* und ihr Verhältnis zu den Tractus
661 des II. und VIII. Tons' **F-25.**146–78 661 Hucke, H. 'Tractusstudien' **F-**
662 29.116–20 662 Schmidt, H. 'Untersuchungen zu den Tractus des zweiten Tones' *KmJb* 42 (1958) 1–25
660 All three groups probably originated from a common psalmodic melody. 661 H concludes that most early Tracts show little melodic relation to Graduals. 662 S discusses structure, formula, and adaptation, and draws tentative chronological conclusions.

Credo

663 Haberl, F. 'Das Choralcredo im 4. Modus in seiner unterschiedlichen Gestalt' **E-7.**28–35

H shows the varied 'stanzaic' character of the melody.

*664 Stein, F. 'Das Credo im ersten und fünften Modus' *Zs für Km* 73 (1953) 55–61

Offertory

665 Ott, Carolus ed *Offertoriale sive versus offertoriorum* (Paris 1935) 197
This is a square-note edition of Offertories, giving the verses, not normally included in the modern repertory.

666 Sidler, Hubert *Studien zu den alten Offertorien mit ihren Versen* GAkF 20
667 (Freiburg 1939) viii + 92 **667** Steiner, R. 'Some Question about the Greg. Offertories and their Verses' *JAMS* 19 (1966) 162–81
666 Sidler analyses 16 chants. **667** Steiner questions parts of **484** and points out some hazards of using non-critical editions.

668 Hucke, H. 'Die Texte der Offertorien' **F-15**.193–203
Distinguishing responsorial and antiphonal types, and suggesting that type is related to age, H seeks more evidence to solve the problem of text repetition, unique in the chant repertory.

Sanctus

669 Thannabaur, Peter J. *Das einstimmige Sanctus der römischen Messe in der handschriftlichen Überlieferung des 11. bis 16. Jh.* EArbMw 1 (Munich 1962) vii + 263 + 2 tables / rev J. Rau *Mf* 17 (1964) 430–1
This includes copious geographical and chronological lists of sources, and thematic and textual indices.

Agnus Dei

670 Schildbach, Martin *Das einstimmige Agnus Dei und seine handschriftliche Überlieferung vom 10. bis zum 16. Jh.* (Sonneberg 1967) iv + 207
This is a catalogue of sources and melodies with analysis of various aspects.

Communion

671 Levy, K. 'The Italian Neophytes' Chants' *JAMS* 23 (1970) 181–227
L isolates early Communion-cycle chants not present in the later Easter-vigil Mass.

Cycles of the Ordinary

672 Catta, Dom D. 'Aux origines du *Kyriale*' *RG* 34 (1955) 175–82
C examines 13–14c mss for plainsong antecedents of the cyclic grouping of Ordinary chants.

673 Schrade, L. 'The Cycle of the *Ordinarium Missae*' **F-13**.87–96. Cf *JAMS* 8

674 (1955) 66–9 **674** Hoppin, R.H. 'Reflections on the Origin of the Cyclic Mass'
F-32.85–92
673 S offers no evidence for M unification, but claims that liturgical unity
is at least as early as the 14c. **674** Plainsong cycles unified in the M sense do
not antedate the 15c.

675 Fischer, K. von 'Neue Quellen zum einstimmigen Ordinariumszyklus des
14. und 15. Jh. aus Italien' F-32.60–8
The most widespread type of cycle appears to be of Roman Use.

OFFICES

Important material on Antiphons, Responsories, etc, occurs in the entries
under 'Style, form, dialect' (**632–47**).

676 Hucke, H. 'M. Formen der Officiumsantiphonen' *KmJb* 37 (1953) 7–33
H categorizes formal types by melodic style and structural sectionalisation.
See also **711**.

677 Steiner, R. 'The Responsories and Prosa for St Stephen's Day at Salisbury'
MQ 56 (1970) 162–82, 2 facss
This is a basic description.

678 Stäblein, B. ed *Die ma. Hymnenmelodien des Abendlandes: Hymnen* I MMMA
1 (Kassel 1956) xviii + 723, 1 map, 8 facss, indices of texts, melodies, sources,
names, etc / rev B. Rajecky *StuMus* 6 (1964) 271–5
This is basically an anthology, with extensive commentary.

Hymns

679 Mittler, Placidus *Melodieuntersuchung zu den dorischen Hymnen der lateinischen Liturgie im MA* SIEGBURGER STUDIEN 2 (Siegburg 1965) 145
This is an analysis of melodic formula and adaptation of basic tunes.

680 Messenger, Ruth E. *The Med. Latin Hymn* (Washington, DC 1953) x + 138,
681 indices of texts, names, etc, ext b **681** Messenger 'Vernacular Hymnody of
the Late MA' *The Hymn* 16 (1965) 80–6
These are two of the numerous items by Messenger: most deal primarily
with textual matters.

Litanies, Laudes, etc

682 Pfaff, M. 'Die Laudes-Akklamationen des MA' D-12.457–61 **683** Kan-
683 torowitz, Ernst H. *Laudes Regiae: A Study in Liturgical Acclamations and Med.
684 Ruler Worship* UCPH 23 (Berkeley 1964) xxi + 292, 15 facss, indices of mss:
685 Appendix 1, pp 188–221, *The M of the Laudes* was written by Manfred

Bukofzer **684** Hucke, H. 'Eine unbekannte Melodie zu den *Laudes regiae*'
KmJb 42 (1958) 32–8 **685** Hesbert, R.-J. 'L'Evangéliaire de Zara (1114)' *Scrip*
8 (1954) 177–204, pll 20 and 21, facss at end of vol
682 This is a brief history, also mentioning the Litany. **683** K writes a general
liturgical history: Bukofzer transcribes and compares the version in several
sources and comments on the general significance. **684** Hucke compares different versions and transcribes the melody in a Porto ms. **685** Hesbert
describes and roughly inventories the ms, and concentrates on the text and
M of the *Laudes* it contains.

686 Gennrich, F. 'Die *Laudes Sancte Crucis* der Hs Darmstadt Hessische Landes-
bibl. 2777' **F-28**.45–58
G gives facsimiles, a transcription (Rh), and a brief description of the
sources of this 13c votive text.

687 Hammerstein, R. 'Tuba intonet salutaris' *Acta* 31 (1959) 109–29, 14 pll facss
H comments on the M of the Exultet rolls, and the iconography of the *tuba*.
The latter has no bearing on actual practice. Another facsimile of a roll is
in *Conv* 10 (1938), pll on pp 639a–d.

688 Huglo, M. 'Antifone antiche per la "fractio panis"' *Ambrosius* 31 (1955) 85–95
H describes a few of these, and transcribes two.

689 Rokseth, Y. 'La Liturgie de la Passion vers la fin du xe siècle' *RdM* 28 (1949)
1–58 and 29 (1950) 35–52
R describes ritual, texts, and M of Holy Week.

PROCESSIONS

689a Bailey, Terence *The Processions of Sarum and the Western Church* PIMS 21
(Toronto 1971) xv + 208, 1 facs, 14 diagg, index / rev R.W. Pfaff *Spec* 48 (1973)
337–9
B describes sources, liturgical practice, with much quotation of rubrics, and
gives many M examples.

SPECIAL OFFICES

Material on specially composed services and Rhymed Offices is listed here
alphabetically by author.

689b Arlt, Wulf *Ein Festoffizium des Ma aus Beauvais* vol 1 (Cologne 1970) 328, 1 facs,
ext b
Quoting copiously, A describes the M and liturgical forms, including
tropes, conductus, and polyphony.

690 Falvy, Zoltán *Drei Reimoffizien aus Ungarn und ihre M* MUSICOLOGIA

691 HUNGARICA ns 2 (Budapest, Kassel 1968) 170, M exx, thematic and textual
692 incipits, index / rev R. Crocker *Notes* 25 (1968/9) 738–9 **691** Falvy 'Die
Weisen des König Stephan-Reimoffiziums' *StuMus* 6 (1964) 207–69
692 Falvy *'Benedic regem cunctorum*; Der Weg einer ma. Weise' *StuMw* 27
(1966) 8–17, 1 facs
These are analytical and comparative studies.

693 Hesbert, R.-J. 'La Composition M à Jumièges: les Offices de S. Philibert et
de S. Aycadre' **D-10.II.977–90**
H examines the order in which the modes appear in the antiphons and
responsories, and transcribes several chants in order to discuss their use of
original or traditional material. René Derivière considers the literary aspects
on pp 969–76.

694 Hoppin, R.H. ed *Cypriot Plainsong* MSD 19 (1968) 168, 55 facss, index of texts
This is a facsimile of the plainsong Offices to St Hylarion and St Anne, and
of Mass cycles of the early 15c. The formal and stylistic discussion of the services and chants found in them is characterised by too much reliance on 20c
liturgical sources. But this is an invaluable study of which kind many more
are needed.

695 Jammers, E. 'Die Antiphonen der rheinischen Reimoffizien' *EL* 43 (1929)
199–219, 425–51 and 44 (1930) 84–99, 342–68, index of incipits
With some general remarks on the Rhymed Office, J lists some sources and
widespread Offices, transcribes the M of some chants, and describes their
M characteristics.

696 Jammers, Ewald *Das Karlsoffizium 'Regali natus'* SAMMLUNG MW ABH 14
(Strasbourg 1934) iii + 111 + 1–49 M exx and transcc / rev W. Frere *ML* 15 (1934)
353–4 (Frere includes a short history of the Rhymed Office)
This is a M analysis of the Office.

696a Jonsson, Ritva *Historia: Etudes sur la genèse des offices versifiés* AUS, Studia
Latina Stockholmiensia 15 (Stockholm 1968) 259, 6 facss
R deals mainly with sources and styles of texts, including isolated hints at
M matters.

697 Mittler, P. 'Zwei Hss mit dem Offizium zu Ehren des heiligen Erzbischofs
Anno von Köln' *Siegburger Studien* 1 (1960) 61–104, 2 facss
M edits the texts and analyses the M.

698 Ottósson, Róbert A. *Sancti Thorlaci Episcopi officia rhytmica et proprium missae in AM 241a folio* BIBL ARN SUPPLEMENTUM 3 (Copenhagen 1959) 127, 22
facss (pp 10–30, 53), 29 pp transcc (94–122), b / rev S. Corbin *RdM* 46 (1960)
224–5
O edits texts and melodies of this 14c Icelandic Rhymed Office, with commentary on styles and sources.

699 Stevens, D. 'M in Honor of St Thomas of Canterbury' *MQ* 56 (1970) 311–48,
2 facss

S describes the plainsong Offices, polyphony based on the chants, and other pieces.

700 Vecchi, Giuseppe ed *Uffici drammatici padovani* (Florence 1954) xii + 187 + 5 pll, index of texts with M / rev S. Corbin *CCM* 2 (1959) 226–7
This is an edition of text and M with parallel Italian translation.

701 Villetard, Henri ed *Office de Pierre de Corbeil (d.1222)* BIBL MUSICOLOGIQUE
702 4 (Paris 1907) xii + 244 + 2 pll + 4 facss, index of incipits / rev P. Wagner *Zs für schw Kirchengeschichte* 2 (1908) 150–2 702 Villetard ed *Office de Saint Savinien et de Saint Potentien, premiers évêques de Sens* BIBL MUSICOLOGIQUE 5 (Paris 1956) frontispiece facs, xii + 115 / rev R. Weakland *JAMS* 12 (1959) 225–6
These are editions with introductions.

703 Weakland, R. 'The Compositions of Hucbald' *EG* 3 (1959) 155–62, 1 facs
Hucbald (d 930) composed some Offices, one transcribed here, and the *laudes* 'Quae vere ...'

THE TONARY

The best edition of a late medieval Tonary is in Frere, *The Use of Sarum* (**529**).

*703a Huglo, Michel *Les Tonaires; inventaire, analyse, comparaison* (Paris 1971)

704 Becker, A. 'Ein Erfurter Traktat über greg. M' *AMw* 1 (1918/19) 145–65, 1 facs
B describes and prints the treatise, basically a Tonary of ca 1300.

705 Gümpel, Karl-Werner *Zur Interpretation der Tonus-Definition des 'Tonale Sancti Bernardi'* AKW UND DER LITERATUR, Geistes- und sozialwissenschaftliche Klasse, Jahrgang 1959, Abh 2 (Mainz 1959) 27
G examines the melodic modes.

706 Huglo, M. 'Le Théoricien bolognais Guido Fabe' *RdM* 55 (1969) 78–82
H gives a brief biography of Fabe, describing the source and contents of his 13c treatise on plainsong and modes.

707 Huglo, M. 'Le Tonaire de Saint-Bénigne de Dijon' *AnnM* 4 (1956) 7–18, 2 facss
The 11c Tonary exhibits early signs that traditional melodies were 'reformed' to accord with recent modal theory.

708 Huglo, M. 'Un troisième témoin du "Tonaire Carolingien"' *Acta* 40 (1968)
709 22–8 709 Lipphardt, Walter *Der karolingischer Tonar von Metz* LITURGIE-WISSENSCHAFTLICHE QUELLEN UND FORSCHUNGEN 43 (Münster-Westfalen 1965) xii + 309 + 2 facss, lists of antiphons (69–100) / rev M. Huglo *RdM* 51 (1965) 228–30
708 Comparing an 11c Tonary with that of Metz and Reichenau, H deduces a stemma, and the contents of the archetype. 709 L describes the ms, and the information it gives about the liturgy and M at Metz cathedral, 9c.

710 Machabey, A. 'Tonale inédit du Graduel Ms de Nevers (XIIᵉ siècle)' *RdM* 7
(1926) 113–25, 1 facs
M describes and transcribes a Tonary.

711 Sowa, Heinrich *Quellen zur Transformation der Antiphonen* (Kassel 1935) vii
+ 202 / rev K.G. Fellerer *DMk* 1 (1936/7) 247–50
Printing two examples and indexing their terminology, S studies the Tonary
and transposition of antiphons. He then examines the problem of rhythm.

MISCELLANEOUS

712 Douteil, Herbert *Studien zu Durantis 'Rationale divinorum officiorum' als kir-
chenmusikalischer Quelle* KBMf 52 (Regensburg 1969) xxxix + 428, indices, b
Durantis (13c) frequently refers to M. See also *KmJb* 29 (1934) 46–9.

713 Handschin, J. 'Gesungene Apologetik' **F-13**. 117–49
H discusses three examples of doctrinal propaganda: the Sequence *Victimae
Paschali* (anti-Jewish and later anti-Luther); the verse *Dicant nunc Judaei*, its
troping and Greek origin; 4c hymns and psalms with doxological implications.

714 Smits van Waesberghe, J. 'Neue Kompositionen des Johannes von Metz
(um 975), Hucbalds von St Amand und Sigeberts von Gembloux?' **F-15**.
285–303 + 3 facss (after p 304)
The text is in Dutch.

Tropes

The following section includes material on the Sequence, which is treated in detail in **752–83**.

CATALOGUES AND SOURCES

715 RISM, Ser B v, vol 1 *Trope and Sequence Mss* (from Austria, Belgium, Czecho-slovakia, France, Germany, Great Britain, Italy, Netherlands, Poland, Spain, Sweden, Switzerland, Vatican State) ed Heinrich Husmann (1964) 236 / rev E.H. Roesner *JAMS* 21 (1968) 212–15
This basic catalogue includes many indices and an extensive bibliography.

716 *Anglo-French Sequelae* ed Dom Anselm Hughes PMMS (Burnham 1934; repr 1966) iv + 142 / rev J.H. Arnold *ML* 17 (1936) 257–8
Although the basic thesis is now questioned, the book has useful informa-tion and lists of mss and texts, and numerous transcriptions of melodies.

717 *Introitus-Tropen. I: Das Repertoire der südfranzösischen Tropare des 10. und 11. Jh.* ed Günther Weiss MMMA III¹ (Kassel 1970) xlii, 13 facss + 470, index of incipits; separate booklist of 48 pp / rev Andrew Hughes *Notes* 27 (1971) 293
This is a scholarly anthology of melodies, whose parent Introits are given in the separate booklet.

718 Bannister, H.M. 'Une Tropaire-Prosier de Moissac' *R d'hist et de la littérature*
719 *religieuse* 8 (1903) 554–72, 572–81 **719** Huglo, M. 'Un nouveau prosaire
720 nivernais' *EL* 71 (1957) 3–30, 2 facss **720** Husmann, H. 'Ein Prosar-Tropar
721 aus St Frambould in Senlis' **F-36**. 229–30 **721** Irtenkauf, W. 'Das neuerwor-bene Weingartner Tropar der Stuttgarter Landesbibliothek' *AMw* 11 (1954) 280–95
These are all brief descriptions of the mss.

Editions, facsimiles of Tropers and Sequentiaries

722 *Ein deutsches Sequentiar aus dem Ende des 12. Jh.* ed Otto E. Drinkwelder GAkF 8 (Graz, Vienna 1914) xi + 84, 1 facs
D describes and edits the ms.

723 723a 723b *Le Prosaire de la Sainte-Chapelle* (ca 1250); *Le Prosaire d'Aix-*
723a *la-Chapelle* (early 13c); *Le Tropaire-Prosaire de Dublin* (14c) MMS 1, 3, 4 (Mâcon
723b 1952, Rouen 1961, 1966) 1–100, 152 facss, 101–12; 1–96, 99 facss, 97–107; 1–116,
98 facss, 117–24 / rev (of **723** only) G. Beyssac *RHE* 49 (1954) 934–40
These are facsimile editions. Some texts and melodies are printed with
indices and extensive introductions.

724 *Über die schwedischen Sequenzen* ed Carl Allan Moberg 2 vols (Uppsala 1927;
repr 1970?) xx + 276 + 5 facss, indices of texts and names; 8 + 1–171 (not numbered) / rev C. Van den Borren *RUB* 35 (1929/30) 119*–20*
Vol 1: M describes texts, melodies, modality, and form, and lists sources and
literature. Vol 2: he transcribes 69 melodies with ms variants.

725 *The Sequences of the Archbishopric of Nidarós* ed Erik Eggen 2 vols BIBL ARN
21 and 22 (Copenhagen 1968) lxxii–320, 1 facs, indices of incipits and
melodies; viii + 277 facss
With a historical dissertation concerning the liturgical practices of
Trondheim and the Northlands, E publishes Sequence sources in facsimile
(vol 2) and transcription (Rh; see vol 1, p 319).

726 *Das Sequentiar Cod. 546 der Stiftsbibliothek von St Gallen und seine Quellen* ed
Frank Labhardt 2 vols PSMfG ser 2: $8^{1,2}$ (Bern 1959, 1963) 272 + 5 facss, indi-
ces; 122
This is a description, inventory, and transcription of the ms (early 16c).

727 *Troparium, Sequentiarium Nonantulanum (Cod. Casanat. 1741)* ed Ioseph (i.e.
Giuseppe) Vecchi MLMAI-L 1 (Modena 1955) 10 + 193 facss
Presumably an introduction and description will follow in vol 2.

728 *The Utrecht Prosarium* ed Nikolaus de Goede MON MUSICA MEERLANDICA 6
(Amsterdam 1965) cxlviii + 142 + 2 tables / rev J.D. Bergsagel *ML* 48 (1967)
390–1
This is an excellent edition of Sequences, with comprehensive historical
introduction and bibliography. There are indices of sources, Alleluia
verses, melody titles, Sequences mentioned or transcribed. A table shows
the distribution of the melodies.

729 *The Winchester Troper* ed Walter H. Frere HENRY BRADSHAW SOC 8 (London
1894) xlvii + 248 + 33 leaves with 6 pp M transcc and 27 facss (whose numbering is not that of the original), list of mss and printed sources (xliii–xliv),
indices of tropes, Sequences, etc
This is a partial edition of the texts with a still useful general introduction
to troping. F also edits parts of other sources, including a St Martial Troper.

 * Announced: A facsimile of the *Winchester Tropers*, in the Early English Mss
in Facsimile series

ORIGINS, HISTORY, AND SIGNIFICANCE OF TROPES

730 Crocker, R.L. 'The Troping Hypothesis' *MQ* 52 (1966) 183–203

'Trope,' as normally used today, includes impossibly extreme styles and forms. C examines some basic types.

731 Evans, P. 'Some Reflections on the Origin of the Trope' *JAMS* 14 (1961) 119–30
Clarifying terminology, E points to weaknesses in earlier theories.

732 Husmann, H. 'Sinn und Wesen der Tropen' *AMw* 16 (1959) 135–47
In a comparative study H argues persuasively that the earliest tropes were introductory prefaces, a general tendency not peculiar to the West.

733 Stäblein, B. 'Die Unterlegung von Texten unter Melismen: Tropus, Sequenz und andere Formen' **A-4**.I.12–29 (discussed in II.48–52)
With extensive references to previous research, S chronologically reviews the development of textual tropes, distinguishing *sequentia, melodia, jubilus, sequela, neuma, prosa*. See **762**.

734 Weakland, R. 'The Beginnings of Troping' *MQ* 44 (1958) 477–88, 2 facss
W indexes and attempts to categorize the insertions in the earliest known ms with tropes (10c).

Specific troped forms

735 Rönnau, Klaus *Die Tropen zum Gloria in excelsis Deo* (Wiesbaden 1967) vi +
736 282, 14 facss, index of tropes / rev M. Huglo *RdM* 53 (1967) 188–9 **736** Rönnau
'Regnum tuum solidum' **F-29**.195–205, 1 facs
735 Printing texts and some melodies, R analyses St Martial tropes and their sources. **736** R discusses subsequent troping with *prosulae* and the performance of them, and concludes that the less repetitive, melismatic version is older.

737 Smits van Waesberghe, J. 'Die Imitation der Sequenztechnik in den
738 Hosanna-Prosulen' **F-11**.485–90 **738** Thannabaur, P.J. 'Anmerkungen zur Verbreitung und Struktur der Hosanna-Tropen im deutschsprachigen Raum und den Ostländern' **F-29**.250–9
737 S gives examples illustrating identical principles and procedures. **738** T finds the repertory folklike in character.

739 Stäblein, B. 'Zum Verständnis des "klassischen" Tropus' *Acta* 35 (1963)
740 84–95 **740** Weiss, G. 'Zur Rolle Italiens im frühen Tropenschaffen' **F-29**.287–92
Both authors discuss Introit troping in general.

741 Göllner, T. 'Eine mehrstimmige tropierte Weinachtslektion in Polen' *Acta* 37 (1965) 165–78, 1 p facs
In melody and text a 14c troped Reading is related to an Alleluia.

742 Holman, H.-J. 'Melismatic Tropes in the Responsories for Matins' *JAMS* 16 (1963) 36–46
Style and structure of melismas suggests they were later, newly-composed additions.

743 Irtenkauf, W. 'Die Weinachtskomplet im Jahre 1345 in Seckau' *Mf* 9 (1956) 257–62
The *Nunc dimittis* may be troped.

ST MARTIAL AND AQUITAINE

The polyphonic repertory is treated in items **1356–73**.

744 Chailley, Jacques *L'Ecole* M *de Saint Martial de Limoges jusqu'à la fin du XI*ᵉ *siècle* (Paris 1960 [but work on the book was finished in 1954: see p 8]) vi + 440, ext b (383–414), index. The two lists of errata are important: see also rev A. Machabey *Rom* 82 (1961) 125–8.
An extensive study, this deals with the history and liturgical practices of the abbey; the mss, described in detail; the Carolingian lyric; tropes, distinguished by formal type and function; Sequences; *planctus* and *versus*; polyphony; literary aspects and verbal rhythm.

745 Evans, Paul *The Early Trope Repertory of Saint Martial de Limoges* PSM 2 (Princeton 1970) ix + 294, b, index, index of tropes. Pp 129–273 M transcc (N) / rev *TLS* 4 June (1971) 645
This deals with the history, sources, texts, and M structure of tropes in Ms Paris BN lat. 1121.

746 Spanke, H. 'St Martial-Studien: Ein Beitrag zur frühromanischen Metrik' *ZfSL* 54 (1931) 282–317, 385–422
In the first part S describes and inventories, with analysis, important sections (mainly conductus and tropes) of the four most significant mss. In the second he relates the contents to the Codex Calixtinus, to the works of Abelard and Hilarius, and to the liturgical drama.

747 Elfving, Lars *Etude lexicographique sur les séquences limousines* AUS, Studia Latina Stockholmiensia 7 (Stockholm 1962) 283, b, index / rev J. Szövérffy *MAe* 35 (1966) 130–1
This is a literary study: on pp 203–59 E discusses the performance of Sequences and shows that the M terms used in the texts are mainly symbolic. St Martial is the chief centre.

748 Chailley, J. 'Les Anciens Tropaires et Séquentiaires de l'école de Saint-Martial de Limoges (xᵉ–x1ᵉ siècles)' *EG* 2 (1957) 163–88
C describes and partially inventories 23 mss. See also *Scrip* 16 (1962) 369–72, pl 30 and *Scrip* 23 (1969) 298–312.

749 Weiss, G. 'Zum Problem der Gruppierung südfranzösischer Tropare' *AMw*
750 21 (1964) 163–71 **750** Hughes, D.G. 'Further Notes on the Grouping of the Aquitainian Tropers' *JAMS* 19 (1966) 3–12
749 Using only Introit tropes with two different melodies, W suggests three

broad groups of mss. **750** A statistical comparison of their repertories justifies tentative conclusions about the relations between the sources.

751 Evans, P. 'Northern French Elements in an early Aquitainian Troper'
F-15.103–10
Variants in melodies and notation suggest an early 10c date for Paris BN lat.
1240.

ALLELUIAS AND THE SEQUENCE

Other information, including editions and facsimiles, is under Tropes
(722–9).
Origins **752–5** relation to the Alleluia **753 755 756 765 766 768 771 776** Notker
and St Gall **756 758–60 766 773** texts **752 753 757 762 769–73 775** special texts
and tunes **754 763–8 770 771 778 779** performance, rhythm **757 761 769 773
777**

752 Birkner, G. 'Psaume hébraïque et séquence latin' *JIFMC* 16 (1964) 56–60
B demonstrates numerous textual parallels, and sees the origin of the
Sequence in psalmody.

753 Crocker, R.L. 'The Repertory of Proses at Saint Martial de Limoges in the
10c' *JAMS* 11 (1958) 149–64
C questions the original relation of proses and Sequences to Alleluias and
the notion that the melismatic Sequence existed *prior* to its texted version.
The *versus* (or text of the partially texted Sequence) and *prosa* may be seen
in the literary context of *prosimetrum*. A later relationship with an Alleluia
stabilises their use within the liturgy. See **757**.

754 Dronke, P. 'The Beginnings of the Sequence' *BGSL* (Tübingen) 87 (1965)
43–73
In this important and convincing article, D shows that *Rex coeli* (early 9c)
reveals a fully developed Sequence tradition. Melody titles disclose, sometimes suggest, the pre-existence of Sequence-like secular songs which may
have served as models for sacred *contrafacta*. 'Sequences' possibly
originated in the last years of the Graeco-Roman world.

755 Husmann, H. 'Alleluia, Vers und Sequenz' *AnnM* 4 (1956) 19–53
H examines repetition, variation, and symmetry. He concludes that
Alleluia, verse and Sequence originated from the same tune and always
belonged together. Each extends the Alleluia *initium* by variation.

756 Husmann, H. 'Die Hs Rheinau 71 der Zentralbibliothek Zürich und die
Frage nach Echtheit und Entstehung der St Galler Sequenzen und Not-
kerschen Prosen' *Acta* 38 (1966) 118–49
Comparing the occasions of their liturgical use, in various sources, H
examines the relations between Alleluia melody, melody titles, Sequences,
and proses. In *Acta* 39 (1967) 100–2, Irtenkauf comments and H replies.

757 Husmann, H. 'Sequenz und Prosa' *AnnM* 2 (1954) 61–91
Sequentiae are melismatic forms of *prosae* sung as repetitions of the texted *prosae*; *prosa* is the texted and Sequence is the melismatic form of the composition, both types having double versicles. Partially texted Sequences are textual tropes to be inserted into *prosae*. See **753**.

758 Duft, J. 'Le *presbyter de Gimedia* apporte son Antiphonaire à Saint-Gall' D-10.II.925–36, 2 facss
D prints and confirms the authenticity and accuracy of Notker's letter (ca 884) acknowledging the inspiration for his work on the Sequence to the *versus* from Junièges.

759 Crocker, R.L. 'Some Ninth-Century Sequences' *JAMS* 20 (1967) 367–402
760 (*JAMS* 21 (1968) 124 clarifies the examples) **760** Stäblein, B. 'Notkeriana' *AMw* 19/20 (1962/3) 84–99
759 C examines the problem of establishing a critical text by comparing some Notker Sequences with their French sources. He concludes that major variants are deliberate revisions. **760** S transcribes and discusses not previously identified Sequence melodies used by Notker.

761 Spanke, H. 'Aus der Vorgeschichte und Frühgeschichte der Sequenz' *ZdA* 71 (1934) 1–39
S discusses titles, performance, Byz. influence, and geographical origin.

762 Stäblein, B. 'Zur Frühgeschichte der Sequenz' *AMw* 18 (1961) 1–33, 2 pll
Extending **733**, S deals with the partially texted Sequence, isolating earlier nuclear versus by means of textual and M characteristics. He mentions organum (pp 31–2).

763 Stäblein, B. 'Psalle symphonizando' F-36.221–8 **764** Stäblein 'Una
764 sconosciuta sequenza dello stile arcaico in Italia' D-8.289–94
S discusses the pieces, illustrating the 'archaic' Sequence.

765 Husmann, H. 'Die Alleluia und Sequenzen der Mater-Gruppe' D-12.276–84
H discusses and relates a complex of names, texts, and tunes, concluding that the Mater group is *Mater omnium sequentiarum*.

766 Husmann, H. 'Iustus ut palma. Alleluia und Sequenzen in St Gallen und St Martial' *RBdM* 10 (1956) 112–28
H discusses the origins, development, and use of the tune. Cf **563 658**.

767 Stäblein, B. 'Der Sequenzmelodie 'Concordia' und ihr geschichtlicher Hintergrund' F-10.364–92
Listing bibliography and editions, S deduces a possible stemma for the complex of texts to this melody.

768 Stäblein, B. 'Das sogenannte aquitanishe 'Alleluia Dies sanctificatus' und seine Sequenz' *Hans Albrecht in Memoriam* ed Wilfried Brennecke and Hans Haase (Kassel, 1962) 22–6

Comparing Aquitainian and Roman versions, S explores the difference between an Alleluia trope and a Sequence. Cf *StuMw* 25 (1962) 504–15.

769 Kunz, L. 'Textrhythmus und Zahlenkomposition in frühen Sequenzen' *Mf* 8 (1955) 403–11
Concluding that the essence of the early Sequence lies in the text, K uses an apparently arbitrary textual analysis to show that the rhythm was not formless.

770 Husmann, H. '*Ecce puerpera genuit*; zur Geschichte der teiltextierten Sequenzen' **F-5**.59–65
H compares Italian with French and Spanish versions, concluding that the latter are older but not original.

771 Schlager, K.-H. 'Ein beneventanisches Alleluia und seine Prosula'
772 **F-29**.217–25 **772** Steiner, R. 'The Prosulae of the Ms Paris BN F. lat. 1118' *JAMS* 22 (1969) 367–93
771 Schlager concludes that southern practice observed no relation between text and M. **772** With transcriptions, Steiner illustrates the relation of prosula to the original text and M. See also **F-28**.157–67.

773 Husmann, H. 'Die St Galler Sequenztradition bei Notker und Ekkehard'
774 *Acta* 26 (1954) 6–18 **774** Smits van Waesberghe, J. 'Zur ursprünglichen Vortragsweise der Prosulen, Sequenzen und Organa' **A-3**.251–4, 1 facs
773 Discussing Notker's letter and Ekkehard's evidence, H concludes that the choir sang the melismatic version, and that only soloists sang the texted version. **774** S suggests that the relationship of prosula to Sequence could clarify the development from organum to motet.

775 Evans, P. 'The *Tropi ad Sequentiam*' **F-30**.73–82
From St Martial sources, E lists, transcribes, and discusses separate interpolations of text and M introducing the *sequentia* (or *prosa*), itself an addition.

776 Husmann, H. 'Alleluia, Sequenz und Prosa im altspanischen Choral' **F-2**.1.407–15
After a useful general introduction to the form of the Alleluia H briefly examines the differences between Greg., Ambrosian, and Mozarabic Sequence.

777 Jammers, E. 'Rhythmische und tonale Studien zur älteren Sequenz' *Acta* 23 (1951) 1–40
J attempts to determine characteristics of rhythm and tonality.

778 Hoppin, R.H. '*Exultantes collaudemus*: a Sequence for St Hylarion' **F-23**.392–405
This early 15c piece borrows traditional patterns. H suggests research into the formulae of Sequences.

779 Bent, I. 'A New Polyphonic *Verbum Bonum et Suave*' *ML* 51 (1970) 227–41, 2 facss

B describes a new English source and, with two transcriptions, compares polyphonic settings of the Sequence (see **1667**).

779a Anglès, H. 'Die volkstümlichen Melodien in den ma. Sequenzen' **F-36**.214–20
A gives a number of Sequences whose melodies are, from his experience with (Spanish) folksong, folklike in quality. See also **F-15**.9–17.

Adam of St Victor

780 Spanke, H. 'Die Kompositionskunst der Sequenzen Adams von St Victor' *SM* ns 14 (1941) 1–29
S lists and analyses Adam's works.

781 *Les Proses d'Adam de Saint-Victor* ed Pierre Aubry and L'Abbé E. Misset MMC 2 (1900) frontispiece facs, vii + 166 (introduction), 167–224 (edition of texts, with index), 225–322 (edition of M (Sq)), 323–7 (indices)
This is the only edition giving the whole melodies.

782 *Adamo di San Vittore, Liriche Sacre* ed Giuseppe Vecchi (Bologna 1953) vii + 123, 2 facss
V edits the texts, with the first phrase of the melody, where known.

783 Benton, J.F. 'Nicolas of Clairvaux and the 12c Sequence, with special Reference to Adam of St Victor' *Traditio* 18 (1962) 149–79
The regular Sequence was established by mid-12c, before Adam. This is a literary study, but B transcribes 4 tunes.

Liturgical drama

784 Schuler, Ernst A. *Die* M *der Osterfeiern, Osterspiele und Passionen des MA* (Kassel 1951) 400
This is a basic catalogue of sources, of individual works, scenes, and texts.

GENERAL HISTORIES

Most major publications are textual studies with minor, sometimes no reference to the M. There are no comprehensive and primarily M studies.

785 Young, Karl *The Drama of the Medieval Church* 2 vols (Oxford 1933) frontisp
786 facs, xxii + 708, 12 pll and facss; frontisp facs, vi + 611, 12 pll and facss, ext
787 index / rev G.R. Coffman *Spec* 9 (1934) 109–17 **786** Donovan, Richard B. *The*
788 *Liturgical Drama in Med. Spain* PIMS 4 (Toronto 1958) 229 / rev S. Corbin *CCM* 2 (1959) 224–6 **787** Chambers, Edmund K. *The Med. Stage* 2 vols (Oxford 1903; repr 1963) xliii + 419, frontisp; vi + 480, frontisp **788** Hardison, Oscar B. *Christian Rite and Christian Drama in the MA* (Baltimore 1965) xvi + frontisp + 328, appendices, index / rev A. Williams *Spec* 41 (1966) 539–41; R. Marshall *Comparative Literature Studies* 3 (1966) 362–6
785 This is a standard reference work, with numerous references to M, complemented by **786**. **787** C gives information about minstrelsy and the troping origin of drama. **788** H, contrary to accepted theories, believes that the *Quem Quaeritis* originated not in troping but in the Easter Vigil service. See **793**.

789 De Boor, Helmut *Die Textgeschichte der lateinischen Osterfeiern* (Tübingen 1967) xi + 371

Liturgical, musical, and dramatic elements

790 Kretzmann, Paul E. *The Liturgical Element in the earliest forms of the Med. Drama* U OF MINNESOTA STUDIES IN LANGUAGE AND LITERATURE 4 (Minneapolis 1916) vii + 171
This is useful for sources, bibliography and descriptions. There is nothing about M.

791 Smoldon, W. L. 'The Easter Sepulchre Music-Drama' *ML* 27 (1946) 1–17 792
792 Smoldon 'The M of the Med. Church Drama' *MQ* 48 (1962) 476–97, 1
793 facs 793 Smoldon 'The Melodies of the Med. Church-Dramas and their Sig-
794 nificance' *Comparative Drama* 2 (1968) 185–209 794 Smoldon 'Med. Lyric
795 Melody and the Latin Church Dramas' *MQ* 51 (1965) 507–17 795 Liuzzi, F.
795a 'L'Espressione M nel dramma liturgico' *SM* ns 2 (1929) 74–109 795a Stevens,
John 'M in Some Early Med. Plays' *Studies in the Arts* ed Francis Warner (Oxford 1968) 21–40

791 Stressing its M content, Smoldon outlines the development. 792 Smoldon reviews the M and comments on the use of instruments, for which he
finds little evidence. 793 Emphasising the M qualities, and discussing the
actual M, Smoldon points to Hardison's errors (788) resulting from ignor-
ance of or indifference to the M. 794 Smoldon describes some of the
melodies. 795 L studies plainsong themes and motives in a number of liturgical dramas, giving M examples and suggesting how various 'aesthetic
effects' in the M of the dramas are achieved. 795a Stevens points to the
changing role of M in three Latin and vernacular dramas.

796 Stemmler, Theo *Liturgische Feiern und geistliche Spiele: Studien zu
Erscheinungsformen des Dramatischen im MA* BUCHREIHE DER ANGLIA, ZS FÜR
ANGLISCHE PHILOLOGIE 15 (Tübingen 1970) vii + 339, 24 pll, b, index / rev
E. Simon *Spec* 47 (1972) 356–61
This certainly refers to the M.

797 Jodogne, O. 'Recherches sur les débuts du théâtre religieux en France' *CCM*
8 (1965) 179–89

798 Entry deleted

799 Marshall, M.H. 'The Dramatic Traditions Established by the Liturgical Play'
800 *PMLA* 56 (1941) 962–91 800 Marshall 'Aesthetic Values of the Liturgical
Drama' *English Inst Essays* ed Alan S. Downer vol 9 (1950) (New York 1951)
89–115

801 Vecchi, G. 'Innodia e dramma sacro. I: Nodi drammatici nella lirica innodia
de Paolino d'Aquileia. II: Una prosa-conductus del processionale C II di
Cividale' *Studi mediolatini e volgari* 1 (1953) 225–37
V investigates Paolino's hymns and one conductus, which resemble liturgical plays in their dramatic character.

FACSIMILES AND EDITIONS

Excluded are performing editions: see items 823–9.

* Announced (1962): Dreimüller, Karl *Die M des ma. Dramas*, in *Das Musik-
werk*, the German original of AnthM

802 Coussemaker, Edmond de *Drames liturgiques du MA* (Rennes 1860; repr New
York 1964) xix + 347, facss (dipl ?)

C edits the text and transcribes (Sq) the M of 22 dramas, many not otherwise published. There are no suggestions for performance.

The Fleury Play-book

803 *Sacre rappresentazioni nel manoscritti 201 della Bibl Municipale di Orléans* ed
804 Giampiero Tintori INST ET MON, ser 1: 2 (Cremona 1958) lxxxvii +84 M transcc
805 +85–103 facss / rev R. Weakland *Notes* 17 (1959/60) 465–7 **804** Corbin, S. 'Le
Ms. 201 d'Orléans. Drames liturgiques dits de Fleury' *Rom* 74 (1953)
1–43 **805** Donovan, R.B. 'Two Celebrated Centers of Med. Liturgical
Drama: Fleury and Ripoll' *The Med. Drama and its Claudelian Revival* ed E.
Catherine Dunn, Tatiana Totitch, and Bernard M. Peebles (Washington
1970) 41–51
803 T describes the 13c ms, edits texts and M (Rh). The introduction by R.
Monterosso describes the basis for the transcriptions. **804** St Lomer de Blois
is a more likely provenance than Fleury. **805** D attributes Orléans 201 to
Fleury on the basis of links between Winchester and Fleury. He also considers Ripoll and Vich as dramatic centres, and discusses the appearance
of the merchant scene in liturgical plays.

Sponsus plays

806 Thomas, Lucien-Paul Le *'Sponsus' (Mystère des vierges sages et des vierges*
807 *folles) ... Etude critique, textes, M, notes et glossaire* (Paris 1951) 251 / rev J.
808 Chailley *RBM* 6 (1952) 153–9 **807** Thomas 'La Versification et les leçons
809 douteuses du *Sponsus* (texte roman)' *Rom* 53 (1927) 43–81 **808** Thomas 'Les
810 Strophes et la composition du *Sponsus* (textes latin et roman)' *Rom* 55 (1929)
45–112 **809** Liuzzi, F. 'Le Vergini savie e le vergini folli' *SM* ns 3 (1930)
82–109, 4 pll **810** *Sponsus. Dramma delle vergini prudenti e delle vergini stolte*
(12c) ed D'Arco Silvio Avalle and Raffaello Monterosso DOCUMENTI DI
FILOLOGIA 9 (Milan 1965) v + 136, 6 facss
806 This primarily linguistic and dramatic study includes one chapter (x,
149–70) on the M and an edition with translation (173–87). **807 808** Both articles are literary studies; the second includes a discussion of the M and its
relation to T's thorough consideration of the poetic structure and form. **809**
L studies the M of the play, formally, structurally, and stylistically. **810** This
is an edition, with separate sections for text and M (Rh). There is a historical
and analytical commentary. See also *AMf* 3 (1938) 80–95, 180–92.

Miscellaneous plays

811 Luzarche, Victor ed *Office de Pâques ou de la Résurrection* (Tours 1856) 4
unnumbered pp + xxxii + 16 facss + 70
This is an edition of texts.

812 Göllner, T. 'The Three-Part Gospel Reading and the Med. Magi Play' *JAMS*
24 (1971) 51–62

G gives an abbreviated edition of the play, which originated in the performance of Gospel readings.

813 Irtenkauf, W., and H. Eggers 'Die Donaueschinger Marienklage' *Carinthia (Geschichtliche und Volkskundliche Beiträge zur Heimatkunde Kärntens)* 1, *Mitteilungen des Geschichtsvereins für Kärnten* 148 (1958) 359–82
The authors describe and transcribe some of the M of a 15c Austrian source of dramatic *planctus*. See also *MMg* 9 (1877) 1–4 and 17–29.

814 Osthoff, H. 'Deutsche Liedweisen und Wechselgesänge im ma. Drama' *AMf* 7 (1942) 65–81, 2 facss
The *Ludus Mariae Magdalenae* (ca 1400, vernacular) includes a number of songs in secular style and some interesting dialogue forms. O transcribes the melodies (Rh, long note values).

815 Bernard, M. 'L'Officium stellae nivernais' *RdM* 51 (1965) 52–65 **816** Corbin,
816 S. 'Le *cantus sibylae*: origine et premiers textes' *RdM* 31 [101–4] (1952) 1–10.
817 See also **1836**. **817** Jeanroy, Alfred and Th. Gérold *Le Jeu de Sainte Agnès*,
818 *drame provençal du XIVe siècle* LES CLASSIQUES FRANÇAIS DU MA (Paris 1931)
819 xxiv + 83 / rev C. Van den Borren *RUB* 37 (1931/2) 99*–100* **818** Hoepffner,
820 E. 'Les Intermèdes M dans le Jeu provençal de Sainte Agnès' *Mélanges d'his-*
821 *toire ... offerts à Gustave Cohen* (Paris 1950) 97–104 **819** Kettering, H. 'Die
822 Essener Osterfeier' *KmJb* 36 (1952) 7–13 **820** Krieg, Eduard *Das lateinische Osterspiel von Tours* LMw 13 (Würzburg 1956) xvi + 131 and 29 pp M / rev W.F. Michael *DVLG* 32 (1958) 470–2 **821** Lipphardt, W. 'Das Herodesspiel von Le Mans nach den Hs Madrid, Bibl. Nac. 288 und 289 (11. und 12. Jh.)' F-28.107–22 **822** Smits van Waesberghe, J. 'A Dutch Easter Play' *MD* 7 (1953) 15–37, 2 pll
815 B describes and transcribes the play. **816** C gives a brief general survey, with sources, but does not deal with the M. **817** This is an annotated edition, with the melodies transcribed (Rh) separately. **818** The play uses songs popular and well known at the time. **819** K edits a brief *Visitatio Sepulchri* from a 14c ms. **820** This is an analysis of the ms and the M, which is transcribed (Rh). **821** L gives a transcription (Sq) with copious commentary, showing the ms relations. **822** S describes the sources and identifies the provenance of this 12–13c play. He appends a transcription.

PERFORMING EDITIONS

823 *The Play of Daniel, a 13c M Drama* ed Noah Greenberg, transc Rembert Weakland (Oxford, 1959) frontisp, x + 118, incl miniature facss and line illuss / rev *TLS* (1960) 76
This is a performing edition with an English translation appended, with suggestions for performance and illustrations of costumes.

824 *Herod. A Med. Nativity Play* (13c) ed William L. Smoldon (London [1960]) xii and 13–46, and 1 facs / rev L. Ellinwood *Notes* 18 (1960/1) 476–7

This edition, in English translation, has additional M and stage directions inserted to make an acting version. S gives a good practical introduction. Cf Bailey, Terence ed *The Fleury Play of Herod* (Toronto 1965) 72 and 1 facs.

825 *Officium Pastorum* ed William L. Smoldon (Oxford nd) x + 12
This is an acting version of a 13c Christmas play, transcribed into modern notation and with a parallel translation. There is a brief but useful introduction to liturgical drama, description of the source of this play, and hints about production.

826 827 828 *Peregrinus, a 12c Easter M-Drama; Planctus Mariae, a 14c Passiontide*
827 *M-Drama; Visitatio Sepulchri* (12c) ed William L. Smoldon (London nd; nd;
828 1964) xi + 23; x + 14; xiv, 1 facs + 34
These are 'acting versions' with English translations appended and suggestions for performance.

829 *The Son of Getron* ed Colin C. Sterne (U of Pittsburgh Press 1962) 54 / rev R. Weakland *Notes* 21 (1963/4) 227–8
This is a performance edition of the drama, including English translation, for modern instruments.

THE MUSIC

830 Bowles, E.A. 'The Role of M Instruments in Med. Sacred Drama' *MQ* 45
831 (1959) 67–84, 1 pl 831 Gamer, H.M. 'Mimes, Musicians, and the Origin of the Med. Religious Play' *DBGU* 5 (1965) 9–28, 6 facss
830 Instruments symbolize dramatic and iconographical features of the plays. B quotes many contemporary accounts. 831 Illustrations of musicians playing instruments and dancing cannot be used as evidence of [secular?] origin of the drama, but are in strict ecclesiastical tradition.

832 Brandel, R. 'Some Unifying Devices in the Religious M Drama of the MA'
833 F-23.40–55, 1 facs (pl 1a, 1b) 833 Wagenaar-Nolthenius, H. 'Sur la construction M du drame liturgique' *CCM* 3 (1960) 449–56
832 B discusses recurrent melody types and motives. 833 W shows some association of melody with dramatic character and situation.

834 Elders, W. 'Gregorianisches in liturgischen Dramen der Hs. Orléans 201' *Acta* 36 (1964) 169–77
In four plays E lists connections with plainchant melodies or melody types.

835 Weakland, R. 'The Rhythmic Modes and Med. Latin Drama' *JAMS* 14 (1961) 131–46
W defends the use of modal rhythms for non-liturgical items.

836 Abert, A.A. 'Das Nachleben des Minnesangs im liturgischen Spiel' *Mf* 1 (1948) 95–105
A finds *contrafacta* in the Bordesholmer 'Lament of Mary.'

837 Stäblein, B. 'Zur M des *Ludus de Antichristo*' **F-21**.312–27
The ms has no M. S suggests that M for one item may be found elsewhere, and compares four versions.

Eastern Europe

BIBLIOGRAPHIES, CATALOGUES, SURVEYS

838 Coover, J.B. 'A Bibliography of East European M Periodicals' *Fontes* 3 (1956) 219–26 (Introduction, Bulgaria); 4 (1957) 97–102 (Czechoslavakia); 5 (1958) 44–5 (Estonia, Finland), 93–9 (Hungary); 6 (1959) 27–8 (Latvia, Lithuania); 7 (1960) 16–21 (Poland); 8 (1961) 75–90 (USSR); 10 (1963) 60–71 (Index of titles and editors)
This refers to US libraries holding the publication.

839 McCredie, A.D. 'New Perspectives in European M Historiography. A Bibliographical Survey of Current Research in Med. and Renaissance Slavic and Byz. Sources' *MiscM-A* 4 (1969) 22–127 (to be continued)
M describes research into med. M in Poland (24–35), Bulgaria (71–7), Roumania (78–82), Yugoslavia (Serbia 96–108; Slovenia 116–17).

840 Stefanović, D 'Einige Probleme zur Erforschung der slavischen Kirchenmusik' *KmJb* 43 (1959) 1–7
S reviews the literature (including that in Slavic languages) and problems, commenting especially on Zagiba's work (for which see also *StuMw* 26 (1964) 222–3; 27 (1966) 244).

841 Salmen, W. *Die Schichtung der ma. Musikkultur in der ostdeutschen Grenzlage* DIE M IM ALTEN UND NEUEN EUROPA 2 (Kassel 1954) 154, ext b / rev I.F. Finlay *JIFMC* 7 (1955) 70
This is a comprehensive survey up to the 16c.

842 Djaparidzé, David *Med. Slavic Mss: a Bibliography of Printed Catalogues* MAA 64 (Cambridge, Mass. 1957) frontisp facs, 134, 8 facss / rev E. Bláhová *Bsl* 25 (1964) 109–10: the reviewer says this is the first of its kind, useful in the history of Slavic M.
Pp 1–21 contain general information listing the most important works and periodicals on M texts, etc.

843 Radó, Polycarpe *Répertoire hymnologique des mss liturgiques dans les bibliothèques publiques de Hongrie* AZ ORSAZÁGOS SZÉCHÉNYI KÖNYVTÁR KIADVÁNYAI 20 (Budapest 1945) 59

This is a list of 10–16c mss, with alphabetical index of hymns, proses, Sequences, etc.

844 Hutter, Joseph *Notationis bohemicae antiquae specimina selecta* (Prague 1931) This contains 30 loose leaves of photographic facsimiles of plainsong mss.

Byzantine influence

845 Høeg, C. 'The oldest Slavonic Tradition of Byz. M' *Proceedings of the British Academy* 39 (1953) 37–66, 4 facss
H compares Novgorod, Greek, and Byz. notations, and discusses cultural relationships. He transcribes the Canon by John the Damascene.

846 Koschmieder, E. 'Wie haben Kyrill und Method zelebriert?' E-1.7–22, 4 facss
Considering language and rite, and examining accents and neumatic notation, K concludes that the missionaries (9–10c) used Roman (or vernacular?) rather than Greek-Byz. forms.

847 Levy, K. 'The Byz. Communion-Cycle and its Slavic Counterpart'
848 C-1.II.571–4 848 Levy 'The Slavic Kontakia and their Byz. Originals'
849 E-8.79–87 849 Levy 'Die slavische Kondakariennotation' E-1.77–92
847 Slavic Communion cycles are borrowed from the Use of Constantinople ca 1100. The Kontakia, which are similar in style, may likewise have been borrowed from originals now lost. 848 L asserts that the Slavic Kontakia descend from an Asmatic recension of the original melodies. 849 L compares different notations and concludes that Slavic melismatic chant is derived from Byzantium.

850 Milojković-Djurić, J. 'A Papadike from Skoplje' *SEC* 1 (1966) 50–6, 2 facss
This treatise on notation confirms that Byz. M theory was known in Serbia.

851 Stefanović, D. 'The Beginnings of Serbian Chant' E-1.55–64, 4 facss
852 852 Stefanović 'The Earliest Dated and Notated Document of Serbian Chant' *Recueils de Travaux de l'Inst d'Etudes Byz.* 7 (1961) 187–96, 1 facs, 5 pp transcc
851 S concludes, from his list of remaining sources (15c at earliest), that Serbian was an offshoot of Byz. chant. 852 The 16c *sticheron* is almost identical with its 13c Byz. original.

853 Velimirović, M. 'The Influence of the Byz. Chant on the M of the Slavic Countries' C-2.119–40
Textual translations preserve, as far as possible, the M features. Transmission and translation took place in the 11c. Russian chant derives from 11c Byzantium. On pp 141–7 D. Stefanović extends the information to Bulgaria and Serbia.

854 Velimirović, Miloš *Byz. Elements in Early Slavic Chant: The Hirmologion* MMB-S 4 (1960) xii + 140; 10 + lxxvi + portfolio of 12 pll

V deals with history, textual differences, formulae and forms, and problems in transcription.

855 Verdeil, R.P. *La M byz. chez les Bulgares et les Russes* MMB-S 3 (1953) 250 + portfolio of 21 pll

856 Falvy, Z. 'Spielleute im ma. Ungarn' *StuMus* 1 (1961) 29–64, 2 facss, 1 map
F reviews med. references, terms, names, instruments, etc.

857 Kamiński, W. 'Beiträge zur Erforschung der früh-ma. Musikinstrumente der Nordwest- und Ostslaven' E-1.139–46
K briefly describes archaeological remains, and comments generally on the *instrumentarium* of the area.

*858 Kos, K. 'Muzički instrumenti u srednjevjekovnoj likovnoj umjetnosti Hrvatske' *Rad* 351 JUGOSLAVENSKA AKADEMIJA ZNANOSTI I UMJETNOSTI (Zagreb 1969)
Examining art in Istria, K draws conclusions about instrumental practice in solos and in groups. Croatia was by no means lacking in contact with contemporary western culture. This annotation is paraphrased from *Arti Musices* (1970) 16–17, 140. Cf also *Arti Musices* (1970) 77–93, 8 plates (M instruments in med. Istrian paintings).

859 Pejović, R. 'Instruments de M dans l'art serbo-macédonien et byz.' C-1.II.589–99, 5 pll.

INDIVIDUAL COUNTRIES

Bulgaria: see index

Czechoslovakia (Bohemia, Moravia)

Histories, literature, sources
860 Batka, Richard *Geschichte der M in Böhmen. I: Böhmen unter deutschem Einfluss (900–1333)* (Prague 1906) xii + 167, several pll, diagrams and facss
This is a comprehensive history.

861 Nejedlý, Zdeněk *Dějiny husitského zpěvu* 6 vols ČESKOSLOVENSKÁ AKADEMIE VĚD 40–5 (revd ed Prague 1954–6) / rev: see 863 and A-3.150–2
Of this history of Hussite M in Czechoslovakia, first written 1904–13, only vols 1 and 2 are relevant.
Vol 1 (1954, pp 479, num exx, *Pre-Hussite Song*) pp 36–140 plainsong; 141–225 artsong; 226–94 liturgical drama; 295–314 secular folksong; 315–88 sacred folksong; 389–97 transcription of monophonic liturgical M of Magister Záviš (14c); 398–400 transcription of Sequences of Jana z Jenštejna (late 14c); 401–5 transcription of Marian *planctus*; 406–8 transcription of Easter drama songs; 409–33 edition of treatise of Jana z Holešova'; 435–77 indices of texts, names, mss, etc, bibliography.

Vol 2 (1954, pp 233, M exx, *Predecessors of the Hussite Reformation*) pp 24–52 sacred folksong; 53–77 heretics; 78–129 preaching; 130–65 reform at Prague University; 166–99 secular attitude to M; 201–7 transcriptions; 209–31 indices of texts, names, mss, etc.

862 Vanický, J. 'Czech Med. and Renaissance M' **D-2**.69–79 **863** Schoenbaum,
863 C. 'Hymnologische Forschung in der Tschechoslowakei' *JbLH* 5 (1960) 157–65
These are reports on the literature dealing with the MA.

864 Fischer, Kurt von 'Elementi arsnovistici nella M boema antica' **D-4**.77–83
F examines 14c and 15c Bohemian sources and styles. Cf **891**.

865 Fischer, Kurt von 'Repertorium der Quellen tschechischer Mehrstim-migkeit des 14. bis 16. Jh.' *Essays in Musicology in Honor of Dragan Plamenac* ed Gustave Reese and Robert J. Snow (Pittsburgh 1969) 49–60
F describes sources of Czech polyphony.

Czech composers, manuscripts, and songs

866 Svejkovský, F. 'Musejní rukopis XIV E 7 jako pramen k dějinám hudby z doby husitské' AUC-PH 2 (Prague 1965) 45–55
The German summary says this 15c ms contains polemic Hussite strictures against polyphony, secular song, etc, and much information about early Hussite practice.

867 Vanický, J. 'Frater Domaslav (Domaslaus), der älteste bekannte Sequenz-dichter Böhmens' *JbLH* 5 (1960) 118–22, 2 facss
Domaslav lived ca 1300.

868 Mužík, F. 'Systém rytmiky české pisně 14. stoleti' *MiscM-C* 20 (1967) 7–48
M examines a score of 14c Czech songs and concludes that they employ modal rhythms (see *JbLH* 14 (1969) 260).

868a Plocek, V. 'Nově nalezená sekvence o svaté Dorotě a její poměr k Jenštejnově *Decet huius*,' *Ročenka universitní knihovny v Praze 1956* (Prague 1958) 67–95
Jenstein's Sequence takes over the melody of *Salve virgo generosa* (this anno-tation is paraphrased from *JbLH* 8 (1963) 275).

869 Nejedlý, Z. 'Magister Záviše und seine Schule: Zur Musikgeschichte Böh-
870 mens im 14. Jh.' *SIMG* 7 (1905/6) 41–69 **870** Mužík, F. 'Závišova píseň'
871 *Sbornik prací filosofické fakulty brněnské university, Ročník 14* (Brno 1965) 167–82, pl 2 (end of vol) **871** Zatočil, L. 'Závišova píseň ve světle minnesangu a její předloha' *Sbornik prací filosofické fakulty brněnské univer-sity, Ročník 2* (1956) 110–26
869 This is the only basic information readily available. **870** The German summary (p 182) says it is not possible to identify Záviš as the composer of *Jižť mne*, which is transcribed. The problem of identifying Záviš is dis-cussed. **871** The German summary (p 126) says that Z discusses Záviš' songs

in relation to the minnesingers, concluding that they show the direct influence of Frauenlob.

Czech theory

872 Reiss, J. 'Pauli Paulirini de Praga *Tractatus de musica*,' *ZMw* 7 (1924/5)
873 259–64 873 Mužíková, R. 'Pauli Paulirini de Praga *Musica Mensurabilis*' AUC-PH 2 (Prague 1965) 57–87, 4 facss (German summary p 87)
Neither article gives a complete edition of the 15c treatise: each complements the other, and includes a discussion.

*874 Mušíková, R. 'Hudebně teoretický traktát Mikuláše z Kozlí' *MiscM-C* 13 (1960) 7–26

Hungary

875 Szabolcsi, Bence *Geschichte der ungarischen* M (2nd ed, transl Georg Knepler,
876 Budapest 1965) 11–24 and 103–111 (M transcc) 876 Szabolcsi *A Concise History of Hungarian* M transl Sára Karig (London 1964) 1–23 and 97–105

877 Falvy, Z. 'M in Ungarn bis zum Ende des XVI Jh.' D-2.237–57
This is a general review, mentioning sources and quoting examples. The footnotes give copious references to Hungarian publications.

878 Szigeti, K. 'Denkmäler des greg. Chorals aus dem ungarischen MA' *StuMus* 4 (1963) 129–72, 10 facss, 1 map, 1 table of Hungarian-German present-day place names
S gives many footnotes to material in Hungarian. He describes sources, centres, scriptoria, and notation, concluding that square notation was adopted only by monks. See also D-12.176–82.

879 *Melodiarium Hungariae Medii Aevi* ed Benjamin Rajeczky (Budapest 1956), only the first vol has been issued to date. Vol 1 (1956) *Hymnen und Sequenzen*, ed Polykarp Radó) lii + 344, indices of texts and melodies
There is an introduction and description of sources in Hungarian and German, with tables showing sources, distribution, etc. R transcribes the melodies (Sq) with variants.

880 Rajeczky, B. 'Mittelalterliche ungarische Musikdenkmäler und das neue
881 Volkslied' *StuMus* 3 (1962) 263–9 881 Wiora, W. 'Mittelalterliche Parallelen zu altungarischer Melodik' *StuMus* 3 (1962) 379–99
880 R sees similarities in form between some Hungarian chants and folksongs. 881 W claims his copious transcriptions reveal significant melodic relationships among folksong, plainsong, and minnesong.

882 Mužík, F. *Die Tyrnauer Hs* (Budapest, *Országos Széchenyi Könyvtár*
883 *c.l.m.ae.243*) AUC-PH 2 (Prague 1965) 5–44 + 12 facss 883 Rajeczky, B. 'Spätma. Organal-kunst in Ungarn' *StuMus* 1 (1961) 15–28, 3 facss
882 M describes a 15c ms and its repertory, including 14c polyphonic styles.
883 R describes Renaissance sources of retrospective polyphony. For other

references to polyphony in Hungary see **D-2**.223–36; *ML* 29 (1948) 356–65.

884 Falvy, Z. 'Un "Quem queritis" en Hongrie au XIIᵉ siècle' *StuMus* 3 (1962) 101–7
The trope appears before Holy Saturday Vespers and is slightly different
from the western version.

Lithuania

884a Salmen, W. 'Zur Mg am litauischen Hofe unter Grossfürst Witold (1350–
1430)' *MOst* 1 (1962) 80–2
This is the only information available about Lithuania.

Poland

884b *Missale Plenarium, Bibl. Capit. Gnesnensis Ms 149* ed Krzysztof Biegański and
Jerzy Woronczak ANTIQUITATES MUSICAE IN POLONIA, ser 1: 12 (Warsaw 1970)
474 pp facss

*Announced: In the series ANTIQUITATES MUSICAE IN POLONIA ed Heironim
Feicht (Warsaw 1963–   ), ser 1, vols 13 and 14 *Mediaeval Polyphony in Poland*
(facsimiles and transcription)

885 Feicht, Heironim ed *Muzyka Staropolska* (Old Polish Music) (Krakow 1966)
1–12
This is a selection of hitherto unpublished works from the 12–18c, with an
introduction in Polish and English.

886 Feicht, H. 'Mittelalterliche Choralprobleme in Polen' *MOst* 2 (1963) 84–90
F mentions important sources. See also **D-2**.277–80.

887 Biegański, K. 'Gnieźnieńskie "Missale plenarium" jako przykład zabytku
izolowanego' (11–12c) *MuzK* 11 no.3–4 (1966) 75–81

888 Sutkowski, A. 'Nieznane zabytki muzyki wielogłosowej z polskich
889 rękopisów chorałowych XIII i XV wieku' *MuzK* 3 no.3 (1958) 28–36, 2
890 facss 889 Sutkowski 'Początki polifonii średniowiecznej w Polsce w
świetle nowych źródeł' *MuzK* 6 no.1 (1961) 3–22, 1 facs (English summary p
22) 890 Sutkowski 'Surrexit Cristus Hodie – najdawniejszy w Polsce
zabytek muzyki wielogłosowej' *MuzK* 4 no.2 (1959) 3–11
S describes and transcribes polyphony from Poland, mostly from the 13c.

891 Perz, M. 'Die Einflüsse der ausgehenden italienischen Ars Nova in Polen'
D-5.465–83
P isolates local pieces in mss presently in Poland and describes little known
fragments. Considerable French and Italian influence is present. See also
864.

Russia and Ukraine

892 Gardner, Johann von, and Erwin Koschmieder *Ein handschriftliches Lehr-*

892a *buch der altrussischen Neumenschrift*. I: *Text* BAYERISCHE AKW, p.h.Kl., Abh,
893 neue folge 57 (Munich 1963) xix + 20 facss + 330 transcc / rev K. Fellerer *KmJb*
894 47 (1963) 153–4 **892a** Gardner, Johann von *Das Problem des altrussischen demestischen Kirchengesanges und seiner linienlosen Notation* SLAVISTISCHE BEITRÄGE 25 (Munich 1967) ix + 270 + 12 leaves M exx **893** Karmann, R. 'Der einstimmige altrussische Kirchengesang' *MK* 23 (1953) 145–9 **894** Yasser, J. 'References to Hebrew M in Russian Med. Ballads' *Jewish Social Studies* 11 (1949) 21–48

892 After a short historical review of notation, sources, and styles, G transcribes examples with parallel diplomatic facsimile. **892a** G describes the notation. **893** The information is very scant. **894** 'Songs from Jerusalem must have formed a quite substantial store in the repertory of Russian med. minstrels': Y presents the evidence.

894a Antonowycz, M. 'Ukrainische Hirmen im Lichte der byz. Musiktheorie' *MOst* 5 (1969) 7–22
The use of both scale and formula underlines the relationship between Ukrainian and Byz. practice.

Yugoslavia (Croatia)

There is little material available, especially in English. The yearbook *Arti Musices* (Zagreb 1970–   ) summarises research and publications.

895 Hudovsky, Z. 'Benedictionale MR 89 of the Metropolitan Library in Zagreb'
896 *StuMus* 9 (1967) 55–75, 9 facss **896** Novak, Viktor *Zadarski Kartular* (Zagreb
897 1959) 283 + 65 facss + 13 misc pll and facss **897** *Sakramentar* MR 126 *Metropolitanske knjižnice u Zagrebu* ed Albe Vidaković *Rad* 287 JUGOSLAVENSKA AKADEMIJA ZNANOSTI I UMJETNOSTI (Zagreb 1952)
895 H describes the 11c ms and its notation, with literature on Zagreb sources. **896** This is an edition of the Cartulary: the polyphonic Sanctus is at the end of the facsimile edition, the transcription is pl 11 of the miscellaneous plates. **897** This is a musico-paleographic study of the oldest known liturgical document (11c) of North Croatia.

898 Žganec, V. 'Folklore Elements in the Yugoslav Orthodox and Roman Catholic Liturgical Chant' *JIFMC* 8 (1956) 19–22
There are no written records of Croatian chant: information must be gleaned from ethnomusicological studies.

899 Šaban, L. 'Musicians in North Croatia in the 13c' *Arti Musices* (1970) 61–75, 1 facs
Š discusses local centres and documents.

Treatises

In general this section does not include theoretical discussions of individual problems such as rhythm, notation, polyphony. The subsections on individual works and writers are arranged in approximate chronological order, but this aspect of medieval M has only recently been examined with the paleographical and biographical care necessary for firm dates to be established: consequently all dates must be regarded as tentative, and within centuries a number of arbitrary decisions has had to be made.

CATALOGUES, SOURCES

900 901 RISM, Ser B III: this series is devoted to mss of M theory. Each volume has indices of libraries, authors, and incipits of anonymous works. Published so far are:

900 *The Theory of M (9–14c)* ed Joseph Smits van Waesberghe et al RISM, Ser B III¹ (1961) 155 / rev J.A. Westrup *ML* 43 (1962) 371
This volume describes mss from Austria, Belgium, Denmark, France, Luxembourg, the Netherlands, and Switzerland.

901 *The Theory of M (9–14c). Mss from Italy* ed Pieter Fischer RISM, Ser B III² (1968) 148 / rev M. Huglo *RdM* 55 (1969) 228–31

Authorship

902 Reaney, G. 'The Question of Authorship in the Med. Treatises on M' *MD* 18 (1964) 7–17
Pointing to deficiencies in Coussemaker (**925**) and Gerbert (**926**), R cites numerous cases of badly mistaken attributions. See also **B-4**.353–4.

Bibliography

902a Gallo, F.A. 'Philological Works on M Treatises of the MA' *AM* 44 (1972) 78–101

This is an excellent bibliographical report, listing editions and studies, including the liberal arts, Judeo-Arabic works, glosses, and other lesser known material. G summarises conclusions and lists sources. The sections of the article are: Early MA – *ars musica, musica plana, mensure instrumentorum, organum*; Late MA – France and England, Italy, Spain, Central and Eastern Europe.

903 Coover, J.B. 'M Theory in Translation: a Bibliography' *JMTh* 3 (1959) 70–96 and 13 (1969) 230–48
Few med. treatises have been translated: the bibliography is not exclusively med., but recent interest is reflected in the 1969 supplement. See also the series MthT.

Terminology, etymology

904 Appel, Margarete *Terminologie in den ma. Musiktraktaten* dissertation (Bottrop 1935) 109 / abstract in *Literarisches Zentralblatt* 86 (1935) 1138
This is a well documented and useful study concerning the meaning of a number of common terms, e.g., *vox, sonus, tonus*. It includes a valuable index of treatises and terminology in general.

905 Gysin, Hans P. *Studien zum Vokabular der M-th im MA* (Basel 1958) 167, indices of names and terms
This is a chronological investigation of numerous important terms.

906 Schmid, H., and E. Waeltner ' "Lexicon Musicum Latinum," ein Unterneh-
907 men zur Erforschung der M Fachsprache des MA' F-28.145–8 907 Eggebrecht, H.H., and F. Reckow 'Das Handwörterbuch der M Terminologie' *AMw* 25 (1968) 241–77
906 This reports the progress in compiling a dictionary of M terms. Each author gives a similar report in **B-4**.349–52. 907 This describes the history, progress, and methods of compiling a terminological dictionary, and its relation to 906. So far devoted to med. terms, the dictionary has indexed words in the works listed on p 247: periodical updatings are in *Jb der AkW und der Literatur in Mainz*. Examples are given to illustrate the entries which cover etymology (false and correct), history, contexts in original sources, usage, contemporary and modern references, and explanations. The three entries exemplified are *diapason, diapente, diatessaron; rondellus /rondeaurota; sonus*. Historians are invited to contribute articles.

908 Reaney, G. 'Terminology and Med. M' **F-5**.149–53
R stresses the flexibility of terms, and the overprecision of modern definitions.

909 Eggebrecht, H.H., W. Frobenius, and F. Reckow 'Bericht II über das Handwörterbuch der M Terminologie' *AMw* 27 (1970) 214–22 + 15 leaves
This includes articles on *cantus firmus, character, clavis, semibrevis*.

910 Waeltner, E.L. 'Die Methode terminologischer Untersuchungen früh-ma.

Musik traktate dargestellt an einem Beispiel des Aurelianus Reomensis' F-8.48–60
W examines the meaning of several terms.

911 Swerdlow, N. *'Musica Dicitur A Moys, Quod Est Aqua,'* JAMS 20 (1967) 3–9
S explains a common etymology of the word 'music.'

912 Bautier-Regnier, A.-M. 'A propos des sens de "neuma" et de "nota" en latin méd.' *RBM* 18 (1964) 1–9
B accumulates and interprets lexicographical evidence.

913 Avenary, H. *'Musica Analecta* aus Isidors *Etymologiae: campana, tubae ductiles, puncti,'* Mf 21 (1968) 38–9
A comments briefly on the terminology.

914 Handschin, J. 'Réflexions sur la terminologie' *RBM* 6 (1952) 7–11
H discusses *organum* and *diskantlied/chanson.*

915 Utley, F.L. 'The Chorister's Lament' *Spec* 21 (1946) 194–202 916 Françon, M.
916 'Notes on the Use of Guidonian Nomenclature by Machaut and Rabelais' *Spec* 22 (1947) 249–50
915 U transcribes and translates the poem, which illuminates practical music-making. 916 Inspired by Utley, F explains passages in Machaut and Rabelais.

917 Vivel, P. Cölestin M *Termini in der Benediktiner-Regel* STUDIEN UND MITTEILUNGEN ZUR GESCH DES BENEDIKTINER-ORDENS UND SEINER ZWEIGE, ns 6 (37, whole ser) (Salzburg 1916) 611–27
V concludes that certain terms refer to melodic singing, others to reciting on a tone, and that the Rule uses accurate terminology.

HISTORIES

918 Brinkmann, R. 'Die Tagung zum Projekt einer "Geschichte der Musiktheorie" im Staatlichen Institut für Musikforschung Berlin (1970)' *Mf* 23 (1970) 458–60
This reports on a proposal for a multi-volume history: vol 1 is projected for 1974.

919 Riemann, Hugo *History of* M *Theory* transl and ed Raymond H. Haggh (U of Nebraska Press, Lincoln 1962) xx + 431, M exx, b, index, translation of excerpts / rev F.Ll. Harrison *ML* 44 (1963) 394–6 and L.A. Gushee *JAMS* 17 (1964) 395–400
This is is a translation with commentary and notes of the first two books of Riemann's *Geschichte der Musiktheorie im* IX–XIX. *Jh.* (2nd ed Berlin 1920). It is included because it is the only survey of med. M theory. The original was a pioneering attempt to deal with this exceedingly difficult field before sufficient reliable information was available and before the known original

documents had been properly assessed and edited. There are errors of dating, attribution, comprehension, and translation. Haggh's translation preserves most of the errors and has many more in the added commentaries. The most reliable section is probably the translator's annotated bibliography. The information and conclusions in this book must be checked at every step with more reliable sources. Only polyphonic theory is discussed, other areas appearing very incidentally, but there are chapters on modes (pp 3–10); rhythm (131–57, 183–208); mathematical acoustics (280–328); *ficta* (329–39). See **235**.

920 Tello, Francisco J.L. *Estudios de Historia de la Teoria* M (Madrid 1962) xxiv + 695, 21 facss, b / rev A. Machabey *RdM* 50 (1964) 123–5
Part I (pp 1–187) reviews the treatises of all major writers up to 1400, with liberal quotations from the originals.

921 Wolf, J. 'Die Musiktheorie des MA' *Acta* 3 (1931) 53–64
W summarises the most important developments up to ca 1350.

922 *Musikerziehung. Lehre und Theorie der* M *im MA* ed Joseph Smits van Waesberghe, MgB Bd III, fasc. 3 (Leipzig 1969) 214, index, b / rev M. Huglo *RdM* 56 (1970) 232–3
Including a chronological table of M treatises and very numerous facss, S traces the history of theoretical writings.

923 Pietzsch, Gerhard W. *Die Klassifikation der* M *von Boethius bis Ugolino von*
924 Orvieto STUDIEN ZUR GESCH DER M-TH IM MA (Halle 1929) v + 124 / rev C. Van den Borren *RUB* 35 (1929/30) 120*–1* **924** Pietzsch *Die* M *im Erziehungs- und Bildungsideal des ausgehenden Altertums und frühen MA* STUDIEN ZUR GESCH DER MUSIKTH IM MA (Halle 1932) iii + 142 / rev C. Van den Borren *RUB* 38 (1932/3) 16*–17*
923 Listing sources and literature, P traces the descent and modification of concepts through over 30 writers, concluding that they were not bound by *auctoritas* and that *ratio* excercised an influence. **924** P discusses the transmission of theory to the 12c. The reviewer says he traces two themes in M education: practical study and theoretical knowledge.

EDITIONS AND ANTHOLOGIES

Coussemaker *Scriptorum* ... (**925**) and Gerbert *Scriptores* ... (**926**) are standard collections of editions, despite their dates of publication. Editions which can be placed in one of the chronological sections (**928–1016**) are noted in those sections. Editions are also listed under polyphony (**1336–89**), 14c France (**1611–30**), 14c Italy (**1727–48**), British Isles (**1810–15**), Spain (**1847–8**), the Germanic countries (**1849–75**).

925 Coussemaker, Edmond de *Scriptorum de Musica Medii Aevi* (often abbr

CousS or CS 4 vols (Paris 1864–76; repr Hildesheim 1963) xxiii + 467; xxviii + 515, 36 dipl facss, index of terms and names; xl + 530, index of terms and names; xiv + 498, index of terms and names
This is an inaccurate and incomplete but still invaluable collection of med. treatises on M. There is a brief and out of date introduction, in Latin, to each vol but no explication of original texts. Information should always be checked elsewhere. A number of the works here published have appeared in more recent editions. The vols include the following (short titles only):

Vol I: 1 Jerome of Moravia; 94 *Discantus positio vulgaris;* 97 Johannis de Garlandis; 117 Franco, *Ars cantus mensurabilis;* 136 Petrus Picardus; 154 *Compendium discantus;* 157 *Introductio musice secundum Magistrum de Garlandia;* 175 Johannis de Garlandia, *De musica mensurabili;* 182 Walter Odington; 251 Pseudo-Aristotle; 282 Petrus de Cruce; 292 *Abbreviatio Magistri Franconis;* 296 Anon I; 303 Anon II; 319 Anon III; 327 Anon IV; 366 Anon V; 369 Anon VI; 378 Anon VII, *De musica libellus;* 383 Robert de Handlo; 403 *Summa Magistri Johannis Hanboys*

Vol II: 1 Regino Prum, *Tonari;* 74 Hucbald, *Quaedam e musica enchiriade inedita;* 78 Guidonis Aretini; 115 Guido, *De sex motibus vocum;* 117 Odo, *Tonari;* 150 Guy de Charlieu; 193 *Speculum musicae* (in fact Jacobus de Liège); 434 Carthusian monk, *Tractatus de musica plana;* 484 Anon, *Tractatus de musica*

Vol III: 1 Marchettus of Padua; 12 *Optima introductio* attr. Garlandia; 13 P. de Vitry, *Ars nova;* 23 *Ars contrapunctus secundum P. de Vitry;* 28 *Ars perfecta secundum P. de Vitry;* 35 *Liber musicalium secundum P. de Vitry;* 46 *Libellus cantus mensurabilis secundum J. de Muris;* 59 *Ars contrapuncti secundum J. de Muris;* 68 *Ars discantus secundum J. de Muris;* 113 Henrici de Zelandia, *Tractatus de cantu perfecto et imperfecto;* 116 Magistri Phillipoti Andreae, *De contrapuncto quaedam regulae utiles;* 118 Philippi de Caserta, *Tractatus de diversis figuris;* 124 Magistri Aegidii de Murino, *Tractatus cantus mensurabilis;* 129 Johannis Veruli de Anagnia, *Liber de musica;* 177 Fratris Theodorici de Campo, *De musica mensurabili;* 193 Prosdocimus, *Tractatus de contrapuncto;* 200 Prosdocimus, *Tractatus practice de musica mensurabili;* 228 Prosdocimus, *Tractatus practice de musica mensurabili ad modum italicorum;* 248 Prosdocimus, *Libellus monocordi;* 258 Prosdocimus, *Brevis summula proportionum;* 262 Nicasii Weyts, Carmelite, *Regule;* 264 Christiani Sadze de Flandria, *Tractatus modi, temporis et prolationis;* 273 Guilielmi Monachi, *De preceptis artis musice;* 307 Antonii de Leno, *Regulae de contrapuncto;* 328 Johannis Hothby, *Regulae super proportionem;* 330 Johannis Hothby, *De cantu figurato;* 333 Johannis Hothby, *Regulae supra contrapunctum;* 334 Anon I, *De musica antiqua et nova;* 364 Anon II, *De musica antiqua et nova;* 370 Anon III, *Compendiolum artis veteris ac novae;* 376 Anon IV, *Compendium artis mensurabilis tam veteris quam novae;* 379 Anon V, *Ars cantus mensurabilis;* 398 Anon VI, *De musica mensurabili;* 404 Anon VII, *De diversis*

maneriebus in musica mensurabili; 409 Anon VIII, *Regulae de contrapuncto;*
411 Anon IX, *De musica mensurabili;* 413 Anon X, *De minimis notulis;* 416
Anon XI, *Tractatus de musica plana et mensurabili;* 475 Anon XII, *Tractatus de
musica;* 496 Anon XIII, *Tractatus de discantu*

Vol IV: 1 Johannis Tinctoris, *Tractatus de musica;* 298 Joannis Gallici, dicti
Carthusiensis seu de Mantua, *Ritus canendi vetustissimus et novus*

926 Gerbert, Martin *Scriptores ecclesiastici de musica sacra potissimum* (often abbr
GerS or GS) 3 vols (St Blasien 1784: repr Milan 1931) l + 350 + frontisp; x
+ 394 + frontisp; viii + 416 + frontisp, index
This is an inaccurate and incomplete but still invaluable collection of med.
treatises on M. There is a brief and out of date introduction, in Latin, to
each vol but no explication of original texts. Information should always be
checked elsewhere. A number of the works here published have appeared
in more recent editions. The vols include the following (short titles only):

Vol I: 1 Abbot Pambo; 4 *Monacho qua mente sit psallendum;* 5 *Instituta patrum de modo psallendi;* 9 S. Nicetius; 15 Cassiodorus; 19 Isidore; 26 Alcuin;
27 Aurelian; 63 Remy; 95 Notker Lamberto; 103 Hucbald, *Harmonica
institutione;* 125 *Alia musica;* 152 *Musica enchiriadis;* 213 *Commemoratio brevis;* 230 Regino Prumiensis; 251 Odo, *Dialogus;* 265 *Musica artis disciplina;*
285 *Rhythmimachia;* 296 *Regulae domni Oddonis;* 303 *Organistrum;* 303
Adelbold; 312 Bernelinus; 330 Anon I; 338 Anon II; 343 Anon III; 344
Mensura monochordi Boetii

Vol II: 1 Guido, *Micrologus;* 25 *Regulae musicae rhythmicae;* 34 *Ignoto cantu;*
43 Guido, *Epistola;* 50 *Collectorius multorum errorum;* 61 Berno; 79 *Tonarius
Bernonis;* 91 *Varia psalmorum;* 114 *Consona tonorum diversitate;* 125 Hermann; 154 William of Hirsau; 182 Theogeri; 197 Aribo; 230 Cotton; 265
Tonale S. Bernardi; 279 Eberhard; 283 Anon, *De mensura;* 287 Engelbert;
370 Aegidius Zamora

Vol III: 1 Franco; 16 Salomon; 64 Marchettus, *Lucidarium;* 121 *Pomerium;*
189 Muris according to Gerbert (actually *Summa musicae* by Jacobus of
Liège); 249 *Musica speculativa* (Muris); 284 *De numeris;* 286 *De propor-
tionibus;* 292 *Musica practica* (Muris); 301 Joannis de Muris (?) *Quaestiones;*
316 *Tractatulus* Arnulph de St Gilles; 319 Keckii; 329 Adam of Fulda;
382 *Constitutiones;* 397 *Ars psallendi*

927 *Source Readings in M History* comp and ed Oliver Strunk (New York 1950)
xxi + 919, index, M exx / rev L. Schrade *JAMS* 4 (1951) 249–51
This was reissued in 1965 in 5 smaller volumes: only vol 1, containing sections I–IV, pp 1–190, of the original is relevant here. Section I deals with
Greek M theory and philosophy, which continues into the MA: section II
deals with the early Christian view of M: sections III and IV with early and
late MA. S presents selected passages with a brief description of the theorist

and treatise. The original Latin is not given, and the translations are moderately free. This is the only comprehensive collection of theoretical writing in translation and is thus a standard work. Nevertheless each excerpt should be related to its original context.

THEORY AND THEORISTS UP TO 800

This section is approximately chronological. Major theorists and treatises are given headings.

928 Coleman-Norton, P.R. 'Cicero Musicus' *JAMS* 1 (1948) 3–22
Discussing Cicero's references to M, C lists terms, many of which passed into the MA from the Latin authors.

929 Richter, L. 'Griechische Traditionen im Musikschrifttum der Römer' *AMw* 22 (1965) 69–98
R compares the references in Censorinus (3c) with earlier and later writers, including Martianus Capella.

Martianus Capella

930   *Martianus Capella* (fl 430) ed Adolfus Dick (Leipzig 1925; repr with additions
930a by Jean Préaux Stuttgart 1969) *Liber* IX: *De Harmonia* (in other editions *De Musica*) pp 469–535 930a Stahl, William H. *Martianus Capella and the Seven Liberal Arts* I: *The Quadrivium of Martianus Capella. Latin Traditions in the Mathematical Sciences, 50 B.C.–A.D. 1250* RECORDS OF CIVILIZATION, Sources and Studies 84 (New York & London 1971) xiv + 274, index
930 This is an edition. 930a Without clearly distinguishing translation from commentary, S presents a very useful section on Martianus' Book IX (pp 202–27). All modern terminology is accompanied by its Latin original. Some caution is probably necessary.

Augustine

931 *Œuvres de Saint Augustin* (354–430) 1ᵉ ser *Opuscules* VII. *Dialogues*
932 *philosophiques* IV: *La Musique* ed Guy Finaert and F.-J. Thonnard (Bruges
933 1947) 546 932 *Aurelii Augustini: De Musica* ed Giovanni Marzi COLLANA DI CLASSICI DELLA FILOSOFIA CRISTIANA 1 (Florence 1969) 688, 2 facss, indices of terms 933 Vecchi, Giuseppe ed *Praecepta artis musicae collecta ex libris sex A. Augustini 'De Musica'* ACCADEMIA DELLE SCIENZE DELL'IST. DI BOLOGNA, Classe de Scienze morali, Mem ser v¹ 1950 (Bologna 1951) 91–153, 2 facss
931 This is an annotated Latin/French edition. 932 M edits all six books with a facing Italian translation. 933 This is a scholarly edition of the *De Musica* and the *Lexicon*.

934 *St. Augustine on* M transl R. Catesby Taliaferro (Annapolis 1939) iii +
935 198 935 Jackson Knight, W.F. *St Augustine's De Musica: a Synopsis* (London
936 1949) 125 / rev A.E. Beau *Humanitas* 3 (1950/1) xxx-xxxii 936 Davenson,
    Henri (pseudonym of Marrou, Henri I.) *Traité de la* M *selon l'esprit de Saint
    Augustin* LES CAHIERS DU RHÔNE, Ser blanche 2 (Neuchâtel 1942) 191 / rev S.
    Clercx *RBM* 1 (1947) 32–3
    934 This is a translation: occasionally the original Latin is given. 935 This
    is in the nature of an English summary or paraphrase of the treatise. 936 This
    is a modern (1940) gloss, with contemporary references. It has a useful 're-
    prise' of Augustine's main views (pp 185–9).

Boethius

937 *A. M. T. S. Boetii. De institutione arithmetica libri duo. De institutione musica
938 libri quinque* ... ed Gottfried Friedlein (Leipzig 1867; repr Frankfurt 1966) viii
938a + 492 + 7 tables of M diagrams, index of words and names 938 Bragard,
939 R. 'Boethiana' *Hommage à Charles Van den Borren* ed Suzanne Clercx and
    Albert Vander Linden (Antwerp 1945) 84–139, 4 pll 938a Masi, M. 'Mss con-
    taining the *De Musica* of Boethius' *Msct* 15 (1971) 89–95 939 Potiron, Henri
    Boèce, théoricien de la M *grecque* TRAVAUX DE L'INST CATHOLIQUE DE PARIS 9
    (Paris 1961) 186 / rev J. Chailley *RdM* 47 (1961) 207–8
    937 This is a scholarly edition. The *Musica* is on pp 175–371 + 6 tables. 938
    Listing European mss, B gives preliminary results of work towards a new
    edition. He describes the sources in Belgium, and comments on earlier edi-
    tions, including 937. 939 Boethius (fl 500) concerns himself exclusively with
    concepts of antiquity.

Isidore

940 Hüschen, H. 'Der Einfluss Isidors von Sevilla auf die Musikanschauung
    des MA' **F-2.1.**397–406
    Isidore fl 600: H notes the sources and descent of some important theoretical
    concepts.

THE NINTH AND TENTH CENTURIES

Aurelian of Réomé

941 Ponte, Joseph transl *Aurelian of Réomé (ca. 843) The Discipline of* M COLORADO
942 COLLEGE M PRESS TRANSL 3 (Colorado Springs 1968) errata slip, v + 64 / rev
    D. Wulstan *ML* 50 (1969) 417–18 942 Waeltner, E.L. 'Die "Musica Discip-
    lina" des Aurelianus Reomensis' **A-3.**293–5
    941 The original text is not given and there is no commentary: the reviewer
    thinks the translation good. 942 W describes the treatise, the earliest to
    include both theory and practice.

Musica Enchiriadis

943 Sowa, H. 'Textvariationen zur *Musica Enchiriadis*' ZMw 17 (1935) 194–
944 207 **944** Schmid, H. 'Die Kölner Hs der *Musica Enchiriadis*' **A-3**.262–4
943 Sowa prints the text and a German translation, with comments. **944**
Schmid describes the mss and their relations. There is no recent edition
of this treatise of major importance for the polyphony of the 9c.

945 Smits van Waesberghe, J. 'La Place exceptionelle de l'Ars Musica dans le
développement des sciences au siècle des Carolingiens' RG 31 (1952) 81–104
S categorizes treatises and discusses the outstanding importance of John
Scottus Eriugena and of *Musica Enchiriadis*.

John Scottus Eriugena

946 Jones, Percy *The glosses de musica of John Scottus Eriugena* (Rome 1957) 115
J edits and comments on 9c Irish annotations of Martianus Capella.

Alia Musica

947 Chailley, Jacques ed *Alia Musica (traité de M du IXᵉ siècle)* PUBL DE L'INST DE
MUSICOLOGIE DE L'U DE PARIS 6 (Paris 1965) 224 + errata slip / rev M. Huglo
RdM 51 (1965) 230–2 and H. Potiron EG 7 (1967) 165–8
This is a comprehensive study, followed by a 'glossed' scholarly edition.

Regino of Prüm

948 Hüschen, H. 'Regino von Prüm, Historiker, Kirchenrechtler und Musiktheoretiker' **F-11**.205–23, 2 pll
H lists Regino's works (9–10c) and their sources, and with quotations discusses the contents and authenticity of the M treatises.

Hucbald

949 Weakland, R. 'Hucbald as Musician and Theorist' MQ 42 (1956) 66–84, 4
facss
Translating some important passages, W concludes that the *De Institutione
Harmonica* of Hucbald (d 930) begins a new concept of practical rather than
speculative theory.

Notker Labeo

950 Nef, W. 'Vom Musiktraktate des Notker Labeo' *Schw Musikzeitung* 87 (1947)
323–6
Notker (950–1022) still keeps separate the theory of antiquity and contemporary practice, especially concerning the modes.

THE ELEVENTH AND TWELFTH CENTURIES

951 Gallo, F.A. 'La M e le *Artes* in Italia attorno al mille' *Quad* 5 (1962) 101–7,
   2 pll
   An Italian treatise of ca 1000 seems to show that M theory was less traditional
   than the others arts.

951a Huglo, M. 'Der Prolog des Odo zugeschreibenen "Dialogus de Musica" '
   AMw 28 (1971) 134–46
   H edits the prologue to an antiphonal in alphabetic notation and sees in
   it a source for the work of Odo and Guido of Arezzo.

Guido of Arezzo

952 *Guidonis Aretini Micrologus* ed Joseph Smits van Waesberghe CSM 4 (1955)
   243, 16 pll / rev W. Waite *JAMS* 9 (1956) 146–9
   This is a scholarly edition of the *Micrologus* (ca 1030).

953 Oesch, Hans *Guido von Arezzo* PSMfG, ser II vol 4 (Bern 1954) xvi + 125,
   b / rev H. Hüschen *Mf* 11 (1958) 357–9
   O accumulates biographical and historical evidence, and reviews Guido's
   theories.

954 Smits van Waesberghe, Joseph *De musico-paedagogico et theoretico Guidone
   Aretino* (Florence 1953) 247, 24 facss, 1 table, index, list of mss / rev J. Hourlier
   EG 2 (1957) 221–5
   This is a detailed and documented account, in Latin, of Guido's innovations
   in notation, solmisation, etc, assessing their importance and authenticity.

955 Smits van Waesberghe, J. 'Guido of Arezzo and Musical Improvisation' *MD*
   5 (1951) 55–63
   Citing a properly edited text, S explains Guido's method of elementary ear-
   training and melodic composition.

956 Wiora, W. 'Zum Problem des Ursprungs der ma. Solmisation' *Mf* 9 (1956)
   263–74
   W discusses possible origins and symbology of the syllables.

Odo of Cluny

957 Thomas, Dom P. 'Saint Odon de Cluny et son oeuvre M' *A Cluny. Congrès*
958 *scientifique ... en l'honneur des saints abbés Odon et Odilon* (Dijon 1950) 171–80,
   2 facss 958 Huglo, M 'L'Auteur du *Dialogue sur la* M attribué à Odon' *RdM*
   55 (1969) 119–71, 1 pl
   957 Odo is not the author of the *Dialogue*, nor of the *Enchiridion* cited by
   Guido. 958 Analysing sources and contents, H shows that the treatise
   originated near Milan, shortly after the year 1000.

Hermannus Contractus

959 Ellinwood, Leonard ed *Musica Hermanni Contracti* (b 1013) ESM 2 (Rochester,
959a NY 1936) 71, 3 pll / rev W.H. Frere *ML* 18 (1937) 81–2 **959a** Crocker, R.L.
'Hermann's Major Sixth' *JAMS* 25 (1972) 19–37
959 Describing the life and work of Hermann and the Rochester ms source,
E edits the treatise with parallel translation. **959a** C comments on hexachords, modes, and finals in theory, 9–11c. See also **F-13**.170–4 and *Acta*
7 (1935) 160.

960 Smits van Waesberghe, Joseph ed *Aribonis De Musica* CSM 2 (1951) xxx +
961 74 + 5 pll / rev L. Schrade *JAMS* 9 (1956) 214–17 **961** Rawski, C.H. 'Notes
962 on Aribo Scholasticus' **F-17**.19–29 **962** Kreps, Dom J. 'Aribon de Liège: une
légende' *RBM* 2 (1948) 138–43
960 This an edition of the treatises (1068–78). **961** R complements and corrects S's edition, and gives a good feeling of Aribo's style: he discusses
the *caprea aribonis*, a new graphic representation of the gamut. **962** K, writing before either of the above, strongly disputes the evidence of Aribo's
activity at Liège.

School of Liège

963 Smits van Waesberghe, J. 'Some M Treatises and their Interrelation. A
School of Liège c.1050–1200?' *MD* 3 (1949) 25–31, 95–118, 2 facss
S describes the contents and relations of a dozen treatises, concluding that
they originated from Liège.

Wilhelm of Hirsau

964 Fellerer, K.G. 'Zum Musiktraktat des Wilhelm von Hirsau' *Fs Wilhelm*
965 *Fischer* INNSBRUCKER BEITR ZUR KULTURWISSENSCHAFT, Sonderheft 3
(Innsbruck 1956) 61–70 **965** Fellerer 'Untersuchungen zur *Musica* des
Wilhelm von Hirsau' **F-2**.1.239–52
964 F describes the 11c treatise and its contents. **965** F compares Wilhelm's
discussion of the modes with that of other theorists.

Minor eleventh-century works

966 Vivell, P.C. ed *Frutolfi: Breviarium de musica et Tonarius* AKW IN WIEN,
p.h.Kl., Sitzungsberichte Bd 188, Abh 2 (Vienna 1919) 188, several facss
With a brief description and index of terms V edits the treatise of Frutolf
(d 1103).

967 Sowa, H. 'Zur Hs Clm 9921' *Acta* 5 (1933) 60–5, 107–20
S prints and discusses briefly several 11c treatises.

968 Huglo, M. 'Un Théoricien du xiᵉ siècle: Henri d'Augsbourg' *RdM* 53 (1967) 53–9
H describes the treatise.

969 Oesch, Hans *Berno und Hermann von Reichenau als Musiktheoretiker* PSMfG, ser II: 9 (Bern 1961) 251, ext b / rev H. Hüschen *KmJb* 48 (1964) 156–7
O describes the life, works, and M treatises of these 11c writers.

John of Afflighem (John Cotton)

970 *Johannis Afflighemensis: De Musica cum Tonario* ed Joseph Smits van Waes-
971 berghe CSM 1 (1950 or 1951) 207, num facss / rev in **971** Ellinwood, L. 'John
972 Cotton or John of Afflighem?' *Notes* 2nd ser 8 (1950/1) 650–9, 4 facss **972**
973 Smits van Waesberghe 'John of Afflighem or John Cotton?' *MD* 6 (1952)
139–53 **973** Flindell, E.F. 'Joh[ann]is Cottonis' *MD* 20 (1966) 11–30 and 23 (1969) 7–11
970 This is an edition with biographical information. **971** Introducing a ms not available to S, E concludes that John (early 12c) was indeed English. **972** S takes issue with Ellinwood's readings and reconfirms his position supporting Afflighem. **973** With extensive documentation F also refutes S's arguments and shows that John is English. He avers that John Cotton and Anon IV's *Johannes filius Dei* are identical.

Minor twelfth-century works

974 Oury, G. 'M et louange de Dieu d'après Hervé de Bourg-Dieu' *EG* 8 (1967) 15–20
Hervé (early 12c) deals with M terms in his exegetical works.

975 Steglich, Rudolf *Die Quaestiones in Musica* PUBL DER IMG, ser 2 Beihefte 10 (Leipzig 1911) viii + 190
S edits this 12c text with extensive commentary.

976 *Expositiones in Micrologum Guidonis Aretini* ed Joseph Smits van Waesberghe
977 (Amsterdam 1957) v + 175, 4 facss / rev A. Machabey *RdM* 39 (1957) 103–4 **977** *Commentarius anonymus in Micrologum Guidonis Aretini* ed P. Cölestin Vivell KAISERLICHE AWK IN WIEN, p.h.Kl., Sitzungsberichte Bd 185, Abh 5 (Vienna 1917) 92
976 S edits 4 tracts (11–13c) with copious notes. **977** V edits a 12c commentary on the *Micrologus*.

Giraldus Cambrensis

978 Hibberd, L. 'Giraldus Cambrensis on Welsh Popular Singing' **F-31**.17–23
979 **979** Hibberd 'Giraldus Cambrensis and English "Organ" M' *JAMS* 8 (1955) 208–12

978 H examines the technical terms upon which the meaning depends. 979 He provides more accurate translations and explanations for Giraldus' statements (ca 1146–ca 1223).

Guglielmo Roffredi

979a Seay, A. 'Guglielmo Roffredi's *Summa musicae artis*' MD 24 (1970) 69–77
S edits this practical treatise of the late 12c.

ARABIC INFLUENCE

980 Farmer, H.G. 'Clues for the Arabian Influence on European м Theory' *JRAS* (1925) 61–80
This is a standard article, referring to most of the important facts. There is much indisputable influence.

981 Chailley, J. 'Elmuahym et Elmuarifa' F-3.61–2
C offers possible Arabic terms as origins of Anon ɪv's words.

982 Reaney, G. '*Quid est musica* in the *Quatuor principalis musicae*' B-3.177–9

Concepts in the *Quatuor principalis* derive through Lambertus from Arabic transmission of Greek theories.

THE THIRTEENTH CENTURY

Vincent of Beauvais

983 *Vinzenz von Beauvais O.P. (um 1194–1264) und sein Musiktraktat im Speculum doctrinale* ed Gottfried Göller, KBMf 15 (Regensburg 1959) iv + 127 / rev G. Reaney ML 41 (1960) 269–70
G discusses and edits the largely speculative text.

John of Garlandia

983a Reimer, Erich ed *Johannes de Garlandia: de mensurabili musica* 2 vols, AMw, Beihefte 10/11 (Wiesbaden 1971)

  * Announced: Rasch, Rudolf A. transl *Johannes de Garlandia: de mensurabili musica* MThT

984 Rasch, Rudolf A. *Johannes de Garlandia* мs 20 (New York 1969) xiii, 8 facss
985 + 333, index of names and terms 985 Waite, W.G. 'Johannes de Garlandia, Poet and Musician' *Spec* 35 (1960) 179–95
984 This is an investigation in Dutch of Garlandia's identity, supposed compositions, and theoretical treatises. There are German (pp 311–17) and English (319–25) summaries. 985 In writings attributed to John there is much

interaction between poetic and music theory. The latter is more than usually concerned with *musica practica*.

Jerome of Moravia

986 *Hieronymus de Moravia*, O.P. *Tractatus de Musica* ed Simon M. Cserba, FREIBURGER STUDIEN ZUR MW 2; Ver. des mw Inst der U Freiburg i. d. Schweiz, Reihe 2 (Regensburg 1935) lxxxv + 293
This is an edition of the 13c treatises collected by Jerome with introduction and notes (German).

Dietricus

986a Müller, Hans *Eine Abhandlung über Mensuralmusik* ... (Leipzig 1886) v + 24
M edits and comments on the 13c treatise of Dietricus.

Anonymous IV

987 Reckow, Fritz ed *Der Musiktraktat des Anonymus 4* 2 vols, AMw, Beihefte 4/5
988 (Wiesbaden 1967) x + 118; iv + 107, b, index / rev Jack A. Westrup *ML* 50
989 (1969) 312–14 **988** *Anonymous IV* transl Luther A. Dittmer, MThT 1 (New York 1959) 72 + addendum on back cover / rev G. Reaney *JAMS* 12 (1959) 226–33 **989** Hiekel, H.O. 'Zur Überlieferung des Anon IV' *Acta* 34 (1962) 185–91
987 Vol 1 describes the sources and edits the text, with comments and an index of names, compositions, and terminology; vol 2 discusses the problems of modal rhythm and consonance in *organum purum*. **988** This is an unsatisfactory English translation. **989** Describing the sources, H suggests that the theorist may have written ca 1300, rather than mid-thirteenth century.

Petrus Picardus

990 *Petrus Picardus*. *'Ars motettorum compilata breviter'* ed F. Alberto Gallo CSM 15 (1971) 9–30
This is an edition.

Franco of Cologne

991 *Magistri Franconis. Ars Cantus Mensurabilis* MwSb 15/16 (1957) 15 + 4 separate booklets (pp 117–35 reprinting the edition from **925**.I; 1–8 dipl facss reproducing concordances of Franco's examples; 6 leaves facss; 6 leaves facss)

992 Rieckenberg, H.J. 'Zur Biographie des Musiktheoretikers Franco von Köln'

993 *Archiv für Kulturgeschichte* 42 (1960) 280–93 / rev J.Torsy *Kölner Domblatt* 20 (1961/2) 227 **993** Frobenius, W. 'Zur Datierung von Francos *Ars cantus mensurabilis' AMw* 27 (1970) 122–7
992 R believes that (1) the Scholaster and deacon of St Kunibert, (2) the Dom-scholaster, and (3) the theorist are one and the same. The reviewer thinks his conclusion very doubtful, and gives good reasons. **993** Franco wrote ca 1280, after Lambertus and the Anon St Emmeram theorists.

Minor thirteenth-century works

994 Sowa, Heinrich ed *Ein anonymer glossierter Mensuraltraktat 1279* (Kassel 1930) lii + 138, 1 facs
S edits the text with an introduction. He gives an index of terms used in the treatise.

995 Kromolicki, Joseph ed *Die Practica Artis Musicae des Amerus und ihre Stellung*
996 *in der M-th des MA* (Berlin 1909) vii + 43 + 2 tables **996** Blanchard, D.P. 'Alfred le musicien et Alfred le philosophe' *Rassegna Gregoriana* 8 (1909) columns 419–32, 1 facs
995 K edits the 13c treatise, then discusses it and the mensural theory of the time. **996** B describes the treatise, which is the *Practica artis musicae* of Amerus.

997 Müller, H. 'Der Musiktraktat in dem Werke des Bartholomaeus Anglicus *De proprietatibus rerum'* **F-24**.241–55
M prints the 13c treatise.

998 Huglo, M. 'Le Théoricien bolognais Guido Fabe' *RdM* 55 (1969) 78–82
This is a basic introduction which briefly describes the treatise of Fabe (d 1245).

999 Goldine, N. 'Henri Bate, chanoine et chantre de la cathédrale St-Lambert à Liège et théoricien de la M (1246–après 1310)' *RBM* 18 (1964) 10–27, 1 pl
G describes the life, duties, and writings of Bate.

1000 Waite, W.G. 'Two M poems of the MA' **F-27**.13–34
The author discusses M theory written in the form of poetry, concentrating on two sources. He tentatively attributes one to Alexander de Villa Dei.

Johannes de Grocheo

1001 Rohloff, Ernst ed *Der Musiktraktat des Johannes de Grocheo* (Leipzig 1943) 151
1002 / rev J. Wolf *Mf* 2 (1949) 72–7, complemented by H. Besseler, pp
1003 229–31 **1002** Wolf, J. 'Die Musiklehre des Johannes de Grocheo' *SIMG* 1 (1899/1900) 65–130 **1003** Johannes de Grocheo *Concerning M (De musica)* transl Albert Seay (Colorado Springs 1967) iii + 42 / rev A. Clarkson *JMTh* 12 (1968) 281–9

1001 R edits the text, with German translation and copious notes and introduction. **1002** W edits the treatise, ca 1300, with parallel German translation. **1003** This is an English translation without comments and without the original.

Minor thirteenth-century works

1004 *Ars musicae mensurabilis secundum franconem* ed Gilbert Reaney and André Gilles CSM 15 (1971) 31–58
This is an edition.

1005 *Compendium musicae mensurabilis artis antiquae* ed F. Alberto Gallo CSM 15 (1971) 59–73
This is an edition.

THE FOURTEENTH AND FIFTEENTH CENTURIES

Treatises definitely assignable by virtue of author or content to a specific country are listed under the relevant geographical heading. New information could result in some of the items listed below being so assigned. The more interesting are listed first.

1006 Crocker, R.L. 'A new source for med. M theory' *Acta* 39 (1967) 161–71, 2 facss, complemented by M. Bent 'A Postscript on the Berkeley theory ms' *Acta* 40 (1968) 175
Quoting significant passages and transcribing the M pieces, C describes and discusses this 14c source. B finds a concordance in London.

1007 Leibowitz, René transl *Un traité inconnu de la technique de la variation (XIVᵉ siècle)* (Liège 1950) 15
L gives a French translation after the Latin. The treatise refers to ornamentation possibly carried out in performance.

1008 Federhofer-Königs, R. 'Ein anonymer Musiktraktat aus der 2. Hälfte des
1009 14. Jh. in der Stiftsbibliothek Michaelbeuern/Salzburg' *KmJb* 46 (1962) 43–60, 2 facss **1009** Federhofer-Königs 'Ein unvollständiger Musiktraktat des 14. Jh. in Ms 1201 der Universitätsbibliothek Graz' *KmJb* 44 (1960) 14–27, 2 facss
F edits and discusses these tracts.

1010 Gallo, F.A. 'Alcune fonti poco note di M teorica e pratica' **D-4**.49–76 + 4 facss
G describes and inventories four 14c and early 15c mss.

1011 Kellner, A. 'Ein Mensuraltraktat aus der Zeit um 1400' ÖSTERREICHISCHE AKW, p.h.Kl., Anzeiger 94 (1957) 72–85, 2 facss
This is an edition.

1012 Bartha, D.V. 'Studien zum M Schrifttum des 15. Jh.' *AMf* 1 (1936) 59–82, 176–99
Referring to older studies, B describes some problems and eight copies of late sources of med. theory, and edits a text.

1013 Anglès, H. 'Dos tractats med. de M figurada' *Fs Johannes Wolf* ed Walter Lott, Helmuth Osthoff, and Werner Wolffheim, Mw Beitr (Berlin 1929) 6–12
A edits the treatises from an early 15c ms.

1014 Schmid, H. 'Zur sogenannten *Musica Adelboldi Traiectensis*' *Acta* 28 (1956) 69–73
The treatise is a copy of Boethius dating from the 15c.

1015 Seay, Albert ed *Anonymous Treatise from the Codex Vatican, Lat. 5129 (ca 1400)* CSM 9 (1964) 48
This is an edition.

1016 Wolf, J. 'Ein Breslauer Mensuraltraktat des 15. Jh' *AMw* 1 (1918/19) 329–45, 1 facs
W prints the early 15c treatise, which deals with 14c practice.

Music in Islam

BIBLIOGRAPHY, SOURCES, HISTORIES

1017 Collangettes, X.M. 'Etude sur la M arabe' *J Asiatique,* 10 sér: 4 (1904) 365–422;
8 (1906) 149–90
This is a general but well exemplified study. The first article includes a list
of Arabic scholars and of ms sources (pp 381–8).

1018 Farmer, Henry G. *A History of Arabian M to the XIIIth Century* (London 1929)
xvii + 264, index, b, 3 pll / rev F. Tauer *Archiv Orientální* 1 (1929) 259–60
This is a standard work. It does not deal with influences on Europe.

1019 *Islam* ed Henry G. Farmer MgB Bd III, fasc. 2 (Leipzig 1966) 206, indices,
b / rev Emmy Wellesz *ML* 49 (1968) 73–4
Including extensive chronological tables and numerous plates, F traces the
history of Islamic art, philosophy, treatises, instruments, and music in
general.

1020 Farmer, H.G. 'Arabic M Mss in the Bodleian Library' *JRAS* (1925) 639–54
This is a catalogue.

PHILOSOPHICAL, SCIENTIFIC, AND AESTHETIC CONCEPTS

1021 Farmer, H.G. 'The Influence of M: from Arabic Sources' *PRMA*52 (1925/6)
1022 89–124 **1022** Farmer 'The M of the Arabian Nights' *JRAS* (1944) 172–85; (1945)
1023 39–60, 1 facs **1023** Farmer 'The Song Captions in the Kitāb al-aghāni al-
kabīr' *GUOS* 15 (1953/4) 1–10
1021 This is an excellent introduction to the magical, speculative, and
mathematical theories of M given by Arabians in the MA. **1022** The tales contain much information about practices and aesthetics. F transcribes the
earliest known piece of Arabic M (13c). **1023** The captions refer to rhythmic
and melodic modes: F identifies the latter.

1024 Shiloah, Amnon *Caractéristiques de l'art vocal arabe au ma.* (Tel Aviv 1963)
23 / rev H.D. *Musical Opinion* 87 (1963/4) 347

S quotes literary and theoretical allusions concerning the social and psychological aspects. See also *CCM* 5 (1962) 463–74.

1024a Manik, Liberty *Das arabische Tonsystem im Ma* (Leiden 1969) xii + 140, b, index
This is a technical discussion of Arabic theory, mathematics, and acoustics.

INSTRUMENTS

1025 Farmer, H.G. 'Ibn Khurdādhbih on Musical Instruments' *JRAS* (1928)
1026 509–18 1026 Farmer 'A Maghribī Work on Musical Instruments' *JRAS* (1935)
1027 339–53 1027 Farmer' 'Abdalqādir ibn Ġaibī on instruments of M' *Oriens* 15 (1962) 242–8, 1 facs
1025 This is the earliest extant account. 1026 The work dates from 1301. 1027 The theorist describes more than 40 instruments.

THEORY

1028 Erlanger, Rodolphe d' *La* M *Arabe* 6 vols (Paris 1930, 1935, 1938, 1939, 1949, 1959) xxviii + 329; 310; xiv + 618; 531; xv + 426; ix + 644 / rev vols 1–4 A. Gastoué *RdM* 12 (1931) 299–301; 17 (1936) 199–200; 20 (1939) 53; 21 (1942) 18–19: vols 5, 6 H. Husmann *Mf* 6 (1953) 401–2; 13 (1960) 364–5
Vol 1: French translation of Al-Farabi's treatise, brief introduction. Vol 2: Vol 1 cont., Avicenna's tract, mathematical appendix. Vol 3: Ṣafiyu-d-Dīn al-urmawī and Mawlānā Mubārak Šāh's commentary. Vol. 4: Anon 15c treatise; Al-lādhiqī (16c). Vol 5: Editor's commentary with numerous transcriptions and b. Vol 6: More commentary and transcriptions.

Al-Farabi

1029 Farmer, Henry G. ed transl *Al-fārābī's Arabic-Latin Writings on* M COLLECTION OF ORIENTAL WRITERS ON M 2 (2nd ed London 1960) frontisp facs, vi + 65
F edits 9–10c Arabic texts and 12c Latin translations, and gives English translations. He discusses their influence on Europe.

Al-Kindi

1030 Farmer, H.G. 'Al-Kindi on the *Ethos* of Rhythm, Colour, and Perfume' *GUOS* 16 (1955/6) 29–38
F translates the 9c passages which relate rhythm and lute strings to the time of the day, humours, the zodiac, colours, and perfumes.

Abu'l-Ṣalt

1031 Avenary, H. 'Abu'l-Ṣalt's Treatise on M' *MD* 6 (1952) 27–32
This describes the source and contents of the 12c treatise and includes a short b.

Avicenna

1032 *Avicenna. Al-Shifā', mathématiques, 3. Musique (Jauāmi' 'ilm el-mūsiqā)* ed
Zakariyya Yousef (revd A.F. El-Ahwani and M.A. El Hefni) (Cairo 1956) vi +
176, tables, M exx, indices (in English)
This is an edition in Arabic.

Other writers and treatises

1033 Farmer, Henry G. *Sa'adyah Gaon on the Influence of* M (London 1943) xi +
1034 109, 2 pll, indices / rev E. Werner *Jewish Social Studies* 6 (1944) 406–7 **1034**
1035 Farmer 'The Science of M in the Mafātīḥ al-ʿUlūm' *GUOS* 17 (1957/8) 1–9
1035 Farmer 'M: the Priceless Jewel' *JRAS* (1941) 22–30; and 127–44
1033 F edits, translates, and comments on original texts concerning 10c Jewish and Arabic views of M. **1034** F translates the relevant section of this
useful 10c encyclopaedia. **1035** F translates much of Ibn ʿAbd Rabbihi's treatise (860–940), partly a defence of the practical execution of M.

1036 Shiloah, A. 'Deux textes arabes inédits sur la M' *Yuval* 221–48 + 1 facs
1037 **1037** Shiloah 'L'Epître sur la M des Ikhwān al-Safa'' *REI* 32 (1964) 125–62;
34 (1966) 159–93
1036 S edits with French translation the Hebrew and Arabic originals of
a speculative and practical treatise, respectively. **1037** This is an annotated
translation. The treatise is speculative, dealing with the magic, moral, and
therapeutic powers of M, deriving from the notion of *musica mundana*.

The lyric in Latin
and the vernacular

Most histories and reference books give only the briefest mention of the predecessors of the lyric in the ninth, tenth, and eleventh centuries, which are little known: moreover only in a very few cases is there evident any direct link with the lyrics of the twelfth century. As a consequence most of the items of a general nature in the following section refer mainly to the lyric from the twelfth century. Items relating to more specific topics such as Troubadour, Trouvère, should be sought under those headings.

SURVEYS

1038 Westrup, J.A. 'The Significance of Melody in Med. and Renaissance M' **F-18.**317–22
We have been led to overemphasise the importance of polyphony.

1039 *A History of Song* ed Denis Stevens (London 1960) / rev A. Hutchings *ML* 42 (1961) 67–70
Pp 15–64, *The MA*, by Gilbert Reaney, is an elementary but comprehensive survey of single-line songs, with and without accompaniment.

1040 Dronke, Peter *The Med. Lyric* (London 1968) 266, b, index / rev R.C.D. Perman *MLR* 64 (1969) 842–3
This is a general introduction, in which M is not ignored, to the sacred and secular lyric, ca 850–1300. Pp 231–40 contain melodies transcribed in various manners from various sources. D gives translations of all texts.

1041 Machabey, A. 'Introduction à la lyrique M romane' *CCM* 2 (1959) 203–11, 283–93
This is a good general survey, mentioning obscure works and problems.

Formal studies

1042 Spanke, Hans *Untersuchungen über die Ursprünge des romanischen Min-*
1043 *nesangs.* I: *Beziehungen zwischen romanischer und mittellateinischer Lyrik ...*

1044 II: *Marcabrustudien* AKW ZU GÖTTINGEN, p.h.Kl., 3. Folge, Abh 18, 24 (Berlin
1045 1936, Göttingen 1940) iv + 189; viii + 119 / rev of I by J. Storost *ZrPh* 62
(1942) 398–406 and A. Långfors *NeuphMit* 40 (1939) 342–50 **1043** Gennrich,
Friedrich *Grundriss einer Formenlehre des ma. Liedes* (Halle 1932; repr with
foreword by Werner Bittinger, Tübingen 1970) xiii + 288 + 1 table, indices
of incipits, names / rev W.H. Bruford *MLR* 29 (1934) 476–9 **1044** Gennrich
Aus der Formenwelt des MA MwSb 7 (2nd enl ed 1962) xxiii + 40 dipl facss
1045 Gennrich 'Die M Formen des ma. Liedes' *Du* 11 (1959) Heft 2 60–80,
2 tables
1042 The title *Untersuchungen ... Minnesangs* was not attached to the first
part of this study. S analyses chansons in 8 categories by form, subdivided
according to the presence of a refrain. Certain forms and melody schemes
are common to Latin and Romance songs. By means of Marcabru's songs
(listed on pp 112–13) S illustrates this thesis, raising the question whether
there was a truly Romance metre. In Romance lyrics the melody has priority;
in Latin this is not so. **1043** G discusses the origin and development of secular forms, in which M and poetry are indivisible. **1044** This is a brief examination of the forms according to type (Litany, hymn, refrain, Sequence).
1045 G categorizes formal principles.

Words

1046 Einstein, A. 'The Conflict of Word and Tone' *MQ* 40 (1954) 329–49
There is no conflict: text, either as an acoustical sound or as a meaningful
communication, and M are inseparable in the MA.

Popular and folk styles

1047 Salmen, W. 'Über das Nachleben eines ma. Kanonmodells' *Mf* 7 (1954)
1048 54–7 **1048** Wiora, W. 'Elementare Melodietypen als Abschnitte ma. Lied-
1049 weisen' **F-2**.II.993–1009 **1049** Wiora 'Der ma. Liedkanon' **B-1**.71–5
1047 In children's songs, dance songs, etc, from the 13–20c, S notes similar
melodies and sees a continuity. **1048** With international examples from
many monophonic repertories, 12–16c, W relates the reappearance of
melodic shapes to oral transmission, stressing the affinity among aristocra-
tic, popular, and folk cultures. **1049** When symmetrical song forms and simple harmonic vocabulary exist contemporaneously, monophony often holds
canonic potential.

Attribution

1050 Machabey, A. 'Comment déterminer l'authenticité d'une chanson méd.?'
F-9.II.915–20
M denies the value of attributions based on textual study alone.

Anthologies

1051 Gennrich, Friedrich ed *Troubadours, trouvères, minnesang and meistergesang*
1052 transl Rodney G. Dennis, AnthM 2 (Cologne 1960) 72 / rev R.L. Crocker
Notes 11 (1953/4) 269 **1052** Taylor, Ronald J. *Die Melodien der weltlichen Lieder des MA* 2 vols (Stuttgart 1964) viii + 72; 76 (transcc 17–36, facss 65–75), b, index / rev E. Jammers *German Quarterly* 39 (1966) 230–1
1051 G gives a good general selection of 79 songs in rhythmic transcription. There is historical and biographical introduction, commentary, and bibliography. The texts are not translated. **1052** This a general survey, with transcriptions of 24 songs.

THE EARLIEST LYRICS, EPICS, ETC

classical texts **1053–7** Anglo-Saxon [**1752–5**] French (chansons de geste, rotrouenge) **1066–9** [also **1180 1826**] German (epics) **1058–65** Italian **1070–1** Provençal **1072–4** others **1075**

Classical texts

1053 Corbin, S. 'Notations M dans les classiques latins' *R des études latines* 32
1054 (1954) 97–9 **1054** Corbin 'Comment on chantait les classiques latins au MA' *Mélanges d'histoire et d'ésthétique* M *offerts à Paul-Marie Masson* (Paris 1955) vol 1, 107–13
1053 Carolingian mss, but not the earlier capital-script sources, transmit what appears to be a traditional tune for parts of Virgil's *Aeneid* and a 'sapphic' melody for the Odes of Horace. **1054** Features of the pre-12c settings of Horace's Odes suggest that they were performed metrically.

1055 Combarieu, Jules *Fragments de l'Enéide en* M *d'àpres un ms inédit* EPM (Paris
1056 1898) v + 88 + 8 facss **1056** Liuzzi, F. 'Notazione M del sec. XI in un ms dell'*Enéide*' SM ns 5 (1932) 67–80, 1 page facss
1055 C describes a 10–11c ms and its notation and transcribes the M (N, Rh, Sq). His 19c harmonisation must be ignored. **1056** L describes and transcribes the piece.

1057 Lagorio, V.M. 'Three Vatican Mss containing Neumes' *Msct* 13 (1969) 40–1
L complements Bannister's list of sources (**72**) with classical texts. The sources she mentions include poems by Martianus Capella, Virgil, Lucan, Horace, etc.

German epics

1058 Jammers, E. 'Grundbegriffe der altdeutschen Versordnung' *ZdA* 92 (1963/4)
1059 241–8 (repr **F-16.**172–8) **1059** Bertau, K. 'Epenrezitation im deutschen MA'
· *Etudes germaniques* 20 (1965) 1–17, 1 p facss

1058 J discusses length, accent, and number of syllables in an attempt to demonstrate some underlying scheme which could illuminate the M rhythm. **1059** B shows very clearly how epics from different eras might have been performed.

1060 Hofmann, D. 'Die Frage des M Vortrags der altgermanischen Stabreimdichtung in philologischer Sicht' *ZdA* 92 (1963/4) 83–121 and E. Jammers ('Der Vortrag des altgermanischen Stabreimverses in musikwissenschaftlicher Sicht' *ZdA* 93 (1964) 1–13 (repr **F-16**.179–91)
I do not know of any other attempts to deal with the M setting of alliterative verse.

1061 Jammers, E. 'Das ma. deutsche Epos und die M' *Heidelberger Jahrbuch* 1 (1957) 31–90, 7 facss (repr **F-16**.105–71, 3 pll)
J describes early German sources with hints of notation, and interprets them. He shows that they were sung, suggesting 'singstimme' using various models, of which the *Accentus Moguntinus* was one (see **643**). K.H. Bertau and R. Stephan confirm, complement, and correct J's conclusions in *AdA* 71 (1958/9) 57–74. See also *DU* 11 (1959) Heft 2, 98–116 and *ZdA* 87 (1956/7) 253–70, 1 facs.

1062 Stavenhagen, L. 'Das *Petruslied*. Sein Alter und seine Herkunft' *WW* 17
1063 (1967) 21–8, 2 pp facss **1063** Hucke, H. 'Die Neumierung des althoch-
1064 deutschen *Petruslieds*' **F-28**.71–8 **1064** Ursprung, O. 'Das Freisinger *Petruslied*,' *Mf* 5 (1952) 17–21
1062 A date prior to 850 is possible. **1063** H examines the notation of this song, the earliest known song from Germany. **1064** U offers a transcription.

1065 Petzsch, C. 'Otfrids *cantus lectionis*,' *Euph* 56 (1962) 397–401
P argues that M is implied.

Chanson de geste and Rotrouenge

1066 Gennrich, Friedrich *Der M Vortrag der altfranzösischen Chansons de geste* (Halle 1923) 40
This is a general summary of the genre and its problems. See also *Acta* 27 (1955) 1–12.

1067 Van der Veen, J. 'Les Aspects M des chansons de geste' *Neophilologus* 41 (1957) 82–100, 1 facs
Matins readings of saints' lives, troped, removed from the church and sung in the vernacular, provide the most likely origin of the form and its M. See also *RdM* 27 (1948/9) 1–27; *ZrPh* 19 (1895) 370–4.

1068 Gennrich, Friedrich *Die altfranzösische Rotrouenge* (Halle 1925) v + 84 / rev
1069 J. Müller-Blattau *ZrPh* 45 (1925) 382–4 **1069** Gennrich 'Zu den altfranzösischen Rotrouenge' *ZrPh* 46 (1926) 335–41
1068 This gives the basic information. **1069** G examines the form by means of *contrafacta*. See also **1180**.

Italian songs

1070 Vecchi, G. 'I *Carmina mutinensia,*' *Conv* ns (1949) 729–39 **1071** Vecchi 'Il
1071 *Canto delle scolte modenesi*. La notazione M' *CNl* 10 (1950) 49–62
   1070 Comparison with liturgical texts, as well as the M, confirms the
ecclesiastical destination of the piece, as a vigil. **1071** V complements Ron-
caglia's literary studies in *CNl* 8 (1948) 5–46 and 205–22, by discussing and
transcribing the M of the 9c *ritmo* (transcribed also in **63**). The 'canto' and
the 'carmina' are the same piece: *O tu qui servas*.

Provençal songs

1072 Vecchi, G. 'Osservazioni ritmico-meliche sull'Alba bilingue del Cod.
1073 Vaticano Regina 1462' *SM* ns 18 (1952) 111–20 **1073** Camilli, A. 'L'*alba* del
1074 codice vaticano reginense 1462' *Studi di filologia italiana* 12 (1954)
335–44 **1074** Stäblein, B. 'Eine Hymnusmelodie als Vorlage einer provenzalischen Alba' **F-2.**II.889–94
   1072 V gives the literature, discusses and transcribes (N) the 11c song. **1073**
This is a literary study, with thorough bibliography. **1074** S claims to see
a melodic relationship. There is a facsimile in **72**, and an edition in **63**.

Latin songs

1075 Frei, W. 'Ein weltliches Neumen-Dokument aus dem 9. Jh. in Codex 36
der Burgerbibliothek Bern' *Schw Musikzeitung* 105 (1965) 7–10, 1 facs, 1 pl
   F offers an unrhythmicised transcription (N) of *Disticon in filomena*.

CONTINUATIONS OF THE SEQUENCE

Formally, and sometimes melodically, the Sequence appears to be continued in secular lyrics such as the *lai*, in elegies and *planctus*, and in dances
such as the *estampie*.

Lai

1076 Spanke, H. 'Zur Geschichte der lateinischen nichtliturgischen Sequenz'
1077 *Spec* 7 (1932) 367–82 **1077** Spanke 'Über das Fortleben der Sequenzenform
1078 in den romanischen Sprache' *ZrPh* 51 (1931) 309–34 **1078** Spanke 'Sequenz
und Lai' *SM* ns 11 (1938) 12–68
   1076 S discusses the continuation of the Sequence. **1077** Summarising with
a diagrammatic *stemma*, S tries to relate Sequence, lai, planctus, estampie,
trope, conductus. **1078** S analyses numerous lais: some are like Sequences
in form.

1079 Stäblein, B. 'Von der Sequenz zum Strophenlied' *Mf* 7 (1954) 257–
1080 68 **1080** Stäblein 'Die Schwanenklage. Zum Problem Lai-Planctus-

1081 Sequenz' F-11.491–502, 1 table   **1081** Vecchi, G. 'Sequenza e lai. A proposito di un ritmo di Abelardo' *SM* ns 16 (1943–50) 86–101, 4 pp facss
1079 S shows how an archaic Sequence is used to set a strophic poem. **1080** Referring to difficulties in deriving the lai from the Sequence, S sees the *planctus* as a possible intermediary. **1081** The *Lai de Pucelles* is a contrafactum of Abelard's *Planctus virginum Israel*: V transcribes them both.

1082 Reaney, G. 'Concerning the origins of the med. lai' *ML* 39 (1958) 343–6
Summarising the theories of its origin (German: from the Sequence; French: from Breton minstrelsy), R sees the influence of the Sequence no earlier than the 14c.

1083 Maillard, J. *Evolution et esthétique du lai lyrique* (Paris 1963) xvii + 395,
1084 indices, list of mss (xiv–xvii) **1084** Maillard 'Le Lai lyrique et la tradition
1085 celtique' *Ar Falz* 18 (1956) 58–61 **1085** Maillard 'Le Lai lyrique et les légendes
1086 arthuriennes' *Bull de la bibl soc intern. arthurienne* 9 (1957) 124–7 **1086** Mail-
1087 lard 'Problèmes M et littéraires du lai' *Quad* 2 (1958) 32–44 **1087** Maillard
'Le *Lai* et la *Note* du Chèvrefeuille' *MD* 13 (1959) 3–13
1083 This is a comprehensive survey of literary and M aspects. **1084** M gives the evidence pointing to Celtic influence, quoting from Romance and Gaelic-Irish literature. He transcribes *Le Lai de Tristan* (dipl) **1085** M transcribes (Rh) one example. **1086** M lists, with comments and sources, the known lais and, under the heading *descorts*, some *contrafacta* in the repertory. **1087** M thinks the lai which he transcribes may be an adaptation of the one *que Tristans fist*.

Planctus, conductus, dance

1088 Spanke, H. 'Ein lateinisches Liederbuch des 11. Jh.' *SM* ns 15 (1942)
1089 111–42 **1089** Schumann, O. 'Die jüngere Cambridger Liedersammlung' *SM*
ns 16 (1943–50) 48–85
1088 Spanke describes the contents of the older Cambridge *Liederbuch*, which include Sequences, *planctus*, political and love songs. **1089** Schumann describes the 12c musical leaves of the more recent Cambridge *Liederbuch* with an analytical inventory. He emphasizes the paleographical features and prints each of the texts.

1090 Spanke, H. 'Eine ma. Musikhs' *ZdA* 69 (1932) 49–70
Describing and inventorying a 13c ms, S shows the close connections between dance, trope, Sequence, conductus, and German lyric.

1091 Irtenkauf, W. 'Das Seckauer Cantionarium vom Jahre 1345 (Hs Graz 756)' *AMw* 13 (1956) 116–41
I inventories the source and discusses its tropes, cantiones, and conductus.

Peter Abaelard: Planctus

1092 Weinrich, 'Peter Abaelard as Musician' *MQ* 55 (1969) 295–312, 464–

1093 86 **1093** Weinrich 'Dolorum solatium. Text und M von Abaelards Planctus
1094 David' MlatJb 5 (1968) 59–78 **1094** Pietro Abelardo: I 'Planctus' ed G. Vecchi
1095 IST. DI FILOLOGIA ROMANZA DELL' U DI ROMA, Testi e Manuali 35 (Modena
1951) 119 + xxi, index **1095** Dronke, Peter Poetic Individuality in the MA (Oxford 1970) x + 234
1092 W discusses Abaelard's hymns and planctus, reconstructing the melodies from neumatic sources and describing rhythm and notation. Noting Abaelard's influence as a composer, he sees the planctus (elegies in content, Sequences in form) leading to the Marian liturgical planctus as well as the French secular lai. In **1093** W gives a comparative transcription of 3 sources illustrating this conclusion. **1094** This is an edition of the texts, with a musical appendix (Rh-N transcription). **1095** Ian Bent supplies an appendix, pp 202–31, in which he transcribes (Rh and N) the newly found planctus of Abaelard and the songs of Hildegard.

1096 Vecchi, G. 'Metodo compositorio e centonazione nella lirica del Medio Evo (Il Mundi renovatio di Adamo di S. Vittore)' Conv ns 22 (1954) 129–39
There are similarities of thought and language among Mundi renovatio, Veris grato tempore (Abaelard), and Victime paschali (Wipo).

Hildegard

1097 Gmelch, Joseph Die Kompositionen der hl. Hildegard (Düsseldorf 1913?) 37
1098 + 32 facss **1098** Hildegard von Bingen, Lieder ed Pudentia Barth, M.
1099 Immaculata Ritscher, Joseph Schmidt-Görg (Salzburg 1969) 328 + 2 facss, indices of songs and melodies **1099** Ritscher, M.I. 'Zur M der heiligen Hildegard' F-25.309–26
1097 There is a brief discussion of Hildegard, the ms and the M. **1098** After a brief introduction the songs are edited in diplomatic facss, and the texts printed with German translation. A critical commentary by R is to be published separately. **1099** R describes the sources and character of Hildegard's songs.

Miscellaneous

1100 Huglo, M. 'Une Elégie sur la mort de Guillaume le Conquérant' RdM 50
1101 (1964) 225–8 **1101** Vecchi, G. 'Il planctus di Gudino di Luxeuil: un ambiente
1102 scolastico, un ritmo, una melodia' Quad 1 (1956) 19–40 **1102** Wagenaar-Nolthenius, H. 'Der Planctus Iudei und der Gesang jüdischer Märtyrer in Blois anno 1171' F-9.II.881–5
1100 H describes and transcribes the planctus (Late 11c). **1101** V prints the text and melody (11c) and discusses the context at length. **1102** W sees considerable Jewish influence in this piece, which she transcribes (N).

1103 Peebles, B.M. 'O Roma Nobilis' American Benedictine Review 1 (1950) 67–92
P discusses this famous song.

1104 Suttina, L. 'Una cantilena med. contro la donne' *SM* 2 (1906/7) 457–60, 1 facs
S prints the text and a facsimile of the misogynist poem, set to M (12c?).

Conductus

This section concerns the monophonic and polyphonic conductus.

REFERENCE, SOURCES

1105 Gröninger, Eduard *Repertoire-Untersuchungen zum mehrstimmigen Notre Dame-Conductus* KBMf 2 (Regensburg 1939) 163
Dealing with the conductus repertory limited as in the title, G gives extensive concordance tables with bibliographical references. This is the only published tool giving access to the polyphonic Notre Dame repertory of conductus.

1106 Falck, Robert A. *The Structure of the Polyphonic and Monophonic Conductus Repertories* 3 vols (unpub diss, Brandeis U 1970) xii + 218; viii + 127; iv + 36
Vol 1: F concludes that larger ms collections are retrospective anthologies of smaller repertories. Vol 2 contains catalogues which are the most comprehensive on the repertory. It facilitates and complements **1105** by including the monophonic conductus and the polyphonic conductus outside Notre Dame. Pp 1–15 list 97 ms sources; 16–39 give concordance tables for the 9 largest mss; 41–127 list 390 compositions in alphabetical order. Vol 3 includes 13 transcriptions not previously published.

Surveys

1107 Ellinwood, L. 'The Conductus' *MQ* 27 (1941) 165–204 incl 15 pp transc +
1108 2 facss **1108** Handschin, J. 'Conductus-Spicilegien' *AMw* 9 (1952) 101–19
1107 E surveys the 12c and 13c repertory. **1108** H discusses the concept, liturgical use, terminology, and repertory.

1109 Steiner, R. 'Some Monophonic Latin Songs Composed Around 1200' *MQ* 52 (1966) 56–70
The conductus in the 10th fascicle of the Florence Ms vary widely in subject matter and M style.

1110 Rokseth, Y. 'Le Contrepoint double vers 1248' *Mélanges de musicologie offerts à M. Lionel de Laurencie* SOC FRANÇAISE DE MUSICOLOGIE 2e ser III and IV (Paris 1933) 5–13
R notes some general stylistic and textual points concerning the conductus.

Editions

1111 *Thirty-Five Conductus* ed Janet Knapp COLLEGIUM MUSICUM 6 (New Haven 1965) viii + 148 / rev L. Ellinwood *Notes* 23 (1966/7) 327–8
An easy to use performing edition of this Notre Dame style of ca 1200. Similar publications are needed throughout the field.

Specific repertories and pieces

1112 Falck, R. 'New Light on the Polyphonic Conductus Repertory in the St. Victor Ms' *JAMS* 23 (1970) 315–26
Disagreeing with 1110, F finds evidence that the repertory is contemporaneous with, or earlier than, Notre Dame.

1113 Schrade, L. 'Political Compositions in French M of the 12 and 13c' *AnnM* 1 (1953) 9–63 and 409: repr **F-27**.152–211
The author relates M, text, and culture, referring to topical allusions in conductus. After mentioning the difficulty of transcribing rhythm, he shows how three conductus are related to each other, to plainsong, to clausulae (cf 1114), and to the coronation service.

1114 Bukofzer, M.F. 'Interrelations between Conductus and Clausula' *AnnM* 1 (1953) 65–103
In this important article B shows that techniques of the clausula appear also in the conductus and proves that the latter does indeed sometimes borrow pre-existent material, whether secular, plainsong, or clausula itself. He discusses rhythmic transmutation.

1115 Spanke, H. 'Das Mosburger Graduale' *ZrPh* 50 (1930) 582–95
S describes a 14c ms which contains tropes, Sequences, and conductus, and gives an inventory of these with a brief analysis of each piece.

1116 Anderson, G.A. 'A Troped Offertorium-Conductus of the 13c' *JAMS* 24 (1971) 96–100
A transcribes and discusses a 'conductus,' unusual in that it is constructed on a borrowed melody. (Falck and Flindell criticise in *JAMS* 25 (1972) 120–2). Cf 1113 1114.

1117 Knapp, J. '*Quid tu vides, Jeremia*: Two Conductus in One' *JAMS* 16 (1963) 212–20 (M transc pp 219–20)
Text and concordances point to the conflation of independent compositions.

* Announced: *The Conductus Collection in Ms Wolfenbüttel 1206* ed Ethel Thurston and *The Unpublished Unica 3-part Conductus in the Florence Ms* ed Gordon Anderson

RHYTHM

Polyphonic conductus have problems similar to those of secular song, since neither texts nor M notation provide clear indications of rhythm. A particular difficulty is the relation between sections with text, set syllabically, and those without text, the two often using identical M: (a) does the modal rhythm of melismas provide the model for setting of a text, or (b) does the rhythm of the poetry provide the model for melismatic rhythm, or (c) do melismatic and syllabic sections have their own criteria? (See **1106**.19.)

1118 Reaney, G. 'A Note on Conductus Rhythm' **A-3**.219–21
Consonance can clarify rhythm.

1119 Husmann, H. 'Zur Grundlegung der M Rhythmik des mittellateinischen Liedes' *AMw* 9 (1952) 3–26
H discusses the application of rhythmic modes to the conductus.

1120 *Musica sine littera MwSb* 13/14 (1956) 38, 1 facs + separate booklet, xi + 32 dipl facss
The notation and rhythm of textless passages in organa, clausulae, and conductus are examined.

1121 Handschin, J. 'Zur Frage der Conductus-Rhythmik' *Acta* 24 (1952) 113–30
H concentrates on the interpretation of *longae*.

1122 Flindell, E.F. 'Syllabic Notation and Change of Mode' *Acta* 39 (1967)
1123 21–34 **1123** Anderson, G.A. 'Mode and Change of Mode in Notre-Dame
1124 Conductus' *Acta* 40 (1968) 92–114 **1124** Flindell, E.F. 'Puncta equivoca and Rhythmic Poetry: a Reply to G. Anderson' *Acta* 42 (1970) 238–48
1122 F discusses the adaptation of rhythmic mode to text. **1123** Correcting and complementing Flindell, A thinks change of mode is usually *extensio* or *fractio modi*. He includes transcriptions. **1124** F crucifies Anderson.

Arabic influence

There are two irreconcilable points of view represented by Ribera and Farmer opposed to Schneider, Spanke, and Li Gotti: the problem of the Arabic influence on the lyric has been investigated by few musicologists in print in the past decade. The following items have major references to the topic within a more general history: **1181 1182 1818**. Whatever the case, there can be no doubt that a majority of instruments and their names derive from Islam.

Surveys: pro **1127–30 1135**; anti **1136–9**   forms **1131–4**

1125 Farmer, H.G. 'Crusading Martial M' *ML* 30 (1949) 243–9 **1126** Farmer 'The
1126 Canon and Eschaquiel of the Arabs' *JRAS* (1926) 239–56
1125 Med. names for trumpets, drums, and many other instruments derive

from the Arabic. **1126** F justifies his derivation of the terms from Arabic and describes the instruments.

Authors in favour of Islamic influence

1127 Farmer, Henry G. *Historical Facts for the Arabian M Influence* (London 1930;
1128 repr Hildesheim 1970) xii + 376, b, footnotes **1128** Farmer 'The Arabic Influence on European M' *GUOS* 19 (1961/2) 1–15; repr as *The Oriental M Influence* (London 1964)
1127 This is still a standard work: F expands in book form many of his earlier articles, and comments on adverse reaction. **1128** Referring to and correcting the work of previous scholars, F demolishes their criticisms of his earlier work, reasserts the evidence, and gives additional arguments.

1129 Ribera, Julian *M in Ancient Arabia and Spain* transl and abridged Eleanor Hague and Marion Leffingwell from **1818**.III (London and Stanford 1929) frontisp facs, xvii + 283 + 4 pll (7 facss), ext index / rev O. Strunk *Art and Archaeology* 29 (1930) 143
The translator supplies a useful chronological table, pp xvi–xvii. As in the original, the M transcc (pp 237–62) should be disregarded. The author's claims for Arabic influence are regarded as extravagant. See also **1130**.

1130 Ribera, Julian *Historia de la M árabe med. y su influencia en la Española* BIBL HISPANIA, Colección de Manuales Hispania, ser G vol 1 (Madrid 1927) frontisp, 355
See also *Volkstum und Kultur der Romanen* 3 (1930) 258–78.

Specific relationships in form

1131 Salazar, A. 'Poesía y Música en las Primeras Formas de Versificación Rimada en Lengua Vulgar y sus Antecedentes en Lengua Latina en la Edad Media' *Filosofía y Letras* (U of Mexico) vol 4, no. 8 (1942) 287–349
The form of the zéjel (or muwaššah) underlies Spanish forms up to the 16c *villancico*, and is related to the earlier French rondeau, virelai, and ballade and to the Italian ballata, as well as to 12c troubadour and Latin forms. S refers to estampies and other secular types. He relates the *volta* to interjections (e.g., Eya; O! O! O!) and to catalectic lines in Sequences, tropes, etc. Less convincingly, he tries to show a connexion between the *piedi* and the *pes* of *rondellus* forms.

1132 Le Gentil, Pierre *Le Virelai et le Villancico. Le problème des origines arabes* COLLECTION PORTUGAISE 9 (Paris 1954) v + 279
L refers constantly to M forms but not to the M.

1133 García Gómez, E. 'La lírica hispano-árabe y la aparicíon de la lírica
1134 románica' *Al-Andalús* 21 (1956) 303–38 **1134** García Gómez 'La canción famosa "Calvi vi Calvi/Calvi aravi"' *Al-Andalús* 21 (1956) 1–18, 215–16
1133 G traces the literary evolution of the muwaššah and the relations

between it and the jarŷa and zéjel. **1134** G recognizes the song as a jarŷa, a souvenir of the muwaššah.

1135 Furness, C.J. 'The Interpretation and Probable Derivation of the M Notation in the "Aucassin et Nicolette" Ms' *MLR* 24 (1929) 143–52
F comments on previous transcriptions and discussions of the M. Experience with present-day Arabian M suggests possible answers to some problems.

Authors opposed to Islamic influence

1136 Schneider, M. 'A Propósito del Inflúyo Arabe' *AnuarioM* 1 (1946) 31–141, 1 map
With copious documented examples S maintains that similarities between Spanish and Arabic M reflect only a culture common to all the Mediterranean. See also **B-2**.175–81.

1137 Chailley, J. 'Notes sur les Troubadours, les Versus et la Question arabe'
1138 F-12.118–28 **1138** Spanke, H. 'La Teoría Arabe sobre el Origen de la Lírica Románica' *AnuarioM* 1 (1946) 5–18
1137 C reviews previous opinions. He reconfirms the influence of *versus* on troubadour, which eliminates the need for direct Arab influence. **1138** The troubadours did not need Arabic influence.

1139 Li Gotti, E. 'La "tesi araba" sulle "origini" della lirica romanza' *Studi medievali in onore di Antonino De Stefano* SOC SICILIANA PER LA STORIA PATRIA (Palermo 1956) 297–339 / rev I. Pope *Spec* 34 (1959) 477–81
This is mainly a literary study, with excellent bibliography. L believes that Arabic M was example rather than ancestor.

Vernacular song in Provence and northern France

This section concerns the Troubadour and Trouvère repertories. Since 1950 literary scholars have thoroughly re-examined the Provençal and Old French lyric, rendering much older material less useful or obsolete. Re-examination of the musical repertories has not yet been undertaken in a similarly comprehensive fashion.

REFERENCE, BIBLIOGRAPHY, SOURCES

These items describe the manuscripts, the distribution of the repertory, and list texts and refrains.

1140 Schwan, Eduard *Die altfranzösische Liederhandschriften, ihre Verhältniss, ihre Entstehung, und ihre Bestimmung* (Berlin 1886) viii + 275

This is a comparative examination of the sources of vernacular songs, whose conclusions have formed the basis for all subsequent work. S's ms sigla, still in use, are listed on pp 2–4.

1141 *Gaston Raynauds Bibliographie des altfranzösischen Liedes* ed and completed Hans Spanke 1st part MUSICOLOGICA 1 (Leiden 1955) viii + 286 / rev W. Ziltener *ZrPh* 77 (1961) 70–4 (complementary, correcting, and textual) and J. Chailley *RdM* 39 (1957) 104–6
S completes only vol 2 of Raynaud's work and was killed before writing parts 2 and 3. This catalogue lists sources, editions, poets, and songs (alphabetically by rhyme), with their location and poetic scheme.

1142 *Bibliographisches Verzeichnis des französischen Refrains des 12. und 13. Jh.* SMMA 14 (1964) viii + 68
This consists mostly of reprints of refrain indices published earlier by Gennrich (the refrain numbers are consecutive from index to index, except from index 1 to index 2, where the numbering jumps from 1276 to 1281. Pp 1–36 reprint the list in vol 2 of 1143; 37–49 reprint the one in 1144, which refers to 1392, unpublished when 1144 appeared; 50–9 list refrains in *chansons à refrain*, indexing 1143.II.255–90 and referring to 1141; 60–8 list addenda. The editor says, with some justice, that all four lists should be combined in a single index. The work is complemented and corrected by 1145.

1143 Gennrich, Friedrich *Rondeaux, Virelais und Balladen aus dem Ende des XII., dem XIII. und dem ersten den über Drittel des XIV. Jh., mit überlieferten Melodien* 2 vols GES FÜR ROMANISCHE LITERATUR 43, 47 (Dresden 1920 or 1921, Göttingen 1927) xvi + 388; xvi + 352 / rev Y. Rokseth *SM* ns 4 (1931) 204–9
These volumes are confusing and complex to use, although indispensable for work in the 13c. There are detailed chapter headings in the list of contents, but only brief bibliographical references. Vol 1 presents the texts and melodies (Rh), sometimes reconstructed, of 12–14c secular songs thought to be in rondeaux, virelai, or ballade form (but see 1176). It has an index of texts but not of names or mss. Vol 2 contains editorial notes, biographical and bibliographical information, an index of refrains in both volumes, by rhyme (also printed in 1142), and an index of motets. It has an appendix of material not in volume 1, including transcriptions of refrains in *chansons à refrain*. Indices of refrains in motets are in 1144 and 1142, indices of refrains in *chansons à refrain* are in 1142. A third volume was published much later: see 1175.

1144 Gennrich, F. 'Refrain-Studien' *ZrPh* 71 (1955) 365–90
G claims that refrains did not originate from popular song or folksong but were specially composed and taken over later into chansons and motets. The article includes a list of refrains used in motets, indexed by rhyme.

1145 Van den Boogaard, Nico H.J. ed *Rondeaux et refrains du XIIe siècle au début du XIVᵉ* BIBL FRANÇAISE ET ROMANE, Ser D: Initiation, textes et documents, 3 (Paris 1969) 342

Correcting and complementing **1142**, this indispensable catalogue lists refrains and rondeaux alphabetically with tables showing concordances between them and with motets. Each rondeau is also printed complete. There are also lists of mss containing (a) *chansons à refrain* and *chansons avec des refrains*, (b) motets with refrains, (c) *Romans* with refrains. The catalogue serves as a concordance to **1141**, **1142**, **1143**, and **1392**.

Anthologies

1146 Aubry, Pierre *Trouvères and Troubadours* transl Claude Aveling from the 2nd French ed (revd) (New York 1969) vi + 174, 1 facs
This includes numerous melodies with complete texts and English translations.

1147 *Exempla altfranzösischer Lyrik* MwSb 17 (1958) xv, 3 facss + 51
This is an edition of 40 songs, with index and list of mss.

The poet-musicians

These items deal with terminology, social status, and biography.

1148 Wright, L.M. 'Misconceptions concerning the troubadours, trouvères and minstrels' *ML* 48 (1967) 35–9
W clarifies the terms *jongleur, ménestrel, troubadour,* and *trouvère,* basing conclusions about their social status on contemporary accounts.

1149 Berger, Roger *Le Nécrologe de la Confrérie des jongleurs et des bourgeois d'Arras (1194–1361)* 2 vols MEM DE LA COMMISSION DEPARTEMENTALE DES MON HIST DU PAS-DE-CALAIS 11² and 13² (Arras 1963, 1970) 186 / rev R. Bossuat *MoyA* ser 4, 20 (1965) 342–3
B edits and indexes a 14c ms listing more than 11,000 names. Vol 2 introduces the subject, with a history of the confrérie.

1150 Boutière, Jean, and A.-H. Schutz *Biographies des troubadours* OHIO STATE U CONTRIBUTIONS IN LANGUAGES AND LITERATURE 14 (2nd ed, Paris 1964) xxxii + 451, index of names, etc
This book prints vitas from 13c and 14c Provençal mss.

1151 Pillet, Alfred, and Henry Carstens *Bibliographie der Troubadours* SCHRIFTEN DER KÖNIGSBERGER GELEHRTEN GES, sonderreihe 3 (Halle 1933) xliv + 518, list of mss / rev K. Lewent *Archiv für das Studium der neueren Sprachen und Literaturen* 166 (1934) 120–3
This is a bibliographical dictionary by poet and incipit and by rhyme. It is out of date and difficult to use, but there is nothing better. See **1183**.

1152 Petersen-Dyggve, Holger *Onomastique des trouvères* STT, ser B; 30 (Helsinki 1934) 255 / rev A. Jeanroy *Rom* 63 (1937) 114–15
This catalogue lists names of authors, and names occurring in trouvère chansons. A bibliography is included.

1153 Petersen-Dyggve, Holger *Trouvères et protecteurs des trouvères dans les cours seigneuriales de France* STT, ser B; 50 (Helsinki 1942) 39–247, genealogical tables, etc, index of names, b
P edits chansons with comments and bio-historical remarks. The M is not discussed.

TRANSMISSION AND VARIANTS

1154 Gennrich, F. 'Grundsätzliches zu den Troubadour- und Trouvèreweisen' *ZrPh* 57 (1937) 31–56
G describes errors and distinguishes them from variants.

1155 Gennrich, F. 'Die Repertoire-Theorie' *ZfSL* 66 (1956) 81–108
Variants in 13c secular song must result from oral rather than written transmission.

1156 VanderWerf, H. 'The trouvère chansons as creations of a notationless M culture' *CM* 1 (1965) 61–8
Rejecting Gennrich's and Bittinger's approach, V follows Aubry's suggestion that discrepancies in concordances are legitimate variants rather than errors. The legitimacy of several versions applies also to the rhythmic and (melodic) modal interpretation.

1157 Karp, T. 'The Trouvère Ms Tradition' E-8.25–52
On the basis of limited evidence, K reviews the filiation of the sources, concludes that a written rather than oral tradition is present, and suggests methods of presenting variant readings.

1158 Karp, T. 'Modal Variants in Med. Secular Monophony' *The Commonwealth of M in Honor of Curt Sachs* ed Gustave Reese and Rose Brandel (Glencoe 1964) 118–29
Contrafacta and concordances often have intentional changes in 'modal' characteristics: K examines briefly some concepts of mode.

1159 Zingerle, Hans *Tonalität und Melodieführung in den Klauseln der Troubadours- und Trouvèreslieder* (Tutzing and Munich 1958) 37

RHYTHM

This crucial and controversial issue is explained succinctly by Olive Sayce in her review of 1160. The most commonly held opinion is that, lacking a clear textual rhythm and lacking precise musical notation, songs should be transcribed according to the system of rhythmic modes (see 170–9).

Although there is some question (see *AMw* 10 (1953) **213–22** and **F-2.1.**315–30), Beck is regarded as the originator of this theory, which he expounds in *Die Melodien der Troubadours* (**1191**).

1160 Kippenberg, Burkhard *Der Rhythmus im Minnesang* MTU 3 (Munich 1962) viii + 236 + 4 facss, critical and informative b, index / rev O. Sayce *MLR* 58 (1963) 600–2
K reviews editions and ms sources, their notation and its rhythmic implications, and the various theories and methods of transcription, and lists contrafacta.

1161 Sesini, U. rev of J.B. Beck *Le Melodie dei Trovadori* (Italian transl of **1191**)
1162 *SM* ns 11 (1938) 210–23 **1162** Beck, J.B. 'Der Takt in den Musikaufzeichnungen des XII. und XIII. Jh., vornehmlich in den Liedern der Troubadours und Trouvères' **F-24.**166–84
1161 S cogently characterises the modal theory as untenable. **1162** Replying to S's criticisms, B again argues the case for modal rhythm. See also *RMI* 57 (1955) 23–47.

The rhythmic mode is chosen according to the poetic scheme. Ambiguities result in extensions of the modal system until the original schemes are indistinguishable.

1163 Husmann, H. 'Zur Rhythmik des Trouvèregesanges' *Mf* 5 (1952)
1164 110–31 **1164** Husmann 'Das Prinzip der Silbenzählung im Lied des zentra-
1165 len MA' *Mf* 6 (1953) 8–23 **1165** Husmann 'Das System der modalen
1166 Rhythmik' *AMw* 11 (1954) 1–38 **1166** Anglès, H. 'Der Rhythmus in der Melodik ma. Lyrik' **A-4.1.**3–11 (discussed in II.43–7)
1163 H rejects rhythmically free interpretations and advocates strict use of all rhythmic modes, in relation to the poetic scheme. **1164** H chooses the rhythm on the basis of accent and syllable count. **1165** Giving numerous transcriptions, H widens the usual definition of the modes, and illustrates how different poetic metres may fit their *ordines*. Relating all 6 modes to 1st, 2nd, or 5th by means of upbeats and modifications, H renders them indistinguishable from each other. **1166** Anglès argues that rhythm is to be deduced from the notation rather than from metre or text-accents, but gives little evidence. The discussion is more informative, summarising the different views up to 1961.

Modal freedom is justified by using, surely retroactively, evidence from polyphonic adaptation of the material.

1167 Gennrich, F. 'Grundsätzliches zur Rhythmik der ma. Monodie' *Mf* 7 (1954) 150–76
Disagreeing with Husmann (**1163**), G uses evidence from motet-refrains, conductus quotations, and textual accentuation to support the theory of mixed and freer modal interpretation.

1168 Anglès, H. 'Die zwei Arten der Mensuralnotation der Monodie des MA' **A-3**.56–7
A finds a mensural-modal as well as a non-modal notation.

1169 Gennrich, F. 'Streifzüge durch die erweiterte Modaltheorie' *AMw* 18 (1961) 126–40
Disagreeing with Anglès, G reasserts modal interpretation, stressing the use of *extensio* and *fractio modi*.

1170 *Übertragungsmaterial zur 'Rhythmik der Ars antiqua'* MwSb 8 (1954) 16 + separate booklet of 40 dipl facss
This is a schematization of rhythmic patterns drawn from 101 examples of monophony of the Ars Antiqua. G shows that modal rhythms were not exclusively used.

Modal rhythms are either too free to be meaningful, or too rigid to be usable. VanderWerf transfers the responsibility back to the philologist for assistance with the textual rhythm, but his theory fails to help with melismatic passages.

1171 VanderWerf, H. 'Deklamatorischer Rhythmus in den Chansons der
1172 Trouvères' *Mf* 20 (1967) 122–44 **1172** Maddrell, J.E. '*Mensura* and the Rhythm of Med. Monodic Song' and H. VanderWerf 'Concerning the Measurability of Med. M' *CM* 10 (1970) 64–9 and 69–73
1171 In this important article V rejects previous hypotheses and methods. He concludes that most chansons were in free declamatory rhythm, and in this way transcribes three songs with variants. **1172** Questioning V's conclusion, M claims that Grocheo's *non ita praecise mensurata* does not justify 'free rhythm' but means 'not according to the exact (rhythmic and other) rules of composition.' V replies, points to some faults in M's argument, and turns to the sources of the M rather than theory: his editorial suggestions are more practical. The two authors are not really basically opposed.

THE FORMS

Descort and Lai

1173 *Lais et Descorts français du XIII siècle* ed Alfred Jeanroy, Louis Brandin, and
1174 Pierre Aubry MMC 3 (Paris 1901; repr 1970) xxiv, 3 facss + 171, glossary, index

/ rev A. Restori *RMI* 8 (1901) 1030–43 **1174** Maillard, J. 'Problèmes M et lit-téraires du Descort' **F-12**.388–409

1173 The authors edit the texts and music (Sq) with an introduction. **1174** M lists and analyses Provençal and French examples of the genre.

Rondeau

1175 *Das altfranzösische Rondeau und Virelai im 12. und 13. Jh.* SMMA 10 (1963) vi
1176 + 128, M exx; vol 3 of **1143** **1176** Apel, W. 'Rondeaux, Virelais, and Ballades
1177 in French 13c Song' *JAMS* 7 (1954) 121–30; see also 8 (1955) 77–8 **1177** Spanke,
1178 H. 'Das lateinische Rondeau' *ZfSL* 53 (1930) 113–48 **1178** Aubry, P. 'Refrains
et rondeaux du XIIIe siècle' **F-24**.213–29

1175 This is a formal and poetic discussion. It forms vol 3 of **1143**. In **1176**
A shows that Gennrich's claims (**1143**) are the result of manipulation. **1177**
S lists the pieces in M and textual sources (13c), with the M and metrical
form, text of refrain, and bibliographical references. He then disusses the
form and its origins. **1178** A indentifies M settings of refrains in the *Roman
de Renart le Nouvel.*

Rondellus and rota

1179 Falck, R. '*Rondellus*, Canon and related Types before 1300' *JAMS* 25 (1972)
38–57
Some apparently monophonic songs are in fact canons. The style of the
Summer canon is not peculiar to England nor surprisingly early. F compares
monophonic refrain-forms, and translates theoretical passages.

1180 Orenstein, Herta *Die Refrainformen im Chansonnier de l'Arsenal* MS 19 (New
York 1970) v + 184, num transcc (Rh), index of incipits
O analyses the (melodic) relationship of refrain to other parts of the song,
concluding that it became progressively looser. Formally refrain songs fall
into two groups characterised by the *rotrouenge* and the *chanson avec des
refrains.*

TROUBADOURS

Surveys and catalogues

1180a Baehr, Rudolf ed *Der provenzalische Minnesang* WEGE DER FORSCHUNG 6
(Darmstadt 1967) xi + 531 / rev F. Pirot *MoyA* 75 (1969) 396–8
B reprints articles from various disciplines on research, origins, problems,
etc, and includes comprehensive bibliographies.

1181 Briffault, Robert S. *The Troubadours* transl by the author, ed Lawrence F.
Koons (Bloomington 1965) xvi + 296, 7 facss / rev W. McBain *MLJ* 49 (1965)
446–7

Although B ignores the M, this is a literary survey and deals with the Arabic question at some length.

1182 Davenson, Henri (pseud Henri Marrou) *Les Troubadours* LE TEMPS QUI COURT 23 (Paris 1961) 192, num pll, facss, M exx, maps, etc / rev C.A. *Quaderni, RaM* 3 (1965) 226–7
This is a popular, comprehensive, and interesting survey. Pp 77–95 deal with M, and pp 109–29 with the Arabic theory and St Martial. The author translates the texts of his examples.

1183 *Répertoire métrique de la poésie des troubadours* comp István Frank 2 vols BEHE 302 and 308 (Paris 1953, 1957) lii + 195; 232 /rev J. Maillard *RdM* 42 (1958) 228–30
This is a comprehensive catalogue of the poetic schemes according to metre, syllable-count, rhyme, etc. It has a bibliography, list of poets and their poems, and lists by genre (e.g., *chansons à refrain, refrains, mots-refrains, coblas, ballades, dansas, descorts*).

1184 Lommatzsch, Erhard *Leben und Lieder der provenzalischen Troubadours.* 1: *Minnelieder* 2: *Lieder verschiedener Gattung* (Berlin 1957–9) viii + 216
These are textual editions; in vol 2 L prints Gennrich's M transcriptions (Rh) pp 159–68.

Origins

1185 Chailley, J. 'Les premiers troubadours et les versus de l'école d'Aquitaine' *Rom* 76 (1955) 212–39
C makes a good case for the origin of the troubadour genres in earlier paraliturgical genres of the St Martial school.

1186 Collaer, P. 'Moyen-âge et traditions populaires' **F-36**.205–13
C transcribes some present-day folksongs but leaves it 'to the reader to see if there are analogies with some troubadour songs.' See also *AnuarioM* 14 (1959) 3–23, 7 pp transcc and 15 (1960) 3–20, 13 pp transcc.

Styles and performance: Descantar

1187 Perrin, R.H. 'Some Notes on Troubadour Melodic Types' *JAMS* 9 (1956)
1188 12–18 **1188** Stäblein, B. 'Zur Stilistik der Troubadour-Melodien' *Acta* 38 (1966) 27–46
1187 P translates some relevant song texts. He states the names for poetic forms are not valid for the M. **1188** S tries to deduce stylistic differences.

1189 Perrin, R.H. 'Descant and Troubadour Melodies: A Problem in Terms'
1190 *JAMS* 16 (1963) 313–24 **1190** Perrin 'On Some Musical References in Old Provençal Literature' *JAMS* 9 (1956) 239–40
1189 *Descantar* in the troubadour repertory refers to deliberate imitation by later troubadours, not to polyphonic singing. **1190** The word *descantar* does not nesessarily have implications of polyphony.

Editions and facsimiles

1191 Beck, Jean Baptiste *Die Melodien der Troubadours* (Strasbourg 1908) viii + 202, indices of names and incipits / rev J. Wolf *ZIMG* 10 (1909) 129–33; A. Guesnon *MoyA* 21 (1908) 323–33; see also **1161**
B describes the sources and notation. He outlines the theory of modal rhythm for the songs and gives many transcriptions.

1192 *Der M Nachlass der Troubadours.* I: *Kritische Ausgabe der Melodien*; II: *Kommentar*; III: *Prolegomena* SMMA 3, 4, and 15 (1958; 1960; 1965) xvi + 300, index of songs by type; viii + 91, b, M exx, tables; xx + 212, M exx, indices of names and words
This is a critical edition (Rh) with an introduction on the transmission of med. M and culture, the origins of troubadour M, the authors and their milieu.

1193 Maillard, Jean (with preface by Jacques Chailley) *Anthologie de Chants de Troubadours* (Paris 1967) xvi + 60 + 8 / rev H. VanderWerf *Notes* 25 (1968/9) 585–6
M edits 21 songs (Rh) with French translations and some comments.

Milan Canzoniere

1194 *Le Melodie trobadoriche nel Canzoniere provenzale della Biblioteca Ambrosiana (R.71 sup.)* ed Ugo Sesini (Turin 1942) vii + 281 + 45 facss / rev M. Bukofzer *Spec* 23 (1948) 506–7
S describes the source and its contents, and transcribes the melodies (Rh) with an analysis of each. This is a reprint of *SM* ns 12 (1939) 1–101 and 13 (1940) 1–107 and 14 (1941) 31–105 and 15 (1942) 189–90 + 24 pp facss (because of the 17-year interval between vol 15 (1942) and vol 16 (1950), during which time the author died, plates xxv–xlv, to have appeared in vol 16 (see vol 15.189), were not published: they are in the reprint).

Other editions

1195 *Lo Gai Saber* MwSb 18/19 (1959) viii + 130
This is an edition of 50 songs with notes on Provençal grammar and glossary.

*1196 Sesini, Ugo, and Rachele Maragliano Mori 24 *Canzoni Trobadoriche* (Bologna 1948) / rev F. Egidi *Conv* 11 (1949) 150–3

Bernard de Ventadorn

1197 Wellesz, Egon ed M *of the Troubadours: Six Songs in Provençal by Bernard de Ventadorn* (Oxford 1947) vii + 2–13
W provides translations, and transcriptions (Rh) with simple editorial accompaniment.

Other troubadours

1198 Machabey, A. *'Licet eger'* in 'La M et les musiciens en Normandie ...' *Etudes Normandes* 83 (Rouen 1957) 229–32, 1 facs
M transcribes and discusses Gautier de Chatillon's song (ca 1180) violently attacking Rome.

1199 Anglès, H. 'Les Melodies del trobador Guiraut Riquier' *Estudis Universitaris Catalans* 11 (1926) 1–78
This is an edition (Rh), with introduction, of the 48 songs of the 13c troubadour.

1200 Aston, S.C. *Peirol, Troubadour of Auvergne* (Cambridge 1953) viii + 190, glossary + 19 facss
All the facsimiles are of leaves with M.

1201 Sesini, U. 'Piere Vidal e la sua opera musicale' *RaM* 16 (1943) 25–33, 65–95
S gives biographical information, then transcribes (Rh) 12 chansons, with musical analysis and translation into Italian of the texts.

TROUVERES

Sources

Most of these entries are facsimiles, some including transcriptions.

Chansonnier d'Arras
1202 *Le Chansonnier d'Arras* ed Alfred Jeanroy, SATF (Paris 1925) 19 + fos 152^r–160^v
1203 + 129^r–151^v (pll i–lxiv) **1203** Gennrich, F. 'Der Chansonnier d'Arras' *ZrPh* 46 (1926) 325–35
1202 This is a facsimile of part of a major source: several leaves of the original are lost and the ms is now misbound. The facsimile arranges them in the proper order. **1203** G gives a description, bibliography, inventory, and index of incipits.

Chansonnier de l'Arsenal
1204 *Le Chansonnier de l'Arsenal* ed Pierre Aubry with introduction by Alfred Jeanroy PUBL DE LA SOC INTERN. DE M (Paris ca 1900–10) 64 (transcc) + 384 facss
This was originally intended to be 2 volumes: 1. facsimile, 2. transcriptions and introduction. The latter was not published; vol 1 includes some transcriptions (Rh).

Chansonnier Cangé
1205 *Le Chansonnier Cangé* ed Jean B. Beck 2 vols CORPUS CANTILENARUM MEDII

AEVI, ser 1: 1 (Philadelphia and Paris 1927; repr New York 1965) xxxiii +
287 pp facss; 76 + 343 / rev H. Spanke *ZfSL* 52 (1929) 165–83
Vol 1 is a facsimile, with introduction and description of a major collection
of 13c vernacular chansons. It includes an inventory with concordances and
a list of names of trouvères and editions. Vol 2 is an old-fashioned edition,
with an introduction dealing with the ms, language, and versification. It
has analytical tables of poetic and M forms, and an index of names. The
edition is usable as a basis for performance, but its rhythmic principles
should be reviewed in the light of recent theories.

Chansonnier du Roi, and du Roi de Navarre
1206 *Le Manuscrit du Roi* ed Jean B. Beck and Louise Beck 2 vols CORPUS
CANTILENARUM MEDII AEVI, ser 1: 2 (Philadelphia 1938) xxxi + fos I–IV +
fos 2–209 + fos I–XXI; iii + 209, list of names and miniatures
Vol 1 includes textual inventories of the *Ms du Roi* and an independent section of it, the *Chansonnier du Roi de Navarre*, and gives facsimiles of each
(fos 2–209 and I–XXI). The foliation of this reproduction bears no relationship to that of the original. Vol 2 prints the original index, with a comprehensive description of the source and its contents.

Chansonnier de Saint-Germain-des-Prés
1207 *Le Chansonnier français de Saint-Germain-des-Prés* ed Paul Meyer and Gaston
Raynaud SATF (Paris 1892) ii + 173 fos facss
The second volume, with commentary, never appeared.

Other manuscripts and fragments
1208 Schubert, Johann *Die Handschrift Paris, Bibl. nat. fr. 1591* (Frankfurt am Main
1209 1963) 204 **1209** Spaziani, Marcello *Il Canzoniere francese di Siena (Bibl. Communale, H-X-36). Introduzione, testo critico e traduzione* BIBL DELL' 'ARCHIVUM
ROMANICUM' ser 1: 46 (Florence 1957) v + 356 + 1 facs, index of names, glossary, list of songs, b / rev E. Vuolo *CNl* 17 (1957) 235–75
1208 S describes the ms (13c) and its contents. **1209** S describes the ms, its
concordances, attributions, and language, and edits the texts with their variants.

1210 Dennis, R.G. 'Ein wiedergefundenes Fragment eines Chansonnier aus dem
13. Jh.' *Mf* 12 (1959) 462–6
D relates this to the Frankfurt and Metz fragments. See **1213**.

1211 Karp, T. 'A Lost Med. Chansonnier' *MQ* 48 (1962) 50–67
K shows that an obscure early 19c report refers to the lost Chansonnier de
Mesmes, and examines the relationship of that ms to the extant sources.

1212 Gennrich, F. 'Die altfranzösische Liederhs London, BM, Egerton 274' *ZrPh*
1213 45 (1925) 402–44, 1 facs **1213** Gennrich 'Das Frankfurter Fragment einer
altfranzösischen Liederhs' *ZrPh* 42 (1922) 726–40 (see **1210**)

These include descriptions, inventories, bibliography, and transcriptions (Rh).

Styles

1214 Anglès, H. 'Die volkstümlichen Melodien bei den Trouvères' **F-21**.15-22
From experience A feels the influence of folk-tunes.

1215 VanderWerf, H. 'Recitative Melodies in Trouvère Chansons' **F-36**.231–40
With comparative examples V shows that many songs consist basically of intonation, reciting-note, termination.

1216 Karp, T. 'Borrowed Material in Trouvère M' *Acta* 34 (1962) 87–101
K contrasts borrowing and fortuitous re-use of the same melodic formula.

Texts

1217 Dragonetti, Roger *La Technique poétique des trouvères dans la chanson courtoise*
WERKEN UITGEGEVEN DOOR DE FACULTEIT VAN DE LETTEREN EN WIJSBE-
GEERTE 127° Aflevering (Bruges 1960) 702, ext b
This is a 'contribution to the study of med. rhetoric.'

1218 Steffens, G. 'Die altfranzösische Liederhs der Bodleiana in Oxford, Douce
308' *Archiv für das Studium der neueren Sprache und Literatur* 98 (1897) 59–80
and 343–82; 99 (1897) 77–100, 1 facs and 339–88
This is a 'diplomatic' edition of the texts. The second section begins *Vesci
labecelaire des estampies.*

Anthologies

1219 *Anthologie de chants de trouvères* ed Jean Maillard and Jacques Chailley (Paris
1967) 87
M and C edit 26 songs (Rh) with French translations appended and some
commentary.

Trouvères: Individual composers

Most items are editions with introductions.

Adam de la Halle
1220 *The Lyric Works of Adam de la Hale* (1236–87) ed Nigel E. Wilkins, CMM 44
1221 (1967) xiv + 82, list of mss and previous editions 1221 *Adam de la Halle. Le
1222 Jeu de Robin et de Marion. Li Rondel Adam* MwSb 20 (1962) 58 1222 Chailley,
J. 'La nature M du Jeu de Robin et Marion' *Mélanges d'histoire ... offerts à Gustave Cohen* (Paris 1950) 111–17

1220 This is an edition of the chansons, jeux-partis, rondeaux, and motets with an appendix of possible motets by Adam. **1221** This is an edition with glossary and notes. **1222** Adam did not compose the melodies in the Jeu because he wished, in the usual manner of *refrains-centons*, to use well-known tunes. He draws a wide range.

Charles d'Anjou
1223 *Roi-trouvère du XIIIᵉ siècle, Charles d'Anjou* ed Jean Maillard, MSD 18 (1967; revd repr of *MD* 21 (1967) 7–66) 73 + 3 pll
This is a review of the life, times, and character of Charles and of his relation to the chanson tradition. The author lists the sources of his compositions and prints the M (Rh) and texts with commentary. He briefly mentions the rhythmic problem.

Conon de Béthune
1224 Gennrich, F. 'Zu den Liedern des Conon de Béthune' *ZrPh* 42 (1922) 231–41
G discusses Conon's songs as *contrafacta* and as models.

Ernoul de Gastinois
1225 Maillard, J. 'Lais et chansons d'Ernoul de Gastinois' *MD* 17 (1963) 21–56; repr in MSD 15 (1964) 42
After a brief description of the sources and a biography, M gives an annotated edition (Rh) of all Ernoul's compositions.

Gautier de Coincy
1226 *Les chansons à la Vierge de Gautier de Coinci* ed Jacques Chailley, PUBL DE LA SOC FRANÇAISE DE MUSICOLOGIE, ser 1: 15 (Paris 1959) v + 193 / rev A. Machabey *Rom* 81 (1960) 402–5
With indices and a historical essay C edits the songs in parallel versions (Rh, dipl facss, and N), and then edits the texts.

Henri, duc de Brabant
1227 *L'Oeuvre lyrique d'Henri III, duc de Brabant* ed Albert Henry (Bruges 1948) 120 + 13 pll and facss / rev E.B. Ham *Romance Philology* 3 (1949/50) 206–10
This is mainly a text edition, but each poem is followed by Gennrich's M transcription together with a detailed analysis.

Jacques de Cysoing
1228 Zitzmann, R. 'Die lieder des Jacques de Cysoing' *ZrPh* 65 (1949) 1–27
This is a basic description of the composer (13c) and his works, which are poorly transcribed (Rh).

Jehan Lescurel
1229 *Jehan Lescurel, Collected Works* ed Nigel E. Wilkins, CMM 30 (1966) 10 unnum pp + vii + 12 facss + 40
This is an edition. Another is in SMMA 13 (1964).

Simon d'Authie

1230 Gennrich, F. 'Simon d'Authie, Ein pikardischer Sänger' ZrPh 67 (1951)
49–104
This is a biography and complete edition (Rh).

LATIN LYRICS AND SACRED SONGS

Adam de la Bassée

1231 *Adam de la Bassée. Ludus super Anticlaudianum* ed Paul Bayart (Tourcoing
1232 1930) cvi + 340, 30 facss **1232** Hughes, Andrew 'The *Ludus super Anti-*
claudianum of Adam de la Bassée' *JAMS* 23 (1970) 1–25
1231 This is an edition with substantial introduction. Pp 222–51 have facsimiles of the leaves with M: 254–325 transcribe the M, in old-fashioned
style. In M respects this is superseded by **1232**. The *Ludus* (ca 1280) uses
the framework of Mass and Offices to incorporate an anthology of contemporary M. H includes a complete list of pieces.

John of Garlandia

1233 Machabey, A. 'Jean de Garlande, compositeur' *RM* no. 221 (1953)
1234 20–22 **1234** Machabey and G. Vecchi 'Remarques sur la séquence *Aula ver-*
1235 *nat virginalis*,' *Quad* 2 (1958) 89–96 + 2 facss **1235** Park, B.A. and E.S. Dallas
'A *Sequentia cum Prosa* by John of Garlandia' *MH* 15 (1963) 54–68
1233 M attributes M as well as text of *Aula vernat* to Garlandia. **1234** M raises
the question of attribution to John of Garlandia: V reaffirms the possibility
of John's authorship of both text and M. See also *Quad* 1 (1956) 256–68. **1235**
The M is certainly by Garlandia and demonstrates a practical application
of his poetico-musical theories (see **985**).

1236 *Cantilenae Piae. 31 altfranzösische geistliche Lieder* ... MwSb 24 (1966) xii +
51, 3 facss
This is an edition (Rh) of sacred songs with brief analysis.

The lyric in Germany and Switzerland: Minnesinger

REFERENCE

A standard reference work is B. Kippenberg's *Der Rhythmus im Minnesang*
(**1160**).

1237 Linker, Robert W. *M of the Minnesinger and early Meistersinger: a Bibliography*

U OF NORTH CAROLINA STUDIES IN THE GERMANIC LANGUAGES AND LITERATURES 32 (Chapel Hill 1961) frontisp facs, xvi + 79 / rev O. Sayce *MLR* 58 (1963) 280–2 deplores inaccuracies, and T. Karp *JAMS* 17 (1964) 95–7 is critical of omissions.
This is a list of songs and their sources in med. mss and modern editions, alphabetically by composer and title, supplemented with a list of mss and M literature.

1238 Entry deleted

ANTHOLOGIES

1239 Jammers, Ewald ed *Ausgewählte Melodien des Minnesangs* AT 1 (Tübingen 1963) xii + 289 / rev R.J. Taylor *GLL* ns 18 (1964/5) 237–8
After a comprehensive introduction J transcribes 131 songs, with tacit editorial emendation.

1240 Moser, Hugo, and Joseph Müller-Blattau edd *Deutsche Lieder des MA* (Stuttgart 1968) xii + 360 / rev J.A. Westrup *ML* 50 (1969) 413–16
This is an edition (Rh) of selected melodies (12c–late 15c) with commentary and index of incipits.

1241 Seagrave, Barbara G., and Wesley Thomas edd *The Songs of the Minnesingers* (Urbana and London 1966) x + 232 and one disc with notes, indices of songs and names / rev D. Colton *Notes* 25 (1968/9) 499–500
This is an excellent anthology representing 12–15c. It has a general introduction, and notes on the composers and the forms of their songs, with miniatures from the Manesse Ms. The melodies are transcribed rhythmically. English translations are given.

1242 Taylor, Ronald J. ed *The Art of the Minnesinger* 2 vols (Cardiff 1968) xliv + 182; 301 / rev J.A. Westrup *ML* 50 (1969) 413–16
This is a complete edition (Rh) of songs up to 1300.

1243 *Melodien altdeutscher lieder* MwSb 9 (1954) xi + 24 dipl facss in separate
1244 booklet **1244** *Mittelhochdeutsche Liedkunst* MwSb 10 (1954) xxiv + 22 pp in separate booklet
1243 47 melodies and texts are edited in ms setting. **1244** This is an edition of 24 melodies.

1245 Kuhn, Hugo *Minnesang des 13. Jh.* (Tübingen 1953) xi + 160
This is a selection of texts chosen from Carl von Kraus' *Deutsche Liederdichter* with a few melodies (Rh) edited by Georg Reichert (pp 150–60).

Switzerland

1245a Geering, A. 'Minnesang in der Schweiz' *Schw Musik-Zeitung* 87 (1947) 326–9
Some melodies are preserved in the repertory of the mastersingers.

ORIGINS, CONTRAFACTA

1246 Aarburg, Ursula ed *Singweisen zur Liebeslyrik der deutschen Frühe* (Düs-
1247 seldorf 1956) 48 **1247** Aarburg 'Probleme um die Melodien des Min-
1248 nesangs' *Du* 19 (1967) Heft 2, 98–118 **1248** Aarburg 'Melodien zum frühen
deutschen Minnesang' *ZdA* 87 (1956/7) 24–45, revd in E-4.378–423
1246 Giving original Romance as well as the new German texts, A edits 27
contrafacta of the 12c. In doubtful cases a rhythm is suggested separately.
1247 This is a general introduction. **1248** A discusses and catalogues sources
of the (contrafacta) melodies.

1249 Jammers, E. 'Minnesang und Choral' F-5.137–47
J shows melodic similarities.

1250 Gennrich, F. 'Der deutsche Minnesang in seinem Verhältnis zur Trou-
1251 badour- und Trouvère-kunst' *ZdBildung* 2 (1926) 536–66, 622, 632 **1251**
1252 Gennrich 'Sieben Melodien zu mittelhochdeutschen Minneliedern'
ZMw 7 (1924/5) 65–98, 1 facs, num transcc (Rh) **1252** Gennrich 'Liedkontrafaktur in mhd. und ahd. Zeit' *ZdA* 82 (1948/50) 105–41; repr E-4.330–77
1250 With historical and literary evidence, and with transcriptions of contrafacta, G shows the extensive borrowing of French culture. **1251** G compares Provençal models with German contrafacta which form the basis of
early minnesinger activity. **1252** G discusses rhythmic and melodic changes
caused by the adaptation of melodies to new texts.

1253 *Trouvères et Minnesänger* ed István Frank sus, Schriften der U, philos Fakul-
1254 tät (Sarrebrück 1952) xlv + 209, 8 facss, glossary of Lotharingian forms (pp
196–7), b / rev U. Aarburg *AdA* 68 (1955/6) 172–6 **1254** *Trouvères und Minnesänger* II ed Wendelin Müller-Blattau sus, Schriften der U, philos Fakultät
(Saarbrucken 1956) 138 / rev R.J. Taylor *GLL* ns 10 (1957) 150–1 and U. Aarburg
AdA 70 (1957/8) 12–16
1253 F edits texts with analytical, biographical, textual, and bibliographical
notes, giving German and French translations. **1254** M edits the melodies
and discusses borrowing. The volume is intended to complement Frank's.

1255 Spanke, H. 'Eine neue Leich-Melodie' *ZMw* 14 (1931/2) 385–97, 7 pp transcc
S uses a Latin 'conductus' tune as melody for a German lai.

Form

1256 Gennrich, F. 'Das Formproblem des Minnesangs. Ein Beitrag zur
1257 Erforschung des Strophenbaues der ma. Lyrik' *DVLG* 9 (1931) 285–349 **1257**
Kuhn, H. 'Ulrich von Winterstetten und der deutsche Leich' *Minnesangs
Wende* HERMEA. GERMANISTISCHE FORSCHUNGEN, Neue Folge, 1 (Tübingen
1952) 91–142 + 7 facss (pp 164–70)
1256 The same forms are distributed in all kinds of lyric song. **1257** K analyses four kinds: the Leich, which he distinguishes from the Lai, the
Estampie, and the Sequence type.

1257a Biber, Walter *Das Problem der Melodieformel in der einstimmigen* M *des MA* BERNER VER. ZUR MF 17 (Bern 1951) vii + 136 / rev K. Gudewill *Mf* 7 (1954) 89–91

Melody, text, and instruments

1258 Touber, A.H. 'Zur Einheit von Wort und Weise im Minnesang' *ZdA* 93
1259 (1964) 313–20 **1259** Maurer, F. 'Sprachliche und M Bauformen des deutschen
1260 Minnesangs um 1200' *Poetica. Zs für Sprach- und Literaturwissenschaft* 1
1261 (1967) 462–82 **1260** Gennrich, F. 'Ma. Lieder mit textloser Melodie' *AMw*
1262 9 (1952) 120–36, 2 facss **1261** Bertau, Karl H. *Sangverslyrik* PALAESTRA 240
(Göttingen 1964) 246, index / rev H. Lomnitzer *AdA* 78 (1967) 119–25 **1262**
Beyschlag, S. 'Langzeilen-Melodien' *ZdA* 93 (1964) 157–76
1258 On the basis of limited but provoking evidence, T claims that the melody determines details of the text structure. **1259** M briefly outlines the form and rhyme-structure and shows how melodic and textual metres complement and confirm each other. **1260** G shows methods of co-ordinating text and M when none of the former is underlaid. **1261** B seeks to clarify the metrical relationship between text and M in the *leich*. **1262** Bey relates line, rhyme, and M phrase.

1263 Jammers, E. 'Deutsche Lieder um 1400' *Acta* 28 (1956) 28–54
J interprets the distribution of vocal and instrumental sections.

1264 Gennrich, F. 'Vier deutsche Lieder des 14. und 15. Jh.' *AMw* 11 (1954) 269–79
G discusses and transcribes the pieces.

Tristan and other poetry

1265 Finlay, I.F. 'M in Gotfrid's *Tristan*' *ML* 33 (1952) 50–4 **1266** Finlay 'M Instru-
1266 ments in Gotfrid von Strassburg's *Tristan und Isolde*' *GSJ* 5 (1952) 39–43 **1267**
1267 Gnaedinger, Louise M *und Minne im 'Tristan' Gotfrids von Strassburg*
BEIHEFTE ZUR ZS WW 19 (Düsseldorf 1967) 99
1265 F shows the aesthetic effect of Tristan's performing through translated quotations. **1266** F comments on the references. **1267** G examines the terminology and ideas and concludes that M is an essential element in the poem (ca 1210).

1268 Taylor, R.J. 'The M Knowledge of the Middle High German Poet' *MLR* 49
(1954) 331–8
M can throw light on the poet's education.

SOURCES, EDITIONS, FACSIMILES

A number of important sources do not include M: editions of these are not listed here.

Berlin

1268a Husmann, H. 'Die mittelniederländischen Lieder der Berliner Hs Germ. 8° 190' **A-2**.241–51
Comparing rhythm and notation of these 15c songs with much older systems and with minnesinger songs, H concludes that duple, triple, and free rhythm were used equally.

Carmina Burana

1269 *Carmina Burana* MedMM 9 (1967) 40 + 112 fos col facs + 7 fos facs + 1 leaf
This is a superb colour reproduction.

1270 Machabey, A. 'Remarques sur les mélodies goliardiques' *CCM* 7 (1964)
1271 257–78 **1271** Spanke, H. 'Der Cod. Buranus als Liederbuch' *ZMw* 13 (1930/1) 241–51
1270 M includes a bibliographic list of the poems set to M (not all in the *Carmina Burana* ms). **1271** S discusses items and types which have M in other sources.

1272 Machabey, A. 'Etude de quelques chansons goliardiques' *Rom* 83 (1962)
1273 323–47 **1273** Lipphardt, W. 'Unbekannte Weisen zu den Carmina Burana'
1274 *AMw* 12 (1955) 122–42, 3 facss **1274** Lipphardt 'Einige unbekannte Weisen zu den Carmina Burana aus der zweiten Hälfte des 12. Jh.' **F-5**.101–25 and 537, 7 facss (pll 5–16)
1272 M describes and transcribes three pieces. **1273, 1274** L analyses, dates, and discusses pieces (a) related to the St Martial repertory, and (b) from 1170–90, and transcribes them with the help of concordances.

1275 Entry deleted

1276 Entry deleted

1277 Entry deleted

Colmar and Donaueschingen

1278 *Die Colmarer Liederhs* SMMA 18 (1967) xviii + 214 (209 facss), indices of texts
1279 and names **1279** *Die Sangesweisen der Colmarer Hs und die Liederhs*
1280 *Donaueschingen* ed Paul Runge (Leipzig 1896; repr Hildesheim 1965) xx + 199, 5 col and 1 black and white facss (dipl?), indices of incipits, melody-titles, names **1280** Aarburg, U. 'Verzeichnis der im Kolmarer Liedercodex erhaltenen Töne und Leiche' **F-5**.127–36
1278 This is a facsimile edition of the M leaves. **1279** This is a transcription of minnesinger and mastersinger songs into pseudo-square notation. It includes a list of contents of the related Donaueschingen ms. The only value of this book now is that it presents the whole ms in a M and textual form that is easier to read than the original. **1280** A revises previous inventories.

1281 Eberth, Friedrich *Die Liedweisen der Kolmarer Hs und ihre Einordnung und*
1282 *Stellung in der Entwicklungsgeschichte der deutschen Liedweise im 14.–16. Jh.*
1283 (Göttingen 1933) iv + 115 / rev O.Ursprung *Acta* 8 (1936) 161–2 **1282** Bartsch,
Karl ed *Meisterlieder der Kolmarer Hs* BIBL DES STUTTGARTER LITERARISCHEN
VEREINS 68 (Stuttgart 1862; repr Hildesheim 1962) 734, indices **1283** Zitzmann, Rudolf *Die Melodien der Kolmarer Liederhs* LMw, Bd 9 (Würzburg
1944) xiii + 185, M exx, index
1281 This is a general investigation. **1282** This is an edition of the texts,
with biographies. **1283** Comparing other mss, Z discusses the M, its notation, forms, and rhythms.

Jena

1284 *Die Jenaer Liederhs* ed Karl K. Müller (Jena 1896) viii + fos 2–136 facss (some
1285 leaves missing in original) **1285** *Die Jenaer Liederhs* SMMA 11 (1963) xiv +
1286 140 facss, indices of texts and names **1286** *Die Jenaer Liederhs* ed Georg
Holz, Franz Saran, and Eduard Bernoulli 2 vols (Leipzig 1901; repr Hildesheim 1966) viii + 241, index of names; 200
1284 This is a superb facsimile of the whole ms. More accessible is **1285**,
a facsimile of the M leaves. **1286** Vol 1 is an edition of the texts and M (Sq):
vol 2 includes rhythmic transcriptions of the M with a commentary on
rhythm, form, and melody. This volume also contains a few transcriptions
of the Colmar ms.

Münster and other fragments

1286a Bertau, K.H. and R. Stephan 'Wenig beachtete Frauenlobfragmente' *ZdA*
86 (1955/6) 302–20; 93 (1964) 215–26, 6 facss
The authors describe two small mss.

1286b Jostes, F. 'Bruchstück einer münsterschen Minnesängerhandschrift mit
1286c Noten' *ZdA* 53 (1912) 348–57 + 2 foldout facss **1286c** Molitor, R. 'Die Lieder
des münsterischen Fragmentes' *SIMG* 12 (1910/11) 475–500 + 2 foldout facss
Both authors describes the ms: J prints the texts, M tries to transcribe the
songs.

Vienna and Mondsee-Vienna

1287 *Gesänge von Frauenlob, Reinmar v. Zweter und Alexander* ed Heinrich
Rietsch, DTÖ 41, Jahrgang xx² (1913; repr Graz 1960) xi + 1–54 facss + 55–88
transcc (Rh) + 89–105 notes and description of ms
This is an edition of the minnesinger ms Vienna, NB 2701.

1288 Heger, Hedwig ed *Mondsee-Wiener-Liederhs (aus Codex Vindobonensis 2856)*
CODICES SELECTI 19 (Graz 1968) 46 + fos 166–284 col facs
The introduction describes and inventories the ms. See also *AMw* 5 (1923)
11–30.

1289 Entry deleted

THE POETS

Hugo von Montfort

1290 *Die Lieder des Hugo von Montfort* ed Paul Runge (Leipzig 1906) v + 76 +
1291 1 facs **1291** Jammers, E. 'Die Melodien Hugos von Montfort' *AMw* 13 (1956)
217–35
1290 R edits text and M (Sq). **1291** This is a discussion of the rhythmic and
other problems. J thinks the melismas were meant to be sung.

Monk of Salzburg

1292 Hintermaier, E. 'Die mehrstimmigen Lieder des Mönchs von Salzburg'
ÖMz 25 (1970) 395–7
H describes the M and its sources.

Neidhart

1293 *Neidhart-Lieder* SMMA 9 (1962) xxvi + 53, index of songs / rev F. Kur *AdA*
1294 77 (1966) 68–73 **1294** *The Songs of Neidhart von Reuental* ed A.T. Hatto and
1295 Ronald J. Taylor (Manchester 1958) frontisp facs, xi + 112 / rev G. Reaney
1296 *ML* 40 (1959) 74–5 **1295** Simon, Eckehard *Neidhart von Reuental, Geschichte*
1297 *der Forschung und Bibliographie* HARVARD GERMANIC STUDIES 4 (Paris 1968)
x + 212, indices and ext b **1296** Lomnitzer, H. 'Kritisches zu neueren
Neidhart-Übertragungen' **F-10**.231–44 **1297** Müller-Blattau, W. 'Melodietypen bei Neidhart von Reuental' **F-21**.69–79
1293 This is an edition (Rh) with commentary and a few diplomatic fac-
similies. **1294** The authors edit (Rh) 17 songs with translation, introduction,
and commentary. **1295** S devotes only 12 pages to the M. **1296** L compares
various attitudes to rhythm and transcription, and stresses the need for col-
laboration between textual and M scholars. **1297** Formulaic construction
around strong tonal notes differentiates them from trouvère songs: see also
StuMw 17 (1930) 3–20.

Oswald von Wolkenstein

1298 *Oswald von Wolkenstein* ed Josef Schatz and Oswald Koller, DTÖ 18, Jahrgang
1299 IX[1] (1902; repr Graz 1959) xxi, 3 pll, 4 facss + 1–126 edition of texts + 127–210
1300 edition of M, mainly dipl, with index of text + 211–233 commentary **1299** *Die
Lieder Oswalds von Wolkenstein* ed Walter Weiss, Notburga Wolf, Kurt Klein,
and W. Salmen AT 55 (Tübingen 1962) xxiii + 389, indices of texts by incipit
and rhyme, cross-reference table **1300** Wendler, Josef *Studien zur Melo-*

diebildung bei Oswald von Wolkenstein. Die Formeltechnik in den einstimmigen Liedern (Tutzing 1961) 235 + 7 leaves M exx, ext b / rev W. Bittinger *Mf* 20 (1967) 346–8

1298 A more modern edition is required. **1299** This is a textual edition, with M appendix (Rh) pp 327–44. **1300** W describes composition by formula and melodic pattern.

1301 Salmen, W. 'Werdegang und Lebensfülle des Oswald von Wolkenstein' *MD* 7 (1953) 147–73

Reviewing past research and the sources, S gives a biography and a chronological list of songs. Relating chronology and social status, he shows Wolkenstein's eclecticism in M, rhythmic and textual characteristics.

1302 Petzsch, C. 'Text- und Melodietypenveränderung bei Oswald von Wol-
1303 kenstein' *DVLG* 38 (1964) 491–512 **1303** Petzsch 'Die Bergwaldpastourelle
1304 Oswalds von Wolkenstein. Text- und Melodietypenveränderung II' *ZdPh*
1305 87 (1968) sonderheft 'Mittelhochdeutsche Lyrik' pp 195–222 **1304** Petzsch
'Eine als unvollständig geltende Melodie Oswalds von Wolkenstein' *AMw*
19–20 (1962/3) 100–13 **1305** Petzsch 'Zum Freidank-Cento Oswalds von Wolkenstein' *AMw* 26 (1969) 125–39

In these articles P discusses melodic types and the relation of melody and text.

1306 Göllner, T. 'Landinis *Questa fanciulla* bei Oswald von Wolkenstein' *Mf* 17 (1964) 393–8

G describes Oswald's two contrafacta.

Walther von der Vogelweide

1307 *Die Lieder Walthers von der Vogelweide* 2 vols I: *Die religiösen und die*
1308 *politischen Lieder* II: *Die Liebeslieder* ed Friedrich Maurer AT 43 and 47 (2nd
1309 ed Tübingen 1960, 1962) xii + 88, index of texts by rhyme; 173, index of
1310 texts by rhyme **1308** Huisman, Johannes A. *Neue Wege zur dichterischen*
1311 *und M-Technik Walthers von der Vogelweide* STUDIA LITTERARIA RHENO-
TRAIECTINA 1 (Utrecht 1950) vi + 164, index / rev C.W. Fox *JAMS* 4 (1951)
255–61 **1309** Brunner, W.-H. 'Walthers von der Vogelweide *Palästinalied* als
Kontrafactur' *ZdA* 92 (1963/4) 195–211 **1310** Gennrich, F. 'Die Melodie zu
Walthers von der Vogelweide Spruch: Philippe, Künec hêre' *SM* ns 17 (1951)
71–85 **1311** Aarburg, U. 'Walthers Goldene Weise' *Mf* 11 (1958) 478–82

1307 With full critical apparatus M edits the texts: the M follows the text-rhythms in transcription (N) **1308** This is a mainly a textual analysis to show the presence of symmetrical number-composition. **1309** B compares 3 versions of the song by Jaufre and 2 versions of the Bordesheimer *Marienklage* with the *Palästinalied*. **1310** G points to melodic and textual borrowings in this contrafactum. **1311** A discusses a melismatic *cauda* and the disposition of the text.

Wizlaw of Rügen

1312 *The Songs of the Minnesinger, Prince Wizlaw of Rügen* ed Wesley Thomas
1313 and Barbara Seagrave U OF NORTH CAROLINA STUDIES IN THE GERMANIC
LANGUAGES AND LITERATURES 59 (Chapel Hill 1967) v + 157, 9 facss / rev
R. Harvey *ML* 50 (1969) 185–7 and H. VanderWerf *Notes* 26 (1969)
34–5 **1313**Taylor, R.J. 'A Song by Prince Wizlav of Rügen' *MLR* 46 (1951)
31–7
1312 After a substantial but criticized introduction, the authors transcribe
the songs (Rh) and print texts in original and translation. **1313** The melody
and criteria of numerical proportion determine doubtful points in the text.

SACRED SONG, GEISSLERLIED

Catalogues

1313a Lipphardt, W. 'Die liturgische Funktion deutscher Kirchenlieder in den
Klöstern niedersächsischer Zisterzienserinnen des MA' *Zs katholische
Theologie* 94 (1972) 158–98
L inventories sources and discusses vernacular songs for Easter and Christ-
mas.

Surveys

1314 Müller-Blattau, J. 'Die ältesten deutschen geistlichen Lieder' *Von der Vielfalt*
1315 *der M* (Freiburg im Breisgau 1966) 9–36 **1315** Müller-Blattau 'Zu Form und
Überlieferung der ältesten deutschen geistlichen Lieder' *ZMw* 17 (1935)
129–46
1314 This is a good general survey. **1315** M discusses sources and styles,
with some examples of the original notation, and transcriptions.

1316 Janota, Johannes *Studien zu Funktion und Typus des deutschen geistlichen
Liedes im MA* MTU 23 (Munich 1968) x + 307, b, indices of songs and mss /
rev E. Simon *Spec* 45 (1970) 302–4
The book deals with sacred song in liturgical contexts.

Mosburger Gradual

1317 Stein, F.A. 'Das Moosburger Graduale (1354–1360) als Quelle geistlicher
1318 Volkslieder' *JbLH* 2 (1956) 93–7, 2 facss **1318** Lipphardt, W. 'Das Moosburger Cantionale' *JbLH* 3 (1957) 113–17 and *Tafel* III, facs, facing p 112
1317 S analyses items used later for vernacular German songs (including
Puer nobis nascitur). See **2003**. **1318** Correcting details in **1317**, L gives concordances and further discussion of two pieces. See **56a**.

1319 Lipphardt, W. 'Ein Mainzer Prozessionale (um 1400) als Quelle deutscher geistlicher Lieder' *JbLH* 9 (1964) 95–121, 2 facss (8 photos)
L describes the ms.

1320 *Die Lieder und Melodien der Geissler des Jahres 1349 nach der Aufzeichnung*
1321 *Hugos von Reutlingen* ed Paul Runge (Leipzig 1900; repr Hildesheim 1969) viii + 222, 1 facs **1321** Gümpel, Karl-Werner ed *Hugo Spechtshart von Reutlingen: 'Flores musicae' (1332/42)* AKW UND LITERATUR, ABH DER GEISTES- UND SOZIALWISSENSCHAFTLICHEN KLASSE, Jg 1958, 3 (Mainz 1958) 177, index of terms
1320 This is the only transcription available of Hugo's *Chronicon* with its M items. R transcribes into square notes and has a brief introduction to the songs. Italian and other *geisslerlieder* (flagellant penitential songs) are discussed. **1321** Introducing the life and works of Hugo, and describing the *Flores* and its sources, G edits the text and gives a facsimile of the M from an early print.

1322 Müller-Blattau, J. 'Die deutschen Geisslerlieder' *ZMw* 17 (1935) 6–18
This is a general survey.

The lauda

ORIGINS AND EVOLUTION

There is very little material on the origins of the form.

1323 Vecchi, G. 'Tra monodia e polifonia' *CHM* 2 (1957) 447–64, 1 facs
With transcriptions V compares the Latin laude and the Sequence, and reviews the evidence for 13c polyphonic practice in Italy.

1324 Fortini, Arnaldo *La Lauda in Assisi e le origini del teatro italiano* (Assisi 1961) 560, 133 pll, index, b
Pp 209–39 refer to the M briefly.

1325 Cattin, G. 'Contributi alla storia della lauda spirituale' *Quad* 2 (1958) 45–75, 16 pp transcc
C gives a general survey of M and literary evolution through 14c and 15c.

SOURCES

Cortona

1326 Liuzzi, Fernando ed *La Lauda e i primordi della melodia italiana* 2 vols (Rome

1327 1935) col frontisp facs + xx + 484, 46 facss; col frontisp facs, 429, 89 facss / rev Y. Rokseth *Rom* 65 (1939) 383–94 **1327** Anglès, H. 'The M Notation and Rhythm of the Italian Laude' **F-3.**51–60
1326 Vol 1 contains an extensive survey of Italian lyric monophony and a description of the two major sources. In a useful alternation of facsimile (incomplete) and transcription (Rh) L edits the Cortona 91 *laudario*. Vol 2 has a similar edition of the Magliabecchiano *laudario* from Florence, together with indices of texts and names. See also *AR* 14 (1930) 527–60. **1327** Criticizing L's transcriptions, A substitutes his own arbitrary rhythmic interpretation and transcribes four melodies.

1328 Terni, C. 'Per una edizione critica del "Laudario di Cortona" ' *Chigiana* 21 (1964) 111–29
Referring to the zejel, T discusses the strophic form.

1329 Entry deleted

Turin

1330 Damilano, Don P. 'Laudi latine in un Antifonario bobbiese del Trecento' *CHM* 3 (1963) 15–57, 6 facss, 13 pp transcc
Defining the term *lauda*, D describes the Turin ms (Turin BN F.I. 4) and the non-liturgical texts and M it contains. He edits text and M.

LAUDESI

1331 Fischer, K. von 'Quelques remarques sur les relations entre les Laudesi et
1332 les compositeurs florentins du Trecento' **D-5.**247–52 **1332** D'Accone, F.A. 'Le Compagnie dei Laudesi in Firenze durante l'Ars Nova' **D-5.**253–80
1331 There is documentary evidence hinting at some liaison between the two 'schools.' **1332** Archives of the confraternities give much useful information: the lauda appears to be the means by which polyphony was popularised.

1333 Ghisi, F. 'Gli aspetti M della lauda fra il xiv e il xv secolo, prima metà' **F-17.**51–7
G stresses the new simple, syllabic, and vertical style.

1334 Fischer, K. von 'Die Lauda *Ave mater* und ihre verschiedenen Fassungen' **F-25.**93–9
German, Polish, and Italian sources are significantly different, suggesting an unknown earlier model.

The theory and practice of polyphony

1335 *Mss of Polyphonic* M *(11th to early 14c)* ed Gilbert Reaney RISM, Ser B IV¹ (1966)
876, indices of composers, texts, incipits
This volume lists mss to the beginning of the Ars Nova, including retrospective English sources in Petronian notation, and excluding most Italian sources.

BEFORE THE TWELFTH CENTURY

Much of our specific information is derived from theoretical treatises (**1348 1349 1355**), and from imprecise references in non-technical writings (**1337**). Some hints about performance practices (**1342 1347**) can be deduced from the present M practices of Near Eastern cultures (**1340 1347**) and of non-literate cultures (**1346**), together with evidence about medieval instruments (**1338 1339 1343–6**) and necessary relationships between plainsong and polyphony (**1338a 1340 1341**)

1336 Spiess, L. 'An Introduction to the Pre-History of Polyphony' **F-31**.11–15
1337 **1337** Synan, E.A. 'An Augustinian Testimony to Polyphonic M?' *MD* 18
(1964) 3–6
1336 Spiess concludes there is no evidence proving polyphonic practice before the 9c. **1337** In the philosophical context, *concinere* may refer to polyphony (4c).

1338 Bachmann, W. 'Die Verbreitung des Quintierens im europäischen Volksgesang des späten MA' **F-26**.25–9
Widespread performing in parallel fifths is suggested by literary references, tuning of instruments, etc.

***1338a** Rybarič, R. ' "Primitivna" polyfónia a gregoriánsky chorál' ('Primitive' polyphony and Greg chant) *Musicologica Slovaca* 1 (1969) 283–96

Primitive polyphony and homophonic liturgical singing are related (annotation abbreviated from 13).

1339 Collaer, P. 'Polyphonies de tradition populaire en Europe méditerranéenne' *Acta* 32 (1960) 51–66
With many examples C points to burdens, ostinati, and parallelism in folk music.

1340 Husmann, H. 'The Practice of Organum in the Liturgical Singing of the Syrian Churches of the Near and Middle East' **F-23**.435–9
Syrian practice may be the origin of western polyphony in fourths.

1341 Jammers, Ewald *Anfänge der abendländischen* M SMwAbh 31 (Strasbourg 1955) 188, b, index / rev *KmJb* 40 (1956) 159–60: reviewer says that J seeks to comprehend the relation between polyphony and Greg. M in the Carolingian period and 10c.

1342 Krüger, Walter *Die authentische Klangform des primitiven Organum* MwArb 13 (Kassel 1958) 76, 3 pll / rev L. Spiess *JAMS* 12 (1959) 90–1: S says this is a 'good survey of modern opinions' regarding performance practice.

1343 Schneider, Marius 'Wurzeln und Anfänge der abendländischen Mehrstim-
1344 migkeit' **A-4**.1.161–78 (discussed in 11.107–11) **1344** Schneider 'Kaukasische Parallelen zur ma. Mehrstimmigkeit' *Acta* 12 (1940) 52–61, 6 pp transcc
1343 S concludes that European med. polyphony is similar to, and develops from, non-western forms of M. Differentiating styles, he suggests that the earliest western polyphony was dissonant in essence and that parallelism in consonances is theoretical and artificial. **1344** The examples show similar techniques.

1345 Vogel, M. 'Zum Ursprung der Mehrstimmigkeit' *KmJb* 49 (1965) 57–64
Investigating the relation between *organum* and *organon* (Greek 'instrument'), V examines the role of aulos, bagpipe, and organ.

1346 Wiora, W. 'Zwischen Einstimmigkeit und Mehrstimmigkeit' **F-26**.319–34
W points to similarities between early polyphony and improvised or nonwestern styles in which a single voice is made into pseudo-polyphony with heterophony, parallels, and drones, etc.

1347 Ringer, A.L. 'Eastern Elements in Med. Polyphony' *Studies in Med. Culture* 2 ed John R. Sommerfeldt (Kalamazoo 1966) 75–83
Referring to the high sophistication of earlier Arabic theory, R makes a very strong case for Eastern prototypes inspiring 12c melismatic organum, modal rhythms, and performance practices.

The earliest theories and compositions

These are presented in approximate chronological order.

Musica Enchiriadis and De Organo

1348 Apel, W. 'The Earliest Polyphonic Composition and its theoretical Back-
1349 ground' *RBdM* 10 (1956) 129–37, 1 facs **1349** Spiess, L. 'The Diatonic
'Chromaticism' of the *Enchiriadis* Treatises' *JAMS* 12 (1959) 1–6
1348 A explains contrapuntal theory from the *Musica Enchiriadis* and the
later *De Organo* treatises. **1349** The Dasian scale applies to *vox organalis*,
rather than *principalis*, for the purpose of avoiding diminished fifths.

Monasterium istud

1350 Gushee, Marion 'A Polyphonic Ghost' *JAMS* 16 (1963) 204–11
Monasterium istud (10–11c) is not polyphonic.

Winchester Tropers

1351 Holschneider, Andreas *Die Organa von Winchester* (Hildescheim 1968)
1352 199 + 23 facss, index of incipits, M transcc (156–81) / rev M. Huglo *RdM* 54
1353 (1968) 251–3 **1352** Machabey, A. 'Remarques sur le Winchester Troper'
F-5.67–90 **1353** Handschin, J. 'The Two Winchester Tropers' *J of Theological
Studies* 37 (1936) 34–49, 156–72
1351 The reviewer says this is a rigorous analysis of sources, liturgical background, notation, with an excellent bibliography and detailed tables. **1352**
M gives an inventory of the polyphony, discusses the notation, and transcribes 3 pieces. **1353** H describes the 11c mss and their contents, and concludes that the one with polyphony was for the succentor, the other for the
precentor.

 * Announced: A facsimile of the Winchester Tropers in the EARLY ENGLISH
MSS IN FACSIMILE series

Miscellaneous

1354 Handschin, J. 'L'Organum à l'église et les exploits de l'Abbé Turstin' *RCG*
40 (1936) 179–82 and 41 (1937) 14–19
H discusses the earliest polyphonic pieces, including some which apparently set the choral sections of the chant.

1355 Waeltner, E.L. 'Der Bamberger Dialog über das Organum' *AMw* 14 (1957)
175–83, 2 facss
This 11c treatise links the organum methods of Musica Enchiriadis and
Guido of Arezzo.

THE TWELFTH CENTURY

1356 Waite, W. 'The Era of Melismatic Polyphony' A-4.1.178–83 (discussed in II.107–11)
With many short quotations from St Martial *prosae* W shows the intimate relation between troping and polyphony, claiming that the use of more regular poetry forced the composer into melismatic style.

1357 Ellinwood, L. 'The French Renaissance of the 12c in M' *Intern. Congress of Musicology, New York 1939* AMERICAN MUSICOLOGICAL SOC (New York 1944) 200–11
With M transcriptions, E traces the relation between organum, motet, and conductus. The details must be accepted with caution.

St Martial

The repertory of this Aquitainian 'school,' generally called the St Martial school because many sources were collected there, bridges the eleventh and twelfth centuries. It is largely a monophonic repertory of tropes, and major sources of information are Chailley *L'Ecole* M *de Saint Martial* (**744**), Evans *The Early Trope Repertory* ... (**745**), and Spanke 'St Martial-Studien ...' (**746**). Some trope manuscripts also transmit polyphony. This begins to show characteristic and highly differentiated styles (**1359–64**) in which some rhythmic system probably evolves (**1360 1367–72**).

1358 Spanke, H. 'Die Londoner St Martial-Conductushs 'and Anglès, Higini 'La Música del Ms de Londres, BM Add 36881' *Butlletí de la Bibl de Catalunya* 8 (1928–32) 280–301, 1 facss, 301–14
Printing the texts, S inventories the 12c ms with brief comments and description; A briefly describes the M and transcribes a few items.

* Announced: *Versarius Martialensis. Die ein- und mehrstimmigen Gesänge ... von St Martial* by Bruno Stäblein

Polyphonic styles and theory
1359 Apel, W. 'Bemerkungen zu den Organa von St Martial' F-2.1.61–70
A points out some of the stylistic traits of the polyphony.

1360 Waite, W. 'Discantus, Copula, Organum' *JAMS* 5 (1952) 77–87, with correspondence on pp 272–6
W disputes Apel's thesis about rhythm (**1372**) and tries to define the stylistic differences implied by the terms in his own title.

1361 Schmidt, G. 'Strukturprobleme der Mehrstimmigkeit im Repertoire von St Martial' *Mf* 15 (1962) 11–39, 205–6 (see also p 394 and *Mf* 16 (1963) 173–4)

S interprets M theory of ca 1100 and claims that contemporary practical sources observe the principles he describes.

1362 Eggebrecht, H.H. 'Diaphonia vulgariter organum' **A-3**.93–7 **1363** Handschin, J. 'Zur Geschichte der Lehre vom Organum' ZMw 8 (1925/6) 321–41 **1364** Treitler, L. 'The Polyphony of St Martial' JAMS 17 (1964) 29–42
  1362 Linking *diaphonia* with note-against-note, and *organum* with sustained-note style, E sees implications of inseparable voices in the former term, of voice and accompaniment in the latter. He quotes theoretical passages. **1363** H quotes and discusses early references to polyphony, then prints and examines an important 12c treatise distinguishing organum and discant. **1364** With transcriptions T shows stylistic opposites in both monophony and polyphony, a rhapsodic or organal style, and a syllabic or discant style emphasising symmetrical constructivism. He relates these to Notre Dame compositions. Karp criticises in **1369**; T replies in *Acta* 40 (1968) 227.

Hidden polyphony
1365 Marshall, J.M. 'Hidden Polyphony in a Ms from St Martial de Limoges' JAMS 15 (1962) 131–44 **1365a** Fuller, S. 'Hidden Polyphony – a Reappraisal' JAMS 24 (1971) 169–92 **1366** Hooreman, P. 'Saint-Martial de Limoges au temps de l'abbé Odolric (1025–1040). Essai sur une pièce oubliée du répertoire limousin' RBM 3 (1949) 5–36, 1 facs
  1365 Discrepancies between poetic and M form point to apparently monophonic pieces whose alternate sections combine to form two-part polyphony. M concludes that organum and discant may have been practised as early as mid-11c. She includes transcriptions. **1365a** Concentrating mainly on the St Martial repertory, F isolates characteristics from which hidden polyphony can be identified. **1366** Attributing authorship to Adémar de Chabannes, H transcribes the *Versus de sancto Marciale* and shows that its double notation gives not polyphony, but two versions of the same melody.

Rhythm
1367 Stäblein, B. 'Modale Rhythmen in Saint-Martial-Repertoire?' **F-6**.340–62 **1368** Krüger, W. 'Singstil und Instrumentalstil in der Mehrstimmigkeit der St Martialepoche' **B-2**.240–5
  1367 After a review of the literature, methods of transcription, and sources S examines the notation, concluding that an increase in regularity in later mss can only indicate modal rhythms. **1368** K gives a modal transcription of *Jubilemus, exultemus*, and discusses its style.

1369 Karp, T. 'St Martial and Santiago de Compostela: an analytical speculation' Acta 39 (1967) 144–60

Referring especially to **1364**, K offers his own ideas about the rhythmic interpretation, and his own transcriptions.

1370 Krüger, W. 'Zur Frage der Rhythmik des St Martial-Conductus *Jubilemus*,'
1371 *Mf* 9 (1956) 185–8 **1371** Krüger *'Ad superni regis decus,'* *Mf* 20 (1967) 30–44, 2 pll, 1 table
1370 K criticises Jammers' transcription in **1341**. See also **1368**. In **1371** K presents an interesting and performable transcription, although his evidence especially concerning performance practice appears very tenuous.

1372 Apel, W. 'From St Martial to Notre Dame' *JAMS* 2 (1949) 145–58
Translating theoretical statements, A maintains that the 'principle of consonance' rather than 'of ligatures' stimulates the origin of modal rhythm, resulting in mixtures of free and modal patterns. See also **1360**.

1373 Dahlhaus, C. 'Zur Theorie des Organums im 12. Jh.' *KmJb* 48 (1964) 27–32
D discusses cadence formulae and transposition relative to the *modi organizandi*.

Codex Calixtinus

This Spanish source of the mid-twelfth century also shows the stylistic differentiation observed in the St Martial school, and has close relationships with the Paris area.

1374 *Liber Sancti Jacobi. Codex Calixtinus* I: *Texto*. II: *Musica*. III: *Estudios e Indices* ed Walter M. Whitehill, Dom German Prado, and Jesús Carro García (Santiago de Compostela 1944) iii + 430; iii + 36 facss + 93 transcc and commentary; i–cxvii, 8 facss / rev C. Meredith Jones *Spec* 23 (1948) 713–17
Vol I contains the text, edited complete by W; vol II contains facsimiles and transcriptions of the M sections, edited by P; vol III contains introductions, by all three editors, a section on the miniatures, and indices of names and places.

1375 *Die Gesänge der Jakobsliturgie zu Santiago de Compostela, aus dem sog. Codex Calixtinus* ed Peter Wagner COLLECTANEA FRIBURGENSIA 29 (ns 20) (Freiburg 1931) 173 + 2 facss
This is an edition of texts and M. Both plainsong and polyphony are transcribed in square notation. There is a lengthy commentary.

1376 Anglès, H. 'Die Mehrstimmigkeit des Calixtinus von Compostela und seine Rhythmik' **F-5**.91–100
A reviews previous literature and transcribes 7 pieces.

1377 Krüger, W. 'Zum Organum des Codex Calixtinus' *Mf* 17 (1964) 225–34, 2
1378 pll **1378** Schubert, J. 'Zum Organum des Codex Calixtinus' *Mf* 18 (1965)

1379 393–9 **1379** Krüger, W. 'Nochmals zum Organum des Codex Calixtinus' *Mf*
19 (1966) 180–6
1377 K, pleading for interpretative evaluation of the scanty evidence, gives
useful transcriptions. **1378** With some justified criticisms S takes issue
strongly with K's transcriptions and, with a somewhat doctrinaire attitude,
stresses the need for strictly scholarly methods, and gives alternative versions. **1379** K rebuts S's arguments.

1380 Osthoff, W. 'Die Conductus des Codex Calixtinus' **F-29**.178–86
O analyses the pieces.

Milanese Polyphony

1381 Stäblein, B. 'Zur archaischen ambrosianischen (Mailänder) Mehrstim-
1382 migkeit' *A Ettori Desderi nel suo 70. compleanno* (Bologna 1963) 169–
1383 74 **1382** Gallo, F.A. 'Esempi dell'*Organum* dei *Lumbardi* nel xii secolo'
Quad 8 (1967) 23–6, 2 facss **1383** Handschin, J. 'Aus der alten Musiktheorie.
3: Zur ambrosianischen Mehrstimmigkeit' *Acta* 15 (1943) 2–23
1381 Milanese polyphony in parallel seconds and fourths is a survival of
archaic practices antedating the theoretical refinements of *Musica
Enchiriadis* (see also **1343**). **1382** G examines the oldest document with
characteristic Lombard polyphony. **1383** H prints and discusses relevant
theoretical passages.

Twelfth- and early thirteenth-century polyphonic theory

1384 *Ad organum faciendum. Lehrschriften der Mehrstimmigkeit in nachguidonischer*
1385 *Zeit* ed Hans Heinrich Eggebrecht and Friedrich Zaminer NEUE STUDIEN ZUR
MW, ed Kommission für Mw der AkW und der Literatur, 3 (Mainz 1970) 240
+ 20 facss, indices of terms, places, names, etc **1385** *Ad organum faciendum.
Item de Organo* transl Jay A. Huff, MThT 8 (196?) 67, 4 facss
1384 After an introduction 6 treatises on 12c polyphony are edited with German translation and copious commentaries. **1385** This is an edition and
English translation.

1386 Seay, A. 'An anonymous treatise from St Martial' *AnnM* 5 (1957) 7–42
S re-edits, complete, a 12c treatise devoted to practical knowledge, including polyphony.

1387 Handschin, J. 'Der Organum-Traktat von Montpellier' **F-1**.50–7 **1388** Blum,
1388 F. 'Another Look at the Montpellier Organum Treatise' *MD* 13 (1959) 15–24.
See also *JAMS* 11 (1958) 87–8
1387 H gives the text and compares it with the Milan treatise. Major thirds
occupy a prominent recognised position in the theory. **1388** B introduces,
edits, and translates the 12c tract.

1389 *Der Vatikanische Organum-Traktat* ed Friedrich Zaminer MVM 2 (Tutzing 1959) 203, 10 facss + 2 tables / rev H. Oesch *Mf* 19 (1966) 80–2
This is a description, analysis, edition, and facsimile of an early 13c treatise on melismatic organum of the Notre Dame style. Z compares contemporary treatises.

France: Notre Dame and the thirteenth-century motet

THE *MAGNUS LIBER*

The sources and concordances of this major collection of twelfth- to thirteenth-century Parisian polyphony, and the origins of the thirteenth-century motet to be found in the revisions and additions to the collection, are catalogued in items **1390–2**.

1390 Ludwig, Friedrich *Repertorium Organorum Recentioris et Motetorum Vetustissimi Stili* 2 vols I: *Catalogue Raisonné der Quellen*, part 1 *Hss in Quadrat-Notation* (Halle 1910) viii + 344; part 2 and vol II were still only in page proofs when the author died (1930) and were not printed (but see **1391**). The plates were published, with the original pagination beginning p 345, as follows: part 2 *Hss in Mensuralnotation* ed Friedrich Gennrich SMMA 7 (1961) vi + 345 + 457; II: *Musikalisches Anfangsverzeichnis des nach Tenores geordneten Repertorium* ed Friedrich Gennrich SMMA 8 (1962) iii + 71 (this printing of vol II includes pp 65–71 of the original, even though the author's proof corrections, reproduced in the print, have not been made, and even though the musical incipits are missing – pp 66, 68, 70 are therefore blank). The complete work is being reprinted: so far only vol I, part 1, has appeared, ed Luther Dittmer MS 7 (1964) xx + 344 + 345–8 (Dittmer's reprint adds a detailed list of contents, and an introduction which expands the original p v).
This monumental but complex work is indispensable for any work on 12–13c polyphony: many corrections and additions have been made in recent years. See **1392 1468** and items by Anderson, Karp, and Tischler.
Vol I is a detailed description of the structure, contents, and relationships of the mss transmitting 12–14c polyphony. Part 1deals with the principal sources of Notre Dame M, and includes some motet mss. Ludwig's fundamental organisation of the *Magnus Liber* by liturgical source of the tenor in Office (O) or Mass (M) was based on the Florence Ms (**1416**) and the complete sequence appears on pp 65–8 (O1–O34) and pp 68–78 (M1–M59). This series of chants is used as necessary for the other mss described. The so-called 'substitute clausulae' are thoroughly listed, and for the motet mss the clausula source of each motet is given where traceable. Part 2, incomplete, deals with two of the 13c motet mss, noting the clausula model as in part 1.

Vol II is organised not according to ms order but according to the liturgical origin of the tenors. In a highly abbreviated form a mass of factual information is brought together to show (a) the plainsong, its source and liturgical use, (b) the ms sources of organum based on this chant, with bibliography, (c) the ms sources of clausulae based on sections (*teile*) of the chant, (d) the sources and texts of motets based on sections of the chant. Each text is given a number, used later by Gennrich in **1392**. Complex abbreviations give some details of the notation, and there is a thematic index. This catalogue was not finished and includes only the Mass tenors M1–M50 (in Gennrich's edition) and none of the Office chants. Dittmer in his reprint hopes to complete this volume. The whole work is often referred to as the *Repertorium*, or LudR.

1391 Ludwig, Friedrich 'Die Quellen der Motteten ältesten Stils' *AMw* 5 (1923) 185–222, 273–315
This is an abridgement, by L himself, of vol I, part 2 of his *Repertorium* (**1390**), not printed in his lifetime. The original plates, and the abridgement, are published by Friedrich Gennrich SMMA 7 (1961) iv + 345–457 (original page numbers) + 185–222 + 273–315 (page numbers of *AMw* 5). The article is often referred to as LudQ.

1392 Gennrich, Friedrich *Bibliographie der ältesten französischen und lateinischen Motetten* SMMA 2 (1957/8) lii + 125
Although confusing to use, with its eight lists of abbreviations for terms, periodicals, literature, theoretical writings, and ms sigla, the comprehensiveness of these lists makes the book an indispensable tool for research into 12–13C M. The theoretical and ms sources are briefly but usefully described with bibliographical references. The body of the book is a listing of 13c motets according to the liturgical source of their tenor, following the order established in **1390**, giving ms sources, publications, facsimiles, editions, and literature, and showing the incipits of texts in the upper voices, and referring to refrains. Incipits are cross-indexed according to language and voice. New sources have been discovered, but the work should be in constant use for any study beyond the elementary. Revisions and additions have been made, principally in articles by Anderson, Tischler, and Karp.

Surveys of the Parisian repertory

1393 Sasse, Götz Dietrich *Die Mehrstimmigkeit der Ars antiqua in Theorie und Praxis* (Leipzig 1940) vi + 148 + 12 M appendix
S gives lists of sources, of older literature, and of theoretical definitions of terms relating to 12c and 13c. The analytical information is based on facts available at the time.

1394 Handschin, J. 'Zur Geschichte von Notre Dame' *Acta* 4 (1932) 5–17, 49–55, **1395** 104–5 **1395** Ludwig, F. 'Die liturgischen Organa Leonins und Perotins'

1396 F-24.200–13 1396 Rokseth, Y. 'La Polyphonie parisienne du treizième
siècle' *Les Cahiers techniques de l'art* 1 (1947) 33–47
1394 H emphasises important dates, feasts, and documents. 1395 L conveys
the basic information about the Notre Dame School. 1396 Reviewing 1420,
R gives much basic information.

1397 Tischler, H. 'New historical aspects of the Parisian *organa*' *Spec* 25 (1950)
21–35
Some of the dates have been re-appraised, but this remains a useful summary of the decades about 1200.

1398 Husmann, H. 'Das Organum vor und ausserhalb der Notre-Dame-Schule'
A-5.I.25–35 (discussed in II.68–80)
This presents a wide survey of opinions, from the etymology of the word
organum and its use in poetry, to performance practice and anthropological
comparisons. H goes into more detail concerning the St Victor Ms.

Magnus Liber: Chronology, destination, liturgical information, distribution

British Isles 1404–6

1399 Husmann, H. 'The Origin and Destination of the *Magnus liber organi*' *MQ*
1400 49 (1963) 311–30 1400 Husmann 'Die Offiziumsorgana der Notre Dame-
1401 Zeit' *Jb der M-bibl Peters* 42 (1935) 31–49 1401 Husmann 'The Enlargement
1402 of the *Magnus liber organi* and the Paris Churches of St Germain l'Auxerrois
and Ste Geneviève-du-Mont' *JAMS* 16 (1963) 176–203 1402 Husmann 'St
Germain und Notre Dame' **F-17**.31–6
1399 Reasoning from liturgical evidence, H concludes that the *Liber* was produced for Notre Dame and its Office pieces were for Vespers rather than
Matins. 1400 H claims to ascertain three chronological stages, the first two
destined for Matins, the third for processions. 1401 Liturgical evidence
shows that, for the later layers of the *Liber*, there were several centres of composition in Paris. 1402 H makes a strong case for St Germain as an alternative
to Notre Dame, at least for Perotin.

1403 Hughes, D.G. 'Liturgical Polyphony at Beauvais in the 13c' *Spec* 34 (1959)
184–200, 1 facs
The structure of the ms BM Egerton 2615 discloses that Beauvais took over
or incorporated Parisian styles and cultivated a local style where no Parisian
piece was available.

1404 Ludwig, F. 'Über den Entstehungsort der grossen Notre-Dame-Hand-
schriften' **F-1**.45–9
Scottish and Spanish med. ownership of Notre Dame sources would
illuminate the distribution of the styles.

1405 Sanders, E.H. 'Peripheral Polyphony of the 13c' *JAMS* 17 (1964) 261–87
Mentioning links between second-generation Notre Dame and English

styles, S stresses that decidedly peripheral characteristics are not necessarily English.

1406 Tischler, H. 'Another English Motet of the 13c' *JAMS* 20 (1967) 274–9 and 21 (1968) 120, complemented by G. Anderson on pp 381–3
T describes and transcribes a previously unidentified composition.

1407 Flotzinger, R. 'Beobachtungen zur Notre-Dame-Hs w_1 und ihrem 11. Faszikel' *Österreichische AkW, Wien, Anzeiger der p.h.KL*, 105 Jahrgang (1968) 245–62
F concludes that the 11th fascicle expands the *Magnus liber* for local use and is thus later than the body of the ms; he suggests a date of ca 1265 .

Magnus Liber: Leonin and Perotin

1408 Birkner, G. 'Notre Dame-Cantoren und -Succentoren vom Ende des 10. bis zum Beginn des 14. Jh.' **F-14**.107–26
From archives B gives biographical information, and seeks to identify Leonin and Perotin.

1409 Tischler, H. 'Perotinus Revisited' **F-23**.803–17, revd and complemented in 'The Early Cantors of Notre Dame' *JAMS* 19 (1966) 85–7
T, preferring Notre Dame, questions Husmann's suggestion about Perotin and St Germain (**1402**), but cannot identify either Leonin or Perotin with any of the Precentors or Succentors, whom he lists.

1410 Sanders, E.H. 'The Question of Perotin's Oeuvre and Dates' **F-36**.241–9
S neatly summarises the achievement of Perotin and conjectures that he lived ca 1165–ca 1225.

Magnus Liber: Sources, facsimiles

Berlin
1411 Dittmer, L.A. 'The Lost Fragments of a Notre Dame Ms in Johannes Wolf's Library' **F-23**. 122–33, 12 facss
Publishing photographs of the Berlin part of the Munich source of Notre Dame polyphony, D complements **1417a**.

1412 Entry deleted

1413 Entry deleted

1414 Entry deleted

1415 Entry deleted

Florence
1416 *Firenze, Biblioteca Mediceo-Laurenziana Pluteo 29, 1* 2 vols MedMM 10, 11 (nd) fascicles I–VI (fos 1–262); VII–XI (fos 263–476) + 3 leaves
This is a facsimile edition of the basic Notre Dame source, known as F.

1416a Baltzer, Rebecca A. '13c Illuminated Miniatures and the Date of the Florence Ms' *JAMS* 25 (1972) 1–18, 6 facss
B demonstrates an earlier date, between 1245 and 1255.

Madrid

1417 *Madrid 20486* MedMM 1 (1957) 75 pp facss
This is a facsimile edition, with introduction.

Munich

1417a *Eine Zentrale Quellen der Notre-Dame M. A Central Source of Notre-Dame Polyphony* MedMM 3 (1959) 269, 6 pp facss
Dittmer reconstructs a ms, and gives a facsimile of the surviving leaves with an inventory, discussion, and transcription. See **1411**.

Wolfenbüttel w₁ (St Andrews) and w₂.

1418 *An Old St Andrews M Book* ed. James H. Baxter (Oxford, Paris 1931) xx + 197
1418a leaves facss **1418a** *Index to the St Andrews Ms* comp Dom Anselm Hughes (Edinburgh, London 1939) 41
1418 This is a complete facsimile, with brief introduction, of the w₁ Ms (late 13c). **1418a** This is an inventory of the ms.

1418b *Wolfenbüttel 1099 (1206)* MedMM 2 (1960) 12 + 253 fos facss
This is a facsimile, with introduction, of the manuscript known as w₂.

Magnus Liber: Editions

1418c Waite, William G. *The Rhythm of 12c Polyphony* YALE STUDIES IN THE HIST OF M 2 (New Haven 1954) x + 141 + 1–254 M transcc / rev. L. Ellinwood *MQ* 41 (1955) 250–3 and M.F. Bukofzer *Notes* 12 (1954/5) 232–6
This is a controversial interpretation of a highly complex rhythmic notation, details of which have been severely attacked (see **131 176 1372 1439**). The appended transcription of Leonin's *Magnus liber* has therefore been similarly attacked, but it remains the most complete and consistent to date.

1419 Thurston, Ethel *The Works of Perotin* (New York 1970) vi, 2 facss + 137, b
This is a performing edition of *Viderunt omnes* (à 4), *Sederunt principes* (à 4), *Alleluia ℣ Nativitas* with its clausulae and motets, and several other well known works. T includes comments and suggestions for performance.

1420 Husmann, Heinrich ed *Die drei und vierstimmige Notre-Dame-Organa* PÄM Jahrgang 11 (Leipzig 1940; repr Hildesheim 1967) xxxiv + 149 / rev: see **1396**
H discusses transmission, notation (especially modal rhythm), and chronology, then the techniques of composition. The edition of the M uses C clefs but is otherwise good.

∗1420a Anderson, Gordon ed *The Latin Compositions in Fascicules VII and VIII of the*

Notre Dame Ms Wolfenbüttel, Helmstadt 1099 (1206) MS 24; 1, 2 (New York 1971)
xxi + 384;
This is a study, with translation of the texts, and an edition.

* Announced: Tischler, Hans *Complete Edition of the Parisian Two-part Organa*

Magnus Liber: Styles

The highly difficult problem of rhythm in this polyphony is most comprehensively discussed in Waite *The Rhythm* ... (**1418c**).

1421 Waite, W.G. 'The Abbreviation of the *Magnus Liber' JAMS* 14 (1961) 147–58
For substitution in Leonin's works, Perotin composed both better as well
as shorter clausulae.

1422 Handschin, J. 'Eine wenig beachtete Stilrichtung innerhalb der ma.
Mehrstimmigkeit' *SJbMw* 1 (1924) 56–75 + 1–10 M exx (in copy used these
pages were bound between pp 64 and 65)
Notre Dame settings in which syllabic sections of chant are not set in sus-
tained note style are more recent and probably of northern and not Parisian
origin.

1423 Schmidt, Helmut *Die drei- und vierstimmigen Organa* (Kassel 1933) 72
With numerous M examples S discusses melodic, rhythmic, and phrase
structure, ornamentation, and concepts of vertical sonority, etc.

1424 Karp, T. 'Towards a Critical Edition of Notre Dame Organa Dupla' *MQ* 52
1425 (1966) 350–67, 1 facs **1425** Tischler, H. 'A propos a Critical Edition of the
Parisian Organa Dupla' *Acta* 40 (1968) 28–43
1424 K believes that harmonic structures should be mostly consonant, and
that up-beat modes and ms alignment help to lead to this result. **1425** T
reviews K's statements and proposes additional principles of transcription.

1426 Schmidt, H. 'Zur Melodiebildung Leonins und Perotins' *ZMw* 14 (1931/2)
129–34
S points to patterns such as sequences underlying the melodic structure.

1427 Krüger, W. 'Wort und Ton in den Notre-Dame Organa' **B-3**.135–40
Most of K's assertions do not seem supported by evidence.

Magnus Liber: Specific pieces

1428 Tischler, H. 'The Arrangements of the *Gloria Patri* in the Office Organa of
the *Magnus liber organi*' **F-29**.260–5
T tabulates and discusses polyphonic doxologies of Notre Dame.

1429 *Perotinus Magnus. Das Organum 'Alleluja Nativitas gloriose virginis Marie' und*

seine Sippe MwSb 12 (1955) xi + separate booklet, 32 dipl facss
This presents the plainsong, settings by Leonin and Perotin, and clausulae and motets dependent on them. Some clausulae are to the *ex semine* text.

1430 Gennrich, F. 'Perotins *Beata Viscera Mariae Virginis* und die "Modal-theorie" ' *Mf* 1 (1948) 225–41
G discusses the authenticity and the rhythmic implications of related pieces.

1431 Machabey, A. 'A propos des quadruples Pérotiniens' *MD* 12 (1958) 3–25
With confusing comparisons between different sources, M suggests possible relationships between *Sederunt* and *Mors*.

1432 Husmann, H. 'Ein dreistimmiges Organum aus Sens unter den Notre-Dame-Kompositionen' **F-6**.200–3
H concludes that *Quindenis gradibus* was for use at Sens rather than Paris.

1433 Wagner, P. 'Zu den liturgischen Organa'; Ludwig, F. 'Nochmals "Zu den
1434 liturgischen Organa" '; and Wagner, P. 'Zum Organum *Crucifixum in carne,*'
AMw 6 (1924) 54–7; 245–6; 401–6 **1434** Handschin, J. 'Zum *Crucifixum in carne,*' *AMw* 7 (1925) 161–6
1433 W and L disagree on the liturgical destination. **1434** H transcribes the piece showing the uncertainty of the result, and including variants from concordances. See **1897**

DISCANT, CLAUSULA, MOTET

1435 Flotzinger, Rudolf *Der Discantussatz im Magnus liber und seiner Nachfolge*
WIENER MW BEITR 8 (Vienna 1969) 322, ext b, index + 32 unnumbered pp
m transcc in separate booklet / rev I.D. Bent *ML* 52 (1971) 80–2
This is a comprehensive catalogue and stylistic description of discant, clausulae, and copulae of the Notre Dame mss.

1436 Tischler, H. 'How were Notre Dame clausulae performed?' *ML* 50 (1969) 273–7
T finds a distinction between clausulae which could be independent pieces and others which are no more than 'organa-segments' and describes some not in either category.

1437 *Aus der Frühzeit der Motette.* I: *Der erste Zyklus von Clausulae der Hs w₁ und ihre Motetten.* II: *Der zweite Zyklus* ... MwSb 22 and 23 (1963) xv + 42, 8 facss; xvii + 42, 16 facss
This includes diplomatic transcription of clausulae, motets, etc, with indices, tables, bibliography.

1438 Anderson, G.A. 'Clausulae or Transcribed-Motets in the Florence Ms?' *Acta* 42 (1970) 109–28

Stressing variant rhythmic interpretations, each correct, A gives five principles for 'adequate' transcription of clausulae without reference to a motet
version. Including numerous transcriptions, he concludes that the clausulae
do not depend on pre-existent motets.

1439 Tischler, H. 'A Propos the Notation of the Parisian Organa' *JAMS* 14 (1961)
1–8
Comparing motets with their clausulae, T points to errors in Waite's
theories (**1418c**).

1440 Dittmer, L.A. 'Änderung der Grundrhythmen in den Notre-Dame-Hss' *Mf*
12 (1959) 392–405 (the announced continuation has not been traced)
Using Ludwig's abbreviations (**1390**), D gives the *apparatus criticus* for variants in 16 clausulae and concludes that ms w_1 was not an ancestor of F.

1441 Smith, N.E. 'Tenor Repetition in the Notre Dame Organa' *JAMS* 19 (1966)
329–51
S shows how tenor repeats (normal practice in motets) may arise through
combination of originally separate clausulae, and discusses adjustments
involved in repetition.

St Victor Manuscript: Clausula

1442 Stenzl, Jürg *Die vierzig Clausulae der Hs Paris, BN Latin 15139 (Saint-Victor*
1443 *Clausulae)* PSMfG Ser II: 22 (Bern 1970) 248 + 8 facss **1443** *Die Sankt Viktor*
1444 *Clausulae und ihre Motetten* MwSb 5/6 (2nd ed 1963) 25 + 11 facss
1445 **1444** Thurston, Ethel *The M in the St Victor Ms, BN Lat. 15139* PIMS 5 (Toronto
1446 1959) 46, 40 facss **1445** Thurston 'A Comparison of the St Victor Clausulae
with their Motets' *F-23*.785–802 **1446** Husmann, H. 'Notre-Dame und
Saint-Victor; Repertoire-Studien zur Geschichte der gereimten Prosen' *Acta*
36 (1964) 98–123, 191–221
1442 S describes the ms and corrects earlier publications concerned with it.
He analyses and transcribes the 40 clausulae. **1443** This facsimile edition
includes an inventory with diplomatic facsimiles of the motets in other
sources. The ms has French cues written in the margins next to the textless
clausulae. **1444** This is a facsimile edition, with a description in English,
French, and German. **1445** The notation of *cum littera* (texted) clarifies the
ambiguity of *sine littera* (melismatic) versions. **1446** Comparing the repertories and their distribution, H concludes that the original melodies and
texts stem from Notre Dame, while contrafacta technique was the creation
of St Victor.

CONDUCTUS

This important genre of Notre Dame composition is partly monophonic,
partly polyphonic: see items **1105–24**.

THE THIRTEENTH-CENTURY MOTET

Major reference books and catalogues are Ludwig (**1390 1391**) and Gennrich (**1392**).

Origins and terminology

1447 Handschin, J. 'Über den Ursprung der Motette' **D-1**.189–200
H traces the true roots of the motet concept to the troping principle.

1448 Dammann, R. 'Geschichte der Begriffsbestimmung Motette' *AMw* 16 (1959)
1449 337–77 **1449** Birkner, G. 'Motetus und Motette' *AMw* 18 (1961)
1450 183–94 **1450** Hofmann, K. 'Zur Entstehungs- und Frühgeschichte des Ter-
minus Motette' *Acta* 42 (1970) 138–50
1448 In the med. section (337–54) D cites and comments on important contemporary definitions. Discussing the origin, musical and etymological, he
claims that *mot* can mean 'word' and 'strophe,' and suggests that the -*et* is
not a diminutive suffix. **1449** Suggesting that 'motet' relates not to the
French *mot* 'word' but to Sardinian-Italian *motto* 'strophe,' B clarifies its relationship to the *brevitas* of the 13c and to the *duplum* of a clausula. **1450** Showing that the word originally referred to the refrain technique, H accounts
for the discrepancy between the length of the text and the diminutive form
of the word.

Style, rhythm, and form

More specific techniques are discussed in items **1484–94**.

1451 Mathiassen, Finn *The Style of the Early Motet (ca 1200–1250)* (Copenhagen
1966) 212, frontisp facs, b, index / rev E. Sanders *Notes* 17 (1959/60) 33–6
M investigates the old corpus of the Montpellier Ms.

1452 Tischler, H. 'Some Rhythmic Features in early 13c Motets' *RBM* 21 (1967)
1453 107–17 **1453** Tischler 'English Traits in the early 13c Motet' *MQ* 30 (1944)
1454 458–76 **1454** Tischler 'The Evolution of the Harmonic Style in the Notre-
1455 Dame Motet' *Acta* 28 (1956) 87–95 **1455** Tischler 'The Evolution of Form in
the earliest Motets' *Acta* 31 (1959) 86–90
1452 T claims that statistical analysis suggests the side by side existence of
progessive high art and conservative light genres. **1453** T distinguishes
melodic and harmonic from rhythmic characteristics. **1454** T investigates
development ca 1200. **1455** T isolates six types of formal design and relates
them to stages in the development of the motet.

Texts

1456 Reichert, G. 'Wechselbeziehungen zwischen M und textlicher Struktur in

1457 der Motette des 13. Jh.' **F-14**.151–69 + 4 tables **1457** Nathan, H. 'The Func-
1458 tion of Text in French 13c Motets' *MQ* 28 (1942) 445–62 **1458** Tischler, H.
1459 'Classicism and Romanticism in 13c M' *RBM* 16 (1962) 3–12 **1459** Tischler 'In-
1460 tellectual Trends in 13c Paris as reflected in the Texts of Motets' *MR* 29 (1968)
1461 1–11 **1460** Walther, H. 'Die poetische Anthologie des cod. Oxford Rawl. c
510' *MlatJb* 3 (1966) 218–27 **1461** Hunt, R.W. 'The Collections of a Monk of
Bardney: a Dismembered Rawlinson Ms' *Med. and Renaissance Studies* 5
(1961) 28–42
1456 Text and M are strictly related in the early trope-motet. In clausula or
free motet one element is predominant. Late 13c tenor repetition revives
close relationships between *color*, phrase, and verse length in different
voices. **1457** Conditioned by sound rather than grammar, texts emphasise
upper parts, forcing rhythmic change and textural heterogeneity. **1458** T
outlines stylistic and textual developments in the motet. **1459** Textual topics
change and can clarify chronology. **1460** W prints and analyses the texts not
previously published. **1461** H identifies the provenance of the ms, which
contains texts of Notre Dame conductus and motets, and prints ten texts.

Miscellaneous

1462 Anderson, G.A. 'Notre Dame Bilingual Motets – A Study in the History of
1463 M c. 1215–1245' *MiscM-A* 3 (1968) 50–144 **1463** Anderson 'A Small Collection
of Notre Dame Motets ca. 1215–1235' *JAMS* 22 (1969) 157–96
1462 This is an analytical and descriptive catalogue of the works. **1463** With
bibliography and some transcriptions, A describes in detail the compositions in BM Add 30091. Tischler comments in *JAMS* 23 (1970) 359–60 and A
replies in 24 (1971) 318–20.

1464 Aubry, P. *Recherches sur les 'tenors' français dans les motets du treizième siècle*
1465 (Paris 1907) 40 **1465** Aubry, with Amédée Gastoué *Recherches sur les 'tenors'
latins* (Paris 1907) 20
1464 A prints texts and completes the Montpellier tenors from an Oxford
chansonnier. **1465** A and G identify many of the tenors.

 *Announced: Hofmann, Klaus *Untersuchungen zur Kompositionstechnik der
Motette im 13. Jh., durchgeführt an den Motetten mit dem Tenor 'In seculum'*

MAJOR SOURCES, FACSIMILES, EDITIONS

Bamberg

1466 *Cent Motets du XIIIe Siècle* ed Pierre Aubry 3 vols (Paris 1908; repr 1964) v +
130 facss; v + 233; 1–144 + 13 facss, 145–61 / rev H. Villetard *Rassegna greg.*
8 (1909) columns 29–38
Vol 1 is a facsimile edition of the M section of the Bamberg Ms Ed. IV. 6 (now

Lit. 115). Vol 2 is an edition of the M, using C clefs, and often quite inaccurate in details. In vol 3 A describes the origin and development of the 13c motet, and describes the ms, its notation, and rhythmic practices. He includes 13 plates of contemporary sources, and a chapter on the use of instruments in the performance of motets.

Las Huelgas

1467 *El Codex M de las Huelgas* ed Higini Angles 3 vols BarcCat 6 (Barcelona 1931) xxxii + 388, num pll, M exx, index; xlviii + 4, 1 facs fos 1–168 facss; xvii + 413 / rev W.H. Frere *ML* 14 (1933) 266–8
Vol 1 includes a general introduction to Spanish M and mss, 6–14c, with a comprehensive bibliography of plainsong and polyphonic mss of various European provenance, and of editions of texts, plainsong, and polyphony, and of books. See **1821**. There is a stylistic description of the M in the Las Huelgas Ms, and an index of names and subjects. Vol 2 contains a description of the Las Huelgas monastery, of the ms and its language, with an inventory. There is a complete facsimile. In vol 3 A edits the M in C clefs, with some 'parallel' variants from concordances. He includes a list of pieces, and index of incipits according to language and voice.

1468 Anderson, G.A. 'Newly Identified Clausula-Motets in the Las Huelgas Ms' *MQ* 55 (1969) 228–45
A corrects tenor assignations made by Ludwig (**1390**) and identifies others not traced. He discusses their implications for the repertory of the ms, concluding that it is mostly of central rather than peripheral origin. He suggests principles for a new *Repertorium*.

Madrid

1469 Husmann, H. 'Die Motetten der Madrider Hs und deren geschichtliche Stellung' *AMf* 2 (1937) 173–84
H complements **1390**, describes and transcribes motets from the Madrid Ms (**1417**).

Montpellier

1470 *Polyphonies du XIIIᵉ Siècle. Le Ms H. 196 de la Faculté de Médecine de Montpellier* ed Yvonne Rokseth 4 vols EOL (Paris 1935, 1936, 1936, 1939) fos 1–397 facss; iii + 306; 267; 311 / rev K. Jeppesen *Acta* 21 (1949) 74–5. See also **15**.
The complete facsimile in vol 1 is followed by an edition in vols 2 and 3. The commentary in vol 4 is a thorough survey of the styles, forms, and sources of M from Notre Dame through the 13c as revealed in the different sections of the Montpellier Ms. For an inventory see **51**.

1471 Apfel, Ernst *Anlage und Struktur der Motteten im Codex Montpellier* SUS, Reihe

Philos Fakultät, Bd 10 (Heidelberg 1970) 117
This is a detailed technical analysis of 'harmonic' structure, rhythmic and pitch disposition of the voices, etc.

1472 Kuhlmann, Georg *Die zweistimmigen französischen Motetten des Kodex Montpellier* 2 vols, LMw, Bd I and II (Würzburg 1938) xxii + 214 + 1 table, b, index; 2 facss + 252 pp M transcc and critical apparatus / rev *Allgem. Musikzeitung* 65 (1938) 354
In vol 1 K describes the structure and notation. In vol 2 he transcribes the works, with variants and commentary.

Smaller sources

La Clayette
1473 *Paris, [nouv. acq. fr.] 13521 & [lat.] 11411* MedMM 4 (1959) 74, 48 facss
1474 1474 *Ein altfranzösischer Motettenkodex* SMMA 6 (1958) 72, fos 369–90ᵛ facss
1473 This is a facsimile of the *La Clayette Ms*, with introduction, index, and transcriptions. 1474 This facsimile with introduction and inventory complements 1390.

1475 Rosenthal, A. 'Le Ms de la Clayette Retrouvé' *AnnM* 1 (1953) 105–30 1476
1476 Schrade, L. 'Unknown Motets in a Recovered 13c Ms' *Spec* 30 (1955) 393–412,
1477 repr in F-27.212–40 1477 Bukofzer, M.F. 'The unidentified tenors in the Ms La Clayette' *AnnM* 4 (1956) 255–8
1475 R gives a brief history and description, followed by a detailed inventory with concordances and indices. See *Mf* 9 (1956) 446. 1476 S complements the previous article and transcribes the triple motet. 1477 B identifies two tenors.

Turin
1478 *Les 'Motets Wallons'* ed Antoine Auda 2 vols, often bound in one (Brussels 1953) xii + 92 + 90 facss; 140 pp M transcc, index / rev M.F. Bukofzer *Notes* 11 (1953/4) 266–8
This is a facsimile and edition of the motets in the Turin Ms vari 42, some of which use Liégeois dialect. A documents the history of M in the Liège area, and describes the M in the ms.

Wimpfener (Darmstadt)
1479 *Die Wimpfener Fragmente der Hessischen Landesbibliothek Darmstadt* SMMA 5
1480 (1958) 69, fos 1ᵃʳ–10ᵛ facss and reconstruction in dipl facs 1480 Flotzinger, R. 'Zur Herkunft der Wimpfener Fragmente' F-15.147–51
1479 A ms of 13c motets and conductus is re-assembled, with description and inventory. 1480 F prefers Parisian rather than German origin.

Others
1481 Chailley, J. 'Fragments d'un nouveau Ms d'Ars Antiqua à Châlons-sur-Marne' F-14.140–50

C describes and inventories this source, which contains *mono*textual motets. See also J. Hourlier and J. Chailley 'Cantionale Cathalaunense' *Mém de la Soc d'Agriculture, Commerce, Sciences et Arts du Département de la Marne* 71 ser 2, 30 (1956) 141–7, 1 facs.

1482 Kossmann, E.F. 'Ein Fragment einer neuen altfranzösischen Motetten-Hs' and F. Ludwig 'Versuch einer Übertragung der Motetten Herenthals Nr. 4 und 5' *ZMw* 8 (1925/6) 193–5 and 196–200
K describes and lists the contents: L transcribes two pieces, with comments.

ANTHOLOGIES

1483 *Florilegium Motetorum. Ein Querschnitt durch das Motettenschaffen des 13. Jh.* SMMA 17 (1966) xlii + 204
This is a critical edition of 53 motets, with indices of incipits, tenors, lists of mss and sources of tenors, and some diplomatic transcriptions.

SPECIFIC STYLISTIC CHARACTERISTICS

Refrains

1484 Gennrich, F. 'Trouvèrelieder und Motettenrepertoire' *ZMw* 9 (1926/7) 8–39,
1485 65–85, 3 facss 1485 Gennrich 'Refrain-Tropen in der M des MA' *SM* 16 (1943–50) 242–54
1484 With numerous transcriptions G examines and catalogues the trouvère material used in motets. 1485 *Motets entés*, beginning and ending with pre-existent refrains, demonstrate a form of troping. G transcribes several pieces to make the procedure clear.

Contrafacta

1486 Anderson, G.A. 'Newly Identified Tenor Chants in the Notre Dame Reper-
1487 tory' *ML* 50 (1969) 158–71 1487 Anderson 'A New Look at an Old Motet' *ML* 49 (1968) 18–20
1486 A sees Latin contrafacta motets as an attempt to stem the tide of secular composition in the 13c. He identifies several tenor sources not traced by Ludwig (1390). 1487 A corrects Ludwig's assignment in 1390, showing the motet to be a contrafactum of a French piece.

Imitation and hocket

1488 Harbinson, D. 'Imitation in the Early Motet' *ML* 45 (1964) 359–68
H argues that conscious imitation does indeed occur quite often in the 13c motet.

1489 Schneider, M. 'Der Hochetus' *ZMw* 11 (1928/9) 390–6 1490 Dalglish, W.E.
1490 'The Hocket in Med. Polyphony' *MQ* 55 (1969) 344–63

1489 S gives some basic information. **1490** Criticising S's explanation and citing theoretical evidence, D distinguishes between hocket *super tenorem*, which he sees as either independent or incidental, and hocket *super cantum*, which he shows to be a variation of previous material. He suggests that hocketing might be one form of med. improvisation.

Specific pieces

1491 Husmann, H. 'Der Hoketus "*A l'entrade d'avril*" ' *AMw* 11 (1954) 296–9
H transcribes the piece and discusses its rhythm.

1492 Birkner, G. 'Zur Motette über "*Brumans est mors*" ' *AMw* 10 (1953) 71–80
1493 **1493** Kaspers, W. '*Brumans est mors*,' *Mf* 2 (1949) 177–80
1492 analyses and transcribes the piece. **1493** K explains the word *brumans* 'bridgroom,' 'Christ'.

1494 Stenzl, J. 'Eine unbekannte Sanctus-Motette vom Ende des 13. Jh.' *Acta* 42 (1970) 128–38, 1 facs
S describes the source and transcribes the piece, an unusual type of motet.

France and Flanders: The fourteenth century

ARS NOVA

Bibliography, surveys

1495 Clercx, S. 'Propos sur l'Ars Nova' *RBM* 10 (1956) 77–82, 154–60 and 11 (1957) 67–9
C reviews and relates recent publications.

1496 Schrade, L. 'The Chronology of the Ars Nova in France' **D-14**.37–62
1497 **1497** Bridgman, N.'La M dans la société française au temps de l'Ars Nova'
1498 **D-3**.83–96 **1498** Pirrotta, N.'Ars Nova e Stil Novo' *RIM* 1 (1966) 3–19 **1499**
1499 Schneider, Marius *Die Ars Nova des XIV. Jh. in Frankreich und Italien* (Potsdam nd or Wolfenbüttel 1931) 85 + 4 pp M exx
1496 Schrade points out uncertainties and vagueness in the interpretation of the 14c. **1497** B finds contemporary views about M , musicians, the use of instruments, etc. **1498** P thinks the most important fact of the Ars Nova is the infusion of formal elements and expressive ideals from the oral monophonic tradition into the polyphonic repertory. **1499** This is a thorough although brief survey.

The papal bull

1500 Anglés, H. 'La M sagrade de la capilla pontificia de Avignon en la capilla
1501 real aragonesa durante el siglo XIV' *AnuarioM* 12 (1957) 35–44 **1501** Fellerer,
1502 K.G. 'Zur Constitutio "Docta Ss Patrum" ' **F-15**.125–32 **1502** Fellerer 'La

"Constitutio docta Sanctorum Patrum" di Giovanni xxɪɪ e la ᴍ nuova del suo tempo' **D-3**.9–17
1500 A discusses the effect of John xxɪɪ's bull. **1501 1502** F considers the bull in its effect and in relation to incipient humanistic attitudes.

Sources, facsimiles, editions

These facsimiles, editions, and anthologies are listed in approximately chronological order, depending on their contents.

General catalogues
1503 *Mss of Polyphonic M (ca 1320–1400)* ed Gilbert Reaney ʀɪsᴍ, Ser ʙ ɪᴠ² (1969) 427, indices of composers, incipits
This volume lists Ars Nova sources, excluding Italian, Czech, and Polish mss.

Roman de Fauvel and Philippe de Vitry
For Philippe de Vitry as a composer see items **1547–50**. For his theoretical works see items **1627–30a**.

***1504** *Le Roman de Fauvel* ed Pierre Aubry sᴀᴛF (Paris 1907) ? leaves of col facss
1505 **1505** *The 'Roman de Fauvel.' The Works of Philippe de Vitry. French Cycles of*
1506 *the 'Ordinarium Missae'* ed Leo Schrade ᴘᴍFc 1 (1956) iv + 164 + separately
1507 bound editorial notes (see under ᴘᴍFc) / rev D.G. Hughes *JAMS* 9 (1956) 221–5 **1506** *Le Roman de Fauvel par Gervais de Bus* ed Arthur Långfors sᴀᴛF (Paris 1914–19) cx + 220, glossary, index of names **1507** Reaney, G. 'The "Roman de Fauvel" and its ᴍ' *The Monthly M Record* 89 (1959) 99–103 **1504** This is a coloured facsimile edition of the whole ms, Paris, ʙɴ Fr. 146. **1505** This is an edition of the musical pieces only. **1506** This is an edition of the text of the *Roman* (**1310 1314**), excluding the interpolated ᴍ items, which consist of Latin and French secular and sacred forms of all types. **1507** This is an excellent description of the ms and its importance.

Other facsimiles and editions
1508 *French Secular Compositions of the Fourteenth Century* ed Willi Apel and Samuel N. Rosenberg cᴍᴍ 53 (1970) lxxviii + 230
This is a scholarly edition with lists of sources, compositions, text incipits, and bibliography.

1509 *The Ms London, ʙᴍ Add 29987* ed Gilbert Reaney ᴍsᴅ 13 (1965) 29 + 88 fos facss + 1 unnumbered facs
This facsimile edition includes an inventory and introduction.

1510 *Le Ms de M du Trésor d'Apt* ed Amédée Gastoué soc FʀANÇAISE ᴅE ᴍusɪcoʟoGɪE, Ser ɪ, Mon de la ᴍ ancienne 10 (Paris 1936) xxii + 176 / rev G. de Van *Acta* 12 (1940) 64–9
G describes the source and styles briefly, then edits the ᴍ.

1511 *Zehn datierbare Kompositionen der Ars Nova* ed Ursula Günther
SCHRIFTENREIHE DES MW INST DER U HAMBURG 2 (Hamburg 1959) 27
G edits a good selection of French and Latin pieces, with introduction and
notes.

1512 Kammerer, Friedrich *Die Musikstücke des Prager Kodex XI E 9* VER. DES MW
INST DER DEUTSCHEN U IN PRAG 1 (Brno 1931) 172 / rev C. Van den Borren *RUB*
37 (1931/2) 103*–4*
K describes and transcribes the M section of this 14c ms.

1513 Hoppin, R. 'Some Remarks a propos of *Pic*' *RBM* 10 (1956) 105–11
H finds evidence for a possible centre of M activity in northern France in
the 14c.

Masses

1514 *Fourteenth-Century Mass M in France* ed Hanna Stäblein-Harder CMM 29
(1962) xiv, 3 facss + 144
This is an edition. The commentary and introduction and list of compositions are in MSD 7 (1962) pp 182, under the same title.

Parody and cyclic Masses

See also under Guillaume de Machaut (**1570–6**).

1515 Clercx-Lejeune, S. 'Les Débuts de la Messe unitaire et de la *Missa parodia*
au XIVᵉ siècle et principalement dans l'œuvre de J. Ciconia' **D-3**.97–104, 2
facss
Avignon Mass style, modified by Italian influence, was practised in Liège
by 1388. C asserts that Ciconia invented the parody Mass.

1516 Ludwig, F. 'Die mehrstimmige Messe des 14. Jh.' *AMw* 7 (1925) 417–35
L itemises the repertory, comparing the styles with those of secular M.

Besançon, Ivrea, and Sorbonne Masses
1517 Schrade, L. 'A 14c Parody Mass' *Acta* 27 (1955) 13–39 and 'A note Concerning
1518 "A 14c ..." ' 28 (1956) 54–5; repr **F-27**.241–82 **1518** Chailley, J. 'Autour de la
1519 messe de Besançon' *Acta* 28 (1956) 73–5 **1519** Chailley 'La Messe de Besan-
1520 çon et un compositeur inconnu du XIVᵉ siècle: Jean Lambelet' *AnnM* 2 (1954)
93–103 + 4 facss **1520** Jackson, R. 'M Interrelations between 14c Mass movements' *Acta* 29 (1957) 54–64
1517 Comparing items in the Sorbonne Mass and the Ivrea ms, S suggests
that they are drawn from a common source now lost. **1518** C corrects some
points in S's article. **1519** C describes the source, transcribes part of the
Besançon Mass, and tries to identify the composer. **1520** J complements and
extends S's discoveries.

Toulouse Mass

1521 Harder, H. 'Die Messe von Toulouse' *MD* 7 (1953) 105–28 **1522** Schrade, L.
1522 'The Mass of Toulouse' *RBM* 8 (1954) 84–96
    1521 With transcriptions H discusses the styles especially in relation to the text. **1522** Showing that chant cycles already existed (see **672–5**), S maintains that 14c polyphonic cycles are artistically unified.

Tournai Mass

1523 *The Tournai Mass* ed Charles Van den Borren CMM 13 (1957) xi + 33 **1524** Ang-
1524 lès, H. 'Una nueva versión del Credo de Tournai' *RBM* 8 (1954) 97–9
    1523 This is an edition. **1524** A ms in Madrid has a concordance.

  *Announced: Harder, H. 'Die Messenkompositionen am päpstlichen Hof in Avignon'

Motets

1525 *Motets of French Provenance* ed F.Ll. Harrison PMFC 5 (1968) xix + 217 + 32 separate pages of notes on the texts
This is an edition.

1526 Harbinson, D. 'Isorhythmic technique in the early motet' *ML* 47 (1966)
1527 100–9 **1527** Reaney, G. 'The Isorhythmic Motet and its Social Background'
1528 B-4.25–7 **1528** Apel, W. 'Remarks about the isorhythmic motet' D-14.139–48
1529 **1529** Günther, U. 'The 14c Motet and its Development' *MD* 12 (1958) 27–58
    1526 H finds elements of isorhythmic technique in the 13c motet and tries to suggest that 14c isorhythm 'embodied nothing new.' **1527** R hypothesises about the occasions on which isorhythmic motets were performed. **1528** This mathematical form may be summarised by formula. **1529** Through an (iso-)rhythmic analysis G shows that the motet was conservative compared with the chanson. She includes two transcriptions and their texts.

1530 Reichert, G. 'Das Verhältnis zwischen M und textlicher Struktur in den
1531 Motetten Machauts' *AMw* 13 (1956) 197–216, 5 tables **1531** Günther, U. 'Das wort-Ton-Problem bei Motetten des späten 14. Jh.' F-5.163–78
    1530 Using foldout tables to give complete voices or works laid out to clarify the isorhythmic scheme, R shows a close relation between strophe and *talea*, text-line and M phrase, rhyme and hocket. **1531** With transcriptions G shows that R's conclusions apply also in the Chantilly Ms.

1532 Petrobelli, P. 'Due mottetti francesi in una sconosciuta fonte udinese' *CHM* 4 (1966) 201–14
    P describes the source, prints and translates the texts, and discusses the M.

Secular forms and poetry

Formes fixes: Ballades, rondeaux, and virelais

1533 Reaney, G. 'Concerning the Origins of the Rondeau, Virelai and Ballade

1534 Forms' *MD* 6 (1952) 155–66 **1534** Reaney 'The Development of the Rondeau, Virelai and Ballade Forms from Adam de la Hale to Guillaume de Machaut' **F-11**.421–7
1533 R summarises earlier theories, including those outside the standard M literature, and draws somewhat inconclusive conclusions. **1534** This is a useful general survey of the landmarks.

1535 Wilkins, N. 'The Structure of Ballades, Rondeaux and Virelais in Froissart
1536 and Christine de Pisan' *French Studies* 23 (1969) 337–48 **1536** Wilkins, ed *One Hundred Ballades, Rondeaux and Virelais from the late MA* (Cambridge 1969) viii + 212, glossary, b, indices of names and first lines / rev M. Bent *ML* 50 (1969) 527–8
1535 W shows that *formes fixes* are indeed fixed when examined from the M aspect. He gives examples illustrating clear typographical layout of textual types to agree with the M form. He suggests avoiding the concept of stanza. **1536** This anthology of texts clearly illustrates the *formes fixes*, has notes on poems and poets, and includes an appendix of M.

1537 Entry deleted

Poets: Deschamps and Molinet
1538 Laurie, I.S. 'Deschamps and the Lyric as Natural M' *MLR* 59 (1964) 561–70
L thinks that Deschamps is the first to describe the lyric as poetry rather than song. See **1540a**.

1539 Entry deleted

1540 Entry deleted

1540a MacClintock, C. 'Molinet, M, and Med. Rhetoric' *MD* 13 (1959) 109–21
Molinet (15c) extends Deschamps' ideas (**1538**) to make rhetoric *une espèce de M*. Apparent confusion in passages relating to M hides a rhetorical order.

Specific compositions and techniques
1541 Günther, U. 'Der Gebrauch des *tempus perfectum diminutum* in der Hs.
1542 Chantilly 1047' *AMw* 17 (1960) 277–97 **1542** Günther 'Die Anwendung der Diminution in der Hs Chantilly 1047' *AMw* 17 (1960) 1–21
In these two articles G describes the relations between Italian and French 14–15c sources. From the original notation she shows how coloration and signs produce complex rhythms and proportions. Finding that diminution is essentially a French practice, she confirms Fischer's assertion (**1722**) that Italian augmentation shows French influence.

1543 Bukofzer, M.F. 'Two mensuration canons' *MD* 2 (1948) 165–71
With transcriptions B brings Ghisi's version (**1682**) closer to a solution.

1544 Chailley, J. 'Motets inédits du xɪvᵉ siècle à la cathédrale de Sens' *RdM* 29 (1950) 27–34
C transcribes pieces with curiously intermingled antiphon texts.

1545 Günther, U. 'Eine Ballade auf Mathieu de Foix' *MD* 19 (1965) 69–81
Briefly relating the Chantilly Ms to Avignon, Foix, and Aragon, G identifies
and dates one of the texts.

1546 Günther, U. 'Zwei Balladen auf Bertrand und Olivier du Guesclin' *MD* 22
(1968) 15–45
G identifies topics and dates of 14c secular texts and discusses two ballades
whose subjects are deducible from the evidence of archives, genealogical
tables, acrostics, and seals. She prints a colour facsimile of one piece, and
discusses the M of both, showing that they cannot be by the same composer.

Composers

These are listed chronologically.

Philippe de Vitry
See **1505**, an edition of his works. For his theoretical writings see items
1627–30a.

1547 Schrade, L. 'Philippe de Vitry: Some New Discoveries' *MQ* 42 (1956) 330–54;
repr **F-27**.283–309
S reviews the methods of attributing works to Vitry, assigns several more
on stylistic grounds, and gives a complete list. S summarises some of Vitry's
political texts.

1548 Besseler, H. 'Falsche Autornamen in den Hss Strassburg (Vitry) und Mon-
tecassino (Dufay)' *Acta* 40 (1968) 201–3
B uses stylistic criteria to deny Vitry's authorship.

1549 Zwick, G. 'Deux motets inédits de Philippe de Vitry et de Guillaume de
1550 Machaut' *RdM* 27 (1948) 28–57, 1 facs **1550** Maillard, J., and A. Gilles 'Notes
sur trois motets fantômes de l'*Ars Nova* de Ph. de Vitry' *RdM* 38 (1956) 147–50
1549 Z describes and inventories a ms in Switzerland, prints some texts and
two compositions. **1550** Three motets in Z's list are unknown probably
because their titles were misread.

Guillaume de Machaut
1550a Reaney, Gilbert *Guillaume de Machaut* OXFORD STUDIES OF COMPOSERS 9
(London 1971) 76
This is an excellent, readable, survey.

Machaut: Collected musical works
1551 *Guillaume de Machaut: M Werke* ed Friedrich Ludwig 4 vols: vols 1–3 PÄM
(Leipzig 1926), vol 4 ed Heinrich Besseler from L's notes (publ 1954, when
vols 1–3 were reprinted) iii + 103; 1*–70*; 1–86 (or 105–90, continuing vol 1);

1–83 (or 191–273) / rev vols 1 and 3 M. Cauchie *RdM* 8 (1927) 172–3 and 11 (1930) 224
Vol 1: Ballades, Rondeaux, Virelais. Vol 2: Introduction. Vol 3: Motets. Vol 4: Mass and Lais. This is a heavily scholarly edition using c clefs. The second volume has a long introduction with lists of mss, names, texts, descriptions of sources, but no stylistic discussion. See **1558**.

1552 *The Works of G. de Machaut* ed Leo Schrade 2 vols PMFC 2, 3 (1956) v + 163; vi + 192 / rev D.G. Hughes *JAMS* 11 (1958) 240–3
The first part (vol 2 of PMFC) contains the Lais, Complainte, Chanson royale, and Motets 1–16; the second part (vol 3) contains Motets 17–24, Mass, Double Hocket, Ballades, Rondeaux, Virelais. This is an edition in modern clefs: a typewritten commentary is bound separately; see under PMFC. See **1558**.

Machaut as poet and composer
1553 Machabey, Armand *Guillaume de Machaut, 130?–1377* 2 vols (Paris 1955) 199, 4 pll; 199, 4 pll, chronology, b, index / rev G. Reaney *ML* 37 (1956) 294–8
Vol 1 is biographical and begins a discussion of the works and sources, continued in vol 2, which also includes a section on the instruments mentioned by Machaut.

1554 Reaney, G. 'Guillaume de Machaut: lyric poet' *ML* 39 (1958) 38–51 **1555**
1555 Reaney 'The Poetic Form of Machaut's M Works' *MD* 13 (1959) 24–41
1554 This is a useful general review of Machaut's poetic style and its relation to the *rhétorique* of the time. **1555** Showing 14c principles of scansion in Ballades, Rondeaux, and Virelais, R sees Machaut as the leader of a new school of poets even though he uses traditional devices.

1556 Perle, G. 'Integrative Devices in the M of Machaut' *MQ* 34 (1948) 169–76
Melodic and rhythmic motives unify the M. P compares this with some 20c techniques.

1557 Schrade, L. 'Guillaume de Machaut and the Roman de Fauvel' **F-2.II.843**–50
S shows that some of Machaut's monophony is modelled on pieces in the *Roman*.

1558 Hoppin, R.H. 'Notational Licences of Guillaume de Machaut' *MD* 14 (1960) 13–27
H shows that the transcriptions by Wolf (**129**), Ludwig (**1551**), and Schrade (**1552**) assume licences which Machaut did not commit.

1559 Dömling, W. 'Zur Überlieferung der M Werke Guillaume de Machauts' *Mf* 22 (1969) 189–95
D lists the ms sources, showing some of the interrelationships.

Machaut: Chronology
1560 Reaney, G. 'A Chronology of the Ballades, Rondeaux and Virelais set to M
1561 by Guillaume de Machaut' *MD* 6 (1952) 33–8 **1561** Günther, U. 'Chro-
1562 nologie und Stil der Kompositionen Guillaume de Machauts' *Acta* 35 (1963)
1562a 96–114 **1562** Reaney, G. 'Towards a Chronology of Machaut's M Works' *MD*

21 (1967) 87–96 **1562a** Williams, Sarah J. 'An author's role in 14c book production: Guillaume de Machaut's *Livre ou je met toutes mes choses*,' *Rom* 90 (1969) 433–54

1560 R outlines a chronology according to his suggestion that one of the mss was supervised by Machaut himself. **1561** Using all the available evidence, G reviews the problem of dating. **1562** R summarises the known information. **1562a** Drawing conclusions from a presumed 'working-exemplar,' W refers to the chronology of Machaut's works.

Machaut: Secular lyrics

1563 Dömling, Wolfgang *Die mehrstimmigen Balladen, Rondeaux und Virelais von Guillaume de Machaut. Untersuchungen zum M Satz* MVM 16 (Tutzing 1970) 95 D analyses M and texts.

1564 Reaney, G. 'The Ballades, Rondeaux and Virelais of Guillaume de Machaut:
1565 Melody, Rhythm and Form' *Acta* 27 (1955) 40–58, 2 pp transcc **1565** Reaney 'Fourteenth Century Harmony and the Ballades, Rondeaux and Virelais of Guillaume de Machaut' *MD* 7 (1953) 129–46

1564 This is a good technical analysis. **1565** Although there are some doubtful conclusions, the article explains the compositional process which resulted in harmonic effects.

1566 Williams, S.J. 'Vocal Scoring in the Chansons of Machaut' *JAMS* 21 (1968) 251–7

W uses variations in scoring to show that our concept of one single established version of a composition is inherently foreign to the MA.

1567 Reaney, G. 'The *Lais* of G. de Machaut and their Background' *PRMA* 82 (1955/6) 15–32

The form of the M is largely controlled by the poetry.

1568 Hoppin, R.H. 'An Unrecognized Polyphonic Lai of Machaut' *MD* 12 (1958)
1568a 93–104 **1568a** Hasselman, M., and T. Walker 'More Hidden Polyphony in a Machaut Ms' *MD* 24 (1970) 7–16

1568 Hoppin justifies, then transcribes, the correct version of the *Lay de Consolation*. **1568a** Another lai is unquestionably polyphonic.

Machaut: Motets

1569 Eggebrecht, H.H. 'Machauts Motette Nr. 9' *AMw* 19/20 (1962/3) 281–93 and 25 (1968) 173–95

Comprehensively analysing the text and M, E argues that Machaut through harmonic processes makes the isorhythmic form apparent to the listener.

Machaut: Mass of Notre Dame

1570 *Guillaume de Machaut: Messe de Nostre Dame* SMMA 1 (1957) iii + fos 281 –294 facss + ii

This is a facsimile edition.

1571 *Guillaume de Machaut: Messe de Notre-Dame dite du Sacre de Charles V (1364)*
1572 ed Jacques Chailley (Paris 1948) xi + 48 **1572** *Guillaume de Machault: La*
*1573 *Messe de Nostre Dame* ed Hanns Hübsch (Heidelberg 1953) 32 *1573 *Messe*
1574 *Notre-Dame à quatre voix de Guillaume de Machault* ed Armand Machabey
(Liège 1948) **1574** *Guillaume de Machaut, Mass* ed Guillaume de Van CMM
2 (1949) xxvi + 6 unnumbered pp + 30
These are all allegedly performing editions of the Mass: the edition by
Hübsch is probably the most satisfactory. See **1576.**

1575 Cape, S. 'The Machaut Mass and its Performance' *Score* 25 (1959) 38–57 and
26 (1960) 20–9
Designed to sell the work, this article offers very personal constructive suggestions. It is marred by illogical conclusions, anachronisms (especially in
the instruments suggested), incorrect and overly dogmatic statements.
Reaney offers much more scholarly recommendations in **1958.**

1576 Gombosi, O. 'Machaut's *Messe Notre-Dame,*' MQ 36 (1950) 204–24 (errata on
p 466)
G comments on the editions by Chailley, Machabey, and de Van. The Gloria
and Credo have a structure of varied strophes. With some juggling of bar-
lines G sees in the isorhythmic movements a speculative mathematical symmetry organising the *taleae* on a higher level. He compares the motets.

1577 Dömling, W. 'Isorhythmie und Variation. Über Kompositionstechniken in
der Messe Guillaume de Machauts' *AMw* 28 (1971) 24–32
D analyses the schemes and endorses a late date of composition.

Ars Nova: Later composers
1578 Hoppin, R.H., and S. Clercx 'Notes biographiques sur quelques musiciens
1579 français du XIVᵉ siècle' **D-14**.63–92 **1579** Pedrell, F. 'Jean I d'Aragon,
compositeur de M' **F-24**.229–40
1578 H and C give information about musicians mentioned in 14c motet
texts or known as composers. **1579** Contemporary records throw light on
Jean's activities.

ARS SUBTILIOR

This section concerns the transition from Machaut to the Burgundian school
of the fifteenth century. Stylistically it is dominated by the extreme
rhythmic complexities of the 'mannered school.'

1580 Günther, U. 'Das Ende der Ars nova' *Mf* 16 (1963) 105–20, 1 pl
G sees the end of the *ars nova* about 1377: she quotes theorists to justify her
preference for *ars subtilior*, rather than 'mannered style,' to describe the M
style of ca 1378–1417. See also **B-4**.108–9.

1581 Wilkins, N. 'The Post-Machaut generation of poet-musicians' *Nottingham Med. Studies* 12 (1968) 40–84
This is a well documented and detailed survey, including a biographical list of composers, and a list of textual incipits, and a schematic examination of the *formes fixes* to show their flexibility.

1582 Reaney, G. 'Machaut's influence on late med. M. I: France and Burgundy. II: The Non-Gallic Countries' *The Monthly M Record* 88 (1958) 50–8, 96–101
These are brief but excellent surveys of French influence between Machaut and Dufay.

1583 Besseler, H. 'Hat Matheus de Perusio Epoche gemacht?' *Mf* 8 (1955) 19–23
Questioning Apel (**1587**), B shows that Matheo was too minor a composer to characterize an era: he would prefer the 'Ciconia era.'

1584 Pirrotta, N. 'On Text Forms from Ciconia to Dufay' **F-23**.673–82
P comments on the dissolving of formal structures.

1585 Günther, U. 'Datierbare Balladen des späten 14. Jh.' *MD* 15 (1961) 39–61 and
1586 16 (1962) 151–74 **1586** Günther 'Zur Biographie einiger Komponisten der Ars subtilior' *AMw* 21 (1964) 172–99, 4 pll
1585 After a detailed M analysis of 10 compositions, G briefly compares the style with that of Machaut. **1586** Textual allusions, court, and church records are used to trace several minor composers.

Sources, facsimiles, editions

Anthologies
1587 *French Secular M of the Late 14c* ed Willi Apel MAA 55 (Cambridge, Mass. 1950) xii + 39 + 8 col facss + 133, glossary, list of texts / rev W.H. Rubsamen *Notes* 8 (1950/1) 695–7
A edits 81 pieces of Avignonese French-Italian polyphony, many in *subtilior* style. The introduction, describing sources, styles, and forms is an expanded version of A's article in *Acta* 18 (1946) 17–29.

Chantilly
1588 *The Motets of the Mss Chantilly, musée condé 564 (olim 1047) and Modena, Bib-*
1589 *lioteca estense α.M. 5,24 (olim lat. 568)* ed Ursula Günther CMM 39 (1965) 8 unnumbered pp + lxv +70 **1589** Reaney, G. 'The Ms Chantilly, Musée Condé 1047' *MD* 8 (1954) 59–113 (errata on extra p preceding 59) and a 'Postscript ...' *MD* 10 (1956) 55–9
1588 This is a scholarly edition. **1589** R describes and inventories this source of French late 14c secular M.

Reina
1590 *A Fourteenth-Century Repertory from the Codex Reina* ed Nigel E. Wilkins
1591 CMM 36 (1966) xxii, 2 facss + 69 / rev: see **1593** **1591** Fischer,K. von 'The Ms

1592 BN, nouv. acq. fr. 6771 (*Codex Reina* = PR)' *MD* 11 (1957) 38–78, 3
1593 pll **1592** Wilkins, N. 'The Codex Reina: a revised Description' *MD* 17 (1963)
57–73, pll **1593** Günther, U. 'Bemerkungen zum älteren französischen
Repertoire des Codex Reina (PR)' *AMw* 24 (1967) 237–52
1590 This is a scholarly edition of 52 secular pieces, with index of incipits,
list of mss, etc. **1591** Introducing a complete inventory with concordances,
F describes the structure, scribes, composers, notation, language, and
forms of this 14c source: in **1592** W disagrees with details and corrects some
errors. Neither scholar's assertions about paleographical matters are supported with adequate evidence. F replies on pp 74–7. **1593** Also giving additional information, G corrects many errors in **1590**.

Ivrea
1593a Borghezio, G. 'Poesie M latine e francesi in un codice ignorato della Bibl.
capitolare d'Ivrea' *AR* 5 (1921) 173–86, 2 facss
This is a description and inventory.

Turin: the Cypriot repertory
1594 *The Cypriot-French Repertory* ed Richard H. Hoppin 4 vols CMM 21: vol I
1595 (1960) 8 unnumbered pp + xvi + 4 facss + 95; vol II (1961) 12 unnumb pp
1596 + xxii + 4 facss + 183; vol III (1963) 2 unnumb pp + xxxvi + 4 facss + 180;
vol IV (1963) 2 unnumb pp + xxv + 4 facss + 77 **1595** Hoppin, 'The Ms J.
II. 9 in the Biblioteca Nazionale of Torino' *D-3*.75–82 **1596** Hoppin 'The
Cypriot-French Repertory of the Ms Torino Bib. Nazionale, J. II. 9' *MD* 11
(1957) 79–125
1594 This is a scholarly edition of an early 15c ms. **1595** H gives an excellent
description of the contents. **1596** H shows that Cyprus was not culturally
peripheral and, describing the ms, finds its M and texts in typical late 14c
French style.

Composers

Ciconia
For his theoretical works see items **1613–15**.

1597 Clercx(-Lejeune), Suzanne *Johannes Ciconia: Un Musicien liégeois et son temps*
2 vols I: *La Vie et l'œuvre*. II: *Transcriptions et notes critiques* (Brussels 1960)
xxiii + 144 + 11 pll, ext b; 198 + 16 facss / rev K. von Fischer 'Johannes Ciconia' *RBM* 15 (1961) 168–74 and *Mf* 14 (1961) 316–22
Vol 1 deals with the M and archival sources upon which a comprehensive
biography and stylistic analysis is based. C also refers to texts and their historical allusions, to notation, forms, and genres. She includes a thematic
inventory. Vol 2 is an edition of the works.

1598 Entry deleted

1599 Brown, S.E. 'A possible Cantus Firmus among Ciconia's isorhythmic motets' *JAMS* 12 (1959) 7–15
Stylistic characteristics of a tenor distinguish it from Ciconia's other tenors.

Vaillant and others
For Matteus da Perusio see **1583**.

1600 Günther, U. 'Die Musiker des Herzogs von Berry' *MD* 17 (1963) 79–95,
1601 pll **1601** Günther 'Johannes Vaillant' **F-15**.171–85
1600 From original archives, and from their compositions, G traces biographical details about Vaillant, Molins, and Solage and their possible relationship to the Duke of Berry. **1601** G discusses Vaillant's life and works.

PLACES

This section is not limited to the fourteenth century.

Apt

1602 Gastoué, A. 'Les Anciens chants liturgiques des églises d'Apt et du Comtat' *RCGrég* 10 (1901/2) 152–60, 166–70 and 11 (1902/3) 23–8, 38–40, 56–60, 81–3
G gives sources and prints melodies of local plainsongs and tropes with comments. One of the sources is the Apt Ms (**1510**).

Chartres

1603 *Fragments des Mss de Chartres* ed Yves Delaporte PalMus Ser 1: 17 (1958) 44
1604 + 76 pp facss **1604** Delaporte 'Fulbert de Chartres et l'école chartrain de chant liturgique au xie siècle' *EG* 2 (1957) 51–81, 8 facss
1603 Some of the fragments include polyphony. **1604** D describes and transcribes the works ascribed to Fulbert.

Jumièges

1605 Hesbert, R.-J. 'Les Tropes de Jumièges' **1606** 'Les Mss M de Jumièges'
1606 **1607** 'Les Séquences de Jumièges' **D-10**.II.959–68, 901–12, 2 facss, 943–58
1607 H examines the repertory and its sources. See **534**.

Liège, Aachen, etc

1608 Smits van Waesberghe, Joseph *Muziekgeschiedenis der Middeleeuwen* 2 vols
1609 NEDERLANDSCHE MUZIEKHIST. EN MUZIEKPAEDAGOGISCHE STUDIËN, Ser A (Til-
1610 burg 1939, 1942) 493, 37 facss, list of mss, b, index; 814, 26 facss, list of mss,

1611 b, index + pamphlet of 7 pages (*Brief van Notker Balbulus aan Lantbertus*) / rev C. Van den Borren *Rev belge d'arch et d'hist de l'art* 7 (1937) 89–90; 8 (1938) 185–6; 9 (1939) 278; 10 (1940) 273–5 **1609** Smits van Waesberghe 'M Beziehungen zwischen Aachen, Köln, Lüttich und Maastricht vom 11. bis zum 13. Jh.' *Beitr zur Mg der Stadt Aachen* BRMg 6 (Cologne 1954) 5–13 **1610** Van der Linden, A. 'Les Bibliothèques M du pays de Liège au ma. d'après les catalogues' *Fédération arch et hist de Belgique, Congrès d'Anvers, 1947: Annales* 264–70 **1611** Auda, Antoine *L'Ecole* M *liégeoise au Xe siècle. Etienne de Liège* ACAD ROYALE DE BELGIQUE, CLASSE DES BEAUX-ARTS, Mém Collection in-8°, tome II, fascicle 1 (Brussels 1923) 212 + 5 facss

1608 The reviewer says this refers to the School of Liège, to Jacques de Liège, Aribo, *Micrologus*, bells, John Cotton, and especially to the *litterae significativae*. Vol 1: *De Luiksche muziekschool als centrum van het muziektheoretisch onderricht in de middeleeuwen: Het eerste bloeitijdperk van circa 1050–1125*. Vol 2: *Verklaring der letterteekens (litterae significativae) in het Gregoriaanische neumenschrift van Sint Gallen*. **1609** S documents cultural interchange. **1610** This is a brief but useful article. **1611** Etienne composed prayers and chants. A edits the M items of 3 Offices within a general historical and M discussion.

France: Fourteenth-century theory

Ciconia

1612 Michels, U. 'Der Musiktraktat des Anonymus OP. Ein frühes Theoretiker-Zeugnis der Ars Nova' *AMw* 26 (1969) 49–62
M dates this tract before 1321, making it one of the earliest Ars Nova documents. Briefly discussing the contents, entirely devoted to rhythm, M prints the original text.

1613 Clercx, S. 'Johannes Ciconia théoricien' *AnnM* 3 (1955) 39–75, 9 pp transcc
1614 **1614** Krohn, E.C. 'The *Nova Musica* of Johannes Ciconia' *Msct* 5 (1961)
1615 3–16 **1615** Seay, A. 'Remarks on the *Nova Musica* of Johannes Ciconia' *Msct* 6 (1962) 42–4
1613 C describes the sources and contents of the treatise. **1614** K collates the chapter headings of two sources. **1615** Ciconia's treatise is speculative and thus destined for university use.

Jacobus of Liège

1616 *Jacobi Leodensis Speculum Musicae* ed Roger Bragard 7 vols projected CSM 3:
1617 *Liber* I (1955) xx + 229 + 1 pl; II (1961) vi + 309 + 1 pl; II (Appendix) (1961) vi + lxxi; III (1963) vi + 163; IV (1965) vi + 126; V (1968) vi + 184; others forthcoming **1617** Bragard, R. 'Le *Speculum Musicae* du compilateur

Jacques de Liège' *MD* 7 (1953) 59–104 (errata on extra p preceding 59) and 8 (1954) 1–17
1616 This is an edition, with charts and diagrams. **1617** In part 1 B gives a detailed description of the sources and contents of this early 14c *summa* of M theory: in part 2 he deals with the author and his background.

1618 Clercx, S. 'Jacques d'Audenaerde ou Jacques de Liège?' *RBM* 7 (1953) 95–101
The two names cannot yet be proven to belong to the same man.

1619 *Die einleitenden Kapitel des 'Speculum Musicae' von Johannes de Muris* [recte *Jacobus of Liège*] ed Walter Grossmann SAMMLUNG MW EINZELDARSTEL-LUNGEN, Heft 3 (Leipzig 1924) iii + 100, 1 facs, index of terms, names
After a substantial introduction G edits chapters 1–19 of Jacques of Liège's *Speculum*, at that date thought to be by Muris, and chapter 18 of a treatise by Robert Kilwardby.

1620 Smith, F.J. 'Une Philosophie méd. du nombre: Jacques de Liège et le
1621 *Speculum Musicae*,' *MoyA* 74 (1968) 237–67 **1621** Smith 'Jacques de Liège, an
1622 Anti-Modernist?' *RBM* 17 (1963) 3–10 **1622** Smith *Iacobi leodiensis, Speculum Musicae* 2 vols MS 13, 22 (1966, nd) 130; xvi + 154
1620 Describing the contents and sources of the *Speculum*, S stresses its speculative and philosophical aspects, yet denies it is conservative. The mathematical, and especially the ternary, basis for rational M is empha-sised. The importance of the treatise as a *summa* is exaggerated in chronological scope. See also *MD* 18 (1964) 19–35, *MD* 19 (1965) 83–97, and D-7.1023–39. **1621** The theorist's conservative intentions took second place to the encyclopaedic purpose. **1622** S is basically concerned with intervals and with concepts of consonance and dissonance.

Jean de Muris

1623 *Expositiones tractatus practice cantus mensurabilis magistri Johannes de Muris*
1624 ed F. Alberto Gallo AMIS III; Prosdocimi de Beldemandis Opera 1 (Bologna
1625 1966) 223, 2 facss **1624** Michels, Ulrich *Die Musiktraktate des Johannes de Muris* BEIHEFTE ZUM AMW 8 (Wiesbaden 1970) vii + 133, b, index, list of sources **1625** Gushee, L. 'New Sources for the Biography of Johannes de Muris' *JAMS* 22 (1969) 3–26, 4 pll
1623 This is an edition of Prosdocimus' 15c recension of Muris' treatise. **1624** This is a chapter by chapter explanation and discussion of the theory. **1625** Mainly using astronomical events of the 14c, G establishes much new infor-mation about Muris.

Nicole Oresme

1626 *Nicole Oresme and the Med. Geometry of Qualities and Motions* ed. Marshall Clagett U OF WISCONSIN PUBL IN MED. SCIENCE (Madison, London 1968) part

II, chapters xv–xxv (pp 304–37) and passim (see Index and Introduction, pp 37–40)
This is a parallel Latin/English edition, with copious notes, of 14c treatises including substantial passages on M.

Philippe de Vitry

1627 *Philippe de Vitriaco: 'Ars Nova'* ed Gilbert Reaney, André Gilles, and Jean Maillard CSM 8 (1974) iv + 93
This reprints and combines earlier articles as follows: R, G, and M, in *MD* 10 (1956) 5–33 and 11 (1957) 3, edit the Latin text with commentary on sources, earlier editions, etc; *MD* 11 (1957) 12–30 prints a French translation; G in *MD* 10 (1956) 35–53, 2 pll, gives the text and French translation of an abbreviated version of the *Ars Nova* which also includes the *Ars Vetus*, previously unknown; G and R in *MD* 12 (1958) 59–66 edit a London source including the *Ars Vetus*; R in *MD* 14 (1960) 29–31 edits an abbreviated compendium of the *Ars Nova* from a 15c source; G in *MD* 15 (1961) 27–38 edits the treatise of Anon III (Coussemaker vol 3, see **925**), largely based on *Ars Nova*. All these sources complement each other to give a fuller picture of Vitry's treatise.

1628 Plantinga, L. 'Philippe de Vitry's *Ars Nova*: a Translation' *JMTh* 5 (1961) 204–23
P uses the only complete ms, with minimal notes on variants.

1629 Werner, E. 'The Mathematical Foundation of Philippe de Vitry's *Ars Nova*' *JAMS* 9 (1956) 128–32
To be sure of avoiding ambiguity in his rhythmic innovations, Vitry demands a mathematical proof from Leo Hebraeus (1288–1344).

1630 Gilles, A. 'Contribution à un inventaire analytique des mss intéressant l'*Ars Nova* de Ph. de Vitry' *RBM* 10 (1956) 149–54
G discusses sources of 14c theory.

1630a Gallo, F.A. 'Tra Giovanni di Garlandia e Filippo da Vitry' *MD* 23 (1969) 13–20
G describes the sources of Garlandia's and Vitry's treatises, showing relationships between the two texts.

Italy and Sicily

REFERENCE AND BIBLIOGRAPHY

1631 Hagopian, V.L. *Italian Ars Nova M: A Bibliographic Guide to Modern Editions and Related Literature* UCPM 7 (Berkeley 1964) x + 75, index of names / rev U. Günther *Mf* 20 (1967) 83
Full of abbreviations, this book lists and annotates items under various

categories (history, editions, ms sources, etc). It also lists articles from dictionaries.

1632 Fischer, Kurt von *Studien zur italienischen M des Trecento und frühen Quattrocento* PSMfG, Ser II, 5 (Bern 1956) viii + 132 / rev G. Reaney *ML* 37 (1956) 392–4
This is a basic reference book which includes indices of mss, composers, all known texts with sources and editions, and a substantial bibliography. The relations between sources, composers, styles, and notation are briefly discussed.

Surveys

1633 Nolthenius, Hélène *Duecento, Zwerftochten door Italië's late Middeleeuwen*
1634 transl from the German edition with reference to the original Dutch as *In*
1635 *that Dawn: the thirteenth century in Italy* (London 1968) xx + 268, 48 pll, index, b **1634** Fischer, K. von 'Die Rolle der Mehrstimmigkeit am Dome von Siena zu Beginn des 13. Jh.' *AMw* 18 (1961) 167–82 **1635** Strohm, R. 'Ein Zeugnis früher Mehrstimmigkeit in Italien' **F-29**.239–49
1633 There are M references throughout, most concentrated in chapter 12, pp 189–213. **1634** Quoting references in an Ordinal and comparing the Notre Dame repertory, F shows that both Ordinary and Proper were sung to polyphonic settings for soloists or choir or double choir. He reviews Italian sources preserving polyphony before 1300. **1635** S gives a diplomatic facsimile and deduces a possible transcription which is stylistically archaic compared with contemporary (ca 1200) French M.

1636 Fischer, K. von 'Trecentomusik–Trecentoprobleme. Ein kritischer For-
1637 schungsbericht' *Acta* 30 (1958) 179–99 **1637** Fischer 'Die M des Trecento' *Das Trecento (Theophil Spoerri zum 70. Geburtstag)* Symposium held at the U of Zurich 1959/60 (Zurich 1960) 183–214
These are useful general surveys. See also **D-14**.93–109.

1638 Martinez, Marie L. *Die M des frühen Trecento* MVM 9 (Tutzing 1963) 144 + 12 dipl facss, index / rev A. Wernli *Mf* 23 (1970) 365–6
This is a comprehensive analytical survey.

Origins of trecento music

1639 Fischer, K. von 'Les Compositions à trois voix chez les compositeurs du
1640 Trecento' **D-3**.18–31, revd and enl from *MQ* 47 (1961) 41–57 **1640** Ghisi, F.
1641 'La Persistance du sentiment monodique et l'évolution de la polyphonie italienne du xive au xve siècle' **D-14**.217–31 **1641** Schneider, M. 'Klagelieder des Volkes in der Kunstmusik der italienischen Ars nova' *Acta* 33 (1961) 162–8
1639 Parallelism and other technical features point to the two-part or monophonic conception of pieces in three parts or two parts. Such features

render a derivation from the conductus unlikely. Contratenors in French style sometimes appear in the second half of the century. **1640** G refers to the effect of ornaments in disguising the underlying style. **1641** With transcriptions S tries to show folksongs in polyphony.

Miscellaneous

1642 Bridgman, N. 'Les Illustrations M des œuvres de Boccaccio dans les collections de la BN de Paris' **D-5**.105–30, 11 pll
The lack of illustrations suggests that M was practised only in a limited circle.

1643 Pirrotta, N. 'Scuole polifoniche italiane durante il sec. XIV' *CHM* 1 (1953) 11–18
Evidence for a Neapolitan school is inconclusive.

1644 Vecchi, G. 'Letteratura e M nel Trecento' **D-5**.485–503
Distinguishing 14c *umanesimo volgare* from 15c *u. latino*, V examines the place of M in the former.

Sicily

1645 Anglés, H. 'La M sacra med. in Sicilia' *Bol del Centro di Studi filologici e linguistici siciliani* 3 (1955) 25–34
A refers to sources.

TEXTS AND POETS

1646 Vecchi, G. 'M e Scuola delle Artes a Bologna nell'opera di Boncompagno da Signa (sec. XIII)' **F-29**.266–73
V prints and discusses passages from tracts on rhetoric.

1647 Vecchi, G. 'Teoresi e prassi del canto a due voci in Italia nel Duecento e nel primo Trecento' **D-5**.203–14
V discusses the statements of an unpublished writer of the early 14c: he concludes that Italian polyphony of the 13c was very old-fashioned rhythmically, concerning itself with melodic and harmonic development.

Francesco da Barberino, Antonio da Tempo

1648 Vecchi, G. 'Educazione M, scuola e società nell'opera didascalica di Francesco da Barberino' *Quad* 7 (1966) 5–29
Barberino (1264–1348), following a conservative tradition, describes the moral purposes of M in a courtly society and its role in the education of women.

1649 Ghislanzoni, A. 'Les Formes littéraires et M italiennes au commencement du XIVe siècle' **D-14**.149–63

G discusses the passages relevant to M in the treatises of F. da Barberino and A. da Tempo.

1650 Debenedetti, Santorre 'Un Trattatello del secolo XIV sopra la poesia M' *SM* 2 (1906/7) 59–82
With information about author, sources, and contents, D edits the 'Capitulum de vocibus applicatis verbis' of Antonio da Tempo's *Summa artis* ... See **1698 1701**.

Poetry of the trecento

1651 Li Gotti, Ettore *La Poesia M italiana del sec. XIV* (Palermo 1944) 101 / rev C. Van den Borren *RBM* 2 (1948) 57–8
This is a general review of sources and styles of poetry designed for M.

1652 Liuzzi, F. 'M e poesia del Trecento nel Cod. Vat. Rossiano 215' *Rendiconti. Atti della Pontificia Accademia Romana di arch* 13 (1937) 59–71
L discusses language and forms and prints some texts.

1653 Karp, T. 'The Textual Origin of a Piece of Trecento Polyphony' *JAMS* 20 (1967) 469–73
K shows that a 14c canonic text is more than a century old.

1654 Li Gotti, Ettore, and Nino Pirrotta *Il Sacchetti e la tecnica M del Trecento italiano* (Florence 1935) 107 / rev U. Leo *Deutsche Literarische Zeitung* 57 (1936) 1879–81
This discusses the relation of the lyric, 1350–1400, to contemporary M efforts towards *poesia musicale*, especially with respect to Sacchetti. L and P include transcriptions of 12 of Sacchetti's poems set to two parts.

1655 Pirrotta, N. 'Due sonetti M del sec. XIV' **F-2**.II.651–62
The poems have M references and list musicians, whom P tries to identify.

1656 Thibault, G. 'Emblèmes et devises des Visconti dans les œuvres M du Trecento' **D-5**.131–60, 15 pll
Texts set to M sometimes refer to heraldic devices.

Dante

1657 Baehr, Rudolf *Dante und die M* SALZBURGER UNIVERSITÄTSREDEN, Heft 11
1658 (Salzburg 1966) 23 **1658** Hammerstein, R. 'Die M in Dantes *Divina Commedia*,' *Deutsches Dante-Jb* 41/2 (1964) 59–125. See also 126–43.
These items are concerned with Dante's view of and references to M and the harmony of the spheres.

Boccaccio

1659 Gutman, H. 'Der *Decamerone* des Boccaccio als mg Quelle' *ZMw* 11 (1928/9)

*1660 397–401 *1660 Becherini, B. 'Il Decameron e la M' *Miscellanea storica della Valdelsa* 69 (1963) 178– ? See also the same journal 22 (1914) 65–72.
1659 Concerning performance practices, the Decameron is ambiguous.

Petrarch

1661 Sesini, U. 'Modi petrarcheschi in poesie venete musicate del Trecento' *Studi*
1662 Petrarcheschi 1 (1948) 167–83 1662 Osthoff, W. 'Petrarca in der M des Abend-
1663 landes' *Castrum peregrini* 20 (1954) 1 facs, 6 pp M exx + 5–36 1663 Vecchi, G. 'Melica med., "Ars Nova" e lirica del Petrarca' *Conv* ns (1953) 105–14
1661 Texts in the Rossi Ms 215 are Petrarchian in style. 1662 O considers settings of Petrarch up to the 17c, beginning with Jacopo da Bologna, whose *Non al suo amante* he gives in facsimile and transcription. 1663 V gives good references.

1664 Rawski, C.H. 'Petrarch's Dialogue on M' *Spec* 46 (1971) 302–17
R prints the text, previously unnoticed. Petrarch replaces traditional topics and figures with others from classical antiquity which remained current until the 17c.

SOURCES, FACSIMILES, EDITIONS

Many Italian pieces are to be found in manuscripts which are primarily French in character.

Chronology and comprehensive editions

1665 Fischer, K. von 'Chronologie des mss du Trecento' discussion **D-14**.131–6
F and Schrade, Clercx, Pirrotta discuss the relationships between the sources.

1666 *I Più antichi monumenti italiani di melica mensurale* ed Giuseppe Vecchi (Bologna 1960) 38, 14 facss
V describes the facsimiles of pre-14c mensural works.

1667 *I Più antichi monumenti sacri italiani* ed F. Alberto Gallo and Giuseppe Vecchi 2 vols MLMAI-M 1 (Bologna 1968, –) xxii + 151 facss; – / rev J. Froger *EG* 11 (1969) 219–20
Vol 1 includes indices of mss and texts and facsimiles of measured sacred M from Italy up to 15c. Most is polyphonic. Vol 2, the text, is in preparation.

1668 *Italian Secular M by Magister Piero, Giovanni da Firenze, Jacopo da Bologna* ed W. Thomas Marrocco PMFC 6 (1967) xii + 185
This is an edition, with commentary.

1669 *The M of 14c Italy* ed Nino Pirrotta 5 vols CMM 8: vol I: *The collected works*

of the Florentines, Giovanni Bartolomeo, Gherardello (Amsterdam 1954) xiii +
80; vol II: *The collected works of Maestro Piero, compositions from the Codex
Vatican Rossi 215, and madrigals and cacce from other ms sources* (Rome 1960)
xiii + 68; vol III: *The collected works of the Florentines Lorenzo, Donato, Rosso
da Collegrano and anonymous works* (1962) xvii, 1 facs + 52; vol IV: *The collected
works of Jacobo da Bologna and Vincenzo da Rimini* (1963) xiii + 52; vol V:
*Andreas de Florentia, Guilielmus de Francia, Bonaiutus Corsini, Andrea Stefani,
Ser Feo, Jacopo Piaelaio, Gian Toscano, Anon* (1964) xvii + 45
Each volume contains an introduction, index, lists of sources, and the texts.

1670 *Les Monuments de l'Ars Nova* ed Guillaume de Van EOL (Paris nd) iv + 41
This is an edition of eight Italian liturgical pieces.

Major sources

These are arranged chronologically.

Rossi 215 (and Ostiglia)
1671 *Il Canzoniere M del Codice Vaticano Rossi 215 con uno studio sulla melica italiana*
1672 *del Trecento* ed Giuseppe Vecchi 2 vols MLMAI-M 2 (Bologna 1966, –) 7 + 36
1673 facss; – **1672** Sesini, U. 'Il Canzoniere M trecentesco del cod. vat. Rossiano
1674 215' *SM* 16 (1943–50) 212–36 **1673** Mischiati, O. 'Uno Sconosciuto frammento appartenente al codice vaticano Rossi 215' *RIM* 1 (1966) 68–76, 1 facs
1674 Marrocco, W.T. 'The newly-discovered Ostiglia pages of the Vatican
Rossi Codex 215: the earliest Italian ostinato' *Acta* 39 (1967) 84–91
1671 This is a facsimile: vol 2, in preparation, will contain the introduction.
1672 S inventories the ms, and prints the texts with a glossary. **1673**
Mischiati describes the new fragments and prints the texts. **1674** Including
a transcription, Marrocco complements **1673**. The ms is edited in **1669**.

London 29987
1675 *The Ms London, BM Add. 29987* ed Gilbert Reaney MSD 13 (1965) 29 + 88 fos
1676 facss + 1 unnumbered facs **1676** Reaney 'The Ms BM, Add 29987 (*Lo*)' *MD*
12 (1958) 67–91
1675 This is a facsimile edition, with inventory and concordances. **1676** R
describes the contents, composers, and forms and gives a detailed inventory. One transcription is given.

Modena lat. 568
1677 Pirrotta, Nino 'Il Codice estense lat. 568 e la M francese in Italia al principio
1677a del '400' *ARAP* ser IV, vol V, parte II (Palermo 1946) 101–54 **1677a** Günther,
U. 'Das Ms Modena, Bibl Estense, α.M.5, 24 (*olim* lat.568 = *Mod*)' *MD* 24
(1970) 17–67
1677 1677a P and G describe and inventory the source.

Paris ital. 568

1678 Reaney, G. 'The Ms BN fonds italien 568 (Pit)' MD 14 (1960) 33–63
R describes and inventories the source.

* Announced: Un Codice Trecentesco: BN Paris Ms fonds ital. 568 ed Ursula
Günther DOCUMENTA MUSICOLOGICA, Reihe 2, Bd 3

1679 Günther, U. 'Die 'anonymen' Kompositionen des Ms Paris, BN fonds it. 568
1680 (Pit)' AMw 23 (1966) 73–92, 42 small facss 1680 Clercx, S. 'Johannes Ciconia
et la chronologie des mss. italiens, Mod. 568 et Lucca (Mn)' D-14.110–30
1679 G examines paleography, erasures, and concordances, concluding
that Pit cannot have served as exemplar for the Squarcialupi codex (1685)
and deducing composers for the anonymous works. 1680 Using biographical information about Ciconia (1597), C shows that the two mss are probably
earlier than Pirrotta (1677) suggests. Pirrotta debates the question.

Lucca (and Perugia and Pistoia)

1681 Bonaccorsi, A. 'Un Nuovo Codice dell'Ars nova: Il Codice Lucchese' Atti
1682 dell'Accademia Nazionale dei Lincei: Mem, classe di scienze morali ... Ser VIII,
1683 vol 1 (Rome 1948) 539–615, 1 pl, 1 facs / rev L. Ellinwood Notes ns 6 (1948/9)
1684 163–4 1682 Ghisi, F. 'Italian Ars-Nova M' MD 1 (1946/7) 173–91, 1 facs +
supplement pp 1–24 M transcc 1683 Mancini, A. 'Frammenti di un nuovo
codice dell'Ars nova' Rendiconti. Atti della Classe di Scienze morali, storiche e
filologiche dell'Accademia Nazionale dei Lincei Ser VIII, vol 2 (1947)
85–94 1684 Pirrotta, N., and E. Li Gotti 'Il Codice di Lucca. I: Descrizione
e inventario. II: Testi letterari. III: Il Repertorio M' MD 3 (1949) 119–38, 4 pll
and 4 (1950) 111–52 and 5 (1951) 115–42
1681 This is a general survey of the background and contents of the ms. 1682
G reconstructs the ms (sometimes called the Mancini Codex) from fragments
at Lucca, Perugia, and Pistoia (the result is extremely difficult to follow). G
also discusses other early 15c sources. See 1543. In 1683 M gives a descriptive
inventory. 1684 Li G edits the texts, with annotations: P reconstructs the
source, and describes the contents and composers.

* Announced: Il Codice Mancini dell'Archivio di Stato di Lucca e della Biblioteca
Communale di Perugia ed Kurt von Fischer MLMAI-M 4

Squarcialupi (Florence Pal 27)

1685 Der Squarcialupi-Codex [Florence, Bibl Laurenziana, Pal 87] ed Johannes
Wolf (Lippstadt 1955) 21 + 359 / rev K. von Fischer 'Zu Johannes Wolfs
Übertragung des Squarcialupi Codex' Mf 9 (1956) 77–89
Posthumous by eight years, this edition is of two- and three-voice secular
songs from the large ms anthology compiled in the 15c: it uses c clefs. In
the review F lists errors and, drawing on research done since the editor's
death, corrects many details of dating, biography, etc.

Florence Pan 26
* Announced: *Il Codice Panciat. 26 della Biblioteca Nazionale di Firenze* ed Nino
Pirrotta MLMAI-M 7

Smaller sources

1686 Pirrotta, N. 'Church Polyphony Apropos of a New Fragment at Foligno'
F-30.113–26 + 2 facss
P makes tentative conclusions about a new, puzzling provincial source.

1687 Corsi, G. 'Frammenti di un codice M dell'*Ars nova* rimasti sconosciuti' *Bel*
20 (1965) 210–15
C describes some fly-leaves guarding a ms at Grottaferrata.

1688 Fischer, K. von 'Ein neues Trecentofragment' **F-36**.264–8
F describes and gives a thematic inventory of the fragments Grottaferrata
Abbey Ms E.β xvi (ca 1400).

1689 Plamenac, D. 'Another Paduan Fragment of Trecento M' *JAMS* 8 (1955)
165–81, 6 pp transcc + 8 facss
P examines and transcribes ms 1106.

1690 Ghisi, F. 'Bruchstücke einer neuen M-hs der italienischen Ars nova und
zwei unveröffentlichte Caccien der zweiten Hälfte des 15. Jh.' *AMf* 7 (1942)
17–39, 1 facs (Italian version in *La Rinascita* anno 5. n. 23 (1942) 72–103, 1 facs)
G describes fragments at Perugia, prints the texts and the M, by Ciconia and
Zachara.

1691 Fischer, K. von 'Una Ballata trecentesca sconosciuta – Aggiunte per i fram-
1692 menti di Siena' **D-4**.39–47, 2 pp transcc **1692** Ghisi, F. 'A Second Sienese
Fragment of Italian Ars Nova' *MD* 2 (1948) 173–7
These are descriptions of small, fragmentary sources.

1693 Gallo, F. Alberto *Da un codice italiano di motetti del primo trecento* BIBL DI
'QUAD,' Ser paleografica 13 (Bologna 1969) 25–44, 4 facss
G describes the source and transcribes the pieces, which are motets.

THE FORMS

Madrigal and Caccia

1694 Pirrotta, N. 'Per l'origine e la storia della "caccia" e del "madrigale" trecentesco' *RMI* 48 (1946) 305–23 and 49 (1947) 121–42
P examines the important features.

1695 Li Gotti, E. 'L'*ars nova* e il madrigale' *ARAP*, ser IV, vol IV, parte II (Palermo
1696 1944) 339–89 **1696** Pirrotta, N. 'Una arcaica descrizione trecentesca del
1697 madrigale' **F-5**.155–61 **1697** Marrocco, W.T. 'The 14c madrigal: its form and
contents' *Spec* 26 (1951) 449–57, 1 facs
1695 This is a catalogue of texts, with and without M settings, with dates,

poets, composers, metrical schemes, sources, and editions. L prints a few texts. **1696** P quotes and discusses important sentences, raising the hypothesis of pre-existent clausula-type models for madrigals. **1697** M shows the textual structure, irregular prior to 1350, becoming more standardised.

1698 Pirrotta, N. 'Piero e l'impressionismo M del secolo XIV' **D-3**.57–74
Translating (to Italian) the relevant passage from 'Capitulum de vocibus applicatis verbis' (see **1650**), P discusses Piero's role in establishing the onomatopoeic caccia.

1699 *Fourteenth-century Italian Cacce* ed W. Thomas Marrocco MAA 39 (2nd ed revd Cambridge, Mass. 1961) xxii + 114 + 5 facss / rev G. Haydon *Spec* 38 (1963) 139–42
M edits the canons.

Ballata

1700 Marrocco, W.T. 'The Ballata – a metamorphic form' *Acta* 31 (1959)
1701 32–7 **1701** Pirrotta, N. 'Ballate e "soni" secondo un grammatico del Trecento' **F-19**.III.42–54
1700 The ballata changes from poem to song and dance, to art form, to a model for the 16c frottola. **1701** Quoting the passage and commenting on Debenedetti's interpretation (**1650**), P tries to explain the meaning of *ballade sunt verba applicata sonis* [= *sonettis*].

Motets and Mass movements

1702 Gallo, F.A. 'Mottetti del primo Trecento in un messale di Biella (Codice Lowe)' **D-5**.215–45, transcc (227–40), 5 facss
G describes the source, prints the texts. Motets are extremely rare in the Italian repertory.

1703 Fischer, K. von 'Kontrafakturen und Parodien italienischer Werke des Trecento und frühen Quattrocento' *AnnM* 5 (1957) 43–59
F analyses several Mass movements based on earlier secular pieces.

COMPOSERS

These are listed alphabetically.

Bartolino da Padova, Bonaiutus, Giovanni and Donato da Cascia

1704 Goldine, N. 'Fra Bartolino de Padova, musicien de cour' *Acta* 34 (1962)
1705 142–55 **1705** Petrobelli, P. 'Some Dates for Bartolino da Padova' **F-30**.85–112
G and P assemble evidence for the composer's life and works.

1706 Wolf, J. 'Bonaiutus de Casentino, ein Dichter-Komponist um 1300' *Acta* 9 (1937) 1–5
W briefly introduces the composer, transcribing his few works.

1707 Casimiri, R. 'Giovanni da Cascia e Donato da Cascia musicisti umbri?' *NASM* 11 (1934) 207–10.

Jacopo da Bologna

For his theoretical work see **1731**.

1708 *The M of Jacopo da Bologna* ed W. Thomas Marrocco UCPM 5 (Berkeley 1954)
1709 xi + 162 + 8 facss / rev J. Ward *JAMS* 8 (1955) 36–42 **1709** Fischer, K. von 'Drei unbekannte Werke von Jacobo da Bologna und Bartolino da Padua?' F-2.I.265–81
1708 M edits a treatise of Jacopo, and his M works. **1709** Partly on stylistic grounds F convincingly attributes anonymous works.

Francesco Landini

1710 *The Works of Francesco Landini* ed Leo Schrade PMFC 4 (1958) v + 222 / rev
1711 R.H. Hoppin *JAMS* 15 (1962) 85–90 **1711** *The Works of Francesco Landino* ed
1712 Leonard Ellinwood MAA, Publ 36 (Cambridge, Mass. 1939) xliii + 316, 2 pll,
1713 6 facss / rev U. Sesini *SM* 12 (1939) 221–4 and J. Beck *Spec* 15 (1940)
1714 503–7 **1712** Fischer, K. von 'EinVersuch zur Chronologie von Landinis Werken' *MD* 20 (1966) 31–46 **1713** Nolthenius, H. 'Een autobiografisch madrigal von F. Landini' *Tijdschrift voor Muziekwetenschap* 17 (1948–55) 237–41, 1 facs **1714** Schachter, C. 'Landini's Treatment of Consonance and Dissonance: a Study in 14c Counterpoint' *The M Forum* 2 (1970) 130–86
1710 1711 These are complete editions, with introductions, lists of works, etc. **1712** By considering biographical, stylistic, ms, and textual information, F summarises the chronological evidence. **1713** N discusses *Mostrommi amor*. **1714** In a detailed technical study S isolates specific practices, some of which he believes account for the spontaneity of Landini's M.

Matteo da Perugia and Giovanni Mazzuoli

1715 Fano, Fabio *Le Origini e il primo maestro di cappella: Matteo da Perugia* vol 1 of *La Cappela Mdel Duomo di Milano* IST E MON DELL'ARTE M ITALIANA ns 1 (Milan 1956) xv + 503, 20 pll and facss (some in col), index, M transcc (191–405)
This is an archival and stylistic monograph introducing the works of Matteo and some contemporaries. The transcriptions are in long note values.

1716 D'Accone, F. 'Giovanni Mazzuoli: a late representative of the Italian *Ars Nova*' **D-4**.23–38
D gives biographical information about the composer (ca 136?–1426)

Paolo Tenorista

1717 *Paolo Tenorista* ed Nino Pirrotta (Palm Springs 1961) col facs frontispiece +
1718 85, 10 facss / rev R.H. Hoppin *MQ* 48 (1962) 129–31 **1718** Pirrotta, N. 'Paolo
1719 da Firenze in un nuovo frammento dell'Ars Nova' *MD* 10 (1956)
1720 61–6 **1719** Pirrotta, and E. Li Gotti 'Paolo Tenorista, fiorentino "extra
moenia"' **F-20**.III.577–606 **1720** Fischer, K. von *Paolo da Firenze und der
Squarcialupi-Kodex* BIBL DI QUADRIVIUM, Ser Musicologica 9 (Bologna 1969)
24 + 4 pll and facss
1717 This is a facsimile edition of a ms now in the library of E.E. Lowinsky,
with an introduction, inventory, catalogue of Paolo's works, and transcription of five pieces. **1718** P describes the ms. **1719** Paolo's revival of the madrigal and other evidence suggest that he did not work in Florence. The texts of his songs are printed on pp 592–606. **1720** New documents support the hypothesis of a close relation between Paolo and the Squarcialupi Ms: see
D-3.141–96.

Others

1721 Li Gotti, E. 'Per la biografia di due minori musicisti italiani dell'Ars-Nova'
Restauri trecenteschi. Saggi di letteratura italiana 9 (Palermo 1947) 98–105
The Mancini Codex (**1681–84**) contributes information relating to the lives of Andrea Stefani and Bonaiuto Corsini.

SPECIFIC PIECES AND TECHNIQUES

1722 Fischer, K. von 'Zur Entwicklung der italienischen Trecento-Notation'
AMw 16 (1959) 87–99
With specific examples and theoretical evidence F shows that augmentation arises through French influence.

1723 Günther, U. ''Zur Datierung des Madrigals *Godi, Firenze* und der Hs Paris,
BN fonds it. 568 (*Pit*)' *AMw* 24 (1967) 99–119, 4 facss
Including facsimiles and a transcription, G shows from M and other evidence that Pirrotta's statements about the date and ownership of the ms must be questioned: cf **1678 1679**. See also *CHM* 4 (1966) 185–93.

1724 Marrocco, W.T. 'Integrative Devices in the M of the Italian Trecento'
D-5.411–29
M points to techniques such as sequence, imitation, and ostinato.

1725 Pirrotta, N. 'M polifonica per un testo attribuito a Federico II' **D-4**. 97–112, 4 pp transcc
P describes the piece.

1726 Schering, A. 'Das kolorierte Orgelmadrigal des Trecento' *SIMG* 13 (1911/12) 172–204, pp. 193–204 M transcc
Although carried to extremes, and with minimal evidence to support them, the principles which this article sets out to demonstrate make reasonable sense (cf **1958**). S believes 14c and 15c mss transmit highly ornamented instrumental versions of underlying 'folk-like' songs: in parallel transcriptions, he gives ms and conjectural unornamented versions.

ITALIAN THEORY, FOURTEENTH AND FIFTEENTH CENTURIES

1727 Gallo, F. Alberto *La Teoria della notazione in Italia dalla fine del XIII all'inizio del XV secolo* AMIS, Subsidia theorica (Bologna 1966) 103, list of mss
This is a comprehensive examination, with quotations, of all important theoretical discussions.

Theorists are listed alphabetically.

Anonymous

1728 *Mensurabilis musicae tractatuli* ed F. Alberto Gallo AMIS I: 1 (Bologna 1966) 85 + 2 facss
G edits 8 brief treatises.

1729 *Notitia del valore della Note del Canto Misurato* ed Armen Carapetyan CSM 5
1730 (1957) 63 + 2 pll **1730** Carapetyan 'A 14c Florentine Treatise in the Vernacular' *MD* 4 (1950) 81–92, 2 pll
C edits and describes a tract representing 'an oral tradition of M teaching.'

Jacopo da Bologna

1731 Wolf, J. 'L'Arte del biscanto misurato secondo el maestro Jacopo da Bologna' *Theodor Kroyer-Fs* (Regensburg 1933) 17–39
W edits the treatise in original Italian and parallel German translation. See **1708**.

Marchettus of Padua

1732 *Marchettus of Padua. Pomerium* ed Giuseppe Vecchi CSM 6 (1961) xxiii + 200,
1733 5 facss / rev A. Seay *JAMS* 15 (1962) 212–13 **1733** Vecchi, G. 'Su la composizione del *Pomerium* di Marchetto da Padova e la *Brevis compilatio*' *Quad* 1 (1956) 153–205

1732 This is an edition, with a list of authors. **1733** V edits and summarises the *Brevis c.*, comparing it with *Pomerium*, and attributing it to Marchettus.

1734 Strunk, O. 'Intorno a Marchetto da Padova' *RaM* 20 (1950) 312–15 **1735** Pir-
1735 rotta, N. 'Marchettus de Padua and the Italian Ars Nova' *MD* 9 (1955)
1736 57–71 **1736** Monterosso, R. 'Un Compendio inedito del *Lucidarium* di
1737 Marchetto da Padova' *SM* Ser 3, 7 (1966) 914–31 **1737** Martinez-Göllner, M.
'Marchettus of Padua and Chromaticism' **D-5**.187–202
    1734 The dates demonstrated for Marchettus' *Lucidarium* (1318) and
Pomerium (1318–19) antedate the earliest *Ars Nova* theory. **1735** P shows that
Marchettus' treatises cannot have been influenced by Vitry or Muris and
that they illuminate the state of Italian polyphony ca 1300–20. **1736** M
describes and edits a 15c compilation. **1737** Marchettus' illogical and
mathematically incorrect division of the tone into semitones of three different sizes influences some important 15c and 16c writers.

Paolo da Firenze

1738 Seay, A, 'Paolo da Firenze: a Trecento Theorist' **D-3**.118–40
    S prints and describes Paolo's treatise, concerned with extemporisation of
polyphony and reflecting Italian emphasis on practical rather than traditional speculative aspects.

Anselmi Parmensis

1739 *Georgii Anselmi Parmensis 'De Musica'* ed Giuseppe Massera (Florence 1961)
209 + 3 pll / rev A. Seay *JAMS* 15 (1962) 214–17 and S. Clercx *RBM* 15 (1961)
161–7
This is an annotated edition.

Petrus Frater

1740 Wolf, J. 'Ein Beitrag zur Diskantlehre des 14. Jh.' *SIMG* 15 (1913/14) 504–34,
1 facs
    W edits the treatise *Compendium de discantu mensurabili compilatum a fratre
Petro dicto Palma ociosa*.

Philipoctus da Caserta

1741 Wilkins, N. 'Some Notes on Philipoctus da Caserta' *Nottingham Med. Studies*
8 (1964) 82–99
    W gives biographical information, prints the ballade texts set to M by
Philippe, and edits his treatise.

Prasdocimus de Beldemandis

1742 Sartori, Claudio *La Notazione italiana del trecento in una redazione inedita del*

1743 'Tractatus practice cantus mensurabilis ad modum Ytalicorum' di Prosdocimo de
1744 Beldemandis (Florence 1938) 159 / rev A. Einstein ML 19 (1938) 357–8 **1743**
Gallo, F. Alberto 'La Tradizione dei trattati M di Prosdocimo de Beldemandis' Quad 6 (1964) 57–84 +3 facss **1744** Stellfeld, B. 'Prosdocimus de
Beldomandis als Erneuerer der Musikbetrachtung um 1400' F-17.37–50
1742 S edits and comments on the different versions of the treatise. Cf
Expositiones tractatus practice cantus mensurabilis (**1623**). **1743** G describes the
sources. **1744** Generally reviewing the theoretical writings, St stresses Prosdocimus' practical rather than speculative attitude.

Teodono de Caprio

1745 Casimiri, R. 'Teodono de Caprio non Teodorico de Campo, teorico M
italiano del sec. xv: un suo trattato inedito' NASM 19 (1942) 38–42, 93–8
Theodorico de Campo is an erroneous reading. C edits the treatise.

Ugolino of Orvieto

1746 Ugolino of Orvieto 'Declaratio Musicae Disciplinae' ed Albert Seay 3 vols CSM
1747 7 (1959, 1960, 1962) viii, 1 pl + 230 + 5 facss + separate booklet of 32 pp; viii
1748 + 266 + booklet of 24 pp; viii + 253 **1747** Seay, A. 'Ugolino of Orvieto,
Theorist and Composer' MD 9 (1955) 111–66 and 11 (1957) 126–33 **1748**
Hughes, Andrew 'Ugolino: the Monochord and Musica Ficta' MD 23 (1969)
21–39
1746 This is an edition, with charts and diagrams and M examples, to which
1747 serves as an introduction: S describes sources, contents, and biography, and transcribes and discusses two of the theorist's compositions.
1748 H discusses the way in which Ugolino (ca 1430) organizes his treatise
on the monochord, giving translations of numerous passages.

The British Isles

REFERENCES AND SURVEYS

1749 Harrison, Frank Ll. *M in Med. Britain* (London 1958) xix + 491, m exx, 26 pll, indices / rev D. Stevens *ML* 40 (1959) 172–4
Pp 1–103 have a useful and heavily factual account of religious institutions and their rituals and plainsongs. Pp 104 to the end have a similarly detailed discussion of polyphony by function, institution, style and form, up to the Reformation. This is comprehensive and invaluable as a reference book.

1750 Padelford, Frederick M. *Old English M Terms* BONNER BEITR ZUR ANGLISTIK 4 (Bonn 1899) xii + 112
The introduction is well documented. The glossary itself is complemented with tables of equivalences to Latin and modern English.

1751 Carter, Henry H. *A Dictionary of Middle English M Terms* INDIANA U HUMANITIES SER 45 (Bloomington, Indiana 1961; repr New York 1968) xv + 655, b / rev R.L. Greene *MAe* 32 (1963) 80–2
This astonishing compendium could serve as the starting-point for further research.

BEFORE THE TWELFTH CENTURY

Beowulf

1752 Pope, John C. *The Rhythm of Beowulf* (revd ed New Haven 1966) xxxvi + 409 / rev J. Oakden *MLR* 38 (1943) 136–7
The rhythm of the lines can be expressed in M note-symbols, the harp filling in the poetic rests. Part of the book is a catalogue of the various rhythmic patterns.

1753 Entry deleted

1754 Bessinger, Jess B. '*Beowulf* and the Harp at Sutton Hoo' *U of Toronto Quar-*
1755 *terly* 27 (1957/8) 148–68 **1755** Wrenn, C.L. 'Two Anglo-Saxon Harps' *Comparative Literature* 14 (1962) 118–28

B and W discuss instruments and the oral performance of Anglo-Saxon M and poetry. See 357.

Miscellaneous

1756 *Early English Harmony* ed H.E. Wooldridge vol 1 PMMS (London 1897) x + 60 facss
This is an anthology of facsimiles from 10–15c with brief description.

1757 Bent, I. 'The English Chapel Royal before 1300' *PRMA* 90 (1963/4) 77–95
B describes the chapel's organization and its function, especially with regard to *laudes regiae* and polyphonic singing: he refers to the evidence of Anon IV.

1758 Bergsagel, J. 'An English Liquescent Neume' **F-34**.94–9, 1 pl
This symbol is known only in English plainsong sources.

1759 Wellesz, E. 'Eastern Elements in English Ecclesiastical M' *J of the Warburg and Courtauld Inst* 5 (1942) 44–55, 1 p facss
The Winchester Tropers contain some Greek texts: W investigates their origins.

THE TWELFTH AND THIRTEENTH CENTURIES

Surveys

1760 Jusserand, Jean J. *English Wayfaring Life in the MA* transl Lucy Toulmin
1761 Smith (4th ed London 1950; repr 1961) 315, 9 pll, index **1761** Salmen, W. 'Die Beteiligung Englands am internationalen Musikantenverkehr des MA' *Mf* 11 (1958) 315–20
1760 Pp 103–119 give a very general, but documented account of the social position and functions of minstrels in England. **1761** Records and poems indicate the role of English musicians.

1762 Chaytor, Henry J. *The Troubadours and England* (Cambridge 1923) vii + 164 / rev G. Lavergne *MoyA* 34 [ser 2:25] (1923) 312–13
There is nothing else on this topic.

1763 Hughes, Anselm 'The Topography of English Med. Polyphony' **F-14**.127–39,
1764 1 map **1764** Hughes, Andrew 'Continuity, Tradition and Change in Eng-
1765 lish M up to 1600' *ML* 46 (1965) 306–15 **1765** Apfel, E. 'England und der Kontinent in der M des späten MA' *Mf* 14 (1961) 276–89
1763 Archival references and known or suspected provenances for mss suggest a geographical shift in M activity, from north- and west-country (before 1350) south- and eastwards. **1764** The author tries to show the long maintenance of certain stylistic features, relating alternation of melismatic and syllabic passages, voice exchange technique, change in metre, and perfor-

mance medium. **1765** A overemphasises the influence of northwestern Europe on 'central' M, but has a useful summary of English works in continental mss.

Sources, pieces, and styles

1766 Dittmer, L.A. 'An English Discantuum Volumen' *MD* 8 (1954) 19–58, 6 pll (errata between pp 18 and 19)
Placing it in historical and stylistic context, D describes the Bodleian Ms Rawl. c 400* and its relation to the lost Reading Ms and to the Worcester Fragments.

Sumer is icumen in

1767 Bukofzer, M.F. '*Sumer is icumen in*'; *a revision* UCPM 2, no. 2 (Berkeley 1944)
1768 vi + 79–113, 3 facss / rev E.B. (A.H. Fox Strangways?) *ML* 26 (1945) 113–15
1769 and Anselm Hughes *MLR* 40 (1945) 327–8 **1768** Handschin, J. 'The Summer
1770 Canon and its Background' *MD* 3 (1949) 55–94 and 5 (1951) 65–113 **1769** Schofield, B. 'The provenance and date of "Sumer is Icumen in" ' *The M Review* (1948) 81–6 **1770** Pirrotta, N. 'On the Problem of "Sumer is Icumen in" ' *MD* 2 (1948) 205–16
1767 Including a transcription, B tries to show that the piece is from ca 1310 rather than ca 1240. Otherwise B gives valuable information. **1768** To conclude that the work is mid-13c H writes a comprehensive but discursive study. He describes the source in detail, the notation and its alteration, and the implications of binary rhythm, including theoretical evidence (cf **178 179**). He investigates the whole question of English M in continental and other sources, collating the lost Reading Ms, Montpellier, Worcester, Huelgas, and others. **1769** S advances paleographic and much other evidence asserting the traditional date and provenance. He corrects some readings in **1390**. **1770** P tries to reconcile the positions of Bukofzer and Schofield, and discusses the diffusion of the piece.

Styles: Rota and rondellus

1771 Sanders, E.H. 'Tonal Aspects of 13c English Polyphony' *Acta* 37 (1965) 19–34
S stresses English predilection for tonally cohesive composition, citing their preference for rondellus and voice exchange as opposed to canon, and their tonal modification of plainsong sections used in polyphonic pieces.

1772 Apfel, Ernst *Studien zur Satztechnik der ma. englischen M* 2 vols HEIDELBERGER AKW, p.h.Kl., Abh 5 (Heidelberg 1959) 107; 145, 16 facss, indices of texts and mss / rev N.C. Carpenter *JMTh* 5 (1961) 303–6
A analyses technical procedures: vol 2 has unreliable diplomatic transcriptions.

1773 Harrison, F. Ll. 'Rota and Rondellus in English Med. M' *PRMA* 86 (1959/60)
98–107
H distinguishes the two and shows that *Sumer is icumen in* combines them.

Worcester school

1774 *Worcester, Add 68, Westminster Abbey 33327, Madrid Bibl Nac. 192* MedMM
1775 5 (1959) 89, 55 facss **1775** *Oxford, Lat. lit.* D 20, *London, Add Ms 25031, Chicago
Ms 654 App* MedMM 6 (1960) 75, 45 facss
These are facsimile editions, with transcriptions and introductions, of various mss transmitting M in the style of the so-called Worcester school.

1776 *The Worcester Fragments. A Catalogue Raisonné and Transcription* ed Luther
1777 A. Dittmer MSD 2 (1957) 185, 6 facss, index of incipits / rev R.L. Crocker *JAMS*
1778 12 (1959) 71–4 and W. Waite *MQ* 44 (1958) 531–4 **1777** Dittmer, L.A. 'The Dating and the Notation of the Worcester Fragments' *MD* 11 (1957) 5–11 **1778**
Dittmer 'Beiträge zum Studium der Worcester-Fragmente' *Mf* 10 (1957)
29–39
1776 D confounds confusion in this catalogue, but it is the only attempt to
organize and edit this important material, scattered in numerous mss. **1777**
D offers no substantial new evidence to justify his conclusions. **1778** After
relating rondellus to conductus and voice-exchange motet, D describes two
fragmentary mss and transcribes two pieces: Worcester is not the only
provenance of such styles.

THE FOURTEENTH AND FIFTEENTH CENTURIES

1779 Reaney, G. 'The Musician in Med. England' *The Monthly* M *Record* 89 (1959)
3–8
This is a good general survey, mainly devoted to the late 14c.

Styles: Gymel and discant

1780 Apfel, E. 'Zur Entstehung des realen vierstimmigen Satzes in England'
AMw 17 (1960) 81–99
Showing that the fourth voice is often grammatically superfluous, A dis-
tinguishes English and continental practices. See also *AMw* 18 (1961) 34–51.

1781 Bukofzer, M.F. 'The Gymel, the Earliest Form of English Polyphony' *ML* 16
(1935) 77–84
In a now discredited theory (cf **1749**), B projects a 15c term back into the practice of the MA.

1782 Bukofzer, Manfred F. *Geschichte des englischen Diskants und des Fauxbourdons
nach den theoretischen Quellen* (Strasburg 1936) xi + 163 + 20 pp M transcc
Attempting to clarify theoretical statements, B traces the continuity up to
the 16c.

1783 Sanders, E.H. 'Cantilena and discant in 14c England' *MD* 19 (1965) 7–52
Comprehensively collating sources, S absorbs and disputes previous
scholarship in a general and diffuse discussion of styles and forms. Giving
many examples, he deals extensively with the treatment of plainsong.

Chaucer

1783a Olson, C.C. 'Chaucer and the M of the 14c' *Spec* 16 (1941) 64–91 **1783b** Moore,
1783b A.K. 'Chaucer's Lost Songs' *J. of English and Germanic Philology* 48 (1949)
1783c 196–208 **1783c** Preston, R. 'Chaucer and the *Ballades notées* of Guillaume de
Machaut' *Spec* 26 (1951) 615–23
1783a Chaucer's references to M do not indicate special knowledge or abil-
ity. **1783b 1783c** Chaucer's poetry is its own M in the M *naturelle* sense of
Deschamps (1538).

Old Hall manuscript

1784 *The Old Hall Ms* ed Andrew Hughes and Margaret Bent 3 vols CMM 46 (1969,
1785 1969, 1973?) xxxii + 1–188 and separately bound 189–428; xviii + 124; 3rd vol
1786 to follow **1785** Hughes, Andrew 'The Old Hall Ms: a Reappraisal' and with
1787 Margaret Bent 'An Inventory' *MD* 21 (1967) 97–147 **1786** Bent 'Initial Letters
1788 in the Old Hall Ms' *ML* 47 (1966) 225–38 + 2 pll **1787** Bent 'Sources of the
Old Hall M' *PRMA* 94 (1967/8) 19–35 **1788** Scott, A.B. 'The Performance of
the Old Hall Descant Settings' *MQ* 56 (1970) 14–26
1784 This is a performing edition, with practical suggestions in vol 1. Vol
1 also contains indices and a long section on editorial accidentals. English
translations of the texts are given. Vol 3 will contain an extensive analytical
commentary. **1785** The reappraisal summarises stylistic, biographical, and
chronological information and offers some new suggestions. The inventory
corrects earlier lists and has much new material. **1786** B traces the history
of the ms and draws conclusions about the M. **1787** This is an excellent article
involving inter-disciplinary study of physical and other non-M features to
show the date, provenance, scribal procedure, and compilation of this
major source of late med. English M. B deals with concordances, texts, and
styles, concluding that Roy Henry is Henry V. **1788** Certain features suggest
the participation of the organ.

1789 Hughes, Andrew 'Mass Pairs in the Old Hall and other English Mss' *RBM*
19 (1965) 15–27
Stylistic and formal criteria are used to identify items which are linked
musically.

1790 Hughes, Andrew 'Mensuration and Proportion in Early 15c English M' *Acta*
27 (1965) 48–61
H shows how English composers modified French rhythmic practice of the
late 14c.

Dunstable

1791 Reaney, G. 'John Dunstable and late med. M in England' *Score* 8 (1953) 22–33
R points to insular characteristics and foreign influences in the M of 14c England. Dunstable introduces a new subjective element.

Carols and Benedicamus Domino

1792 *Mediaeval Carols* ed John Stevens MUSICA BRITANNICA 4 (revd ed London 1957) xxi + 145 / rev T. Dart *ML* 34 (1953) 78–9
This is an edition of all known carols of the early 15c with M.

1793 Sahlin, Margit *Etude sur la carole méd.* (Uppsala 1940) xi + 243, b / rev P.
1794 Zumthor *ZrPh* 64 (1964) 182–4 **1794** 'The English Carol' Round Table
1795 A-6.284–309 **1795** Harrison, F.Ll. 'Benedicamus, Conductus, Carol: A Newly Discovered Source' *Acta* 37 (1965) 35–48
1793 Referring to literary aspects of refrains, chansons, dances, chants, etc, this has considerable bearing on M forms. There are numerous quotations from contemporary literature. **1794** Prompted by several main statements, the panel discusses the relations between carol, lauda, procession, *Benedicamus Domino*, and social function. **1795** H lists, transcribes, and discusses the compositions in a ms from Aosta (Seminario 9-E-19), suggesting that conductus and carol were successive replacements for the *Benedicamus Domino*.

SOURCES

These are alphabetical by author. See the RISM volumes: **8b 8c 1503.**

1796 Andrews, H.K., and T. Dart 'Fourteenth Century Polyphony in a Fountains Abbey Ms Book' *ML* 39 (1958) 1–12, 3 facss and D. Stevens 'The Second Fountains Fragment: a Postscript' ibid 148–53
A and D describe the contents, notation, and texts, with some transcriptions. S identifies the ms as a polyphonic troper with additions by later scribes, and describes its place in the Cistercian liturgy.

1797 Bent, M. 'New and Little-known Fragments of English Med. Polyphony' *JAMS* 21 (1968) 137–56, 4 facss
With M examples and some discussion of an uncommon form of notation, B describes several sources.

1798 Greene, R.L. 'Two Med. M Mss: Egerton 3307 and Some University of Chicago Fragments' *JAMS* 7 (1954) 1–34
G uses the provenance of the latter fragments to strengthen his suggestion for the Egerton Ms (ca 1440 – not included in this bibliography).

1799 Harrison, F.Ll. 'Ars nova in England: a New Source' MD 21 (1967) 67–85
H inventories and describes the Durham Cathedral Ms c.I. 20 and its relation to other 14c English sources, and to continental styles, printing numerous M and textual passages.

1800 Hughes, Andrew 'New Italian and English Sources of the 14–16c' Acta 39
(1967) 171–82, 1 facs
H describes fragmentary sources, with some transcriptions.

1801 Levy, K.J. 'New material on the early motet in England: a Report on the
Princeton Ms Garrett 119' JAMS 4 (1951) 220–39 + 2 facss
L describes the fragments and transcribes some of the M.

1802 Reaney, G. 'Some Little-known Sources of Med. Polyphony in England' MD
15 (1961) 15–26
R describes and inventories several 14–15c mss.

1803 Stevens, D. 'A Recently Discovered English Source of the 14c' MQ 41 (1955)
26–40, 2 facss
S describes the source (London, Public Record Office, Ms E. 149/7/23 dorse)
and transcribes four pieces. See also Score 8 (1953) 11–16.

1804 Stevens, D. 'Polyphonic Tropers in 14c England' F-23.768–84, 1 facss (pl 28
a, b)
S inventories and discusses related Gloria tropes in several sources.

1805 Strohm, R. 'Ein englischer Ordinariumssatz des 14. Jh. in Italien' Mf 18
(1965) 178–81
S adduces evidence about a polyphonic Kyrie in a ms at Pisa.

1806 Trowell, B. 'A 14c ceremonial motet and its composer' Acta 29 (1957) 65–75
With copious biographical information T concludes that Sub Arturo plebs
was composed ca 1358, for use at Windsor. This apparently conclusive study
has recently been strongly challenged by Margaret Bent in her doctoral dissertation (Cambridge).

THE CELTIC LANDS

1807 Lewis, T. 'Celtic Songcraft' MLR 41 (1946) 131–43
Examining terminology, L concludes that Welsh practice was much
influenced by the Norman Conquest and the Angevins.

1808 Travis, James Miscellanea Musica Celtica MS 14 (Brooklyn 1968) iv + 78, 4 pll
and facss / rev J. Rimmer Notes 26 (1969/70) 260–2
16c sources may throw light on much earlier harp M. The author challenges
accepted belief about Sumer is icumen in. He finds melodies hidden in Celtic
designs.

1809 Harrison, F.Ll. 'Polyphony in Med. Ireland' F-29.74–8, 1 pl
H transcribes and discusses all the known examples.

Thirteenth- and fourteenth-century theory

1810 Georgiades, Thrasybulos *Englische Diskanttraktate aus der ersten Hälfte des 15. Jh.* SCHRIFTENREIHE DES MW SEMINARS DER U MÜNCHEN, Bd 3 (Munich 1937) 111
G edits and interprets tracts and relates them to continental theory.

1811 *Breviarium Regulare Musicae* and *Tractatus de Figuris sive de Notis* ed Gilbert
1812 Reaney, and with André Gilles *Declaratio Trianguli et Scuti*CSM 12 (1966) 63, M exx, diagrams **1812** Reaney 'The *Breviarium Regulare Musice* of Ms Oxford Bodley 842' *MD* 11 (1957) 31–7
1811 R and G edit short treatises by Willelmus (late 14c), Torkesey? (ca 1350), and Torkesey. **1812** R describes the contents of this 14–15c pedagogical ms and summarises one of the treatises.

Walter Odington

1813 *Walter Odington's 'Summa de Speculatione Musicae'* ed Frederick F. Hammond CSM 14 (1970) 159 + 6 pll, b, indices of incipits and of Odington's sources
This is an edition.

1814 *Robert de Handlo* [*Regulae*] transl Luther A. Dittmer MThT 2 (1959) 44, 1 facs / rev W. Apel *Spec* 35 (1960) 296–8

1815 Reaney, G. 'John Wylde and the Notre Dame Conductus' **F-15**.263–70
R transcribes sections of a 14c treatise which refers to Notre Dame compositions.

The Iberian peninsula

1816 Stevenson, Robert *Spanish* M *in the Age of Columbus* (The Hague 1960) xv +
335, ext b, index / rev P.E. Peacock *ML* 42 (1961) 374–5
There is an excellent factual survey of the med. era (pp 1–49).

1817 *La* M *de las Cantigas de Santa María del Rey Alfonso el Sabio* ed Higinio
Anglés 3 vols in 4 BIBL CENTRAL, PUBL DE LA SECCIÓN DE M 19, 15, 18^1, 18^2
(Barcelona 1964, 1943, 1958, 1958) xvi + 12 + 361 fos facss; xi + 462; xx +
428, index of incipits; xi + 429–675, 36 facss + 1–99 M transcc, index,
b / rev vols 2 and 3 only: A. Machabey *Rom* 81 (1960) 405–8; J. Chailley
RdM 47 (1961) 208–13; and W. Apel *Spec* 22 (1947) 458–60
Vol 1: this is a facsimile edition of Ms Escorial j.b.2, containing monophonic
secular M of 13c Spain, with an introduction, description, and inventory.
Vol 2: A introduces the general background of the *cantigas* with a detailed
description of the notation, indices of texts and melodies, and a transcription (Rh) with parallel variants from concordances. Vol 3^1: this is a general
survey of M culture in Spain up to the 13c, dealing with both secular and
liturgical M and especially with Arabic influence. A gives information about
Alfonso and the culture of his court. There is a long and detailed section on
notation, rhythm, poetic and M form, with an *Abhandlung* on metre and
form by Hans Spanke. Vol 3^2: this contains more detailed studies on Arabic
influence, Santiago de Compostela, Martín Códax, *Les Miracles de Notre
Dame* by Gautier de Coincy, etc. A also discusses the Italian lauda,
Provençal songs, and the trouvères. There are facsimiles and transcriptions,
indices of texts, subjects, etc, and a comprehensive bibliography.

1818 Ribera, Julian *Cantigas de Santa Maria* 2 vols (Madrid 1889) and vol 3 *La* M
de las Cantigas (Madrid 1922) (vol 3 transl in item **1129**) iii + 226 (R describes
the sources and their historical context) + i–cxxviii (R summarises the narra-
tives of the poems) + i–xxxv (rough inventory of Ms Escorial j.b.2) + 1–214,
9 col facss continued in vol 2; 215–805 (R edits the poems with a glossary
(611–799); 159, 13 facss + 118 facss + 119–345 (R edits the M with an introduction and complete facsimile of Ms Madrid 10069)

R is a strong Arabist, but not a musician: some transcriptions are provided with a 19c piano accompaniment. Anglès (**1821**) says the publication is an inexhaustible arsenal of historical documentation on Arabic M culture in Iberia, but R's theories are strongly open to question from the M standpoint.

1819 Bell, A.F.G. 'The "Cantigas de Santa Maria" of Alfonso X' *MLR* 10 (1915) 338–48
B introduces the literary aspects.

1820 Anglés, Higini *La M en la España de Fernando el Santo y de Alfonso el Sabio*
1821 REAL ACAD DE BELLAS ARTES DE SAN FERNANDO (Madrid 1943) 71 **1821** Anglés 'Hispanic M Culture from the 6–14c' *MQ* 26 (1940) 494–528
1820 This is a general survey. **1821** This is an abbreviation and translation of the commentary to **1467**.

Texts

1822 Le Gentil, Pierre *La Poésie lyrique espagnole et portugaise à la fin du ma*. I: *Les Thèmes et les genres*. II: *Les Formes* (Rennes 1949, 1953) 617, 505 / rev vol 1 W.J. Entwistle *MLR* 46 (1951) 532–3 and vol 2 W.C. Atkinson *MLR* 49 (1954) 524–5
This deals comprehensively with primarily the literary aspects, but vol 2 relates the forms to M.

Interaction with other cultures

1823 Anglès, H. 'La M juive dans l'Espagne méd.' *Yuval* 48–64 ***1824** Anglès 'La
*1824 M anglesa dels segles XIII–XIV als Països Hispànics' *Miscellània Finke:*
1825 *Analecta Sacra Tarraconensia* (Barcelona 1935) 219–33 **1825** Anglès 'M Beziehungen zwischen Deutschland und Spanien in der Zeit vom 5. bis 14. Jh.' *AMw* 16 (1959) 5–20
1823 There is little firm evidence. A thinks the Jews more influential than the Arabs. **1824** This item was not seen. **1825** A cautiously surveys the evidence, which is mainly in texts and court records rather than in the M.

1826 Gerson-Kiwi, E. 'On the M Sources of the Judaeo-Hispanic *Romance*' *MQ* 50 (1964) 31–43
G suggests possible sources of the M for *romance* melodies: chanson de geste, its eastern parallels, Iberian folk idioms, and Hebrew traditions amalgamating in an oral tradition.

1827 Salmen, W. 'Iberische Hofmusikanten des späten MA auf Auslandsreisen' *AnuarioM* 11 (1956) 53–7

1828 Stern, Samuel Miklos ed *Les Chansons mozarabes: les vers finaux (kharjas) en espagnol dans les muwashshahs arabes et hébreux* U DI PALERMO. IST. DI FILOLOGIA ROMANZA, Collezione di testi 1 (Palermo 1953) xxviii + 67
This is a literary study and analysis.

SOURCES

The most important sources are the Codex Calixtinus (1374–80), the Escorial Ms j.b.2 (1817 1818), Las Huelgas (1467 1468), the Llibre Vermell (1831), Madrid 10069 (1818), Madrid 20486 (1417), and the Martin Codax Ms (1844–6).

1829 Angles, H. 'Die mehrstimmige M in Spanien vor dem xv. Jh.' *Beethoven-Zentenarfeier. Intern. Musikhist Kongress* (Vienna 1927) 158–63; also in *Revista M Catalana* 24 (1927) 138–44
This is a general review of the sources known at the time.

1830 Anglès, H. 'Die altespanische Mensuralnotation' **D-12**.7–17
Using transcriptions with original notation, A compares Spanish, Provençal, northern French, and Italian rhythmic practices. Spanish notation is less ambiguous.

1831 Anglès, H. 'El *Llibre Vermell* de Montserrat y los cantos y la danza sacra de los peregrinos durante el siglo xiv' *AnuarioM* 10 (1955) 45–78, 8 pp M transcc
A gives the basic information about this ms.

1832 Aubry, P. 'Iter Hispanicum. Notices et extraits de mss de Mancienne. I: Un
1833 "discantuum volumen" parisien du xiiie siècle à la cathédrale de Tolède. II: Deux chansonniers français à la Bibliothèque de l'Escorial. III: Les Cantigas de Santa Maria de don Alfonso el Sabio. IV: Notes sur le chant mozarabe. V: Folk-lore M d'Espagne' *SIMG* 8 (1906/7) 337–555, 2 facss, 517–34, 1 facs and 9 (1907/8) 32–51, 1 facs, 157–75, 175–83 (repr Paris 1908 84 + 4 pll) 1833 Sablayrolles, Dom M. 'A la recherche des mss grég. espagnols' *SIMG* 13 (1911/12) 205–47, 5 facss, 401–32, 2 facss, 509–31, 2 facss
1832 With numerous examples and transcriptions A describes the main sources of Spanish polyphony and mozarabic plainsong. 1833 S describes many sources and transcribes a number of plainsongs.

1834 Harder, H., and B. Stäblein 'Neue Fragmente mehrstimmiger M aus spanischen Bibliotheken' **F-25**.131–41 + 14 facss
The sources are inventoried and described, and are related to the Avignon repertory of the 14c.

AREAS

Andalusia **1842** Aragon **1839** Catalonia **1835–8 1841 1843** Galicia **1844–6** Navarre **1838a** Portugal **1840**

1835 Anglès, H. 'Els Cantors i organistes franco-flamencs i alemanys a Catalunya els segles xiv–xvi' *Gedenkboek ... Scheurleer* ('s-Gravenhage 1925) 49–62
A quotes archival references. See also **D-1**.56–66.

1836 Anglès, Higini *La* M *a Catalunya fins al segle* XIII BarcCat 10 INST D'ESTUDIS CATALANS (Barcelona 1935) xvi + 447, 25 pll, 67 facss, num transcc, tables, indices of texts, names, etc / rev I. Pope *Spec* 12 (1937) 404–7
This is a general history, dealing with chant and singers, theorists, instruments, mss, polyphonic and monophonic secular M and its relations with French and Provençal song. A describes forms and styles, and gives a long section on liturgical drama. There is no bibliography, but the book is well documented.

1837 Anglès, H. 'La M aux xe et xie siècles. L'Ecole de Ripoll' *La Catalogne à l'époque romane* U DE PARIS, INST D'ART ET D'ARCH, BIBL D'ART CATALAN, Fondation Cambó 2 (Paris 1932) 157–79
A describes sources and centres of M cultivation.

1838 Anglès, H. 'Die Sequenz und die Verbeta im ma. Spanien' *Svensk Tidskrift: (Studier tillägnade Carl-Allan Moberg)* 43 (1961) 37–47
Catalonia is the centre of cultivation. A points to instances of Sequence (and Alleluia) being used in the Offices and compares the Verbeta (trope to a Responsory).

1838a Anglès, Higionio *Historia de la* M *med. en Navarra* DIPUTACION FORAL DE NAVARRA, Inst Principe de Viana (np 1970) 463, 7 facss, index of names
This is a comprehensive history: there are sections on Visigothic-mozarabic chant, learned and popular M (9–12c), the courtly lyric, pilgrimage M, *Ars Nova*, instrumental M.

1839 Baldelló, F.deP. 'La M en la casa de los Reyes de Aragón' *AnuarioM* 11 (1956) 37–51
B examines and quotes archival references, 1308–1444, to musicians, instruments, and dances.

1840 Corbin, Solange *Essai sur la* M *religieuse portugaise au ma.*, 1100–1385 COLLECTION PORTUGAISE 8 (Paris 1952) xl + 436, 18 facss, M exx, b / rev M.F. Bukofzer *Notes* 12 (1954/5) 240–1 and A.T. Luper *JAMS* 8 (1955) 50–4
This is a comprehensive, but quite detailed, history.

1841 Figueras, J.R. 'El Cantar paralelístico en Cataluña' *AnuarioM* 9 (1954) 3–55
F discusses the influence and distribution of Provençal poetry.

1842 Ribera y Tarragó, Julián *La* M *Andaluza med. en las canciones de trovadores, troveros y minnesinger* 3 fascicles (Madrid 1923, 1924, 1925) 1–31 + 1–73; 1–40 +1–62; 1–64 + 1–68 / rev W. Gurlitt *Literarische Wochenschrift* (1926) 1006
R rhythmicizes, or adds 19c accompaniments to melodies from 13c chansonniers. Each volume has an introduction. There is nothing else which ostensibly deals with Andalusia.

1843 Ursprung, O. 'Spanisch-katalanische Liedkunst des 14. Jh.' *ZMw* 4 (1921/2) 136–60
U describes and transcribes the pieces in the *Llibre Vermell*. See also **1831**.

Martín Códax

1844 Vindel, Pedro ed *Martin Codax. Las Siete Canciones de Amor: Poema* M del
1845 *Siglo XII* (Madrid 1915) 14 + 31 unnumbered pp, 7 facss + 2 foldout facss
1846 **1845** Pope, I. 'Med. Latin Background of the 13c Galician Lyric' *Spec* 9 (1934)
3–25 + 4 facss **1846** Bell, A.F.G. 'The Seven Songs of Martin Codax' *MLR*
18 (1923) 162–7
1844 This is a facsimile edition, with introduction and transcription of the
seven songs. **1845** P describes and transcribes the songs. **1846** B translates
the songs.

TREATISES

1847 Anglès, H. *'De cantu organico*. Tratado de un autor catalán del siglo xiv'
AnuarioM 13 (1958) 3–24, 1 facs
A edits the text, explaining its contents and context.

1848 Gümpel, K.-W. 'Zur Frühgeschichte der vulgärsprachlichen spanischen
und katalanischen Musiktheorie' *Spanische Forschung der Görresges. Ser I:
Gesammelte Aufsätze zur Kulturgesch Spaniens* 24 (1968) 257–336, 1 facs
Including a vocabulary of terms and a bibliographical list of sources, G edits
the *Arte de canto llano*.

The Germanic countries

LYRIC SONG AND MINNESINGER

See **1058–65** and **1237–1322**.

CATALOGUES AND SOURCES OF POLYPHONY

1849 Geering, Arnold *Die Organa und mehrstimmigen Conductus in den Hss des*
1850 *deutschen Sprachgebietes vom XIII bis XVI Jh.* PSMfG ser 2, vol 1 (Bern 1952)
1851 xvi + 99 / rev W. Apel *Spec* 29 (1954) 803 **1850** Göllner, Theodor *Formen*
1852 *früher Mehrstimmigkeit in deutschen Hss des späten MA* MVM 6 (Tutzing 1961)
201 + 10 facss **1851** Pietzsch, G. 'Übersehene Quellen zur ma. Orgel-
geschichte' *AnuarioM* 12 (1957) 83–96 **1852** Stephan, R. 'Einige Hinweise
auf die Pflege der Mehrstimmigkeit im früheren MA in Deutschland'
B-1.68–71
1849 Including some transcription, G describes and inventories sources and
styles, many of which are archaic. **1850** Göllner relates vocal and instrumental practice and theory. He edits with a complete facsimile and translates
a 15c organ-playing treatise. **1851** 13c and 14c documents show that organ
playing and polyphony were cultivated in German churches. English
influence is possible. **1852** S mentions second-hand sources of literary references.

Theory

1853 *Das Cantuagium des Heinrich Eger von Kalkar, 1328–1408* ed Heinrich
Hüschen, BRMg 2 (Cologne 1952) 67, 1 facs / rev S. Clercx *RBM* 10 (1956) 72–4
H prints and comments on the treatise.

Switzerland

1854 Handschin, J. 'Bis zur Wende des MA' *Gesch der M in der Schw* SCHW
1855 MUSIKBUCH 1 (Zurich 1939) 11–53, 2 facss **1855** Handschin 'Die Anfänge

1856 des Kirchengesanges in der Schweiz' **F-13**.188–91 **1856** Handschin 'Mittelalterliche Kulturprobleme der Schweiz' **F-13**.175–87
These are all quite general articles.

1857 Handschin, J. 'Die ältesten Denkmäler mensural notierter M in der Schweiz' ·
1858 *AMw* 5 (1923) 1–10 **1858** Handschin 'Die Schweiz, welche sang' **F-22**.102–33
+ 7 pp transcc
1857 H describes sources. In **1858** H comments on the monophonic pieces, especially the *cantio*, conductus, and rondeaux, in several Swiss mss, including the Engelberg Ms (**314**). He defines the terms.

1859 Entry deleted

Towns and areas

Braunschweig
1860 Härting, Michael *Der Messgesang im Braunschweiger Domstift St Blasii (Hs Niedersächsisches Staatsarchiv in Wolfenbüttel VII B Hs 175)* KBMf 28 (Regensburg 1963) 237, 15 facss, ext b
This is a description of sources, notation, and transmission of chants. H inventories the main ms, and includes lists of incipits.

Cologne
1861 Pietzsch, Gerhard *Fürsten und fürstliche Musiker im ma. Köln. Quellen und Studien* BRMg 66 (Cologne 1966) 195
This gives archival and biographical information.

1862 Werner, Hans-Josef *Die Hymnen in der Choraltradition des Stiftes St Kunibert zu Köln* BRMg 63 (Cologne 1966) 252
With indices and bibliography W discusses sources and characteristics of the hymns.

Erfurt, Essen, Euskirchen
1862a Handschin, J. 'Erfordensia I' *Acta* 6 (1934) 97–110
H describes sources.

1863 Kettering, Heinz *Quellen und Studien zur Essener Mg des hohen MA* BRMg 17 (Essen 1960) 344
K refers to sources and church practices.

1864 Kremp, Werner *Quellen und Studien zum Responsorium prolixum in der Überlieferung der Euskirchener Offiziumsantiphonare* BRMg 30 (Cologne 1958) 346, 6 facss
This consists of sources, analyses, indices.

Freiburg, Kremsmünster, Münster, Reichenau
1865 Fellerer, Karl G. *Mittelalterliches Musikleben der Stadt Freiburg im Uechtland* FREIBURGER STUDIEN ZUR MW 3 (Regensburg 1935) 108

1866 Kellner, Altman *Musikgeschichte des Stiftes Kremsmünster* (Kassel 1956) 827, num facss, M exx, index
Pp 1–109 deal with the MA, concentrating on the sources.

1866a Ossing, Hans *Untersuchungen zum Antiphonale Monasteriense (Alopecius-*
1866b *Druck 1537): Ein Vergleich mit den Hss des Münsterlandes* 2 vols KBMf 39 (Regensburg 1966) 322, num facss; 133 **1866b** Aengenvoort, Johannes *Quellen und Studien zur Geschichte des Graduale Monasteriense* KBMf 9 (Regensburg 1955) iv + 281 / rev D. Mintz *Notes* 16 (1958/9) 63–5
1866a O's study includes alphabetical lists of plainsongs and is basically a comparative catalogue of sources. **1866b** With indices and commentary A describes the sources from ms to print.

1867 Stephan, R. 'Aus der alten Abtei Reichenau' *AMw* 13 (1956) 61–76, 2 facss
S identifies M sources from the song school.

St Gall

1868 Van Doren, Dom Rombaut *Etude sur l'influence* M *de l'Abbaye de Saint Gall*
1869 *(VIIIᵉ au XIᵉ siècle)* U DE LOUVAIN, RECUEIL DE TRAVAUX, ser 2, fascicle 5 (6, according to title page) (Louvain 1925) 160 + 3 facss, onomastic, geographical, and ms indices / rev A. Gastoué *MoyA* sér 2: 27 (1926) 394–8 **1869** Wagner, P. 'St Gallen in der Musikgeschichte' *Die Dichterschule von St Gallen* ed Samuel Singer DIE SCHW IN DEUTSCHEN GEISTESLEBEN 8 (Leipzig 1922) 8–26

1870 Marxer, Otto *Zur spätma. Choralgeschichte St Gallens: Der Cod. 546 der St Galler Stiftsbibliothek* GAkF 3 (St Gall 1908) vii + 248 + 10 facss / rev J. Wolf ZIMG 11 (1910) 120–1
Although the ms dates from 1507, it is the culmination of the med. tradition of the monastery. M describes and inventories the ms and transcribes many melodies (dipl and Sq).

1871 Husmann, H. 'Die älteste erreichbare Gestalt des St Galler Troparium'
1872 *AMw* 13 (1956) 25–41 **1872** Wellnitz, Adalbert *Die Alleluia-Melodien der Hs Sankt Gallen 359* (Bonn 1960) 399
1871 H lists some of the tropes to establish a stemma of the six main mss, and finds two distinct groups. **1872** W describes the source and analyses the contents.

Salzburg, Silesia

1873 Zagiba, F. 'Die irisch-schottische Mission in Salzburg im 8. Jh. und die Anfänge der Choralpflege in den Alpenländern' *KmJb* 41 (1957) 1–3.

1874 Feldmann, Fritz M *und Musikpflege in ma. Schlesien* DARSTELLUNGEN UND QUELLEN ZUR SCHLESISCHEN GESCH 37 (Breslau 1938) x + 212, 4 facss + 1–31 M appendix + 5 tables
This is a general survey, listing liturgical mss (195–8), musicians (199–206), and with an index. On pp 155–94 F edits two treatises.

Vienna

1875 Mantuani, Josef *Die M in Wien* in *Geschichte der Stadt Wien* Bd III, 1. Hälfte, ed Albert Starzer ALTERTHUMSVEREINE ZU WIEN (Vienna 1907) 119–458, num M exx, pll, and facss / rev B Scharlitt *Die M* 22 (1906/7) 50–3

This is a comprehensive history up to the 16c, dealing with much off-the-beaten-track material. M includes 54 transcriptions.

Scandinavia

1876 Hammerich, Angul *Med.* M *Relics of Denmark* transl Margaret W. Hamerik
1877 (Leipzig 1912) viii + 124, num facss **1877** Handschin, J. 'Das älteste Doku-
1878 ment für die Pflege der Mehrstimmigkeit in Dänemark' and 'Noch eine
stimmtauschmässige Hymnenkomposition' *Acta* 7 (1935) 67–9, 70–1
1878 Hammerich 'Das Volkslied-Fragment in *Codex Runicus*,' *ZMw* 3
(1920/1) 513–18
1876 Hammerich describes Danish mss and prints texts and melodies
(mostly Sequences). **1877** Referring to refrains and conductus, Handschin
notes the wide distribution of polyphonic voice-exchange versions of
melodies, especially the hymn *Nunc sancte nobis.* **1878** Hammerich describes
and transcribes the 13c fragment.

1879 Husmann, H. 'Die Oster- und Pfingst-Alleluia der Kopenhagener Liturgie
1880 und ihre historischen Beziehungen' *Dansk aarbog for musikforskning* 4
(1964/5) 3–62 **1880** Husmann 'Studien zur geschichtlichen Stellung der
Liturgie Kopenhagens (unter Zugrundelegung des Missale von 1510)' *Dansk
aarbog for musikforskning* 2 (1962) 3–58
These are comparative textual and liturgical studies, with useful lists of mss.

1881 Hammerich, A. 'Studien über isländische M' *SIMG* 1 (1899/1900) 341–71 + 2
1882 facss **1882** Helgason, H. 'Das Bauernorganum auf Island' **A-3.**132–3 **1883**
1883 Wallin, N.L. 'Hymnus in honorem Sancti Magni comitis Orchadiae: Codex
Upsaliensis C 233' *Svensk Tidskrift (Studier tillägnade C.-A. Moberg)* 43 (1961)
339–54, 1 facs
1881 Hammerich describes and transcribes old 'folk' tunes and polyphonic
pieces, mostly in med. styles but in late survivals. **1882** Helgason describes
the performance of the traditional *tvisöngur*, outlining the similarities to
parallel organum. **1883** W discusses *Nobilis, humilis* in relation to gymel,
tvisöngur, conductus, and carol.

SWEDEN

1884 Norlind, Tobias *Bilder ur svenska musikens historia från äldsta tid till medelti-dens slut* (Stockholm 1947) 271, num illuss, pll, exx, facss
N deals with instruments, with secular, folk, and spiritual cultivation of M, and with ms sources of plainsong.

1885 Moberg, Carl-Allan *Die liturgischen Hymnen in Schweden.* I: *Quellen und Texte. Text- und Melodieregister* (Copenhagen 1947) xxiv + 398, num small facss, list of mss, indices of incipits, names / rev B. Stäblein *Mf* 3 (1950) 309–16
This is a comprehensive examination of the sources and the texts of hymns with alphabetical lists of melodies, etc. Vol 2 seems never to have been published.

1886 Kroon, Sigurd *Ordinarium Missae, Studier kring melodierna till Kyrie, Gloria* ... LUNDS U ÅRSSKRIFT, Nf Avd. 1, Bd 49, Nr 6 (Lund 1953) 231 + 31 facss / rev P. Lefèvre *RHE* 49 (1954) 944–5
There is a French résumé, pp 214–31. The book is basically a catalogue of Swedish sources.

Miscellaneous manuscripts with polyphony

Some of the following items discuss major sources: they are arranged alphabetically by author. Where no annotation is given, the item is a simple description. See also **8b 8c 1335 1503**.

1887 Delft, Metha-Machteld van 'Een Gloria-fragment in de Universiteits-bibliotheek te Utrecht' *TVNM* 19 (1960/3) 84–5

1888 Droz, E., and G. Thibault 'Un Chansonnier de Philippe le Bon' *RdM* 7 (1926) 1–8, 4 facss
D and T give the original list of contents of a major 14c polyphonic ms of which only two leaves remain.

*1889 Engelhardt, Christian M. *Herrad von Landsperg und ihr Werk 'Hortus deliciarum'* 2 vols (Stuttgart, Tübingen 1818)
This includes diplomatic facsimiles, several with M instruments. Table x has the polyphonic piece *Sol oritur* (12c).

1890 Federhofer, H. 'Denkmäler der ars nova in Vorau Codex 380' *Acta* 22 (1950) 1–7
F transcribes the *unicum* work.

1891 Fischer, K. von 'Neue Quellen zur M des 13., 14., und 15. Jh.' *Acta* 36 (1964) 79–97, 4 facss
F inventories and describes several sources, including French and Italian 14c M, and Notre Dame pieces.

1892 Handschin, J. 'Angelomontana polyphonica' *SJbMw* 3 (1928) 64–96 + 26 pp M exx
H describes the contents of 4 mss related to the Engelberger circle, with detailed comments and 26 transcriptions.

1893 Handschin, J. 'Das Fragment Coussemaker' *Acta* 7 (1935) 160–1

1893a Hofmann-Brandt, H. 'Eine neue Quelle zur ma. mehrstimmigkeit' F-29.109–15, 1 facs
H describes Amiens 162.

1894 Hoppin, R.H. 'A M Rotulus of the 14c' *RBM* 9 (1955) 131–42

1895 Huglo, M. 'Trois anciens mss liturgiques d'Auvergne' *Bull hist et scientifique de l'Auvergne* ACAD DES SCIENCES, BELLE-LETTRES ET ARTS DE CLERMONT-FERRAND 77 (1957) 81–104, 1 pl, 1 facs

1896 Irtenhauf, W. 'Zur ma. Liturgie- und Mg Ottobeurens' *Ottobeuren: Fs zur 1200-Jahrfeier der Abtei* ed Aegidius Kolb and Hermann Tüchle (Augsburg 1964) 141–79

1897 Köllner, G.P. 'Eine Mainzer Choral-Hs des 15. Jh. als Quelle zum "Crucifixum in carne"' *AMw* 19/20 (1962/3) 208–12, 2 pll
K describes a 15c source of Notre Dame polyphony. See **1433 1434**.

1898 Koller, O. 'Aus dem Archive des Benediktinerstiftes St Paul im Lavanthal in Kärnten' *MMg* 22 (1890) 22–9, 1 table (between pp 32 and 33), 35–45

1899 Nowak, L. 'Das Melker Marienlied' *Unsere Heimat* ns 7 (1934) 184–95, 1 facss

1900 Petrobelli, P. 'Nuovo materiale polifonico del Medioevo e del Rinascimento a Cividale' *Mem storiche Forogiuliesi* 46 (1965) 213–15

1901 Reaney, G. 'New Sources of *Ars Nova* M' *MD* 19 (1965) 53–67

1902 Seay, A. 'Le Ms 695 de la bibliothèque communale d'Assise' *RdM* 39 (1957) 10–35, 4 pp transcc
Describing and inventorying the 13c ms, S concludes it was a careful compilation from three other mss.

1903 Spanke, H. 'Die Stuttgarter Hs H. B. I. Ascet. 95' *ZdA* 68 (ns 56) (1931) 79–88

1904 Stenzl, J. 'Das Dreikönigsfest in der Genfer Kathedrale Saint-Pierre' *AMw* 25 (1968) 118–33
S discusses and transcribes 14–15c monophonic and polyphonic settings of a Gospel, in Geneva Ms L 38b.

1905 Strohm, R. 'Neue Quellen zur liturgischen Mehrstimmigkeit des MA in Italien' *RIM* 1 (1966) 77–87

1906 (Wagenaar-)Nolthenius, H. 'De Leidse fragmenten. Nederlandse polyfonie uit het einde der 14de eeuw' **F-18**.303–15
W describes the ms and transcribes four pieces.

1907 Wolf, J. 'Eine neue Quelle zur mehrstimmigen kirchlichen Praxis des 14. bis 15. Jh.' **F-33**.222–37
W describes, inventories, and partially transcribes this ms now destroyed (Berlin, Staatsbibl. 40580).

Instrumental music, dances

1907a Schrade, Leo *Die handschriftliche Überlieferung der ältesten Instrumentalmusik* (diss 1931; repr with a few changes and an introduction, Tutzing 1968) 128 / rev N. Bridgman *RdM* 55 (1969) 85–6: reviewer says this is a description of mss and notation which has not been brought up to date and remains a 1931 publication.

DANCES

1908 Spanke, H. 'Tanzmusik in der Kirche des MA' *NeuphMit* 31 (1930) **1909** 143–70 **1909** Spanke 'Zum Thema "ma. Tanzlieder" ' *NeuphMit* 33 (1932) 1–22

1908 Ecclesiastical dances were widely in use. S examines Sequence, antiphon, conductus, and Latin rondeaux. **1909** S expands the previous item to include evidence from Spain, and transcribes two virelais.

1910 Stephan, R. 'Lied, Tropus, und Tanz im MA' *ZdA* 87 (1956/7) 147–62

In the late MA German songs were interpolated as tropes into plainchants, especially processional chants: some evidence links such interpolations with dances.

1911 Anglès, H. 'La Danza sacra y su M en el templo durante el Medioevo' *Medium Aevum Romanicum: Fs für Hans Rheinfelder* (Munich 1963) 1–20

This is a general survey; A transcribes several rondeaux from the Florence Ms.

1912 Rokseth, Y. 'Danses clericales du XIIIe siècle' *Mélanges 1945*, vol 3 *Etudes Historiques* PUBL DE LA FACULTE DES LETTRES DE L'U DE STRASBOURG, fasc. 106 (Paris 1947) 93–126

R sees the secular vernacular rondeaux and carol existing prior to and providing the model for Latin pieces of the type. She quotes evidence of the sacred 'dance' and transcribes 60 pieces from the 11th fascicle of the Florence Ms.

1913 Chailley, J. 'Un Document nouveau sur la danse ecclésiastique' *Acta* 21
1914 (1949) 18–24, 1 facs **1914** Chailley 'La Danse religieuse au ma.' **D-7**.357–80,
11 facss
1913 C investigates the word *balare* and unusual notational signs in a 14c
liturgical ms. **1914** Do constant ecclesiastical prohibitions imply constant
use of dancing? C examines the terms *tripudium, carole, chorea* and finds
literary and M evidence demonstrating continued use of dances for sacred
purposes. Specially composed rondeaux (e.g., as in the Florence Ms), as well
as standard plainsongs, were used for M.

Estampies

1915 Aubry, P. 'Estampies et Danses Royales ...' *Le Mercure* M 2² (1906)
1916 169–201 **1916** Wolf, J. 'Die Tänze des MA' *AMw* 1 (1918/19) 10–42, 24 pp
transcc
1915 A describes dances from a 13c ms: his transcriptions are virtually useless. **1916** W discusses the evidence for instrumental dances, and prints 14c
examples.

1917 Handschin, J. 'Über Estampie und Sequenz' *ZMw* 12 (1929/30) 1–20 and 13
(1930/1) 113–32
With several transcriptions H points to a form occurring in both styles: the
double-cursus with first and second time cadences.

1918 Hibberd, Ll. '*Estampie* and *Stantipes*,' *Spec* 19 (1944) 222–49 **1919** (Wagenaar-)
1919 Nolthenius, H. 'Estampie/Stantipes/Stampita' **D-5**.399–409
1918 This is a standard study: the *stantipes* probably developed out of the
estampie. **1919** There are discrepancies in the evidence and the explanations.
See also *ZMw* 2 (1919/20) 194–206.

1920 Streng-Renkonen, Walter O. ed *Les Estampies françaises* LES CLASSIQUES
FRANÇAIS DU MA 65 (Paris 1930) xiii + 74, glossary, list of incipits / rev A.
Wallensköld *NeuphMit* 33 (1932) 146–51
This is an edition of texts with analytical notes.

1921 Entry deleted

Other dances

1922 Cosacchi, S. 'Musikinstrumente im ma. Totentanz' *Mf* 8 (1955) 1–19
This is a general introduction, dealing especially with the iconography. See
Mf 9 (1956) 189–90.

∗1923 *De dansen van het Trecento* ed Jan ten Bokum SCRIPTA MUSICOLOGICA
ULTRAJECTINA 1 (Utrecht 1967) 47 / rev W. Salmen *Mf* 22 (1969) 534–5

KEYBOARD MUSIC

Faenza Codex

1924 *Keyboard* M *of the 14 and 15c* ed Willi Apel CORPUS OF EARLY KEYBOARD M 1,
American Inst of Musicology (Rome 1963) vii + 52
Pp 1–9 of the edition include pieces from before 1400.

1925 *The Codex Faenza, Biblioteca Communale, 117* foreword by Armen Carapetyan
MSD 10 (1961) 112: repr from *MD* 13 (1959) 79–107; 14 (1960) 65–104; 15 (1961)
65–104
This is a facsimile edition.

1926 Plamenac, D. 'Keyboard M of the 14c in Codex Faenza 117' *JAMS* 4 (1951)
1927 179–201 + 3 facss **1927** Plamenac 'A Note on the Rearrangement of Faenza
1928 Codex 117' *JAMS* 17 (1964) 78–81 and 233 **1928** Plamenac 'New light on
Codex Faenza 117' A-2.310–26, 4 pll
1926 After describing the ms P gives transcriptions (one including the
unembellished original) and a list of the instrumental works with text
incipits. **1927** P describes the reorganization of the ms prior to rebinding
and publishing in facsimile (**1925**). He explains the discrepancies in foliation. **1928** P discusses newly identified paraphrases of vocal originals and
newly observed settings of Organ Masses, with paraphrased plainsong. He
transcribes four pieces.

* Announced: Kugler, Michael *Die Tastenmusik im Codex Faenza* MVM 21

Performance practice

GENERAL DISCUSSIONS

See also Performing Editions, preceding **65**.

1929 Dart, Thurston *The Interpretation of* M (London 1954) x + 11–192, glossary, b, index
This book is full of common sense and practical suggestions. Pp 150–68 deal with med. M and pp 18–28 explain editorial methods.

1930 Haas, Robert *Aufführungspraxis der* M HbMw (Potsdam 1931) 299, num pll,
1931 exx, facss / rev E. Schmitz *Neue Literatur* 34 (1933) 281 **1931** Schering,
1932 Arnold *Aufführungspraxis alter* M MUSIKPÄDAGOGISCHE BIBL, Heft 10 (Leipzig 1931; repr Wiesbaden 1969) **1932** Müller-Heuser, Franz *Vox humana. Ein Beitrag zur Untersuchung, der Stimmästhetik des MA* KBMf 26 (Regensburg 1963) iv + 188 / rev J. Smits van Waesberghe *KmJb* 51 (1967) 168–9
1930 Pp 1–108 deal with oriental, Greek, plainsong, and med. practices. The book provides a useful beginning, but there is little documentation or practical application. **1931** Med M is discussed on pp 1–25: there is little that is specific. **1932** M discusses vocal timbres preferred at different times: there is nothing practical.

MORE SPECIFIC DISCUSSIONS

See also items **1958–62**.

1933 Harrison, F.Ll. 'Tradition and Innovation in Instrumental Usage 1100–1450' F-23.319–35, pll 19a, 19b, 19c
With some details relevant to viella and trumpet H surveys the problems.

1934 Reaney, G. 'Voices and Instruments in the M of Guillaume de Machaut' *RBM* 10 (1956) 3–17, 93–104; revd and enl from **B-2**.245–8
R reviews the whole problem of performing 14c M, showing from contem-

porary statements that M with text may be played on instruments and that without text it may still be sung. He gives evidence for singing styles and for performance of lower parts either vocally or instrumentally. He describes 14c instruments and their presumed capabilities and deduces the probable tone-colour which resulted. Mentioning ornamentation, he gives good practical suggestions. See also **1958 1959**.

1935 Heyde, H. 'Polyphonales Musizieren im späten europäischen MA' *BMw* 7 (1965) 184–96
H examines the *bordun* possibilities for performance practice.

1936 Van den Borren, C. 'La Pureté de style et l'interpretation de la M du ma.' *La R intern de M* 1 (1938) 96–102, 273–9
Surely incorrect in some respects, V nevertheless broaches, tentatively, such intangible features as dynamics and speed changes, on which subjects there is virtually no evidence.

1937 Thibault, G. 'L'Ornementation dans la M profane au ma.' **A**-4.1.450–63 (discussed in II.166–71)
This is mainly concerned with 15c and 16c.

PLAINSONG

1938 Avenary, H. 'Formal Structure of Psalms and Canticles in Early Jewish and
1939 Christian Chant' *MD* 7 (1953) 1–13 **1939** Leeb, Helmut *Die Psalmodie bei*
1940 *Ambrosius* WIENER BEITR ZUR THEOLOGIE 18 (Vienna 1967) 115 **1940** Van Dijk,
1941 S.J.P. 'Med. Terminology and Methods of Psalm Singing' *MD* 6 (1952)
7–26 **1941** Gindele, C. 'Doppelchor und Psalmvortrag im Frühmittelalter'
Mf 6 (1953) 296–300
1938 Translating Talmudic texts, A discusses seven ways of performing psalms. **1939** With contemporary quotation L illustrates form, performance practice, and terminology. **1940** V shows how different terms refer to rhythmic movement and to voice production. **1941** G examines the evidence for performance of psalm and antiphon.

1942 Fellerer, K.G. 'Kirchenmusikalische Vorschriften im MA' *KmJb* 40 (1956) 1–11
With copious quotations and documentation F examines the recommendations about M and its performance to be found in the prescriptions of Councils and Synods.

1943 Van Dijk, S.J.P. 'St Bernard and the *Instituta Patrum* of St Gall' *MD* 4 (1950) 99–109
V comments on the sources and M references in this 13c tract.

1944 Weakland, R.G. 'The Performance of Ambrosian Chant in the 12c' **F**-23.856–66
'... study of the single melodic line is not enough': W shows how an *Ordo* can inform about the M.

1945 More, Mother Thomas 'The Performance of Plainsong in the Later MA and the 16c' *PRMA* 92 (1965/6) 121–134 + 4 pll
Dealing mainly with the 15c and 16c, the author suggests that tempo may be deduced from *alternatim* polyphonic settings and that rhythm may have been influenced by speech-rhythm.

1946 Corbin, S. 'Note sur l'ornementation dans le plain-chant grég.' A-4.I.428–39 (discussed in II.166–71)
C discusses the role of written-down ornamentation, especially with regard to the text. See also *StuMus* 11 (1969) 349–353.

INSTRUMENTS IN CHURCH

There are diametrically opposed views epitomised by Krüger, who favours the use of instruments, and McKinnon who objects. The evidence is in favour of the later opinion. The dispute results from ambiguous and not thoroughly assessed pictorial and theoretical evidence. The extremes can perhaps be reconciled: ideally, traditionally, philosophically, orthodoxically, and legally all instruments except the organ were forbidden in church: abuses and exceptions were sufficiently frequent and widespread to allow composers and performers to take advantage of the situation.

1947 Krüger, W. 'Aufführungspraktische Fragen ma. Mehrstimmigkeit' *Mf* 9 (1956) 419–27; 10 (1957) 279–86, 397–403, 497–505; 11 (1958) 177–89
Concentrating on the Notre Dame school and quoting liberally, K comprehensively reviews the evidence supporting the use of instruments in church. He maintains that prohibitions argue *de facto* practice and demonstrates that *organizare* and *sine littera* may have instrumental implications, and suggests that *Leoninus ... organista* may mean '... organist.' His theoretical and pictorial evidence some would interpret allegorically. K makes a very strong case for instrumental participation.

1948 McKinnon, J. 'The Meaning of the Patristic Polemic against M Instruments'
1949 *CM* 1 (1965) 69–82 **1949** McKinnon 'M Instruments in Med. Psalm Commentaries and Psalters' *JAMS* 21 (1968) 3–20
1948 The polemic was a matter of morality, not of liturgy. Its effect dominated the MA; no evidence is known for the use of instruments in the services. **1949** M demonstrates that references in psalm commentaries and illustrations are allegorical and do not constitute evidence for the use of instruments in the liturgy.

1950 Bowles, E.A. 'The Organ in the Med. Liturgical Service' *RBM* 16 (1962)
1951 13–29 **1951** Bowles 'Were M Instruments used in the Liturgical Service during the MA?' *GSJ* 10 (1957) 40–56. See also 11 (1958) 85–7 and 12 (1959) 89–92

1950 B quotes much contemporary evidence, and outlines the development of the instrument. **1951** Denying the evidential value of M style or of art, B emphasises the definite negative evidence. Only the organ had any regular place in the liturgy. A 17c scholar rebuts the arguments and B replies.

1952 Caldwell, J. 'The Organ in the Med. Latin Liturgy, 800–1500' *PRMA* 93 (1966/7) 11–24
This is a general review of the topic, mentioning most of the important sacred styles of the MA.

1953 More, Mother Thomas 'The Practice of Alternatim' *JEH* 18 (1967) 15–32
M quotes documents relating to the alternation of organ and polyphony. She deals primarily with 15c and 16c, which probably continue earlier practice.

1953a Rastall, Richard 'Minstrelsy, Church and Clergy in Med. England' *PRMA* 97 (1970/1) 83–98
R examines records which unequivocally document instrumental performance in church, referring particularly to bells.

CONDUCTING, TEMPO

1954 Gindele, C. 'Chordirektion des greg. Chorals im MA' *Studien und Mitteilungen zur Gesch des Benediktiner-Ordens und seine Zweige* 63 (1951) 31–44
Translating numerous passages, 11–14c, into German, G concludes that the cantor used both visual and audible signals. The passages give other information about position of the choir, etc.

1955 Huglo, M. 'La Chironomie méd.' *RdM* 49 (1963) 155–71, 2 pll
The med. method of 'conducting' is compared with that of Byzantium and antiquity.

1956 Smits van Waesberghe, J. 'Singen und Dirigieren der mehrstimmigen M im MA' **F-9**.II.1345–54, 4 pll
Some illustrations demonstrate physical contact between performers and director.

1957 Gullo, Salvatore *Das Tempo in der M des XIII und XIV Jh.* PSMfG Ser II: 10 (Bern 1964) xvi + 96, list of theorists, b / rev C. Brown *Notes* 23 (1966/7) 52–4
G concludes that the temporal length of the beat differs according to the amount of subdivision and that the length of the shorter note values is constant. The conventional statement is that the 'beat' (or *tactus*) remains constant.

PRACTICAL SUGGESTIONS

1958 Reaney, G. 'The Performance of Med. M' **F-23**.704–22
Reviewing the whole field, R introduces heterophonic practice and suggests

that the Machaut Mass is an ornamented instrumental score of simpler vocal parts.

1959 White, J.R. 'Performing 14c M'*Symposium. J of the College M Soc* 9 (1969) 85–90
A practical musician comments expertly on the difficulties and offers suggestions.

1960 Geering, A. 'Retrospektive mehrstimmige M in französischen Hss des MA' **F-2.I.**307–14
G shows that the works he lists, being stylistically retrospective, are often for choir rather than soloists.

1961 Krüger, W. 'Jubilemus, exultemus! Aufführungspraktische Fragen zu einem weinachtlichen Organum' *Musica* 6 (1952) 491–4
On the basis of questionable rhythmic interpretation K thinks the upper voice was instrumental. See **1368 1370**.

1962 Bloch, S. 'Note on Med. M' *The Guitar R* no. 29 (1966) 8–14
B attempts performing versions of five pieces, including parts for guitar. This attempt is in the right direction.

The Renaissance

Items **1963–9** deal with the transition to the M of the Burgundian court and fifteenth-century Germany in general (cf Ars subtilior, **1580–1601**). The main source of influence on the former – English M, especially of the Old Hall Manuscript and Dunstable – is presented in items **1784–91**.

1963 Lowinsky, E.E. 'M in the Culture of the Renaissance' *JHI* 15 (1954) 509–53
L concentrates on the period 1450–1600 in order to illuminate the period 1300–1450 and the characteristic differences between med. and Renaissance styles.

1964 'Critical Years in European M History, 1400–1430' Symposium **A-6**.43–76
The panel mention and discuss recent work and ideas, often undocumented, about the period.

1965 Dannemann, Erna *Die spätgotische Musiktradition in Frankreich und Burgund vor dem Auftreten Dufays* SAMMLUNG MW ABH 17 (Strasbourg 1936) 137
With old-fashioned transcriptions D discusses the transition from 14–15c.

1966 Pirrotta, N. ' "Dulcedo" e "subtilitas" nella pratica polifonica franco-italiana al principio del '400' *RBM* 2 (1948) 125–32

1967 Bowles, E.A. 'Instruments at the Court of Burgundy (1363–1467)' *GSJ* 6 (1953) 41–51
B gives documentary evidence relating to the cultivation of M.

1968 Pirro, A. 'Musiciens allemands et auditeurs français au temps des rois Charles V et Charles VI' **F-1**.71–7
P documents M interaction between France and Germany in the late 14–15c.

1969 Göllner, T. 'Die Trecento-Notation und der Tactus in den ältesten deutschen Orgelquellen' **D-5**.176–85
G examines the relation between 15c German organ notation and Italian trecento notation.

SOURCES

Listed alphabetically by location, these are sources which, among fifteenth-century compositions, transmit numerous medieval pieces. See also **8b, 8c**.

Aosta

1970 Van, G.de 'A Recently Discovered Source of Early 15c Polyphonic M'*MD* 2 (1948) 5–74, 2 pll
This is a general description of the Aosta Seminario Ms and its contents and composers. V includes an inventory with concordances and melodic incipits of the *unica*, and transcribes 5 texts and 3 pieces.

Bologna

*1971 Clercx(-Lejeune), Suzanne ed *Il Codice Q 15 del Civico Museo Bibliografico* M
1972 *di Bologna* MLMAI-M 6 (Bologna 1968) **1972** Van, G.de 'Inventory. of Ms Bologna, Liceo M, Q 15 (olim 37)' *MD* 2 (1948) 231–57, 2 facss
*1971 This is presumably a facsimile edition. **1972** This is an inventory, with concordances.

1973 *Il Codice M 2216 della Biblioteca Universitaria di Bologna* ed F. Alberto Gallo
1974 2 vols MLMAI-M 3 (Bologna 1968,   ) ix + 114 facss;   **1974** Besseler, H. 'The
1975 Ms Bologna Bibl Universitaria 2216' *MD* 6 (1952) 39–65 **1975** Gallo, F.A. 'Musiche veneziane del Ms 2216 della Biblioteca Universitaria di Bologna' *Quad* 6 (1964) 107–16, 3 facss + 1–11 M transcc
1973 Vol 2, with an introduction, is in preparation. **1974** This is a general description and inventory. **1975** G briefly describes and transcribes three works of Venetian origin.

Grottaferrata

1976 Strunk, O. 'Church Polyphony apropos of a new Fragment at Grottaferrata'
1977 D-5. 305–13 **1977** Günther, U. 'Quelques remarques sur des feuillets récemment découverts à Grottaferrata' D-5.315–97, 8 pp facss
1976 S describes the ms and discusses concordances with the Foligno fragments (**1686**), in which he sees a very early predecessor of fauxbourdon.
1977 G inventories, transcribes, and describes the polyphony in the ms.

Munich

1978 Dèzes, K. 'Der Mensuralkodex des Benediktinerklosters *Sancti Emmerami* zu Regensburg' *ZMw* 10 (1927/8) 65–105, 2 facss
D describes and gives a thematic inventory of the ms, now in Munich (Mus 3232a).

1979 Emerson, J.A. 'Über Entstehung und Inhalt von MüD' *KmJb* 48 (1964) 33–60
The Ms Munich, Bayerische SB Cgm 716 is from southern Germany. E gives
a complete inventory.

1980 Fischer, K. von 'Eine neue süddeutsche Quelle des frühen 15. Jh.' **F-29**.52–6
F describes and inventories Munich, Bayerische SB Clm 15611.

Oxford

1981 Reaney, G. 'The Ms Oxford, Bodleian Library, Canonici Misc. 213' *MD* 9
1982 (1955) 73–104 **1982** *Polyphonia Sacra, a Continental Miscellany of the 15c* ed
Charles Van den Borren PMMS (Burnham 1932; repr in a 2nd ed revd Pennsyl-
vania State U Press, University Park 1963) lv + 294 / rev *J of Church M* 6 (1964)
14–15
1981 R gives a basic description and inventory. **1982** This edition includes
still otherwise unpublished pieces by late 14c and 15c composers.

1982a Schoop, Hans *Entstehung und Verwendung der Hs Oxford, Bodleian Library,
Canonici misc. 213* PSMfG, ser II: 24 (Bern and Stuttgart 1971) 128, 2 pll

Pavia

1983 Cattin, G. 'Le Composizioni M del ms Pavia Aldini 361' **D-4**. 1–21, 12 pp
transcc
This is an inventory with transcription of 13 pieces.

Strasbourg

1984 Van den Borren, Charles *Le Ms M M.222 C.22 de la Bibliothèque de Strasbourg*
1985 (Antwerp 1924) 219; repr from *Annales de l'Acad Royale d'Arch de Belgique* 71
(1923) 343–74; 72 (1924) 272–303; 73 (1925) 128–96; 74 (1926) 71–152 **1985** Van
den Borren 'La M pittoresque dans le ms 222 c.22 de la Bibl. de Strasbourg
(xvᵉ siècle)' **D-1**.88–105
1984 V reconstructs and inventories this early 15c ms, burnt in 1870, from
a partial copy made by Coussemaker. He gives a comprehensive description. **1985** V describes and transcribes some programmatic pieces.

Trent

1986 *I Codici Tridentini quattrocenteschi del Castello del Buonconsiglio* ed L. Feinin-
1987 ger 7 vols MLMAI-M 5^{1-7} (Rome 1969, 1970, 1969, 1970, 1970, 1970, 1970) 440;
836; 838; 932; 510; 460; 708 **1987** *Sechs* [from 1924 *Sieben*] *Trienter Codices*
DTÖ 14–15, Jahrgang 7 (1900) 22, Jahrgang 11¹ (1904) 38, Jahrgang 19¹ (1912) 53,
Jahrgang 27¹ (1920) 61, Jahrgang 31 (1924) 76, Jahrgang 40 (1933) (repr Graz
1959; 1959; 1960; 1960; 1960; 1960) xxxiv + 294; x + 139; xxxviii + 189; vi +
107; x + 148; viii + 107

1986 These volumes are facsimiles with no introduction, no title pages, etc.
1987 Vols 14–15 and 61 include a thematic inventory of the seven mss: it is
inaccurate but has not yet been revised. All vols include transcriptions (long
note-values, C clefs), introductions, commentaries, and facsimiles.

Trier

1988 Ewerhart, Rudolf *Die Hs 322/1994 der Stadtbibliothek Trier als* M *Quelle* KBMf
7 (Regensburg 1955) xix + 2 facss + 157 / rev D. Mintz *Notes* 16 (1958/9) 63–5
E describes and transcribes the M of this peripheral 15c ms.

Utrecht

1989 Smits van Waesberghe, J. 'Die Hs Utrecht NIKK B 113' *KmJb* 50 (1966) 45–74
Including a complete transcription, S discusses and inventories the retrospective polyphony in this 15c ms.

Venice

1990 Cattin, G. 'Il Ms Veneto Marc. Ital. IX, 145' *Quad* 4 (1960) 1–57 + 7 facss; repr
1990a in BIBL DI ' QUADRIVIUM' (Bologna 1962) **1990a** Cattin *Laudi quattrocentesche*
BIBL DI 'QUAD,' ser paleografica 10 (Bologna 1958) 19, 2 pp facss
1990 C describes the ms and its contents with an inventory and bibliography and (**1990a**) edits 8 polyphonic laudi, late 14c, from the ms.

POLYPHONY IN ARCHAIC STYLE

1991 Dömling, W. 'Überlieferung eines Notre-Dame-Conductus in mensurierter
Notation' *Mf* 23 (1970) 429–31
D transcribes the work from a 15c ms (London, BM Add 27630).

1992 Federhofer, H. 'Eine neue Quelle zur Organumpraxis des späten MA' *Acta*
1993 20 (1948) 21–25, 1 facs **1993** Federhofer 'Archaistische Mehrstimmigkeit im
Spätmittelalter' *Schw Musikzeitung* 88 (1948) 416–19
F describes and transcribes the polyphony from some mss at Graz.

1994 Fischer, K. von 'Neue Quellen mehrstimmigen M des 15. Jh. aus
schweizerischer Klostern' **F-18**.293–301
Describing two sources and transcribing several pieces, F shows that parallel or simple organal polyphony from the MA survived till the 16c (eastern
Europe) and 17c (Iceland).

1995 Gallo, F.A. '*Cantus planus binatim*. Polifonia primitiva in fonti tardive' *Quad*
7 (1966) 79–89, 6 facss
G describes three mss with retrospective polyphony.

1996 Irtenkauf, W. 'Ein neuer Fund zur liturgischen Ein- und Mehrstimmigkeit des 15. Jh.' *Mf* 12 (1959) 4–12
I describes leaves containing chant and retrospective polyphony.

1997 Milveden, I. 'Die schriftliche Fixierung eines Quintenorganums in einem Antiphonar-Fragment der Diözese Åbo' *Svensk Tidskrift för Mf* 44 (1962) 63–5
A late 15c hand added a parallel voice to a Responsory.

1998 Schrade, L. 'Ein neuer Fund früher Mehrstimmigkeit' *AMw* 19/20 (1962/3) 238–56
S describes and transcribes simple polyphony from Ivrea Ms LXVIII.

WELL-KNOWN MELODIES

1999 Lipphardt, W. 'Das älteste Weihnachtslied' *JbLH* 4 (1958/9) 95–101 **2000** Smits
2000 van Waesberghe, J. 'Über den Ursprung der Melodie "Nun siet uns willekommen" ' *StuMw* 25 (1962) 496–503
1999 L traces the history of *Nun siet,* concluding that the *Kyrieleis* was not the germ-cell for the melody. **2000** Opposing L, S shows how the melody is traceable to a Kyrie.

2001 Lipphardt, W. ' "Christ ist erstanden." Zur Geschichte des Liedes' *JbLH* 5 (1960) 96–114, 1 facs
L lists more than 160 sources, 12–16c. The item is sung, *alternatim,* as a trope to the Sequence *Victimae paschali* in the liturgical drama, and derives its melody from that Sequence.

2002 Smits van Waesberghe, J. 'Das Weihnachtslied "In dulci jubilo" und seine ursprüngliche Melodie' *Fs Helmuth Osthoff zum 65. Geburtstage* ed Lothar Hoffmann-Erbrecht and Helmut Hucke (Tutzing 1961) 27–37
The differing Dutch and German-English versions represent corruptions from two-part settings of the original.

2003 Smits van Waesberghe, J. 'Die Melodie der Hymne *Puer nobis nascitur* [Unto us a Child is Born]' *KmJb* 43 (1959) 27–31
S traces the melody to a *Benedicamus Domino* and explains unusual vowels in its text, drawing upon his knowledge of the *prosa-prosula* techniques. See **1317**.

Congresses, Festschriften, and other collections

Congresses

In some years no report was published: in others none of the articles is relevant and the report is not included here. Occasionally no editor is named.

INTERNATIONAL MUSICOLOGICAL SOCIETY (IMS), Reports

INTERNATIONALE MUSIKWISSENSCHAFTLICHE GESELLSCHAFT (IMG), Berichte

SOCIETE INTERNATIONALE DE MUSICOLOGIE (SIM), Comptes rendus

A-1 *IMS. Fourth Congress, Basle 1949* ed Ernest Mohr and Philipp Etter (Basel 1949)

A-2 *SIM. Cinquième Congrès, Utrecht 1952* (Amsterdam 1953)

A-3 *IMG. Siebenter Kongress, Köln 1958* (Kassel 1959)

A-4 *IMS. Eighth Congress, New York 1961* ed Jan LaRue 2 vols (Kassel 1961, 1962)

A-5 *IMG. Neunter Kongress, Salzburg 1964* ed Franz Giegling 2 vols (Kassel 1964, 1966)

A-6 *IMS. Tenth Congress, Ljubljana 1967* ed Dragotin Cvetko (Kassel 1970)

GESELLSCHAFT FÜR MUSIKFORSCHUNG, Berichte

B-1 *[Zweiter] Kongress, Lüneburg 1950,* ed Hans Albrecht, Helmuth Osthoff, and Walter Wiora (Kassel nd)

B-2 *Intern. Mw Kongress, Bamberg 1953* ed Wilfried Brennecke, Willi Kahl, and Rudolf Steglich (Kassel 1954)

B-3 *Intern. Mw Kongress, Hamburg 1956* ed Walter Gerstenberg, Heinrich Husmann, and Harald Heckmann (Kassel 1957)

B-4 *Intern. Mw Kongress, Kassel 1962* ed Georg Reichert and Martin Just (Kassel 1963)

BYZANTINE STUDIES

C-1 *Douzième congrès intern. d'études byzantines, Oochri 1961, Actes* 3 vols (Belgrade 1963, 1964, 1964)
II.563–9 Constantin Floros 'Fragen zum M und metriscchen n Aufbau der Kontakien'; II.575–82 Giovanni Marzi 'Martyria e incipit nella tradizione nomica'

C-2 *Thirteentneenth gintern. Congress of Byzantine Studies, Oxford 1966, Proceedings* ed J.M. Hussey, D. Obolensky, and S. Runciman (London 1967)
Pp 255–66 Giuseppe Schirò 'Problemi heirmologici'

Miscellaneous congresses

Some are held under the auspices of a society; others appear independent. They are listed here by alphabetical order of the city in which they were held.

D-1 *Mw Kongress in Basel 1924* ed W. Merian NEUE SCHW MUSIK-GES, ORTSGRUPPE BASEL (Leipzig 1925)

D-2 *Musica Antiqua Europae Orientalis, Bydgoszcz 1966* ed Zofia Lissa (Warsaw 1966)
This is a report of the concerts and papers presented at 'The First Festival of Old M of Central and Eastern Europe.' Pp 97–102 Slovakian sources of monophony; 281–3 polyphony in Poland; 419–24 Byzantine M in Rumania.

D-3 *L'Ars nova italiana del trecento* I: *Primo convegno intern., Certaldo 1959* ed Bianca Becherini (Certaldo 1962) indexed

D-4 – II: *Convegni di studio 1961–67* ed F. Alberto Gallo (Certaldo 1968)

D-5 – III: *Secondo convegno intern., 1969* ed F. Alberto Gallo (Certaldo 1970)
Pp 11–28 Kurt von Fischer 'M e società nel trecento italiano' (F gives a general introduction to the convention); 67–81 caccia.

D-6 *Erster Mw Kongress der deutschen M-ges in Leipzig 1925, Bericht* (Leipzig 1926)

D-7 *Arts libéraux et philosophie au ma.: IVe congrès intern. de philos. méd., Montréal 1967* (Montreal 1969)
Pp 186–7 medicine, ethos, theology etc, and M in the quadrivium.

D-8 *Congresso intern. di M mediterranea e del convegno dei bibliotecari musicali* (OR *Congresso intern. di M popolari mediterranee ...*), *Palermo 1954* (Palermo 1959)

Pp 259–61 plainsong and improvisation in the *Schola cantorum* (German version in *KmJb* 38 (1954) 5–8).

D-9 *Congresso intern. di M sacra, Roma 1950* ed Igino Anglès (Tournai 1952)
Pp 119–22 Byz. M mss in the monastery of El Escorial; 129–30 oral tradition in Sicily compared with Byz. mss; 172–6, 229–35, 259–64 neumes; 187–91 on a critical edition of the Gradual; 199–201 Cistercian plainsong; 236–9 notation of Metz; 267–70 evolution of psalm tones; 276–8 hexachords and modes; 284–6 rhymed office; 308–10, 315–18 Zacar and parody technique.

D-10 *Jumièges. Congrès scientifique du XIIIᵉ centenaire, Rouen 1954* 2 vols (Rouen 1955)
The vols are paginated consecutively.

D-11 *Zweiter intern. Kongress für katholische Kirchenmusik, Wien 1954, Bericht* (Vienna 1955)
Pp 105–10 plainsong notation; 129–37 and 2 facss preceding 129 description of an Antiphonal ca 1100; 142–5 plainsong dialect of Aquileia, pre-11c.

D-12 *Intern. mw Kongress, Wien Mozartjahr 1956, Bericht* (Graz, Cologne 1958)
Pp 92–8 harmonic development in MA; 192–202 church M pre-8c.

D-13 *The Book of the First Intern. Musicological Congress devoted to ... Chopin, Warsaw 1960* ed Zofia Lissa (Warsaw 1963)
Pp 510–13 Polish Sequences; 551–8 early Polish instruments; 567–71 early polyphony.

D-14 *Les Colloques de Wégimont, 2 (1955). L'Ars nova.* Recueil d'études sur la M du XIVᵉ siècle BIBL DE LA FACULTE DE PHILOS ET LETTRES DE L'U DE LIEGE 149 (Paris 1959) / rev U. Günther *Mf* 14 (1961) 210–14
Each paper is followed by a discussion.

Miscellaneous collections

E-1 *Anfänge der slavischen M* ed Ladislav Mokrý SLOWAKISCHE AKW, INST FÜR MW SYMPOSIA I (Bratislava 1966)
Pp 23–4 Petrus-liturgy; 35–41 the Office of St Demetrius; 43–8 early med. M of Moravia; 49–53 Bulgaria; 65–76 two Chilandari mss; 101–15, 165–71 Russia; 147–64 forms of folk-M.

E-2 Chailley, Jacques ed *Précis de musicologie* (Paris 1958) / rev A. Machabey *Rom* 79 (1959) 272–3
Pp 83–94 P. Fortassier 'La M byz.'; 95–119 S. Corbin 'Le Plainchant'; 115–25 J. Chailley 'La Monodie occidentale hors de la liturgie jusqu'à la fin du XIIIᵉ siècle'; 126–51 A. Machabey 'La Polyphonie occidentale du IXᵉ au XIVᵉ siècle'; 152–6 G. Thibault 'Le XVᵉ siècle: les prédécesseurs de Dufay et de Binchois.'
Each contribution summarises the field, its main problems and sources,

naming scholars and concentrating on the major modern publications and on journals dealing with more detailed research.

E-3 *Etudes grégoriennes.* See Plainsong, before **476**.

Vol 1 (1954) pp 9–45 J. Gajard 'Les Récitations modales des 3ᵉ et 4ᵉ modes et les mss bénéventains et aquitains'; 47–52 E. Cardine 'La Corde récitative du 3ᵉ ton psalmodique ...'; 83–148 H. Gavel 'A propos des erreurs d'accentuation latine ...'; 206–7 index of mss cited.

Vol 2 (1957) pp 5–26 J. Gajard 'Quelques réflexions sur les premières formes de la м sacrée'; 27–35 E. Cardine 'Théoriciens et théoriciens. A propos de quelques exemples d'élision dans la mélodie grég.'; 37–50 H. Potiron 'La Notation grecque dans *L'Institution Harmonique* d'Hucbald'; 189–203 P. Combe 'Bibliographie de Dom André Mocquereau'; 236–9 list of mss cited.

Vol 3 (1959) pp 27–33, 2 facss R. Arnese 'Codici di origine francese della Biblioteca Nazionale di Napoli'; 35–9 H. Gavel 'L'Accentuation des mots du Canon de la Messe dans un ms d'Angers'; 75–82 D. Catta 'Le Texte du Répons *Descendit* dans les mss'; 135–43 R. Ménard 'note sur la mémorisation et l'improvisation dans le chant copte'; 145–54 E. Cardine 'Neumes et rhythme.'

Vol 4 (1961) pp 7–42, 2 facss L. Brou 'L'Ancien Office de Saint Vaast, évêque d'Arras'; 43–54 E. Cardine 'Preuves paléographiques du principe des "coupures" dans les neumes'; 55–63 G. Benoit-Castelli 'L'Antienne *Jam fulget oriens*'; 65–170, 1 table, list of mss and of antiphons R. Le Roux '... Les Antiennes et les psaumes de Matines et de Laudes pour Noël et le 1ᵉʳ Janvier.'

Vol 5 (1962) pp 15–21 E. Cardine 'Paroles et mélodie dans le chant grég.'; 23–71 J. Froger 'L'Epître de Notker sur les "lettres significatives" '; 73–97 G. Oury 'Les Messes de Saint Martin dans les sacramentaires gallicans, romano-francs et milanais'; 109–18 H. Potiron 'Les Modes grég. selon les premiers théoriciens du ma.'; 119–30 R. Le Roux 'Les Graduels des Dimanches après la Pentecôte.'

Vol 6 (1963) pp 39–148, 2 tables, list of mss R. Le Roux 'Les Répons *De Psalmis* pour les Matines, de l'Epiphanie à la Septuagésime'; 149–52, 1 facss J. Hourlier 'Neumes sur des diptyques'; 153–7 J. Hourlier 'Sémiologie м'; 159–64 R. de Morault 'L'Evangéliaire de Saulieu.'

Vol 7 (1967) pp 1–19 C. Szigeti 'Les Formules dans l'ésthétique grég.'; 21–40 G. Oury 'Formulaires anciens pour la Messe de saint Martin'; 41–51 M. Robert 'Les Adieux à l'Alleluia'; 53–6, 2 facss M. Murjanof 'Le Fragment de Léningrad F.v.1.142'; 57–61 H. Potiron 'La Terminologie grecque des modes.'

Vol 8 (1967) pp 29–37 H. Potiron 'Théoriciens de la modalité.'

Vol 9 (1968) pp 25–36 H. Darre 'De l'usage des hymnes dans l'église, des origines à Saint Grégoire-le-Grand'; 37–40 H. Potiron 'Les Equivoques terminologiques'; 41–6 H. Potiron 'La Définition des modes liturgiques.'

Vol 10 (1969) pp 13–28 E. Cardine 'Neume'; 29–86 C. Thompson 'La Traduc-

tion mélodique du trigon dans les pièces authentiques du Graduale Romanum'; 147–50 H. Potiron 'Le Bémol.'
Vol 11 (1970) pp 181–5 H. Potiron 'Les Modes liturgiques d'après Gevaert'; 187–92 H. Potiron 'Complément au traité d'Hucbald: *De Harmonica Institutione.*'

E-4 Fromm, Hans ed *Der deutsche Minnesang: Aufsätze zu seiner Erforschung* WEGE DER FORSCHUNG 15 (Bad Homburg vor der Höhe 1961) indices of poets and texts
F reprints 10 articles (1914–57), some with revisions, describing various aspects of the genre.

E-5 *Musica Medii Aevi* ed Jerzy Morawski INSTYTUT SZTUKI POLSKIEJ AKADEMII NAUK ZAKŁAD HISTORII I TEORII MUZYKI KIEROWNIK: JÓZEF M. CHOMINSKY (Kraków 1965–)
English summaries are included from vol 3 onwards. Vol 1 (1965) 194, 32 facss, indices of names, mss; pp 9–52 H. Feicht 'Liturgical Mss in Med. Poland'; 53–68 A. Sutkowski 'Paleographical Characteristics of M Notations in Med. Polish Mss'; 69–88 J. Morawski 'Studies on Cistercian Sequences in Poland'; 89–95 A. Sutkowski 'Non-choral Compositions in the Gradual of the St Andrew Cloister in Krakow (sign. M 205/594)'; 96–174 J. Lewański 'Liturgical drama and Dramatizations in Med. Poland.'
Vol 2 (1968) 130, 40 facss, indices of names and mss; pp 7–39 W. Kamiński' M Instruments in Med. Poland'; 40–51 J. Węcowski 'The Beginnings of Benedictine Plainsong in Poland'; 52–70 H. Feicht 'Med. Polish Song'; 71–7 J. Morawski 'Silesian Diagrams of the Tone System in the Light of Med. Theory'; 78–92 K. Swaryczewska 'The Organ Mass in Med. Poland'; 98–114 Z. Rozanow 'Med. M Iconography.'
Vol 3 (1969) 164 + errata slip, 49 facss, indices of names and mss; pp 7–29 Z. Bernat 'The Wrocław Pontifical of the 12c as a M Historical Monument'; 30–6 H. Kowalewicz (and 37–42 J. Pikulik) 'The Oldest Sequence on St Adalbert: *Annua recolamus* I. Text (II. Melody)'; 43–58 E. Hinz 'M Notation of the Gradual Ms 118/119 of the Library of the Clerical Seminary of Pelplin'; 59–90 T. Maciejewski 'The Cistercian Kyriale in the Oldest Polish Ms: 13c and 14c'; 91–112 F. Bąk 'Med. Franciscan Graduals'; 113–29 H. Cempura 'The Franciscan *Mandatum* in a Med. Ms of Poland'; 130–51 B. Bartkowski 'The Gradual of the Regular Canons of Czerwińsk.'

E-6 *Studies in Eastern Chant* ed Miloš Velimirović
This journal is intended to complement the series MMB vol 1 (London 1966) xvi + 134. Pp xiii–xvi list the works on eastern chant by Egon Wellesz and Henry Tillyard; 1–8, transcc, and 1 facs G. Dévai 'Akathistos-Prooemia in Byz. M Mss in Hungary'; 9–36 M. Dragoumis 'The Survival of Byz. Chant in the Monophonic M of the Modern Greek Church'; 37–49 G. Engberg 'Greek Ekphonetic Neumes and Masoretic Accents'; 67–88 M. Velimirović and D. Stefanović 'Peter Lampadarios and Metropolitan Serafim of Bosnia';

104–7 C.A. Trypanis 'On the M Rendering of the Early Byz. Kontakia'; 108–29 M. Velimirović 'Unknown Stichera for the Feast of St Athanasius of Mount Athos'; 131 index of Byz. musicians; 132–4 index of mss.

E-7 Tack, Franz ed *Der kultische Gesang der abendländischen Kirche* (Cologne 1950) This has 24 articles on plainsong, and an index. Pp 19–24 rhythm; 36–9 Sanctus; 40–6 Byz. Sanctus; 53–63 OR antiphons; 63–6 Alleluia trope; 66–72 liquescent neumes; 72–5 *Pange lingua*; 76–83 Rhenish antiphonal; 90–3 Augustinian plainsongs; 93–101 word and note, Julian of Speyer.

E-8 *Twenty-fifth Anniversary Festschrift of Queen's College ... New York* ed Albert Mell (New York 1964)

Collections dedicated to, or written by, noted scholars

This section consists mainly of Festschriften. The items are listed alphabetically by dedicatee or author. See **18** for a bibliography and index of M Festschriften.

F-1 *Studien zur Mg. Fs für Guido* ADLER *zum 75. Geburtstag* (Vienna 1930) Pp 58–63 instrumental performance in troubadour M; 64–70 Gacien Reyneau and the Barcelona royal court ca 1400.

F-2 *Miscelánea en homenaje a Monseñor Higinio* ANGLES 2 vols (Barcelona 1958, 1961) *xx* + 500; 495(*sic*)–1054 Rarely has such a galaxy of the finest scholars been gathered in a single collection. Vol 1 includes a list of A's publications. Both vols have numerous illustrations and examples but there is no index.

F-3 *Essays in Musicology: A Birthday Offering for Willi* APEL ed Hans Tischler (Indiana U 1968) v + 191 A's bibliography is on pp 185–91. Pp 25–49 description and inventory of 12c Gradual.

F-4 Apfel, Ernst *Beiträge zu einer Geschichte der Satztechnik von der frühen Motette bis Bach* 2 vols (Munich 1964, 1965) 112; 76 / rev J.D. Bergsagel ML 48 (1967) 80–2: rev says A sketches the difference between English and continental procedures in composition A collects earlier material from various sources.

F-5 *Fs Heinrich* BESSELER ... INST FÜR MW DER KARL-MARX-U (Leipzig 1961) 540 Pp 51, 52, and 537, and pl 4 Collégiale de St-Quentin, to 14c.

F-6 *Fs Friedrich* BLUME ... ed Anna A. Abert and Wilhelm Pfannkuch (Kassel 1963) 426

Borren: see Van den Borren F-32.

F-7 Bukofzer, Manfred F. *Studies in Med. and Renaissance* M (New York 1950) 324, 7 pll, list mss, index / rev D. Stevens *ML* 33 (1952) 65–8
This consists of 7 long essays, 4 dealing with definitely 15c topics. All are linked by the central idea of treatment of a pre-existent melody. Most need bringing up to date. Nevertheless the collection, and especially no. 7, remains a classic of interdisciplinary research. Nos 1, 2, 3 on med. English M (no. 2 is superseded by **1785–9**): nos 4, 5, 6 on 15c: no. 7 on Dufay, Okeghem, Obrecht, and the *Caput* Mass

F-8 *Medium aevum vivum. Fs für Walther* BULST (Heidelberg 1960)

F-9 *Mélanges offerts à René* CROZET ed Pierre Gallais and Yves-Jean Riou 2 vols (suppl to CCM, Poitiers 1966) xxxi + 696; 697–1419

Davison: *see* **F-31**.

F-10 *Fs Hans* ENGEL ed Horst Heussner (Kassel 1964)

F-11 *Fs Karl Gustav* FELLERER, *zum 60.Geburtstag* ed Heinrich Hüschen (Regensburg 1962)

F-12 *Mélanges de linguistique et de littérature romanes à la mémoire d'István* FRANK SUS, Philos Fakultät 6 (Sarrebrücken 1957)
This contains a bibliography of F (mostly in literary fields), pp 7–10, and numerous articles on troubadour and other med. lyrics. There is a partial list of chansonniers (mainly textual), pp 82–6.

F-13 *Gendenkschrift Jacques* HANDSCHIN ed Hans Oesch (Bern, Stuttgart 1957) 397
O reprints articles by Handschin.

F-14 *In Memoriam Jacques* HANDSCHIN ed Higinio Anglès et al (Strasbourg 1962)
H's bibliography is given on pp 1–26.

F-15 *Speculum musicae artis. Festgabe für Heinrich* HUSMANN *zum 60. Geburtstag* ed Heinz Becker and Reinhard Gerlach (Munich 1970) 347

F-16 *Ewald* JAMMERS. *Schrift Ordnung Gestalt* ed R. Hammerstein NEUE HEIDELBERGER STUDIEN ZUR MW 1 (Munich 1969)
This is a collection of J's articles, to celebrate his seventieth birthday. His bibliography is given on pp 279–91.

F-17 *Natalicia Musicologica. Knud* JEPPESEN ed Bjørn Hjelmborg and Søren Sørensen (Oslo, London 1962) 319

F-18 *Renaissance-Muziek 1400–1600. Donum natalicium René Bernard* LENAERTS ed Jozef Robijns MUSICOLOGICA LOVANIENSIA 1 (Louvain 1969)

F-19 *Saggi e ricerche in memoria di Ettore* LI GOTTI 3 vols CENTRO DI STUDI FILOLOGICI E LINGUISTICI SICILIANI, Bol 6, 7, 8 (Palermo 1962)
L's bibliography is given in I, viii–xviii. His publications, and most of those in *Saggi ...*, are primarily on literary topics of the trecento.

F-20 *Estudios dedicados a* MENENDEZ PIDAL 7 vols (Madrid 1950, 1951, 1952, 1953, 1954, 1956, 1957)
The studies include many on the literature of med. Spain. III.361–412 troubadour Cerverí, including references to *estampida, sirventes, descort*; v.165–84 'Juglares ... en el siglo XIV' referring to archives and instruments.

F-21 *Zum 70. Geburtstag von Joseph* MÜLLER-BLATTAU ed Christoph-Hellmut Mahling SAARBRÜCKER STUDIEN ZUR MW 1 (Kassel 1966) 340

F-22 *Fs Karl* NEF *zum 60. Geburtstag* (Zürich, Leipzig 1933) 219

F-23 *Aspects of Med. and Renaissance* M: *a Birthday Offering to Gustave* REESE ed Jan LaRue (New York 1966) xviii + 892 / rev J.A. Westrup ML 48 (1967) 266–7
R's bibliography is given on pp 889–91. Pp 96–110 Aristoxenos and Greek mathematics; 308–13 a trecento fresco; 314–18 performance of early M; 489–99 15c lauda; 545–59 M as a liberal art; 818–31 15c Byz. composers.

F-24 RIEMANN-*Fs. Gesammelte Studien zum 60. Geburtstage* (Leipzig 1909; repr Tutzing 1965) xl + 524
R's bibliography is given on pp xxv–xl.

F-25 *Colloquium Amicorum. Joseph* SCHMIDT-GÖRG *zum 70. Geburtstag* ed Siegfried Kross and Hans Schmidt (Bonn 1967) xxviii + 461

F-26 *Fs Max* SCHNEIDER *zum 80. Geburtstage* ed Walther Vetter (Leipzig 1955) 366
This is for S's eightieth birthday.

F-27 *Leo* SCHRADE. *De Scientia Musicae Studia atque Orationes* ed Ernst Lichtenhahn (Stuttgart 1967) 623
As well as a complete bibliography, this contains reprinted and previously unpublished articles by S. Pp 35–112 Boethius, propaedeutics, and ontology; 113–51 iconography and symbolism at Cluny.

F-28 *Organicae voces: Fs Joseph* SMITS VAN WAESBERGHE ... *60. Geburtstages* (Amsterdam 1963) 180
S's bibliography is given on pp 175–9.

F-29 *Fs Bruno* STÄBLEIN *zum 70. Geburtstag* ed Martin Ruhnke (Kassel 1967) xvi + 326
S's bibliography is given on pp ix–xiii. Pp 1–8 Milanese Offertory; 274–86 text of the Improperia.

F-30 *Studies in* M *History: Essays for Oliver* STRUNK ed Harold Powers (Princeton 1968) x + 527

F-31 *Essays in* M *in Honor of Archibald Thompson* DAVISON ed Randall Thompson et al (Cambridge, Mass. 1957) x + 374

F-32 *Liber Amicorum Charles* VAN DEN BORREN ed Albert Van der Linden (Antwerp 1964) 226

F-33 *Fs Peter* WAGNER *zum 60. Geburtstag* ed Karl Weinmann (Leipzig 1926) vii + 237

F-34 *Essays presented to Egon* WELLESZ ed Jack Westrup (Oxford 1966) viii + 188

F-35 Winternitz, Emmanuel M *Instruments and their Symbolism in Western Art* (London 1967) 240 + 96 pll, index of names and subjects, b-footnotes / rev M. Remnant *ML* 49 (1968) 155–9
W traces the development from 5–16c, stressing the frequency and continuity of unrealistic and allegorical representation.

F-36 *Fs Walter* WIORA ... ed Ludwig Finscher and Christoph-Hellmut Mahling (Kassel 1967) 678

Abbreviations

AA *Acta Antiqua: Academiae Scientiarum Hungaricae*
AB *Art Bulletin*
Abh Abhandlung(en)
ABSA *Annual of the British School at Athens*
Acad Academy
Acta *Acta Musicologica* (in the beginning called *Mitteilungen der IMG*)
AdA *Anzeiger für deutsches Altertum* (the review section of *ZdA*)
Ak Akademie
AkW Akademie der Wissenschaften
ALw *Archiv für Liturgiewissenschaft*
AMf *Archiv für Musikforschung*
AMIS ANTIQUAE MUSICAE ITALICAE SCRIPTORES
AMw *Archiv für Musikwissenschaft*
AnnM *Annales Musicologiques*
anon anonymous
AnthM ANTHOLOGY OF M ed Karl Fellerer
    1– (Cologne 195?–) (originally published as *Das Musikwerk*)
AnuarioM *Anuario Musical*
AR *Archivum Romanicum*
ARAP *Atti della Reale Accademia di Scienze, Lettere e Arti di Palermo*
Arb Arbeit(en)
arch archéologique
Arch *Archeologia*
AT ALTDEUTSCHE TEXTBIBLIOTHEK, Ergänzungsreihe
AUC(-PH) ACTA UNIVERSITATIS CAROLINAE: (PHILOSOPHICA ET HISTORICA)
AUS ACTA UNIVERSITATIS STOCKHOLMIENSIS

b bibliography
BarcCat BARCELONA, BIBL DE CATALUNYA, PUBLICACIONS DEL DEPARTAMENTA DE M
BBG *Bolletino della Badia greca*, Grottaferrata
BEHE BIBL DE L'ECOLE DES HAUTES ETUDES
Beitr Beitrag, Beiträge
Bel *Belfagor. Rassegna di varia umanità*
BGSL *Beitr zur Geschichte der deutschen Sprache und Literatur* (Halle or Tübingen specified)
bibl bibliothèque, bibliotheca, biblioteca
BIBL ARN BIBLIOTHECA ARNAMAGNAEANA
BM British Museum, London
BMw *Beiträge zur Mw*
BN Bibl Nationale, Paris
Bol Bolletino, boletino
BQ *Brass Quarterly*
BRMg BEITRÄGE ZUR RHEINISCHEN MUSIKGESCHICHTE
BrPh *Beiträge zur romanischen Philologie*
Bsl *Byzantinoslavica*
Bull Bulletin
Byz. Byzantine, Byzantium (used throughout, even in quoting titles in which the word is not abbreviated)
BZ *Byzantinische Zeitschrift*

c century, centuries
ca circa

CCM *Cahiers de civilisation méd.*
CHM *Collectanea Historiae Musicae*
ChR *Chaucer Review*
ClMed *Classica et Mediaevalia*
CM *Current Musicology*
CMM CORPUS MENSURABILIS MUSICAE (general ed Armen Carapetyan, INSTITUTE OF AMERICAN MUSICOLOGY, Rome; most vols do not give place of publication)
CNl *Cultura Neolatina*
col coloured
comp compiled by, compiler
Conv *Convivium. Rivista di lettere filosofia e storia*
CSM CORPUS SCRIPTORUM MUSICAE (general ed Armen Carapetyan, INSTITUTE OF AMERICAN MUSICOLOGY, Rome; most vols do not give place of publication)

DBGU *Deutsch Beiträge zur Geistigen Überlieferung*
dipl diplomatic (i.e., facsimiles traced or copied freehand)
DJbMw *Deutsches Jahrbuch der Musikwissenschaft* (1st vol is 48th of *Jahrbuch der Musikbibliothek Peters*)
DMk *Deutsche Musikkultur*
DOP DUMBARTON OAKS PAPERS
DTÖ DENKMÄLER DER TONKUNST IN ÖSTERREICH (general ed Guido Adler, 95 vols, Vienna 1894–1959; repr 1–83, 1959/60)
Du *Der Deutschunterricht*
DVLG *Deutsche Vierteljahrsschrift für Literaturwissenschaft und Geistesgeschichte*

EArbMw ERLANGEN ARBEITEN ZUR MUSIKWISSENSCHAFT
EBM EARLY BODLEIAN MUSIC, various editors, 3 vols (London, 1898, 1901, 1913; repr New York, 1967; Amsterdam, 1963)
ed editor, edited, edition
EG *Etudes grégoriennes: see* **E-3**
EL *Ephemerides liturgicae*
enl enlarged
EOL EDITIONS DE L'OISEAU LYRE

EPM ETUDES DE PHILOLOGIE MUSICALE
ESM EASTMAN SCHOOL OF MUSIC, Studies
Euph *Euphorion. Zeitschrift für Literaturgeschichte*
ex(x) example(s)
ext extensive

facs(s) facsimile(s)
FAM *Fontes Artis Musicae*
FMw *Forschungsbeiträge zur Musikwissenschaft*
fol, fos folio(s)
Fs Festschrift (für)

GAkF GREGORIANISCHE AKADEMIE, FREIBURG (SCHWEIZ), Veröffentlichungen
Ges Gesellschaft
gesch Geschichte
Ges für Mw *see* IMG
GLL *German Life and Letters*
Greg. Gregorian, grégorien (used throughout, even in quoting titles in which the word is not abbreviated)
GSJ *Galpin Society Journal*
GUOS *Glasgow University Oriental Society*

HbMw HANDBUCH DER MUSIKWISSENSCHAFT ed Ernst Bücken (Potsdam 1931); this was issued in numerous unnumbered *Lieferungen*, which are now numbered at the discretion of the owner
hist history, historical, historisch
hs Handschrift
HUCA *Hebrew Union College Annual*

IEM INSTITUTO ESPAÑOL DE MUSICOLOGIA
illus illustrated, illustrations
IMG INTERNATIONALE MUSIKWISSENSCHAFTLICHE GESELLSCHAFT (or GES für Mw): *see* IMS and SIM
IMS INTERNATIONAL MUSICOLOGICAL SOCIETY: *see* IMG and SIM
Inst Institute, Instituto, etc.
intern. international
Ist. Istituto, Istituzione

J Journal

JAAC Journal of Aesthetics and Art Criticism

*JAMS Journal of the American Musicological
   Society*

Jb Jahrbuch

JbLH Jahrbuch für Liturgik und Hymnologie

JbLw Jahrbuch für Liturgiewissenschaft

JEH Journal of Ecclesiastical History

Jh. Jahrhundert, Jahrhunderts

JHI Journal of the History of Ideas

JHS Journal of Hellenic Studies

*JIFMC Journal of the International Folk Music
   Council*

JMTh Journal of Music Theory

JRAS Journal of the Royal Asiatic Society

JRMEd Journal of Research in Music Education

JWAG Journal of the Walters Art Gallery

KBMf KÖLNER BEITRÄGE ZUR MUSIK-
   FORSCHUNG

KmJb Kirchenmusikalisches Jahrbuch

List *The Listener*

LJb Liturgisches Jahrbuch

LMw LITERARHISTORISCH-MUSIKWISSEN-
   SCHAFTLICHE ABH

M music, musical, *Musik, musique,* etc. (used
   throughout, even in quoting titles in
   which the word is not abbreviated)

MA or ma. Middle Ages, moyen âge,
   Mittelalter(s), medii aevi, and adjectival
   forms, mittelalterlich, etc. (used throughout, even in quoting titles in which the
   word is not abbreviated)

MAA MEDIAEVAL ACADEMY OF AMERICA,
   Studies and Documents

MAe Medium Aevum

MD Musica Disciplina (vol 1 appeared as *J of
   Renaissance and Baroque M*)

med. medieval (used throughout, even in
   quoting titles in which the word is not
   abbreviated)

MedMM MEDIAEVAL MUSICAL MANUSCRIPTS

(ed Luther Dittmer, INST OF MEDIAEVAL
   MUSIC, New York)

Mém or mem Mémoires, memorie

Mf Die Musikforschung

Mf (MF) Musikforschung, musikforskning

Mg Musikgeschichte, musikgeschichtlich

MgB MUSIKGESCHICHTE IN BILDERN: see **308**

MGG DIE MUSIK IN GESCHICHTE UND GEGEN-
   WART: *see* **1**

MH Medievalia et Humanistica

MiscM-A Miscellanea Musicologica
   (Australia)

MiscM-C Miscellanea Musicologica
   (Czechoslovakia)

MK Musik und Kirche

ML Music and Letters

MlatJb Mittellateinisches Jahrbuch

MLJ Modern Language Journal

MLMAI-L MONUMENTA LYRICA MEDII AEVI
   ITALICA I. Latina

MLMAI-M MONUMENTA LYRICA MEDII AEVI
   ITALICA III. Mensurabilia

MLN Modern Language Notes

MLQ Modern Language Quarterly

MLR Modern Language Review

MMB-L MONUMENTA MUSICAE BYZANTINAE,
   Lectionaria (published in Copenhagen,
   unless otherwise noted)

MMB-P MONUMENTA MUSICAE BYZANTINAE,
   Principale (published in Copenhagen,
   unless otherwise noted)

MMB-S MONUMENTA MUSICAE BYZANTINAE,
   Subsidia (published in Copenhagen, unless otherwise noted)

MMB-T MONUMENTA MUSICAE BYZANTINAE,
   Transcripta (published in Copenhagen,
   unless otherwise noted)

MMC MELANGES DE MUSICOLOGIE CRITIQUE ed
   Pierre Aubry 4 vols (Paris 1900, 1900, 1901,
   1905)

MMg Monatshefte für Musikgeschichte

MMMA MONUMENTA MONODICA MEDII AEVI
   (general ed Bruno Stäblein, Kassel):
   see **B-1.**52–4 and *StuMus* 6 (1964)
   277–98

MMS MONUMENTA MUSICAE SACRAE, ed Dom Renato-Joanne Hesbert

Mon monumenta

MOst Musik des Ostens

MoyA Le Moyen âge

MQ Musical Quarterly

ms(s) manuscript(s) (used throughout, even in titles in which the word is not abbreviated)

MS MUSICOLOGICAL STUDIES (ed Luther Dittmer, INSTITUTE OF MEDIAEVAL MUSIC, New York)

Msct Manuscripta

MSD MUSICOLOGICAL STUDIES AND DOCUMENTS (general ed Armen Carapetyan, AMERICAN INSTITUTE OF MUSICOLOGY, Rome)

MT Musical Times

MThT MUSICAL THEORISTS IN TRANSLATION (general ed Luther Dittmer, INSTITUTE OF MEDIAEVAL MUSIC, New York)

MTU MÜNCHENER TEXTE UND UNTERSUCHUNGEN ZUR DEUTSCHEN LITERATUR DES MITTELALTERS

Mus Musica

MusMA Musica Medii Aevi: see E-5

MuzK Muzyka Kwartalnik

MVM MÜNCHENER VERÖFFENTLICHUNGEN ZUR MUSIKGESCHICHTE

Mw (MW) Musikwissenschaft(lich)

MwArb MUSIKWISSENSCHAFTLICHE ARBEITEN

MwSb MUSIKWISSENSCHAFTLICHE STUDIENBIBLIOTHEK, ed Friedrich Gennrich 24 vols (vols 1–2 publ Darmstadt; 3–4 Nieder-Modau; 5–6 Darmstadt and Langen bei Frankfurt; 7 Langen b.F.; 8–19 Darmstadt; 20–24 Langen b.F.)

N a neutral transcription not committed to a rhythmic interpretation

NASM Note d'archivio per la storia musicale

nd no date of publication given

NeuphMit Neuphilologische Mitteilungen

np no place of publication given

ns new series

num numerous

ÖMz Österreichische Musikzeitung

OR OLD ROMAN

PalMus PALEOGRAPHIE MUSICALE ed Benedictine monks of Solesmes (1889–   ). The place of publication is Solesmes, unless otherwise noted. Editors are not identified. This is a series of publications of facsimiles of those mss of early Gregorian chant thought to be basic for establishing the authentic version, rhythm, and interpretation of the melodies. It is a basic tool for plainsong research, but the rhythmic theories and general attitude of the Solesmes school have been strongly challenged. Lengthy and informative introductions accompany each facsimile, either in the same or another volume.

PÄM PUBLIKATIONEN ÄLTERER MUSIK

philos philosophisch, etc.

p.h.Kl. philosophische-historische Klasse

PIMG PUBLIKATIONEN DER INTERNATIONALEN MUSIKGESELLSCHAFT

PIMS PONTIFICAL INSTITUTE OF MEDIAEVAL STUDIES (Toronto) Studies and Texts

pl(l) plate(s)

PMFC POLYPHONIC M OF THE FOURTEENTH CENTURY, vols 1–4, general ed Leo Schrade; vols 5–   , general ed Frank Ll. Harrison (EOL, Monaco); the commentary for vols 1–4 is bound separately in 3 vols.

PMLA Publications of the Modern Language Association

PMMS PLAINSONG AND MEDIÆVAL MUSIC SOCIETY

PRMA Proceedings of the Royal Musical Association

PSM PRINCETON STUDIES IN MUSIC

PSMfG PUBLIKATIONEN DER SCHWEIZERISCHEN MUSIKFORSCHENDEN GESELLSCHAFT

publ published, publication

Quad Quadrivium. Rivista di Filologia e musicologia medievale

R Review, Revue
RaM Rassegna musicale
RBAH Revue belge d'archéologie et d'histoire de l'art
RBM Revue belge de musicologie
RCCM Rivista di cultura classica e medievale
RCGrég Revue du chant grégorien
RdM Revue de musicologie
REI Revue des études islamiques
repr reprint of, reprinted
rev reviewed by/in, review of
revd revised
RG Revue grégorienne
Rh a transcription committed to one of a number of rhythmic interpretations
RHE Revue d'histoire ecclésiastique
RIM Rivista italiana di musicologica
RISM REPERTOIRE INTERNATIONAL DES SOURCES MUSICALES (Munich-Duisburg). Series A: alphabetical listing of composers and their works with locations. Series B: systematic-chronological arrangement by specific category with locations. *See* **8b 8c 900 901 1335 1503**. The project is described in *Intern. Inventory of* M *Sources*, Report of the Joint us Committee on Activities to … 1966, prepared by Wayne D. Şhirley (Washington 1966) I.v–vi.
RM Revue musicale
RMI Rivista musicale italiana
Rom Romania
RQ Römische Quartalschrift für Christliche Altertumskunde und Kirchengeschichte
RUB Revue de l'Université de Bruxelles (when asterisked, the page references are to the *Bibliographie*, or review section)

SATF SOCIETE DES ANCIENS TEXTES FRANÇAIS
SB Staatsbibl.
Schw Schweizerisch
Scrip Scriptorium
SE Sacris erudiri

SEC Studies in Eastern Chant: see **E-6**
Ser series
SH Schweizer Heimatbücher
SIM SOCIETE INTERNATIONALE DE MUSICOLOGIE
SIMG Sammelbände der Internationale Musikgesellschaft
SJbMw Schweizerisches Jahrbuch für Musikwissenschaft
SM Studi medievali
SMMA SUMMA MUSICAE MEDII AEVI, ed Friedrich Gennrich 18 vols (vols 1–6 publ Darmstadt; 7–18 Langen bei Frankfurt)
SMwAbh SAMMLUNG MUSIKWISSENSCHAFTLICHER ABHANDLUNGEN (COLLECTION D'ETUDES MUSICOLOGIQUES)
Soc Society, Société
Spec Speculum
Sq a transcription in square note-symbols which are not diplomatic, and whose rhythm is usually non-committal
STT SUOMALAISEN TIEDEAKATEMIAN TOIMITUKSIA (ANNALES ACADEMIAE SCIENTIARUM FENNICAE)
StuMus Studia musicologica
StuMw Studien zur Musikwissenschaft
SUS SAARBRÜCKEN UNIVERSITÄT DES SAARLANDES (ANNALES UNIVERSITATIS SARAVIENSIS)

TLS Times Literary Supplement
transc(c) transcription(s)
transl translation in, translated by
TVNM Tijdschrift van de Vereniging voor nederlandse Muziek; after 1948 called *Tijdschrift voor Muziekwetenschap*

U University
UCPH UNIVERSITY OF CALIFORNIA PUBLICATIONS IN HISTORY
UCPM UNIVERSITY OF CALIFORNIA PUBLICATIONS IN MUSIC

Ver. Veröffentlichung(en)

WS Die Welt der Slaven (Vierteljahrsschrift für
    Slavistik)
WW Wirkendes Wort

Yuval Yuval: Studies of the Jewish Research
    Centre (Jerusalem)

Zd Zeitschrift für deutsche ...
ZdA Zeitschrift für deutsches Altertum und
    deutsche Literatur

ZdPh Zeitschrift für deutsche Philologie
ZfSL Zeitschrift für französische Sprache und
    Literatur
ZIMG Zeitschrift der International
    Musikgesellschaft
ZM Zeitschrift für Musik
ZMw Zeitschrift für Musikwissenschaft
ZrPh Zeitschrift für romanische
    Philologie
Zs (zs) Zeitschrift

Index of authors and editors

AARBURG, Ursula **213a 244 262 1246–8 1280 1311**

ABERT, Anna A. **836**

ABERT, Hermann **80 100**

ABRAHAM, Gerald **30**

ADKINS, Cecil **187**

ADLER, Guido **F-1**

ADLER, Israël **192 383 387**

AEGENVOORT, Johannes **1866b**

AGUSTONI, Luigi **138 483 577**

ALLAIRE, Gaston G. **257a**

ALLWORTH, Christopher **525a**

ANDERSON, Gordon A. **1116 1123 1406 1420a 1438 1462–3 1468 1486–7**

ANDERSSON, Otto **346**

ANDREWS, Herbert K. **1796**

ANGLES, Higinio (the necrology and recent official publications authorise the spelling Higinio Anglés; elsewhere numerous variations are to be found) **F-2 10 166 492 779a 1013 1166 1168 1199 1214 1327 1358 1376 1467 1500 1524 1645 1817 1820–1 1823–5 1829–31 1835–8a 1847 1911**

ANOYANAKIS, Fivos **468**

ANTONOWYCZ, Miroslav **894a**

APEL, Willi **F-3 3a 66 131 224 253 319 484 605 1176 1348 1359 1372 1508 1528 1587 1924**

APFEL, Ernst **F-4 225 287 1471 1765 1772 1780**

APPEL, Margarete **904**

ARBOGAST, Paul M. **148**

ARLT, Wulf **689a 689b**

ARRO, Elmar **35**

ASTON, Stanley C. **1200**

AUBRY, Pierre **277 781 1146 1173 1178 1204 1464–6 1504 1832 1915**

AUDA, Antoine **194 203 1478 1611**

AVENARY(-LOEWENSTEIN), Hanoch **286 338 369 913 1031 1938**

AYOUTANTI, Aglaïa **435–6**

BACHMANN, Werner **297 345 469 1338**

BAEHR, Rudolf **1180a 1657**

BAILEY, Terence **689a 824**

BAINES, Anthony **358**

BALDELLO, Francisco de P. **1839**

BALTZER, Rebecca A. **1416a**

BANDMANN, Günter **307**

BANNISTER, Henry M. **56a 72 718**

BARTH, Pudentia **1098**

BARTHA, Dénes V. **1012**

BARTSCH, Karl **1282**

BATKA, Richard **860**

BAUTIER-REGNIER, Anne-Marie **912**

BAXTER, James H. **1418**

BAYART, Paul **1231**

BECHERINI, Bianca **1660**

BECK, Jean Baptiste **1191 1205–6**

BECK, Johann B. **1162**

BECKER, Adolf **704**

BECKER, Heinz **359**

BEHN, Friedrich **36**

BEICHNER, Paul E. **293**

BELL, Aubrey F.G. **1819 1846**

BENT, Ian **779 1095 1757**

General index

This index is analytical and liberally supplied with cross-references to aid the reader not familiar with the technicalities of the subject. For example, names of composers, theorists, and poets are listed under those headings as well as under the specific name, where the reference numbers are given. Although the index is compiled according to the appearance of a word in an item of the bibliography, this principle is somewhat flexible: where it is quite clear from the annotation or context that a word applies, it has been listed even when it does not itself occur in the bibliographical entry. Similarly, some entries, in particular for 'editions,' 'facsimiles,' and the like, are to some extent selective, noting only items with substantial transcriptions, or reproductions, etc. It is important also to remember that many editions and large works contain indices, lists of sources, and other useful material which could not, because of space, be recorded in the bibliographical entry and which therefore do not show up in the index.

When entries are very numerous, the most important are listed first. Entries of lesser importance follow in brackets: here too are noted some other references not of sufficient weight to be included in the body of the book.

Medieval names like Johannes de Garlandia are generally listed under the first word. Names like Peter Abelard, known more commonly by their last name, are so recorded.

I have used the following devices:

1 names or incipits of musical pieces are printed with a capital letter and italics,
2 names or incipits of treatises are printed in capitals,
3 other titles (e.g., of poems) are within quotation marks,
4 manuscripts referred to by their location and call-number or by a common but distinctive name are preceded by an asterisk (*).

A l'entrade d'avril **1491**
Aachen **1609**
ABBREVIATIO MAGISTRI FRANCONIS **925**
'Abdalqādir ibn Ġaibī **1027**
Abdias. *See* Obadiah
Abelard, Peter **746 1081 1092–6**
Åbo, diocese of **1997**

Abu'l-Salt **1031**
accent
– Latin **60 61 140 632 1058 1164 1166 1167**
  [E-3.1.83, III.35 E-6.1.37]
– French **242**
– German **242**
accents (notation) **130 846**

Toronto Medieval
Bibliographies

Editor: John Leyerle
Director, CENTRE FOR MEDIEVAL STUDIES, University of Toronto

1 OLD NORSE-ICELANDIC STUDIES by Hans Bekker-Nielsen, Editor, *Mediaeval Scandinavia*, Co-editor of *Bibliography of Old Norse-Icelandic Studies* and of *Den Arnamagnæanske Kommissions Ordbog*, Odense University

2 OLD ENGLISH LITERATURE by Fred C. Robinson, Department of English, Yale University

3 MEDIEVAL RHETORIC by James J. Murphy, Chairman, Department of Rhetoric, University of California (Davis)

4 MEDIEVAL MUSIC: THE SIXTH LIBERAL ART by Andrew Hughes, Faculty of Music, University of Toronto

At press

MEDIEVAL CELTIC LITERATURE by Rachel Bromwich, Lecturer in Celtic Languages and Literature, University of Cambridge

In preparation

AIDS TO THE STUDY OF LITERARY HISTORY by Richard H. Rouse, Department of History, University of California (Los Angeles)

ARTHURIAN LEGEND AND ROMANCE by Edmund Reiss, Department of English, Duke University

CHAUCER by John Leyerle, Director, Centre for Medieval Studies, University of Toronto

ITALIAN LITERATURE TO 1400 by John Freccero, Department of Romance Languages, Yale University, and Giuseppe Mazzotta, Department of Romance Studies, Cornell University

LATIN PALAEOGRAPHY TO 1500 by Leonard E. Boyle, OP, Pontificial Institute of Mediaeval Studies, Toronto

MEDIEVAL EXACT SCIENCE AND NATURAL PHILOSOPHY by John E. Murdock, Chairman, Department of the History of Science, Harvard University

MEDIEVAL LATIN LITERATURE by A.G. Rigg, Centre for Medieval Studies, University of Toronto

MEDIEVAL MATERIA MEDICA AND APPLIED BOTANY by Jerry Stannard, Department of History, University of Kansas

MEDIEVAL MONASTICISM by Giles Constable, Henry Charles Lea Professor of Medieval History, Harvard University

MEDIEVAL SCOTS POETRY by Florence H. Ridley, Department of English, University of California (Los Angeles)

MIDDLE ENGLISH LITERATURE by L.D. Benson, Department of English, Harvard University

MIDDLE HIGH GERMAN LITERATURE by R. William Leckie, Jr, Department of German, University College, University of Toronto

OLD PROVENÇAL by Robert A. Taylor, Department of French, Victoria College, University of Toronto

SOURCES AND METHODOLOGY FOR THE INTERPRETATION OF MEDIEVAL IMAGERY by R.E. Kaske, Department of English, Cornell University

SPANISH LITERATURE TO 1500 by James F. Burke, Department of Italian and Hispanic Studies, University of Toronto, and John E. Keller, Director, School of Letters and Languages, University of Kentucky